# EROS AND MAGIC
# IN THE RENAISSANCE

Ioan P. Couliano

# Eros and Magic in the Renaissance

Translated by Margaret Cook

With a Foreword by Mircea Eliade

The University of Chicago Press     Chicago and London

Ioan P. Couliano is a fellow of the Netherlands Institute for Advanced Study (Wassenaar) and associate professor at the University of Groningen in the Netherlands. He has also taught at the University of Chicago and the Catholic University in Milan. He is the author of many books and articles, including *Expériences de l'extase, Gnosticismo,* and *Psychanodia.*

THE UNIVERSITY OF CHICAGO PRESS, CHICAGO 60637
THE UNIVERSITY OF CHICAGO PRESS, LTD., LONDON

© 1987 by The University of Chicago
All rights reserved. Published 1987
Printed in the United States of America
96 95 94 93 92 91 90 89 88 87    5 4 3 2 1

This book was originally published in France under the title *Eros et magie à la Renaissance, 1484,* © 1984, Flammarion, Paris.

LIBRARY OF CONGRESS CATALOGING-IN-PUBLICATION DATA

Culianu, Ioan P.
  Eros and magic in the Renaissance.

  Translation of: Eros et magie à la Renaissance, 1484.
  Bibliography: p.
  Includes index.
  1. Renaissance—Psychological aspects.   2. Magic.
I. Title.
CB367.C6813   1987   133.4'094   87-10882
ISBN 0-226-12315-4
ISBN 0-226-12316-2 (pbk.)

# Contents

# Translator's Note

Because the subtitle of a section of chapter 4 reads *Vinculum vinculorum* (part of the sentence later quoted in full, *Vinculum quippe vinculorum amor est*), I have translated the French *liens* sometimes as "bonds," sometimes as "chains," since *vinculum* means both. Sometimes I have chosen "chains" to avoid a mixed metaphor when the image is to "forge chains." Sometimes "bonds" has been used when the context calls for a less emphatic word. Because "bond" can have a psychoanalytic connotation, as in the reference to Freud in the text, I have tried to avoid using it in other contexts.

In translating quotations from ancient texts, I have sought to render the vivid charm and naïveté of the originals. The prose sounds archaïc, in English as in French.

The quotations in Latin and other foreign languages can be understood by all readers because—with rare exceptions—they only serve to substantiate and emphasize the text. (One exception is pornographic and appears in Spanish only on page 204 of the original text. I have honored the writer's discretion.)

It has been a privilege to translate this remarkable book.

MARGARET COOK

# Foreword

Ioan P. Couliano, a historian of religions and a specialist in Late Antiquity and gnosticism as well as a Romanist and an expert on the Balkans, teaches, among other subjects, the history of Rumanian culture at the University of Groningen. He has become known for many articles in scholarly journals and for three volumes, the most recent being *Religione e Potere* (Turin, 1981), written in collaboration with two young Italian researchers. But it is with *Eros and Magic*—pending the publication of an extensive comparative monograph on myths and techniques relating to ecstasy*—that his most important works begin to appear.

Remembering that the Italian Renaissance was one of my youthful passions and that I had chosen for my thesis the ideas of Marsilio Ficino, Pico della Mirandola, and Giordano Bruno, the author asked me to write a short foreword to *Eros and Magic*. I was tempted to enlarge upon the stages and great names of modern historiography concerning the Renaissance, emphasizing, for instance, recent reevaluations of hermetic, occult, and alchemical traditions. What a fascinating field of study in the history of thought is the analysis of interpretations of the Italian Renaissance, from Jacob Burckhardt and Giovanni Gentile to Eugenio Garin, P. Oskar Kristeller, E. H. Gombrich, F. A. Yates, D. P. Walker, Allen G. Debus, and other distinguished scholars of our day.

Alas! At my age, time and energy are limited. Hence I shall not discuss the author's most significant interpretations but shall confine myself to stressing their originality. I should like to mention, for example, the analysis of a little-known work by Giordano Bruno, *De vinculis in genere* ("Of Enchainment in General"), that Couliano compares to Machiavelli's *The Prince* (see chap. 4, sec. 2). Indeed, if Ficino identified eros with magic (for, he wrote, "the task of Magic consists in comparing things to one another"), Giordano Bruno carries to their final conclusions the operative possibilities of erotic magic. *Everything* can be manipulated by the imagination, that is, by phantasms erotic in origin and

---

*Expériences de l'extase* (Paris: Payot, 1984). An abridged English version was published in Leiden in 1983 (*Psychanodia* I, EPRO 99).

nature that arise in a subject or community, provided the manipulator be immunized through magic against his own phantasms. Quite rightly, the author recognizes in the technique expounded in *De vinculis* the direct forerunner of a modern discipline, applied psychosociology. "The magician of *De vinculis* is the prototype of the impersonal systems of mass media, of oblique censorship, of worldwide manipulation and of the brain trusts which exert their hidden influence upon the masses" (ibid).

I have cited this example, on the one hand, because *De vinculis* is still little known but also because, shortly after Giordano Bruno's death, the Reformation and the Counterreformation successfully imposed total censorship over expression of the imaginative faculty. The reason, of course, was religious: phantasms were idols conceived by "the inner sense" (see chap. 9, sec. 1). And, to be sure, censorship succeeded in wiping out the "sciences" based on the strength of the imagination, especially fanciful eroticism, the art of Memory, and magic. Moreover, according to the author, it was the Reformation's victorious offensive against the imagination that culminated in the destruction of Renaissance culture.

That censorship over the imagination which motivated the Churches of the West might be compared to the Iconoclasts' attack on the Eastern Church in the eighth and ninth centuries. The theological argument was the same: the idolatry inherent in the glorification of images. On the other hand, the iconophilic theologians laid stress on the continuum between the spiritual and the natural: the Incarnation annulled the interdiction against portraying the divine. Fortunately, the synod of 843 definitively reestablished the cult of icons. Fortunately, because it was the contemplation of images that gave the faithful access to a whole universe of symbols. In the final analysis, images could complete and deepen the religious instruction of the illiterate. (Actually, iconography fulfilled this function with regard to all rural populations of eastern Europe.)

Along with most historians, Ioan P. Couliano believes that "on the theoretical level, the gigantic censorship of the products of imagination results in the advent of the exact sciences and of modern technology" (chap. 10, sec. 4). Other researchers, on the other hand, have borne witness to the role of creative imagination in great geniuses of Western science, from Newton to Einstein. It does not behoove us here to address this complex and delicate problem (for creative imagination plays a decisive part especially in the progress of mathematics and theoretical physics, less so in the "natural sciences" and technology). Rather, let us keep to Couliano's observations on the survival, or reappearance, of a certain "magic" in the modern sciences of psychology and sociology. It is significant that this book, which begins with the history of the concept of "inner sense" from Aristotle to the Renaissance, should end with the legend of Faust in the interpretations of Marlowe and Calderón. These two writers exemplify, though in different ways, the rise of Puritanism: their literary imagination was laboriously curbed by what the author calls "an excessive moralism."

MIRCEA ELIADE
*University of Chicago*
*February 1982*

# Acknowledgments

The American edition of this work, appearing now in Margaret Cook's translation, is a revised version of my *Eros et Magie à la Renaissance* (Paris: Flammarion, 1984). Except for the appendixes, ommitted in the present translation, this edition is almost identical to the Italian one, published by Mondadori. The Introduction to both these editions was written in Chicago, where I spent the Spring Quarter 1986 as a visiting professor of history of religions and Hiram Thomas Guest Lecturer. During this period I gave a course on Renaissance magic and profited from stimulating contacts with the students. I also had the privilege of meeting Allen G. Debus on more than one occasion, and this renewed my interest in the Lullian system of memory and in Renaissance astrological medicine.

The good time I spent in Chicago, for which I thank all my colleagues in the Divinity School and especially its dean, Franklin I. Gamwell, was shadowed by a very sad event, the death of Mircea Eliade. He not only wrote the foreword to this book but also encouraged its author, over no less than fifteen years, to continue his researches. It would be impossible to say in a few words all I owe to Mircea Eliade's teaching and example. To friends and disciples he used to give far more than most professors do: he gave love, an unwavering enthusiasm, and positive thinking. Meeting first the work, and then the man himself, was the most decisive event in my formative years.

Fortunately, Mrs. Margaret Cook, who took upon herself the ungrateful task of translating a bulky work filled with technical terms, showed more than a professional interest in it. This would have been rewarding for any author who spends most of his time trying to understand worldviews of the past, an occupation for which he seldom receives public acclaim.

The press has been indulgent with this book, and it was not without satisfaction that I took notice, now and then, of enthusiastic reviews. There has been only one negative reaction to date, and I felt relieved when I read it: if things went too smoothly, the book would be forgotten in no time. After all, it was meant to be provocative on some issues.

Since 1984 I have occasionally given lectures on Renaissance magic, an enterprise from which I shall refrain in the future. In Chambéry, where I was invited by Jean Burgos, three real witches happened to attend my speech and accused me of talking about things I did not know from experience. I admitted it only too gladly and humbly asked for some understanding for a poor historian who was merely doing his job. This was apparently not granted, for strange things happened: a couple of people fainted, while my colleague the Africanist Hans Witte and I each got a terrible headache, which persisted till after we left the place. We found a rational explanation to this in the awsome *mistral* a wind so fatal that Moroccan traditional law used to excuse a husband if he killed one of his wives during the windy season. (Regrettably enough, the reverse does not seem to be true).

Since the last draft of the French version of this book was prepared (1982), I have changed my mind on the causes of the great witch craze in the sixteenth and seventeenth centuries. This was my topic for the first Hiram Thomas lecture on May 5, 1986, before a very friendly audience. Unfortunately, for more than one reason it was impossible to get the manuscript ready for the present translation. I would have liked to include it as a separate chapter in this book.

While staying with the Netherlands Institute for Advanced Study (N.I.A.S.) in Wassenaar (The Hague), I met Walter Gerbino from the University of Trieste, who is engaged in research concerning the psychology of cognitive processes. He explained to me that mnemotechnics are enjoying particular attention today. He himself was trying to establish possible connections between sight (image) and memory. I much regret that I was unaware, at the time this book was written, of the existence of many studies he cited. Without being pessimistic, I cannot help thinking that it is unlikely I shall ever find time to study all those aspects of Renaissance and Reformation culture that have been neglected or only superficially mentioned in the present work. (Even reincarnation would not be a solution, since I would have to start all over again anyway).

I am grateful to Adriana Berger, who, at the request of the University of Chicago Press, read the French text prior to translation and made a number of suggestions.

Last but not least: a special acknowledgment goes to Hillary Suzanne Wiesner, who graciously corrected my many corrections to this book.

I.P.C.
*N.I.A.S., Wassenaar (The Hague)*
*October 1986*

# Introduction

It is still commonly thought that a chasm separates our contemporary view of the world and ourselves from the concepts held by Renaissance man. The manifest sign of this cleavage is supposed to be modern technology, fruit of "quantitative science," which began to develop at the end of the seventeenth century. Though the most eminent authorities on the history of science tell us that the subject matter of a Newton, a Kepler, a Descartes, a Galileo, and a Bacon has absolutely nothing to do with this so-called "quantitative science," nevertheless the same mistaken opinions of our rationalist nineteenth-century forebears continue to be held. They, after all, firmly believed in the idea of reason and of progress, which they defended to the bitter end. To posit the existence of a hiatus between the infancy of mankind, which ended with the Renaissance, and its maturity, culminating with the advent of modern technology, served at that time to bolster the sociopolitical aims of our partisans of progress, who thought they were, or who actually were, surrounded by hostile forces. But nowadays, when the obvious proofs furnished by technology take away the usefulness of too nostalgic a view of the past, it is absolutely essential to overhaul from top to bottom this attitude whose falsity has to be concealed by intolerance.

The concept we moderns have of magic is very strange: we see it as merely a ludicrous heap of recipes and methods stemming from primitive, unscientific notions about nature. Unfortunately, the few "specialists" who venture to explore this realm carry with them, as their only equipment, the same prejudices. The works which break with this persistent pattern can be counted on the fingers of one hand.

Of course, it would be difficult to maintain that the method of magic has something to do with the method of our natural sciences. The structure of matter is completely ignored, and physico-chemical phenomena are ascribed to occult cosmic forces. Yet magic has in common with modern technology that it claims to arrive, by other means, at the same ends: long-distance communication, rapid transport, interplanetary trips are some of the magician's current exploits.

But it is not on this level that magic has continued to exist, mocking those who thought it had disappeared long ago. Indirectly derived from it are today's psychological and sociological sciences. That is why it is necessary first to have a correct picture of the essence and the methodology of magic to be able to form an idea of what we still owe to it.

The magic that concerns us here is theoretically a science of the imaginary, which it explores through its own methods and seeks to manipulate at will. At its greatest degree of development, reached in the work of Giordano Bruno, magic is a means of control over the individual and the masses based on deep knowledge of personal and collective erotic impulses. We can observe in it not only the distant ancestor of psychoanalysis but also, first and foremost, that of applied psychosociology and mass psychology.

Insofar as science and the manipulation of phantasms are concerned, magic is primarily directed at the human imagination, in which it attempts to create lasting impressions. The magician of the Renaissance is both psychoanalyst and prophet as well as the precursor of modern professions such as director of public relations, propagandist, spy, politician, censor, director of mass communication media, and publicity agent.

The workings of phantasy in the Renaissance are more or less complex: eroticism is the most important, already apparent in the natural world without human intervention. Magic is merely eroticism applied, directed, and aroused by its performer. But there are other aspects of the manipulation of phantasms, one of them being the miraculous Art of Memory. The bond between eroticism, mnemonics, and magic is indissoluble to such an extent that it is impossible to understand the third without first having studied the principles and mechanisms of the first two.

In studying imagination at the time of the Renaissance and the changes it was to undergo in the Reformation, I am something of a pioneer. Yet would be naive to maintain that my book has no connection with a whole tradition of studies about history and philosophy of science whose optical illusions it sometimes tries to correct.

It goes without saying that the subject matter whose historical vicissitudes are to be examined in the course of this work is *human imagination* as revealed in documents relating to eroticism and magic in the Renaissance. Sometimes it will be impossible to avoid taking into consideration the magician's pretenses in performing feats which are out of the ordinary. As a result, it will be impossible not to compare such pretense—whose validity is not at issue here—to the accomplishments of modern science and technology. Magic and science, in the last analysis, represent needs of the imagination, and the transition from a society dominated by magic to a predominantly scientific society is explicable primarily by a *change in the imaginary*. In that respect this book is innovative: it examines changes at the level of the *imaginary* rather than at the level of scientific *discoveries;* granted, of course, that a discovery is only made possible by a certain horizon of knowledge and beliefs conducive to it.

Nowadays, if we can boast of having at our disposal scientific knowledge and technology that used to exist only in the phantasies of magicians, we must allow that, since the Renaissance, our capacity to work directly with our own phantasms, if not with those of others, has diminished. The relationship between the conscious and the unconscious has been deeply altered and our ability to control our own processes of imagination reduced to nothing.

It is interesting not only to learn about the relationship between Renaissance man and his own phantasms but also to understand the ideological reasons that caused them to evolve in the way they did. What this amounts to is a correct understanding of the origins of modern science, which could not have appeared without the existence of factors able to cause modification of man's imagination. Those factors were not economic, nor did they stem from a so-called historical "evolution" of our race. On the contrary, the forces that produced them were regressive on the psychosocial level and even "reactionary" on the sociopolitical level. How can it be, then, that we owe to those forces the advent of the spirit that was to lead, step by step, to the rise of modern science? This is the enigma of history that this book attempts to solve.

To forestall uneasiness on the part of the reader when confronted with statements which are too shocking, primarily that we continue to live in a world in which magic still has a part to play and a place of honor, we have let the texts speak for themselves. We have, in the reader's behalf, assumed the burden of understanding them in letter and in spirit. After all, the conclusions we have drawn seem to us adequate recompense for the painstaking study pursued for twelve years without interruption, study involving philology only as a means, not as an end in itself. The fact that unremitting concentration on the *meaning* of documents has here supplanted mere reporting of their contents suffices to explain the individuality of this work, an individuality for which we do not believe we must apologize.

We find ourselves today at the crossroads of two kinds of epistemology: the one, which goes back to the age of Enlightenment, believes that scientific progress is cumulative and that, all things

considered, mankind is supposed to discover Truth; the other, only extant for a quarter-century, believes that all worldviews are valid, that
they are all far from Truth, and that there is no continuity between
them. According to that epistemology, the Renaissance concept of the
world and that of modern science, though chronologically related, are
not so in any other way: they are simply *incommensurable* with one another. Our research tends to confirm this point of view. Science in the
Renaissance—whose most general principles are the only ones under
examination here—is a coherent system, based on the psychic (or
rather, spiritual, *pneumatic*) dimension of things. This dimension, as will
be easily understood, is a real one. But are the intersubjective processes,
that magic says may exist, also real? Yes, in a way. We have proof of it
nowadays when manipulation through picture and speech has reached
an unprecedented level owing to mass communication.

But if there is a certain truth in the sciences at the time of the Renaissance, why did a revolutionary change occur which affected and destroyed them—from the seventeenth century on? Sociology has long
since established the fact of a shift in vocational interests toward science
and technology in Puritan England, bringing about a contact between
scientific vocations and religious Puritanism.[1] So it is that the range of
Puritanism which, according to Max Weber, was to lead to the forming
of the "spirit of capitalism"[2] was broadened to include the creation of
new spheres of social interest able to explain the rise of modern science
and technology.

Yet we must be careful when ascribing to historic causes a definitive
and *primary* character, for, in most cases, it is impossible to avoid circular
reasoning. For instance, if we try to define the scope of capitalism, we
cannot determine whether it is the product of (religious) reason that
accedes to the idea of possession, or whether it is not the latter that
wraps itself in religious reasons for purposes of self-justification. The
dilemma is unanswerable: greedy reason, or reasonable greed? Which-
ever it may be, the European scientific revolution that leads to the annihilation of the Renaissance sciences is caused by *religious* factors which
have nothing to do with the sciences themselves. It is always religion
that carries away European societies into risky ventures whose consequences we are still far from being able to evaluate. The historian with
knowledge, however unpretentious, of different worldviews, the scientific system, technology, and the institutions of any of the great civiliza-
tions of the past must sooner or later reach the disturbing conclusion
that all networks of ideas or collective (or individual) "programs" are
equally valid and, consequently, that the concept of the linear progress

of mankind is essentially false. In the final analysis, every cultural system rests on myths, our own as well as that of the Renaissance—not excepting the "exact sciences," as Stephen Toulmin[3] has brilliantly demonstrated. And who, from the summit of the Palatine, would ever have dreamed that the Roman Empire was not eternal? Who, from the top of many an impregnable fortress or many a cathedral, would not have thought that the medieval world would last forever? This also applies, of course, to Giotto's *campanile*.

I have no time here to indulge in decadent feelings, but I was surprised lately by the question of a young archaeologist when we were admiring the magnificent buildings in Chicago. "Don't you think," she asked, "that some day all this will be nothing but rubble?" I had never thought of it and I have not thought of it since. "There would be a lot of work, *a lot* of work for people like you," was all I replied. But her question opened up unfathomed deeps.

Let the reader look into these deeps of history, by himself.

After all, this book is only a sowing of phantasms destined for an unknown reaper. It is he who will decide how to make use of it.

*Chicago*
*May 1986*

# I Phantasms at Work

*Supprime gl'eminenti, e inalza i bassi*
*Chi l'infinite machini sustenta,*
*Et con veloce, mediocre, et lenta*
    *Vertigine, dispensa*
    *In questa mole immensa*
*Quant'occolto si rende e aperto stassi.*

Giordano Bruno.

# 1| History of Phantasy

## (i) On the Inner Sense

SOME PRELIMINARY CONSIDERATIONS

Our civilization is born of the conjunction of many cultures whose interpretations of human existence were so at variance that a huge historic upheaval along with a fanatic faith were necessary to achieve a lasting synthesis. In that synthesis, matters of diverse origin underwent a reconversion and a reinterpretation marked by traces of the predominant culture of the period: the culture of a conquered people, the Greeks, enhanced by a conquering people, the Romans.

In Greek thought, sexuality was usually a secondary component of love. While granting the link between sexuality and reproduction, no emphasis was placed on a "natural cause," which assigned to the former a purely generative goal; it is also true that woman's role as instrument of reproduction involved no intimacy between the sexes based on love but rather a liaison based on politics: the fruit of intercourse was to become a new citizen useful to the state, a soldier or producer of soldiers. Profane love, that of an Alcibiades for instance, was a mixture of physical attraction, comradeship, and respect inspired by exceptional qualities, a strong attraction more characteristic of a homosexual relationship. Plato, undaunted by the banishment of poets from his ideal city on the pretext that their uncontrollable poetic fervor conceals a danger to the State, certainly poses the question of the social usefulness of the tremendous emotional power that Eros is. The kind of love that Socrates teaches in Plato's dialogues represents a gradual elevation in the nature of the human being from the signs of beauty apparent in the physical world to the ideal forms whence those signs derive, the intellectual cosmos which, as unique and indivisible source of the True, the Good, and the Beautiful, also represents the ultimate goal to which he aspires. Love is the name of that desire with many manifestations which, even in its most decadent form, admixing sexual attraction, still retains its quality of unconscious aspiration to the transcendental Beauty.

Plato, probably the philosopher with the greatest influence on the history of Western thought, separates the sphere of genuine love from the respective (and insuperable) spheres of sexuality and reproduction by endowing Eros with the status—very important though indefinite in the ideal order of things—of *link* between existence and the essence of beings, *ta onta ontos.* The supreme lover is the *philosophos,* he who loves wisdom, that is to say, the art of elevating himself toward the Truth, which is also Goodness and Beauty, by detaching himself from the world.

Both as conscious attraction and as unconscious yearning, even profane love for Plato is imponderable. In any case, physical desire, aroused by the irrational soul and appeased by means of the body, only represents, in the phenomenology of love, an obscure and secondary aspect of love. The body is just an instrument, whereas love, even the kind with a sexual goal, stems from the powers of the soul. In sum, the maieutic endeavor of Socrates puts the emphasis on the convertibility of all love, even physical (that is, psycho-physical) into intellectual contemplation.

Aristotle does not question the existence of the Platonic soul-body dichotomy. But, with an interest in the secrets of nature, he feels the need to define empirically the relations between those two separate entities, whose union, almost impossible from a metaphysical point of view, forms one of the deepest mysteries of the universe. The coming of Aristotle, who was probably inspired by the medical theories of Sicily or Empedocles,[1] produces two results of incalculable importance to the history of Western thought: on the one hand, Eros will be envisaged in the same way as sensory activity, as one of the processes involving the mutual perceptible soul-body relation, thus removing it from the unconditioned dominion of the soul. On the other hand, and as a result, the erotic mechanism, like the process of cognition, will have to be analyzed in connection with its spiritual characteristics and the subtle physiology of the apparatus which serves as intermediary between soul and body.

This apparatus is composed of the same substance—the spirit (*pneuma*)—of which the stars are made and performs the function of primary instrument (*prōton organon*) of the soul in its relation to the body. Such a mechanism furnishes the conditions necessary to resolve the contradiction between the corporeal and the incorporeal: it is so subtle that it approximates the immaterial nature of the soul, and yet it is a body which, as such, can enter into contact with the sensory world. Without this astral spirit, body and soul would be completely unaware of each other, blind as each is to the dominion of the other. For the soul has no ontological aperture through which it can look down, while the body is only a form of organization of natural elements, a form which would disintegrate immediately without the vitality ensured it by the soul. Finally, the soul can only transmit all vital activities, including movement, to the body by means of the *prōton organon*, the spiritual apparatus located in the heart. On the other hand, the body opens up to the soul a window to the world through the five sensory organs whose messages go to the same cardiac apparatus which now is engaged in codifying them so that they may become comprehensible. Called *phantasia* or inner sense, the sidereal spirit transforms messages from the five senses in *phantasms* perceptible to the soul. For the soul cannot grasp anything that is not converted into a sequence of phantasms; in short, it can understand nothing without phantasms (*aneu phantasmatos*).[2] This passage is rendered in Latin by William of Moerbecke, translator of Aristotle, as follows: *Numquam sine phantasmate intelligit anima.* And St. Thomas uses it almost literally in his *Summa theologica*,[3] which was of enormous influence in the succeeding centuries: *Intelligere sine conversione ad phantasmata est (animae) praeter naturam.* The *sensus interior,* inner sense or Aristotelian common sense, which had become a concept inseparable not only from scholasticism but also from all western thought until the eighteenth century, is to keep its importance even for Descartes and reappear, perhaps for the last time, at the beginning of Kant's *Critique of Pure Reason.* Among philosophers of the nineteenth century it had already lost credence, being changed into a mere curiosity of history limited to books specializing on the subject or becoming the butt of ridicule, proof that in intellectual circles it was not forgotten at all. Without knowing that, for Aristotle, intellect itself has the nature of phantasm, that it is *phantasma tis,* it would be impossible to grasp the meaning of Kierkegaard's jest: "Pure thought is a phantasm."

Fundamentally, all is reduced to a question of communication: body and soul speak two languages, which are not only different, even inconsistent, but also *inaudible* to each other. The inner sense alone is able to hear and comprehend them both, also having the role of translating one into the other. But considering the words of the soul's language are phantasms, everything that reaches it from the body—including distinct utterances—will have to be transposed into a phantasmic sequence. Besides—must it be emphasized?—the soul has absolute primacy over the body. It follows that *the phantasm has absolute primacy over the word,* that it precedes both utterance and understanding of every linguistic message. Whence two separate and distinct grammars, the first no less important than the second: a grammar of the spoken language and a grammar of phantasmic language. Stemming from the soul, itself phantasmic in essence, intellect alone enjoys the privilege of understanding the phantasmic grammar. It can make manuals and even organise very serious-minded games of phantasms. But all that will be useful to him principally for understanding the soul and investigating its hidden potentialities. Such understanding, less a science than an art because of the skill which must be deployed to catch the secrets of the little-known country where the intellect travels, involves the assumption of all the phantasmic processes of the Renaissance: Eros, the Art of Memory, theoretical magic, alchemy, and practical magic.

THE PHANTASMIC PNEUMA

The Aristotelian theory of the phantasmic pneuma did not come out of the blue. On the contrary, it can even be said there is nothing original about it except for the way the pieces composing it are fitted together. The system is that of the philosopher of Stagira, though the elements of the system preexisted. Using Aby Warburg's expression, the "selective will" may be attributed to Aristotle but not the creation of the substance of that tenet.

To recall the important periods of the history of the phantasmic pneuma as we are doing here is not merely a collector's foible. It is because they were satisfied with Aristotle and had lost sight of that history that interpreters of the Renaissance, even the most astute, never grasped the essence of many spiritual processes nor their basic unity. So long as the phenomenon itself was not understood, all the erudition in the world is useless, for what it can do comes down to very little, specifically to perfecting our knowledge about the existence and manifestations of a phenomenon without, however, broaching the much more important problem of the cultural presuppositions that keep it in existence at a given time. The doctrine of the phantasmic pneuma is not an isolated oddity produced by the gropings of premodern science. On the contrary, it is the principal theme that will help us to understand the mechanics and goal of that science as well as being the horizon of hope[4] toward which human existence stretched for a long period in the past of our species.

As early as the sixth century the Sicilian physician, Alcemaeon of Croton, like the Pythagoreans, speaks of vital pneuma circulating in the arteries of the human being. The relation of blood to pneuma—the latter being the subtler part of the former—becomes common ground for the school of Sicilian medicine whose chief is the famous Empedocles of Agrigentum, the fifth-century Greek medicine man. As *iatromantis,* healer (*iatros*) and soothsayer (*mantis*), Empedocles was known as the greatest specialist of antiquity in the treatment of catalepsy (*apnous*) or apparent death.[5] We do not know what Empedocles thought of the vital pneuma, but the members of the school who acknowledged him as leader believed spirit to be a subtle vapor from the blood moving about in the arteries of the body, whereas the venous circulation was set apart for the blood itself. The heart, the central depository of the pneuma, holds first rank in the maintenance of the body's vital functions.

Though less refined than the theory of the *prānas* in the Upanishad, the Sicilian doctrine closely resembles it in making use of the concept of rarefied fluids to explain organic functions. As I have shown elsewhere, it is from this subtle physiology, or alongside of it, that the mystical theories and techniques are developed in which the "heart" or the "heart's place" plays a fundamental role.[6]

The Cos school of medicine, founded by Hippocrates, a contemporary of Socrates, differentiated itself from the Sicilian school by ascribing to the pneuma another origin and another location. According to the Hippocratics, the arterial pneuma was merely the air breathed in from the environment, and its center was the brain.

This doctrine was transmitted by Praxagoras of Cos to his disciple Herophilus of Alexandria and doubtless contributed to the synthesis worked out by Erasistrates, a younger countryman of Herophilus. Erasistrates, whose opinions have come down to us through the writings of Galen, tries to reconcile the views of the two medical schools by propounding the decentralization of the pneuma. To satisfy the Empedocleans, he makes of the heart's left ventricle the seat of the *vital* pneuma (*Zōtikon*) and, in order not to oppose the Hippocratics, he locates the *psychic* pneuma (*psychikon*) in the brain. The right ventricle of the heart contains venous blood, whereas the pneuma circulates in the arteries but—according to the Hippocratic theory—is merely air inhaled from the outside, a theory not endorsed by Galen, for whom the arteries contain both blood and pneuma mixed.[7]

If only for the fact that they are probably repeated by Plato, the principles of the Sicilian school already would have deserved careful attention. In addition, two of the most influential thinkers of antiquity, Aristotle and Zeno of Citium, founder of Stoicism, made of those ideas the foundation of their respective doctrines of the soul and, especially in Zeno's case, of a whole interpretation of the microcosm as well as the macrocosm based on analogy.

Two pieces of evidence, unequal in value, indicate a connection between Plato and Sicilian medicine. Around 370–60, a proponent of the latter, Philistion, was sojourning in Athens.[8] That is historical and would be without significance if it were not confirmed by the presence in Plato's work of elements borrowed from teachings of the Sicilians and the Hippocratics. Since the question is only of marginal interest to us, we shall refrain from dealing with it exhaustively.[9] The Stoics's interest in the theory of sensory knowledge is well known, and we shall return to it. We might assume that this is just one of many debts owed to Sicilian medicine, for we shall observe later that the medicine of the "pneumatic school" and of Galen took up such matters. Sometimes it is through the nexus of Stoicism that we can reconstruct the earliest medical thinking where more direct evidence is lacking.

Plato does not adopt the concept of pneuma, but his explanations of the mechanics of sight (*Timaeus* 45b–d) and of hearing (*Timaeus* 67b) with similarities to Stoic and medical ideas at their latest stage of development could derive from the teaching of the Sicilians. The formation of optical images is not without affinity to the principle of radar: the eyes, depositories of an internal fire, project an igneous ray through the pupils, a ray that meets the "external fire" projected by sensory bodies outside themselves. Aristotle (*De anima* 428a) will reduce the number of "fires" to one—specifically the "external fire" which, in the act of seeing, is reflected in the ocular membranes. For Plato, hearing results from the impact of sound wave on the ears, an impact that is transmitted "to the brains and the blood, thus to arrive at the soul" (*Timaeus* 67b). His explanation is akin to the one the Stoics are to give to this phenomenon later, except that, for the Stoics, sound wave is called *vocal pneuma*.[10]

After Plato, more direct contact is established between the Sicilian medical doctrines and the great thinkers of the period, thanks largely to the remarkable work of Diocles of Carystus, a contemporary if not a precursor of Aristotle.[11] It is still premature to make a statement about what the latter owes to Diocles. In any case, by comparing the Aristotelian theory of the phantasmic pneuma with the Stoic concept of *hēgemonikon* or "Principal" of the soul, a concept built up by the Stoics based on hypotheses of Empedoclean medicine, it is possible, if not necessary, to conclude that it was Diocles who inspired Aristotle and not the reverse.

For Zeno, the hypotheses stemming from the teachings of Diocles, especially the medical concept of the pneuma, form the skeleton of a whole micro- and macrocosmic theory representing the greatest attempt by the human mind to reconcile man with the world, the low with the high. Built upon the Stoic synthesis, magic in Late Antiquity—whose principles reappear, perfected, in magic in the Renaissance—is but a practical continuation of the Empedoclean medical theories as reelaborated by the Stoics.

Whereas, for Aristotle, the pneuma was just a thin casing around the soul, for the Stoics, as well as for the doctors, the pneuma is the soul itself, which penetrates the whole human body, controlling all its activities—movement, the five senses, excretion, and the secretion of sperm. The Stoic theory of sensory knowledge is not unrelated to that of Aristotle: a cardiac synthesizer, the hegemonic Principal (*hēgemonikon*), receives all the pneumatic currents transmitted to it by the sensory organs and produced by the "comprehensible phantasms" (*phantasia kataleptikē*) apprehended by the intellect.[12] This has only the means to recognize "prints made upon the soul" (*typosis en psychē*) produced by the Principal, which, like a spider in its web, from its seat in the heart—the body's center—is on the lookout for all information transmitted to it by the peripheral senses.[13] For Chrysippus, "the perception of an object would occur by means of a pneumatic current which, taking off from the hēgemonikon, goes toward the pupil of the eye where it enters in contact with the air situated between the organ of vision and the perceptible object. That contact produces in the air a certain tension which spreads in the shape of a cone whose summit is in the eye and whose base delimits our visual field."[14] A corresponding pneumatic circulation animates the five senses as well as producing voice and sperm.[15] The later Stoics, like Epictetus, perhaps inspired by Platonic radar, even go so far as to say that, in the act of looking, the pneuma outstrips the sensory organ to enter into contact with the tangible object and bring the image perceived back to the hēgemonikon.[16]

Stemming from ancient medical theories but perfected by the Stoics, the theory of pneumatic cognition reenters, by way of the school of the physician Athenaeus, founded in Rome in the first century, the discipline from which it came. According to the doctrine of "pneumatic" physicians whose principal advocate was Archigenes of Apamea in Syria, practicing in Rome under the emperor Trajan, the hegemonikon does not enter directly into the process of sensory cognition. The great Galen, second-century doctor, takes inspiration from the "pneumatics" in that he no longer asserts that the hegemonikon is located in the human heart but contends it is in the brain instead. He accords it, however, the important function of *synaisthēsis*, of "synthetization" of pneumatic information.[17]

I cannot dwell here on the fate of Galen in the Middle Ages. His works were used and thus preserved by Arab medicine. The cultural event that some call the "twelfth-century Renaissance" signals the rediscovery of

Greek Antiquity through Arab channels. Galen reappeared in European culture through translations in Latin of Arab writers.[18] At the beginning of the thirteenth century, medieval encyclopedias record new knowledge, which will become thereafter a common good of that period.

One of the most famous synopses of the time was *De proprietatibus rerum libri XIX*, drafted between 1230 and 1250 by a Friar Minor, Bartholomaeus Anglicus, who had taught at Magdeburg and at the Sorbonne. The countless incunabula, the eighteen editions, and the translation into six vernacular languages are inadequate to give an idea of the prestige—alas, greatly superior to the value—of this mediocre work. A significant fact is that at the beginning of the fourteenth century the copy which had belonged to Pierre de Limoges was chained to the pulpit of the chapel of the University of Paris.[19]

The psychology of intellectual faculties or the theory of "qualities" of the soul is expounded by Bartholomaeus in the third book of his synopsis[20] following Latin translations from the Arabic such as *Hysagoge in medicinam* by Hunain ibn Ishaq, alias Johannitius, Iraqi physician of the ninth century,[21] the writings of Constantine the African or compilations like *De motu cordis* by Alfred the English, and the pseudo-Augustinian *De spiritu et anima*, twelfth-century work now attributed to Hugh of Saint-Victor or (perhaps more likely) to Alcher of Clairvaux.

In that doctrine, rather clumsily summarized by Bartholomaeus, in which Galenism and Aristotelianism commingle, the human soul is divided into three parts: the rational or intellective soul, eternal, incorruptible, or immortal; the sensitive soul, composed of spiritual substance; and the vegetative soul. The vegetative soul is common to men and plants, the sensitive soul is common to man and animals, while the intellective soul belongs to man alone. The vegetative soul produces the generation, conservation, and growth of bodies; it controls nutritive, digestive, and excretory functions (III, 8). The sensitive soul—that which interests us here—has three faculties: *natural, vital,* and *animal.* It seems that through the natural faculty, which resides in the liver and is transmitted to the body through venous circulation, the sensitive soul only takes upon itself the functions of the vegetative soul, those of nutrition, generation, and growth (III, 14). The seat of the vital or spiritual faculty is the heart, which spreads life through the entire organism by means of the spirit circulating in the arteries. As for the animal faculty, its seat is the brain. It is divided in three (III, 16): *ordinatiua, sensitiua,* and *motiua.* The distinction between the first two is quite difficult to grasp, so much so that elsewhere (III, 12) Bartholomaeus himself forgets what it is, dwelling only on the description of the sensory faculty.[22]

The chamber, or anterior ventricle of the brain, seat of the imagination (or, according to Bartholomaeus, of the *virtus imaginatiua*, a branch of the *ordinatiua*), is filled with nerve endings, which establish communication with the sensory organs. The same spirit—here called "sensory"—circulates in the nerves and arteries (III, 9), which makes us believe that originally the doctrines expounded by Bartholomaeus were based on the idea prevalent in Arab medicine that the heart is the unique generator of the vital spirit which, once it has reached the brain, is called sensitive. The messages of the five "external" senses are transported by the spirit to the brain, where the *inner* or *common* sense resides. The action of common sense is, according to Bartholomaeus, that of the *virtus ordinatiua*, which occupies the three cerebral ventricles: the anterior, seat of the imagination; the median, seat of reason; and the posterior, seat of memory. Imagination translates the language of the senses into fantastic language so that reason may grasp and understand phantasms. The data of imagination and of reason are deposited in the memory (III, 10).

Bartholomaeus is merely a faithful reflection of the concepts of an entire period shared by Albert the Great, Roger Bacon, and Thomas Aquinas. Most of his theories were already available in Latin from the second half of the eleventh century, when, after a life of adventure, the Carthaginian physician Constantine the African found peace in the cloisters of Montecassino and devoted himself to the translation of Arab medical works, which circulated for a long time under his own name. Finally, in the twelfth century, the great translator Gerard of Cremona, installed in the college of the archbishop Raymond in Toledo, rendered among other works a Latin vesion of the works of Avicenna in which the theory of phantasmic synthesis and the compartments of the brain were already commonplace.

### (ii) Flux and Reflux of Values in the Twelfth Century

The originality of an era is not measured by the content of its ideological systems but rather by its "selective will," that is, according to the *interpretive grille* it interposes between preexisting contents and their "modern" treatment.[23] The passing of a message through the hermeneutic filter of an era produces two results of a semantic kind: the first, aiming at the very organization of the cultural structure of the time and hence located outside it, is set forth as a complex and subtle mechanism of emphasis or, on the contrary, of suppression of certain ideological contents; the second, which operates in the very interior of the cultural structure, is set forth as a systematic distortion or even a semantic inversion of ideas which pass through the interpretive grille of the era.

All of this means that the crowning wish of the historian of ideas is

not, or should not be, to define the ideological contents of a given period, which are fundamentally recursive in nature, but to glimpse its *hermeneutic filter*, its "selective will," which is, at the same time, a *will to
distort*.

An ideology can be described; a system of interpretation—the only
one that counts because it alone can show what the originality of one
cultural moment in time relative to every other is capable of—is imperceptible. An implicit if not a hidden presence but also an objective and
ineluctible one, it is revealed stealthily in all its complexity only to immediately escape the observation of the investigator. In order for him to
practice the history of ideas, he is called upon to *see* not only what is
preeminently revealed, the *ideas* themselves, but precisely that which is
not revealed, the hidden threads that link ideas to the invisible will of
the time, their producer. Ideas are seen by everyone; the *historian* of
ideas is supposed to look in the wings, to contemplate another aspect of
the theater, the stage seen from within.

It is impossible to observe the Renaissance of the fifteenth century
without having first glanced at the Renaissance of the twelfth.[24] Theories about phantasmic Eros were developed in the course of the latter to
reach their apogee, which soon degenerated into affectation, in the poetry of the *Dolce Stil Novo*.

The "selective will" of the Italian Renaissance pays a good deal of
attention to the often fastidious works of its thirteenth-century precursors in order to fit them into its own system of interpretation. It is not
purely out of kindness that Marsilio Ficino, whose treatise on love was
written for use by a descendant of Guido Cavalcanti,[25] sets forth in detail some of Cavalcanti's erotic theories. As one of the principal representatives of the *fedeli d'amore*, Guido Cavalcanti developed an empirical
psychology of Eros that does not differ essentially from that of Ficino.

The case of Pico della Mirandola, which we shall analyze in chapter 3,
is more complicated: it would be called a striking example of the Oedi-
pus complex if that term had not fallen into disuse through repeated
abuse. Stimulated, or rather irritated, by Ficino's little masterpiece on
love, Pico abandons all courtesy and tries to refute it in toto. That is why
he attacks Guido Cavalcanti for lacking profundity and holds up as a
model for a love poem a *canzona* by his own friend Girolamo Benivieni
on which he undertakes a commentary. The example of Pico is highly
significant. The young man forgets what elsewhere he reveals he knows
only too well, in particular that a cultural era is not defined by the content of the ideas it conveys but by its interpretive filter. It demands of
Guido Cavalcanti that which Ficino, more subtle in this respect, would

never have asked: to wit, that he already use the Platonistic interpretation of the fifteenth century! Benivieni's *Canzona* only differs from a *canzona* by Cavalcanti in that it furnishes *directly* to Pico della Mirandola the interpretation he would have made even in the absence of the poem because it was *his own* interpretation of Eros in general. The Platonistic reading of Cavalcanti signified, to Ficino, a hermeneutic bias which also allowed him to pay tribute to a precursor and to the ancestor of someone he liked. Now, in rejecting a real *object* for interpretation—because the difference between his commentary and the text commentated is only prosodic, the former being in prose, the latter in verse—Pico peremptorily rejects all hermeneutics. For Ficino, Cavalcanti exists to the extent he said something *interpretable*; for Pico, he does not exist since he does not provide something already *interpreted* as was the case with his friend Benivieni. As for the rest of it, there is no great fundamental difference between Ficino's and Pico's theories, although Pico latter constantly censures Ficino for the vulgarity of his approach to questions of love.[26]

Whether expressed in a polite or positive way, as by Ficino, or in the contemptuous and negative manner of Pico, it is certain that the Florentine Renaissance takes chronological precedence over the rediscovery of the other Renaissance, that of the twelfth and thirteenth centuries.

Modern scholars, who sometimes confuse the rediscovery with the summarizing or literal resumption of the same ideas, accord such precedence only to Mario Equicola, interpreter of Provençal poetry in his *Libro de natura de amore*, of which the Latin original—on which the Italian translation of 1509–11 (published in 1525) was based—dates back to the years 1494–96,[27] right after the death of Pico. Now, it is true that Mario Equicola refers directly to the lyric style of the troubadours, whereas Cavalcanti, in whom Ficino discovers a precursor, is only the later representative of an Italian school, which, also profiting from the lessons of the Sicilian school[28] and in competition with the school of Bologna, replaces the code of the troubadours with one that is more rigid and "scientific." Of course, the two examples are not superimposable, but "stilnovism" and Provençal poetry both stem from the same existential root of courtly love.

ACCULTURATION OF THE WEST

The observer of ideas and currents taking place on the twelfth-century stage is frustrated by their variety. A quick foray into the wings, which few have yet dared to attempt, shows us that many strings are held in the same hand, the same "selective will," perhaps.[29]

The phenomenon that characterizes the movements of ideas in the twelfth century might be compared to a huge flux and reflux of data and cultural values. Spain at the time of the *Reconquista*[30] is one of the most important centers. In proportion as the Christian kingdom of Castille advances and the Arabs retreat, "specialists" or adventurers throng the field, fascinated by the wealth and culture of the Moslems, and begin their feverish work of translation in which wonder and religious controversy intermingle. Quickly, due chiefly to the college of translators installed at Toledo, the Latin West comes into contact with the principal records of Arab culture (and of Greek Antiquity) in the fields of medicine, philosophy, alchemy, and religion.

The latter remains subject to rebuttal, and Rodriguez Ximénez de Rada or Peter the Venerable, abbot of Cluny, carry out this task conscientiously. Their philosophy offers food for thought; in any case it was not accepted at once and without changes unless, by chance, a Jewish philosopher of Cordoba such as Solomon ibn Gabirol happened—under the Latinized name of Avicebron, Avencebrol, or Avemcembron—to pass for Christian. But as soon as the Arab Aristotle and the Greek Aristotle were discovered, Scholasticism had found its man. No authority, until the rediscovery of Plato and of pagan Neoplatonism, could give that master any competition. Medicine had the same fate: it was adopted immediately, especially because the Galenism of the Arabs concurred on many points with the doctrines of Aristotle. The time of the great syntheses, or *summae*, had come.

With regard to the Arab culture of Spain, it is more difficult to specify what it carried away in its reflux: perhaps traces of Christian mysticism evident in Ibn 'Arabī, the great Sufi master of the thirteenth century. Be that as it may, those who stood to profit from the exchange of values were primarily the Christians.

This process of acculturation that occurred at the western end of Europe was also accompanied by infiltration of elements from the east, threatening the bases of medieval society with disintegration. Long disguised under other names or simply remaining hidden, the ancient universalistic gnosis of Mani reappeared, in the tenth century, in the teachings of the Bulgarian pope Bogomil. Bogomilism, which had quickly come to Byzantium, showed off the whole arsenal of dualistic gnoses: it held the adversary of God to be the creator of the visible world and inspirer of the Old Testament, which was rejected in one lump, or almost so; it preached *encratism*, or abstention from marriage and sexual relations, in order not to perpetuate Satan's evil doings, and *vegetarianism*, to avoid incorporating the Satanic element present in animals; it also preached antinomianism or nonobedience to laws formulated by the civil and religious authorities.[31]

Catharism, which appears toward the end of the first half of the twelfth century, probably represents the Western branch of Bogomilism.[32] Sporadic traces of dualistic gnosis, however, appear from the beginning of the eleventh century in France and Italy. A group of noblemen and priests from Orléans, around 1015, practiced encratism, vegetarianism, and *docetism*, the idea that Christ never assumed a real human body, this also constituting part of the dualistic dogma.[33] A second example, in Monforte in Piedmont, closely resembles that of Orléans, both in the nature of its beliefs and in the composition of the group. Anticlerical, docetist, antinomian, encratite, and vegetarian, they also presage the Catharan *endura* with the idea that the members of their sect nearing death should be ritually killed in order to spare them death throes.[34] At the beginning of the twelfth century the Bogomil influences are revealed in the anticlerical and iconoclastic heresy of Peter of Bruis and the itinerant preacher Henry,[35] as well as in the profession of dualistic faith of two peasants from Soissons, Clement and Ebrard (1114).[36] Tanchelm of Anvers and Eudo (Eon) of l'Etoile, both very strange people, seem to have been inspired by the gnosticism of the first centuries A.D., the former being especially influenced by Simon the Magician of Samaria. Perhaps this was a spontaneous inspiration—coming from the innermost depths of the collective unconscious, since both men were declared insane by some of their contemporaries as indeed they are by modern scholars.

The Cathars, Puritan dualists of the twelfth and thirteenth centuries, were alone in organizing themselves along the lines of the Bogomils[37] into powerful churches, which, in southern France and northern Italy became a real threat to the Catholic Church. It was in the fight against the Cathars that the Church created and perfected the shocking agency of the Inquisition.

The difference between the Cathars and the heretics of Orléans and Monforte is not to be sought on the ideological level but rather on the level of practical power, which the Cathars attained by means of their active preaching. Although they rationalized their dogma in a different way than the people from Orléans and Monforte, the Cathars professed no less than *anticosmism* or opposition to the evil world created by Satan, docetism, encratism, antinomiansm, anticlericalism, and vegetarianism (or almost, since fish, which they maintained were generated spontaneously and nonsexually, by water, were not excluded from their lean repasts).

All that interests us here is the codification of theories about love in the twelfth and thirteenth centuries, and not the history of medieval dualism. Now, it is very important that the Cathars' code of morals, in principle puritan, did not exclude, in certain cases, licentiousness, a grave form of antinomiansm with respect to the social regulations for Catholics. The Cathars, being encratite, did not permit marriage: *Legitima connubia damnant. Matrimonium est meretricium, matrimonium est lupanar*, they declared in opposing such "legalization of concubinage." "They absolutely proscribe marriage . . . ," the inquisitor Bernardus Guidonis tells us; "they assert that it is a perpetual state of sin. They deny that the good Lord ever instituted it. They declare that carnal knowledge of a wife is no lesser sin than incestuous relations with a mother, daughter, or sister."[38]

On the other hand, given that the path of Cathar initiation went from mere *believer* to the *perfect* one, sexual lapse of believers was openly (*publice*) allowed, provided that it not bear the legal seal of marriage, because it was much more weighty to make love to a wife than to another, *facere cum uxore sua quam cum alia muliere*. This opened the way to a sexual licentiousness that the Catholic Church feared at least as much as the dualistic dogma of the Cathars, because of its antisocial and anti-demographic consequences.[39]

The cultural flux that swamped western Europe from west to east, which resulted in the scholasticism of the early Middle Ages as well as the dualistic sects, can be considered an important phenomenon. When the tide receded, the influences coming from the west and those coming from the east were united in the strange and original ideology of *courtly love.*

Courtly love has in common with Catharism a contempt for marriage and an ambiguous message which, though opposed in principle to sexual intercourse, is contradicted, in practice, by the licentious behavior of the troubadours. Like the Cathar faithful, some of them seem systematically to have indulged in debauchery. The phenomenon of courtly love has, however, more in common with Arab medicine and mysticism, which nevertheless does not negate the hypothesis of a dual origin.

Idealization and even hypostatization of woman, a vital component of courtly love, had long imbued Arab mystical poetry. The latter, moreover, did not escape the charge of dualism, a phenomenon meeting with the same intolerance both by Moslems and Christians. In 783, the poet Bashshār ibn Burd was sentenced to death as a zindīq or crypto-Manichaean (hence a Cathar ahead of his time) "because he had identified the woman, to whom he had dedicated his poem, with Spirit or *rūh*, the intermediary between man and God."[40] Only unattainable womanhood can be deified, and R. Boase recalls, as a Cathar adjunct to the story of Bashshār, that Gervais of Tilbury sent a young girl to the stake only because she had resisted his erotic advances.[41]

In Islam, the identification of woman as suprasensory entity was more or less current, without lacking ambiguity. For the sufi mystic Sanā'ī, who died about 1150, a *Madonna Intelligenza* hidden behind the features of a woman was the pilgrim's guide in the cosmos of the Neoplatonists of Islam;[42] he was, at the same time, the author of one of the most dreadful diatribes against women ever conceived.[43] It is probably a question of the dual aspect of the feminine: the *natural* aspect, which prompts and justifies the misogyny of the ascetic man, and the *essential* aspect, under which woman is the "other half of heaven."

Mitigating the contradiction between those two separate aspects of the feminine, the sufi mystic Ibn 'Arabī of Murcia considers woman merely an ideal species. In Mecca in 1201, he composes a *Dīwān* dedicated to Nezām (Harmony), daughter of an Imam nobleman of Persian origin, Zāhir ibn Rostam.[44] Entitled *The Interpreter of Burning Desires*, the *Dīwān's* prologue contains these intimate confessions:

> Now this sheik had a daughter, a slender and willowy adolescent who attracted the attention of anyone who saw her, whose presence alone was the embellishment of public meetings and struck with amazement all who looked upon her. Her name was Nezām (*Harmonia*) and her surname "Eye of the Sun and of Beauty" ['ayn al-Shams wa'l-Bahā']. Scholarly and pious, with experience of the spiritual and mystical life, she personified the venerable antiquity of the Holy Land and the innocent youth of the prophet's great city. The magic of her glance, the grace of her conversation, was so enchanting that if she happened to be prolix her speech was filled with references; if concise, a marvel of eloquence; holding forth on a subject, clear and lucid. . . . Were it not for petty minds eager for scandal and inclined to slander, I would here comment on the beauty that God lavished on her body as well as on her soul, which was a garden of generosity. . . . At the time I used to visit her I carefully observed the noble qualities of her person besides what the company of her aunt and her father added to it. Thus I took her as the prototype for inspiration of the poems contained in this book, love poems, composed of elegant and sweet phrases, albeit I have not been able to succeed in expressing even part of the emotion in my soul that meeting this young girl aroused in my heart, nor the wholehearted love I felt, nor the stamp that her continuous friendship left on my memory, nor the grace of her spirit and her modesty of demeanor, because she is the object of my Quest and of my hope, the Purest virgin [*al-Adkrā al-batūl*]. Nevertheless, I have succeeded in putting into verse

some of my nostalgic thoughts like precious objects offered here. I have clearly expressed my smitten soul, I have wished to suggest the deep attachment that I felt, the deep solicitude that troubled me during the period that has elapsed and the sorrowful longing that still moves me when I think of the exalted companionship of this young girl.[45]

Although Ibn 'Arabī is at great pains to specify that his poems are symbolic, that the visible beauties only evoke the suprasensory realities of the world of angelic meanings, a doctor from Aleppo accuses him of having concealed a sensual love in order to save his reputation for austerity. This personage, real or fictional, here fills the place he deserved: the moralist who interferes in order to question the purity of intent of the lover and who arouses the very protests of the lover that form the explanation of courtly love. What is involved here is not just a personage but a *function* in the structure of the literary and existential style cultivated by love's faithful, from the troubadours to Dante. To refute these vulgar insinuations, Ibn 'Arabī decides to write his long commentary on the *Dīwān* in which he explains what Henry Corbin calls "the manner of theophanic apperception" typical of love's faithful. Hence, Nezām becomes "a sublime and divine Wisdom [*Sophia*], fundamental and sacrosanct, who reveals herself *visibly* to the author of these poems, with such sweetness as to engender in him joy and rapture, delight and ecstasy."[46]

The intelligential beauty revealed in the sensory beauty of the feminine is the expression, optimistic and moving, of the Platonism of the Andalusian mystic. The corollary of this conception is dual: that which belongs to the intelligential is endowed with feminine beauty, like the angel appearing with the features of a "princess of the Greeks";[47] second, everything influenced by the intelligential shares in the virginal virtues, like St. Fatima of Cordova, who, at the age of ninety, still looks like a young girl.[48] Contrary to Sanā'ī who states that the sensory world is a trap in which beauty does not correspond to an ontological quality, Ibn 'Arabī is completely indifferent to that truth, only retaining the idea of a continuum between sensory beauty and intelligential Beauty.

This said concerning the idealization of feminine beings, it behooves us to return to the believers in love in the West. One of the most striking aspects of courtly love is the "vocation of suffering" on the part of the faithful. The occultation of love represents an essential element of the ritual of eroticism. In this process of voluntary withdrawal from the love object, a withdrawal that causes the indefinite postponement of the consummation of desire, is to be seen one of the secrets of Western tradition. No obstacle is too great in this case, including one set up by the lover himself in adopting fickle conduct conveying a mood of public defiance. His purpose in this voluntary fickleness is to obtain not the favors but rather the contempt of the beloved so that this may increase her unattainability. Instead of assuaging his pangs of passion, the faithful lover employs every means to increase them. He has a divine call to be ill and refuses to be cured by the vulgar method of appeasing desire either furtively, like lovers, or legally, like married people.[49]

That Eros can take pathological forms is not new in the history of medicine. An allusion to the *cogitatio immoderata* aroused by a female image even appears in the very conventional treatise *On Love* by Andreas Capellanus, a twelfth-century puritan who had the misfortune to be mistaken for a Cathar:[50]

> When a man sees a woman deserving of erotic attentions, he at once begins to desire her with his whole heart. Then, the more he thinks of it, the more he feels himself imbued with love until he reconstructs her in her entirety in phantasy. Then he begins to think of her figure, he perceives her limbs, imagines them in action and explores [*rimari,* lit: splits] the private parts of her body.

The feminine phantasm can then take entire possession of the pneumatic system of the lover, producing—unless desire finds its natural outlet—somatic disturbances of a quite vexing sort. Called *'ishq,* this syndrome of love is described by Avicenna, whose *Liber canonis* was the manual of medicine in use in the early Christian Middle Ages. But previously, Constantine the African had spoken of it in his translation of the *Liber regius* of Alī ibn 'Abbas al-Majūsī, called Haly Abbas. After Constantine, the semiology of the pathological Eros is described by Arnaldus of Villanova and by Vincent of Beauvais,[51] who classify it among the varieties of melancholia.[52]

The name of the syndrome is *amor hereos* or, Latinized, *heroycus,* as its etymology is still in doubt: it might be derived from the Greek *erōs,* corrupted *herōs* (love),[53] or directly from *herōs* (hero),[54] for heroes represented, according to ancient tradition, evil aerial influences, similar to devils.[55]

The relationship between *melancholia nigra et canina* and *amor hereos* is explainable by virtue of the fact that abnormal erotic phenomena were associated, ever since Aristotle, with the melancholic syndrome. According to that tradition, St. Hildegarde of Bingen (d. 1179) attributes to melancholics unlimited sexual capacities:

Melancholics have big bones that contain little marrow, like
vipers. . . . They are excessively libidinous and, like donkeys,
overdo it with women. If they desisted from this depravity,
madness would result. . . . Their love is hateful, twisted and
death-carrying, like the love of voracious wolves. . . . They
have intercourse with women but they hate them.[56]

Ficino himself admits the relationship between melancholy and erotic
pathology,[57] and Melanchthon makes them one and the same thing in
his turn of phrase *melancolia illa heroica*.[58]

The most complete etiology of the illness is found in the section *De
amore qui hereos dicitur* in the *Lilium medicinale* of Doctor Bernard of Gordon (ca. 1258–1318), professor at Montpellier:[59]

The illness called *hereos* is melancholy anguish caused by love
for a woman. The *cause* of this affliction lies in the corruption
of the faculty to evaluate, due to a figure and a face that have
made a very strong impression. When a man is in love with a
woman, he thinks exaggeratedly of her figure, her face, her
behavior, believing her to be the most beautiful, the most
worthy of respect, the most extraordinary with the best build,
in body and soul, that there can be. This is why he desires her
passionately, forgetting all sense of proportion and common
sense, and thinks that, if he could satisfy his desire, he would
be happy. To so great an extent is his judgment distorted that
he constantly thinks of the woman's figure and abandons all
his activities so that, if someone speaks to him, he hardly
hears him. And since this entails continuous contemplation,
it can be defined as melancholy anguish. It is called *hereos*
because noblemen and lords of the manor, because of plenty
of pleasures and delights, often were overcome by this
affliction.

The semiology of the syndrome is as follows: "The *symptoms* are lack of
sleep, food, and drink. The whole body weakens, except the eyes." He
also mentions emotional instability, irregular pulse and "ambulatory
mania." The prognosis is worrisome: "If they are not treated, they become maniacal and they die." Finally, the treatment should begin with
"gentle methods" such as persuasion, or "strong" ones such as whip-
ping, travel, the pursuit of erotic pleasures with several women, natural
diversions (*coito, digiuno, ebrietà e esercizio* as Ficino is to recommend).
Only "if there is no other remedy," the doctor Bernard de Gordon, professor and practitioner, advises that there be recourse to the talents of an
old and horrible shrew, to stage a dramatic scene. Under her clothes the

old woman should wear a rag soaked in menstrual blood. In full view of the patient she should first utter the worst invectives regarding the woman he loves and, if that proves useless, she should remove the rag from her bosom, wave it under the nose of the unhappy man, and shout in his face: "Your friend, she is like this, she is *like this!*" suggesting that she is only—as the *Malleus maleficarum* is to say—"a bane of nature."

Exhausted, the doctor draws his conclusion: "If, after all that, he does not change his mind, then he is not a man but the devil incarnate."[60]

### HOW A WOMAN, WHO IS SO BIG, PENETRATES THE EYES, WHICH ARE SO SMALL

If we closely examine Bernard of Gordon's long description of *amor hereos*, we observe that it deals with a phantasmic infection finding expression in the subject's melancholic wasting away, except for the eyes. Why are the eyes excepted? Because the very image of the woman has entered the spirit through the eyes and, through the optic nerve, has been transmitted to the sensory spirit that forms common sense. Tranformed into phantasm, the obsessional image has invaded the territory of the three ventricles of the brain, inducing a disordered state of the reasoning faculty (*virtus estimativa*), which resides in the second cerebral cell. If the eyes do not partake of the organism's general decay, it is because the spirit uses those corporeal apertures to try to reestablish contact with the object that was converted into the obsessing phantasm: the woman.

The second thing worthy of note is that the erotic syndrome only represents the medical semiology—of necessity, *negative*, since we are in the realm of psychosomatic pathology—of the courtly love glorified by "the faithful." Indeed, they seem to use every means not only to escape that baneful infection but, on the contrary, *to catch it*. Quite rightly, mention has been made of a "semantic reversal," a reverse valorization of the pathologic symptoms described by the Greco-Arab *materia medica*.[61] Even the *locus amoenus*, recommended in the treatment of *hereos* love, reappears in Provençal poetry, as we know.

We must deduce from this that the phenomenon of courtly love results from a warped purpose that brought about a shift of emphasis concerning the concept of *health* as defined by medical science at the time. Through this *Umwertung*, the gloomy equilibrium of psychic forces recommended by learned treatises was transformed into a sickness of the intellect, whereas, on the contrary, the spiritual sickness induced by love ended by being extolled as the real health of body and soul.

But—and here we disagree with G. Agamben—this reversal of evaluation did not take place in Provencal poetry beginning with the syn-

drome of *amor hereos* but well before, in Sufi mysticism with the equivalent concept of *'ishq* described by Avicenna. Even the paradoxical attitude of love's faithful, which consists in feigning frivolous and licentious behavior the better to keep the pure flame of passion burning, is
presaged by the Sufi attitude called *malāmatīya*, which consists—according to the definition received by Ibn 'Arabī from the magician Abu
Yahya al Sinhachī[62]—in "concealing holiness beneath apparent licentiousness of behavior."[63]

The semantic reversal of the concept of psychophysical health is spell-
ed out in the *dolce stil novo*, which describes in detail the process of phantasmic infection caused by the feminine image. In the fact that this
symptom becomes the object of a supreme spiritual experience resides
the secret of love's faithful; it amounts to saying that the "gentle heart,"
far from following the precepts of medical science, becomes ennobled in
proportion as it turns to account the delights of the sickness that con-
sumes it.

That sickness is precisely the experience described by Guido Cavalcanti, continuing from the moment the visual spirit intercepts the woman's image and transmits it to the anterior cell of the brain, seat of the
imaginative faculty, until the moment the feminine phantasm has infested the whole pneuma and spreads from now on through the spiritual canals of the febrile organism. No one will be astonished that the
poet Giacomo da Lentino should ask this seemingly childish question:
How can it be that so large a woman has been able to penetrate my eyes,
which are so small, and then enter my heart and my brain?[64] The physicians of antiquity, like Galen, were also fascinated by the same phenomenon: *Si ergo ad visum ex re videnda aliquid dirigitur . . . quomodo illum
angustum foramen intrare poterit?*[65] Averroës answers the astonishment
(feigned) of both parties: it is not a corporeal impression but a phantasmic one. Common sense receives the phantasms on this side of the
retina and transmits them to the imaginative faculty.[66]

Dante goes farther in his erotic pneumophantasmology. In sonnet 21
of his *Vita nova*, he envisages the Lady as the recipient of spirit overflowing through eyes and mouth, *miracolo gentil.*[67] His experience does not
pine away in an interior pneumatic circle but represents, in a certain
way, a decanting of spirit which takes for granted, albeit involuntarily,
some reciprocity of desire. Through a kind of *significatio passiva,*[68] what
was the object of covetous desire is transformed into a subject whence
Love emanates, but emanates without being aware of it. Virginal innocence that only increases the pangs of passion, the exquisite torment of
love's faithful.

With his *Vita nova*, Dante also enters a mysterious realm that our rudiments of medieval psychology are inadequate to explain: dream, vision.

### (iii) The Vehicle of the Soul and Prenatal Experience

That empirical psychology regarding Eros which will recur in Ficino was inadequate to satisfy Renaissance demands for depth in thought. The theory of phantasmic knowing merely represented the last link in a huge body of dogma relating to the pneuma and the soul.

As we shall see, the connection between Eros and magic is so close that differentiation between them is a matter of degree. A phantasmic experience carried out through the spiritual channels with which we are already acquainted, magic makes use of the continuity between the individual pneuma and the cosmic one. It is this same universal pneumatic "combination" that justifies the depth psychology of Eros (see below, chap. 4, sec. 2).

Through the doctrine of incorporation of the soul, not only is the continuity of the pneuma demonstrated but also the cosmic nature of all spiritual activity. It is of course a rather refined form of speculation on the relations between microcosm and macrocosm, along with a dual projection that leads to the cosmization of man and to the anthropomorphization of the universe. This principle, which historians of science never cease to repeat, unaware that it is a simple schema permitting countless variations, is so generic that it does not succeed in explaining anything at all. How can man be a compendium of the cosmos, and, after all, a compendium of *what* cosmos? Those are problems whose solution is far from univocal, and one need only have read a good history of philosophy to know it.

The Renaissance knows not only one but at least four types of cosmos: the geocentric and finite cosmos of Aristotle, Ptolemy, and St. Thomas; the infinite cosmos of Nicholas of Cusa of which God is the omnipresent center; the cosmos of Aristarchus and the Pythagoreans as exemplified by the "heliostatic"[69] theory of Copernicus;[70] finally, the infinite universe of Giordano Bruno, which integrates our heliocentric planetary system. We might add to the above the ancient geo-heliocentric theory of Plato's disciple, Heracleides Ponticus, never wholly discarded in the Middle Ages and taken up again by Tycho Brahe.[71] None of those cosmological systems excludes the hypothesis of magic since it is based on the idea of *continuity* between man and the world which could not be upset simply by changing theories about the structure of the world. Magicians such as Giordano Bruno or Pythagorean astrologers like Kepler have no difficulty in conforming to the new philosophy. What does change, from one cosmos to another, is only the idea of the dignity of the earth and of man, and there, too, considerable doctrinal variations exist. In the Aristotelian universe, the earth occupies the _lowest_ position, actually corresponding to its ontological inferiority since it is the site of impermanence, rapid changes, of generation and corruption. Everything existing this side of the sublunar sphere is relegated, so to speak, to a kind of cosmic hell from which escape can only be made by going beyond the moon.[72] On the other hand, the planetary spheres are divine, and beyond the sky of fixed stars begin the dwelling places of God.

Perhaps as a joke, but also as a result of the fact that the earth was only a "fallen" heavenly body, Nicolas Oresme was already wondering (in the fourteenth century) if the idea of the _fixedness_ of the earth was not incompatible with its inferiority. Actually, fixedness means stability, and it is the stars of the eighth sky that are fixed because they are superior to the moving stars. That is why Nicolas Oresme hypothesizes the movement of the earth, which is too vile to be immobile.[73]

The profound philosophic reason for which Nicolas of Cusa maintains the idea of the infinity of the universe stems from a conception diametrically opposed to that of Oresme. Cusanus rejects the Aristotelian theory of the elements. For him, there is no differentiation in the cosmos, neither ontological nor spatial, between "high" and "low," "above" and "below." There is no incorruptible world of ether and pure fire beyond the lunar sphere, nor is there a corruptible one formed of the four elements this side of the moon. The world is spherical and turns on its axis. Aristotle's concept, according to which "this earth is very vile and low," _terra ista sit vilissima et infima,_ is untrue. "The earth is a noble star with its light, its heat, and its own influence, which differs from the other stars."[74]

Cusanus's effort, like that of Giordano Bruno, later his disciple, was directed toward the reevaluation of the metaphysical prestige of the earth, hence of man—a prestige it had lost through Aristotelian-Ptolemaean cosmology. A fundamental reform of Christianity is envisaged in this new concept of the world; but a reform whose humanistic, not to mention anthropocentric, nature accepts and encourages magic.

Ficino, the classic source of the revival of magic, is only dimly aware of Cusanus's ideas.[75] But once it was accepted that there was no incompatibility between Cusanus's system of the world and the ancient astrological magic espoused by Ficino, it is of small importance that Ficino himself adopted the traditional Ptolemaic cosmology and astrology. With the ideas he endorsed, Nicholas of Cusa[76] might easily have worked on magic, but that was probably of slight interest for a pure metaphysician of his kind. As to Ficino, except for his Thomism and his

Platonism which force the cosmological system upon him, he is not so far from Kepler, who studies Pythagorean astral music.[77] The concepts of the world, the inner aspirations and motivations of a Ficino and a Kepler, do not essentially differ from one another: on that point contemporary historians of science no longer have any doubt.[78] We shall attempt, in the second part of this book, to examine the true ideological causes that produced the change in human imagination without which the transition from qualitative scientific principles to obviously quantitative principles would not have been possible.

For the present, let us go back to the sources of Ficino's doctrine of incorporation, a doctrine that explains to some degree the close relation between man and the world. As with pneumato-phantasmology—an ancient discipline—this time astrology engendered the hypothesis of a prenatal cosmic knowledge impressed on the soul and determining the destiny of the individual person. Beginning in the second century B.C., this idea coalesced with the story of the incorporation of the soul, its descent onto earth, and its return to the heavens. Now we fancy that the soul, on entering the world, assimilates planetary concretions it will yield only on its exit from the cosmos, in the course of the ascension that takes it to the place of its birth. Perfected by the Neoplatonists, the doctrine of the "vehicle of the soul" will make its glorious reentry in the astromagic of Ficino and his disciples.

Popular Hellenistic astrology, purportedly fathered by the Egyptian god Hermes Trismegistus, or by Egyptian figures such as the Pharaoh Nechepso and the priest Petosiris, comprised several books, mostly lost or only surviving in Latin versions of the Renaissance. It dealt with various questions, like *genika* or universal astrology, the *apokatastaseis* or cosmic cycles, *brontology*, or divination by thunder, New Year predictions (*kosmika apotélesmata*), individual and iatrological (*salmeschoïniaka*) astrology, "fortunes according to the planets" (*kléroi*), *melothesy* or correspondence between the planets and the astral information contained in the microcosm (actually the medical branch of the discipline was called *iatromathematics*), pharmacopeia and pharmacology, etc.[79]

In a series of articles of too specialized a kind to permit us to detail the contents here, we have shown that the vulgar gnosis of the second century A.D. had already incorporated the astrological dogma of *kléroi* or "fortunes," transforming it into a real passage of the soul through the planets, the soul assimilating increasingly material concretions that link it to the body and to the world here below. The Alexandrian doctor Basilides and his son Isidore, as well as the popular gnosis of the third and fourth centuries, which has come down to us through treatises in Coptic discovered at Nag Hammadi and elsewhere, provide us with

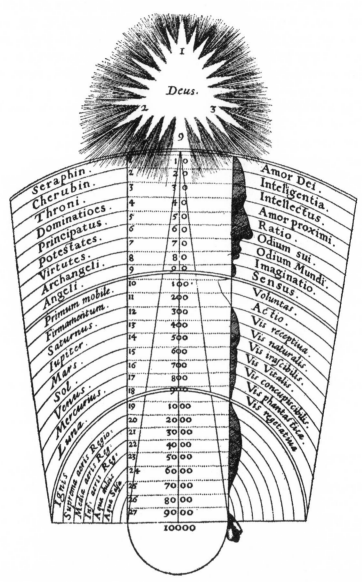

FIGURE 1. Relationship between the parts of the soul and the parts of the macrocosm. From Robert Fludd, *Utriusque cosmi . . . historia* (1617–21), II, a, 1, p. 259.

adequate data concerning this process of corruption of the soul. The *Corpus hermeticum*, a collection of pseudo-epigraphic writings composed A.D. 100–300, also relates the descent of primordial man into the cosmos and the passage of the soul through the planets in its reentry to the heavenly homeland. Reverberations of this purely negative version of incorporation or *ensōmatosis* are still preserved in some passages of the commentary on the *Aeneid* by the grammarian Servius, who wrote toward the end of the fourth century.

On the contrary, the Neoplatonists, from Porphyry to Proclus, do not attribute to the planets any demonic influence but only certain *qualities*, such as the contemplative faculty, practical intelligence, etc., extending to the begetting of children and growth of the body; qualities the soul reappropriates in the course of its descent and discards in the course of its reentry into heaven.

It is very important that this Neoplatonic vehicle (*ochēma*) of the soul, whose history has been outlined by G. Verbeke, H. Lewy, E. R. Dodds, etc., will in time be confused with Aristotle's pneumatic synthesizer, the sidereal *pneuma*, which is innate and transmitted in the act of procreation (*De partu animalium*, 659b16). It matters little that to resolve the contradiction between a vehicle acquired in the skies and a purely terrestrial outer wrapping for the soul, the late Neoplatonists, especially Proclus, have recourse to the theory of *two* vehicles of the soul. In one way or another, the astral garments of the soul and the rarefied spirit generated by the human heart become as one—which enables Synesius, for instance, pupil of the Neoplatonist Hypatia, who will later become a Christian bishop, to endow this whole phantasmic process with cosmic importance. Actually, the organ of the human imagination is not a substance bereft of other qualities; on the contrary, it entails a system in which prenatal information stemming from the celestial bodies, the cosmic gods, is rigorously recorded.[80] Now this spiritual relationship of man with the divine has two sides: the one, restrictive, set forth in Ficino's doctrine about eroticism, and the other, reciprocal, allowing the working of magic.

Reciprocity, or the principle of inversion of action, is the guarantee that a process that takes place in the phantasmic mind and spirit of the individual will result in obtaining certain gifts the stars grant us by virtue of the consubstantiality and intimate relationships existing between us and them.

In the case of Eros, the theory of the astral vehicle makes it possible to establish not only the *how* of the phenomenon of love but also its *why*. It supplies the profound, transcendental reasons for our choice.

# 2| Empirical Psychology and the Deep Psychology of Eros

### (i) The Empirical Psychology of Ficino and Its Sources

The focal concept in Ficino's astrology and psychology is spirit. It might even be said that Ficino redefines spirit in every treatise, avoiding exact repetition through the use of new, concise, and careful turns of phrase. "The soul," he says in his *Theologia platonica* (VII,6),

> being completely pure, conjoins with the solid and terrestrial body so removed from it [by dint of its nature] through the intermediary of a very airy and luminous corpuscle called spirit, generated by heat of that part where the blood is thinnest, whence it penetrates the whole body. The soul, easily sliding into this kindred spirit, at first propagates everywhere within it and then, through its intermediary, throughout the whole body and confers life and movement, thus bringing it to life. And through spirit it rules the body and moves it. And everything transmitted by the body to this spirit is perceived by the soul, which inheres in it; this act we call perception. Afterward the soul observes and judges that perception and such observation is called phantasy.

More details are given in the treatise *De vita sana:*[1] spirit is

> defined by physicians as a vapor: sanguineous, pure, subtle, hot and shiny. Produced from the thinnest blood by the heart's heat, it flies away to the brain and enables the soul to use actively both the internal and external senses.

The most elaborate definition is in the treatise *De vita coelitus comparanda:*[2] spirit is

> a very thin body, almost nonbody and already almost soul; or almost nonsoul and almost body. In its composition there is a minimum of a terrestrial, a little more of an aquatic, and still more of an aerial nature. But most of it partakes of the nature of stellar fire. . . . It is altogether shiny, hot, humid, and invigorating.

Also, the theory of the impossibility of knowledge *sine conversione ad fantasmata*, without reducing sensory language to phantasmic language, is proclaimed in this passage from *Sopra lo Amore*, or commentary on Plato's *Symposium* (VI,6):

> Using the senses, [spirit] grasps the images of external bodies; now, the soul itself cannot perceive those images directly, given that incorporeal substance, superior to that of the body, cannot be induced by the latter to receive images. Omnipresent in spirit, the soul can easily contemplate images of bodies, reflected in it as in a mirror. It is through those images it can appraise the bodies themselves.

The metaphor of the mirror applied to the pneuma is to appear at greater length in the chapter devoted to theurgical purifications (IV, 1 and 3). In any case, it is useful to recall that, for a phantasm to form on the polished and reflective surface of spirit, it is first necessary that the object be *seen* and its image carried to common sense through the pneumatic canals. It goes without saying that the phantasm is not only visual or audiovisual; it is, so to say, *synesthetic*, engendered by the collaboration of several or all senses simultaneously. Nevertheless, sight certainly plays the most important part in forming the phantasm: it is one of the reasons why it is believed to be, throughout the Platonic tradition, "the noblest of the senses."

We recall that, in Plato's theory of optics, the image was produced by a circuit bringing the visual ray from the eyes to its place of origin and thence to the brain. Aristotle simplified that theory, denying that an igneous ray could emanate from the eyes. The Stoics and the pneumatic doctors chose one of those two positions. For some, like Epictetus or Galen—but also for Epictetus's contemporary, the Platonist Plutarch of Chaeronea (*Quaestiones conviv.*, V, 7)—the pneuma comes out of the sensory organ to enter into contact with the sensory object and carry its image to the "hegemonikon."[3] For the others, that image spreads through the surrounding air.

Ficino remains of the same opinion as Plato and Galen: in the act of seeing, "the internal fire" is externalized through the eyes, mixed with the pneumatic vapor and even with the thin blood that engendered spirit. That theory is confirmed by Aristotle himself, who relates that menstruating women who look at themselves in the mirror leave little drops of blood on its surface. This can only mean that it is the thin blood brought to the eyes along with the pneuma (*Amore*, VII, 4).

This phenomenon is the origin of two related spiritual activities: the evil eye and love. The ungodly, regardless of whether he undergoes or causes the resulting infection, is unaware of what is going on. It is enough that someone looks at him: the pneumatic ray emitted by the

other person will penetrate through his pupils into his spiritual organism and, on arrival at the heart, which is its center, it will cause an
agitating disturbance and even a lesion, which can degenerate into a
bloody infection. In the opposite case, for instance when the subject is
fascinated by the beautiful eyes of a woman and cannot stop looking at
them, he emits through his pupils so much spirit mixed with blood that
his pneumatic organism is weakened and his blood thickens. The subject will waste away through lack of spirit and through ocular hemorrhage (*Amore*, VII, 4).

"Love's arrows," held in high esteem by the French poets of the
Pléiade, were not, for Ficino, a mere metaphor. They were equipped
with invisible pneumatic tips able to inflict severe damage on the person
shot. Had not Plato already said that love was a kind of ocular sickness
(*ophthalmia: Phaedo*, 255c–d)? And did not Plutarch ascribe to sight a "miraculous force"?[4]

Regarding the "evil eye," fascination or *jettatura*, its etiology is the
same:

> Fascination is a force which, emanating from the spirit of the
> fascinator, enters the eyes of the fascinated person and pene-
> trates his heart. Spirit is therefore the instrument of fascina-
> tion. It emits from the eyes rays resembling itself, bearing
> with them spiritual quality. Hence rays emanating from eyes
> that are bloodshot and bleary, on meeting the eyes of the be-
> holder, carry with them the vapor of the spirit and of tainted
> blood, thus spreading the contagion to the beholder's eyes.[5]

So speaks Agrippa of Nettesheim, after Ficino; but Girolamo Cardan,
Della Porta, and Johannes Wier[6] share the same opinion, as does
Leonardo da Vinci, who informs us that there are some who declared
such a phenomenon to be impossible because, they said, "no spiritual
force can emanate from the eye for it would use up the faculty of vision. . . . Even if it were as big as the body of the earth it would use itself
up by looking at the stars." Among others, Leonardo compares the popular belief—also expressed by Ficino—"that the eyes of virgins have the
power to attract the love of men."[7]

The spreading infection of the blood and ocular hemorrhage are merely the least subtle of the pathological effects of Eros. It is at the level of
phantasmic techniques that Ficino's empirical psychology presents us
with the most interesting concepts.

Circulating through the same pneumatic passage in which contagion
of the blood is spread are images that, in the mirror of common sense,

are changed into phantasms. When Eros is at work, the phantasm of the loved object leads its own existence, all the more disquieting because it exerts a kind of vampirism on the subject's other phantasms and thoughts. It is a morbid distension of its activity which, in its results, can be called both concentration and possession: concentration, because the subject's entire inner life is reduced to contemplation of one phantasm only; possession, because this phantasmic monopoly is involuntary and its collateral influence over the subject's psychosomatic condition is highly deleterious.

Interestingly, the love object plays a secondary role in the process of establishing the phantasm: it is only a pretext, not a real presence. The true object, omnipresent, of Eros is the phantasm, which has taken permanent possession of the spiritual mirror. Now, this phantasm represents a *perceived* image that has gone beyond the threshold of consciousness, but the reason it has assumed such obsessional dimensions lies in the deepest part of the individual unconscious. We do not love *another* object, a stranger to ourselves, Ficino thinks (*Amore*, VI, 6), thus anticipating the analytic psychology of Carl Jung. We are enamored of an unconscious image.

"The lover carves into his soul the model of the beloved. In that way, the soul of the lover becomes the mirror in which the image of the loved one is reflected": *Amans amati suo figuram sculpit in animo. Fit itaque amantis animus speculum in quo amati relucet imago* (ibid., II, 8). That entails rather a complicated dialectic of love, in which the object is changed into the subject ousting the subject who, tormented by the anxiety of prospective annihilation due to being deprived of his state as subject, desperately claims the right to a form of existence.

The phantasm that monopolizes the soul is the image of an object. Now, since man is soul, and since soul is totally occupied by a phantasm, the phantasm *is* henceforth the soul. It follows that the subject, bereft of his soul, is no longer a subject: the phantasmic vampire has devoured it internally. But it also follows that the subject has now grafted itself onto the phantasm which is the image of the other, of the beloved. Metaphorically, therefore, it can be said that the subject has been changed into the object of his love.

A strange situation without a conclusion if it continues thus: a person without a soul decays and dies (Ficino's subtlety does not go so far as to imagine what happens to that soul after death; he only avers that the beloved exists in duplicate and the lover no longer in any form). A solution does exist, however: that the beloved accept, in his turn, the offer of love. In this case he will also allow the phantasm of the lover to enter into his pneumatic mechanism, to establish itself there and take the place of his soul; in other words, to grant the annihilated subject a place where his identity as subject can emerge from nothingness and gain existence. This is a good thing, since the soul as subject had already been substituted for the soul of the other: if he gives a soul back, he still keeps one. "A" has become "B," "B" has become "A," and everyone is satisfied.

Quite elaborate dialectic and, when all is said and done, quite materialistic. But, at the same time, very close to the dialectic *animus-anima* in the analytic psychology of Carl Jung, in which the relationship between the sexes is envisaged in terms of the conscious domination of one of them compensated by a subjection of the same at the level of the unconscious. The metaphors vary but the general schema stays the same: changed into "B," "A" loves himself, and vice versa. Heterosexual relations are fundamentally a form of narcissism, Ficino believes. In the event that the object who has been substituted for the subject prevents the latter from loving himself, takes away from him the pneumatic mirror without which he is practically reduced to nonexistence, the beloved can be called the murderer of his lover. After knocking hopelessly at the door of the other's eyes, this Narcissus will die through lack of access to the glossy surface of a spirit on which (or on whom) he can be reflected.

A Narcissus without a mirror is a contradiction in terms. It follows that the meaning of the medieval expression *dangerous mirror* does not have reference to the pneumatic mechanism of another but to that of the subject himself. Having too rashly welcomed the phantasm of the devourer, the imagination of the subject then chased the subject from its own dwelling place, turning it loose on the roads to nothingness where bodies have no shadow and mirrors reflect nothing.

### (ii) The Art of Memory

The Art of Memory, also a phantasmic process whose principles and history Paolo Rossi and Frances Yates have dealt with in their excellent books, forms an intermediary link between Eros and magic. It concerns us here only to the extent that, without a general idea of it, we would be at a loss to understand the ideological scope of Ficino and other theoreticians of phantasmic love such as Francesco Colonna and Giordano Bruno.[8]

The Art of Memory is a technique for the manipulation of phantasms, which rests on the Aristotelian principle of the absolute precedence of the phantasm over speech and of the phantasmic essence of the intellect (see above, chap. 1, sec. 1). The precise inference drawn from it, expounded by St. Thomas in his commentary on Aristotle's *De memoria et reminiscentia*, is that whatever is seen, thanks to its intrinsic quality of image, is easy to remember, whereas abstract concepts or linguistic sequences require some phantasmic support or other to charge the memory.[9] This is why St. Thomas recommends recourse to the mnemotechnical rules contained in *Ad Herennium*, wrongly attributed to Cicero and also called *Rhetorica secunda*.

It is certain that the Art of Memory had been utilized in the Middle Ages in cloisters to foster teaching of abstract concepts but also as a very important element of the monk's inner discipline. In the fourteenth century, two treatises in Vulgar Italian deal with it, and even Petrarch was acquainted with its rules.[10]

But times change, and, with the discovery in 1416 of Quintilian's *Institutio oratoria* (which, by the way, does not endorse mnemotechnics), the humanists place the arts and virtues of the ancients on a pedestal. Whereas the Middle Ages utilized the pseudo-Ciceronian treatise *ad maiorem gloriam Dei*, the better to bring to mind the majestic structure of theological concepts, humanism sees in the *Ars memoriae* an important weapon for social success, to ensure, by means of an infallible memory, advantage over others.[11] It is along these lines that the jurist Peter of Ravenna's treatise *Phoenix, sive artificiosa memoria* (Venice, 1491) was written.

The reader of Rossi's or Yates's books doubtless recalls the function of Art, which we shall try to reconstruct freely here without going into detail. Owing to the fact that perceptions have an intrinsically phantasmic character, and are thus readily committed to memory, the task is to superimpose any contents linguistic or conceptual—for instance a poem or classification of virtues—onto a succession of images. Now, those images can come from some *place*, but this does not prevent them from being, as well, phantasms produced for the circumstances by the imaginative faculty. In the first instance, the place must be chosen with care: truly, this Art demands a total concentration only possible in solitude. It follows that mnemonic activity can only be pursued in a church, a cemetery, a deserted palace, or at home, avoiding all company and diversion. The *parts* of the place must be memorized in a certain *order*. On each part the individual will superimpose a sequence to the message or the conceptual series, which must be learned by heart. The indissoluble unity formed by the two discourses—phantasmic discourse and linguistic discourse—will be forever engraved in the memory, due to the imaginary character of the first. There is no limit, either of what can be memorized or in the choice of phantasms to be put to use. Finally—and here is the origin of the emblems, *impresae* and emblematic legends of the Renaissance—phantasms can, as we have already said, stem directly from the imaginative faculty without an objective support. In this case they will be constructed in such a way as to cover, through their parts, the segments of the message to be memorized.

The principle of the priority of phantasm to speech has, in some cases, led to results of doubtful usefulness and applicability, such as the alphabets propounded in 1520 by Johan Romberch in his *Congestorium artificiose memorie*;[12] in one of these each letter of the alphabet is replaced by a bird whose name starts with the appropriate letter: "A = *anser*, B = *bubo*," etc.[13] The Florentine Dominican Cosimo Rosselli replaces birds with animals; in that way the word AER, air, is memorized by means of a donkey (*asinus*), an elephant, and a rhinoceros![14]

Here we are dealing with extreme examples of degeneracy of mnemotechnics, not to be confused with the real processes or with the amazing achievements of that Art. Humanism highlighted the utilitarian rather than the speculative and intellective side, which, however, Marsilio Ficino seems to understand and appreciate. That said, we cannot discard the hypothesis that in the Western Middle Ages, or at least in the early Middle Ages, the Art of Memory was analogous to the preliminary stages of yoga in India: a perfected technique of meditation, with or without objective support, which, in creating a phantasmic world according to traditional rules, claimed nevertheless that, in its approximation, this world was an imperfect equivalent of realities existing on an ontological level inaccessible to direct experience.

The Renaissance knew two Arts of Memory: one, strictly utilitarian, was soon to degenerate into the alphabets of Romberch and Rosselli and even into some *impresae* and emblems of a playful sort; the other was a continuation of medieval mnemotechnics and the universal Art of Ramon Llull, who, by various methods, intended to construct a world of phantasms supposed to express approximately the realities of intelligible order of which our world is but a distant and imperfect copy. *Quidquid recipitur, ad modum recipientis recipitur*: "everything that is accepted is accepted according to the object or person accepting it." Now, the method characteristic of human beings is the phantasm reflected in the mirror of the pneuma. That is the only means at humanity's disposal for understanding reality clearly. It is fundamentally a question of performing a symmetrical maneuver in relation to the process of sensory knowing. This is the translation of the surrounding world into make-believe language so that the soul may learn about it. On the contrary, clear knowledge represents the translation into phantasmic language of

real truths, which are engraved in the soul in order that discursive reasoning—an objective though impotent process—may have the means to
grasp and monopolize them.

Ficino's *hieroglyphics*, which we shall take up later, are symbols of intelligential awareness. But Ficino's successors go much farther: they
even assert that the rules of the phantasmic language that translates
intelligential relationships can be represented in the form of *theater*, to be
meditated upon and learned by anyone who so wishes. The idea of theater came from the Friulan Giulio Camillo Delminio, born around 1480,
who spared no pains to see it realized. A professor at Bologna, Giulio
Camillo was not a charlatan. He managed to interest Francis I in his
theater and, subsidized by the king, settled in Paris in 1530. In 1532 he
was in Venice where Viglius Zuichemus, who corresponded with Erasmus, came to see him. His letter to Erasmus mockingly describes the
theater of our artist with the heavenly memory, which the humanist of
Rotterdam could neither appreciate nor understand. The year 1534
found Giulio Camillo again in Paris but never able to perfect his construction, a wooden structure which, according to a letter of Gilbert
Cousin, Erasmus's secretary, was still at the French court in 1558. Mean-
while, he was invited in 1543 to the court of Alfonso Davalas, marquis of
Vastos, the Spanish governor of Milan. Giulio Camillo lived just long
enough to arrive there, for he died in 1544.[15]

Giulio Camillo, a modest and unassuming man whose Latin made
him the butt of Zuichemus's jokes, left us few writings. He worked on
rhetoric and translated *Le Idee, overo Forme della Oratione*, attributed to
Hermogenes of Tarsus,[16] but it seems he had also studied the work of
Pico della Mirandola[17] and perhaps also that of the Venetian Brother
Francesco Giorgi,[18] which is based on Ficino. His main preoccupation
was adequately to depict a cosmic model. This cosmic model certainly
stems from Florentine Platonism.

Camillo set forth his schema in an obscure little treatise published in
Florence in 1550, *L'Idea del Teatro*. His construction, which had the form
of an amphitheater of seven sections, aspired to be an *imago mundi* in
which all ideas and objects might find their appropriate place by virtue
of their planetary classification. Like any artificial system, this was
doomed to be no longer understood as soon as the sets linking terrestrial
phenomena to corresponding planets fell into disuse. We shall see later
that they were constructed according to correlations between a planet
and certain animals, plants and stones and were transmitted by tradition
with inevitable changes from the very beginnings of Hellenistic astrology. For the Renaissance mind there existed still a kind of internal evi-

dence inherent in the fact that the lion, gold, and the heliotrope belonged to the solar set, but this was only evidence of a cultural kind, becoming invalid as soon as astrology began to lose credibility. Giulio Camillo's schema, as Frances Yates discerned,[19] was magical. He was inspired less by Pico della Mirandola's speculations[20] than by Ficino's treatise *De vita coelitus comparanda* (see below, chap. 4, sec. 3). The subject matter symbolized by the dramatic figures also came from Florentine Platonism. For example, the idea of the incorporation of the soul was represented by the image of Pasiphae and the Bull on the door of the fifth level. Pasiphae symbolized the soul attracted by the body (the Bull), a theme associated with black magic, *goeteia*,[21] by Plotinus and also by the Church Fathers. In its descent among the planetary spheres, the soul was supposed to invest itself with an aerial quality (the pneuma) enabling it to become incarnated in the material body.[22] We can readily understand that working out all the details of that plan, including not only images but also cryptic formulas, was too much for one man. Once he vanished, no one else could take his place to continue his work. At bottom, Giulio Camillo's ambition amounted to no less than to forge a *figura universi*,[23] a cosmic form *ex qua tamen beneficium ab universo sperare videntur*, through which it was hoped some profit might be obtained from the universe.

Ficino himself, who describes in detail the realization of an *universi figura*, was not one of those who, like Giulio Camillo, cultivated the art of oratory. This is probably why it never occurred to him that the *imago mundi* could have the aspect of a theater. For him, the phantasmic expression of the intelligential world did not assume forms as concrete as Camillo's dolls. On the contrary, it ought to be something mysterious, unreachable by the profane.

Egyptian hieroglyphics fulfilled those requirements wonderfully. In the first place, they had the prestige of tradition: Plato himself had spoken of them (*Phaedo*, 274c–75b) and Plotinus too, in his *Enneads* (5.8):

> The Egyptian priests, in symbolizing divine mysteries, did not use small characters but whole forms of plants, trees, and animals, for it is clear that God's system of knowledge of things does not take the form of multiple fancies [*excogitationem multiplicem*] about the thing but sees the thing itself in its simple, stable essence.[24]

Ficino does not end his commentary on Plotinus with this; he continues with a reference—arbitrary, moreover—to one of the hieroglyphics of Horapollon.[25]

The treatise, *Hieroglyphica*, attributed to Horapollon and "translated" into Greek by an unknown writer called Philip, was an attraction in Florence of rather recent appearance. The codex had been discovered by Cristoforo Buondelmonti on the island of Andros and taken to Florence. The Greek text was only published in 1505, followed, in 1515, by a Latin translation, but Ficino's contemporaries were well acquainted with it, since Leon Battista Alberti had extracted from it some whimsical explanations of hieroglyphics in his *De architectura* (1452). The fashion of pseudo-Egyptology made a big hit, especially in the art of emblems that Giovanni Andrea Alciato (1492–1550), in his *Emblematum Pater et Princeps*, was to develop in the sixteenth century, not without debt to his precursor Pierio Valeriano (Giovan Pietro della Fosse, 1477–1558), author of *Hieroglyphica sive sacris Aegyptiorum aliarumque gentium literis commentarii*.[26]

Hieroglyphics, symbols endowed with the dual preferential claim of having aroused the interest of Platonic diviners and also of being fashionable with Ficino's contemporaries, assume particular importance in his concepts, as pointed out by André Chastel in his fine book *Marsile Ficin et l'Art*.

Ficino, as Eugenio Garin tells us, conceived of philosophy as an initiation into mysteries,[27] consisting of a gradual rise in intellectual loftiness receiving in response from the intelligential world a phantasmic revelation in the form of *figurae*.[28] These *figurae*, characters of an inner phantasmagoria staged by the soul itself, represent the modality by means of which the vision of the soul opens before the *oculus spiritalis*, the organ that has taught the inner consciousness about existence, through diligent meditation.[29] This experience, so well described by P. O. Kristeller,[30] has to do with the formation of an "inner awareness," interpretable as a phantasmic process, a *visio spiritalis* in the Augustinian sense.[31] It is, in fact, a need to discover a means of communication between reason and intellect (the soul), and this means is provided by the spiritual eye, the mysterious organ that permits us to look upward toward the higher ontological levels.[32]

André Chastel believes that the term *hieroglypha*, as used by Ficino, does not refer to a form communicated by the soul to the faculty of reason through the intermediary of the pneuma. Rather, it is a symbol of meditation "keeping the spirit in a state of tension propitious to a kind of meditation close to ecstasy, the talisman of the *oculus mentis*."[33]

Pseudo-Egyptian hieroglyphics, emblems, and *impresae* were wonderfully suited to the playful spirit of Florentine Platonism, to the mysterious and "mystifying" quality Ficino believed it had. "Pythagoras,

Socrates, and Plato had the habit of hiding all divine mysteries behind the veil of figurative language to protect their wisdom modestly from the Sophists' boastfulness, of joking seriously and playing assiduously, *iocari serio et studiosissime ludere.*"[34] That famous turn of phrase of Ficino's—translation of a remark by Xenophon concerning the Socratic method—depicts, at bottom, the quintessence of every phantasmic process, whether it be Eros, the Art of Memory, magic, or alchemy—the *ludus puerorum*, preeminently a game for children. What, indeed, are we doing in any of the above if not playing *with* phantasms, trying to *keep up with* their game, which the benevolent unconscious sets up for us? Now, it is not easy to play a game whose rules are not known ahead of time. We must apply ourselves seriously, assiduously, to try to understand and learn them so that the disclosures made to us may not remain unanswered by us.

In the *Ball Game (De ludo globi, 1463)* by Nicholas of Cusa, these verses have been inserted although they do not belong to the author:[35]

> *Luditur hic ludus; sed non pueriliter, at sic*
> *Lusit ut orbe novo sancta sophia deo . . .*
> *Sic omnes lusere pii: Dionysus et qui*
> *Increpuit magno mystica verba sono.*

The *ludus globi* is the supreme mystical game, the game the Titans made Dionysus play in order to seize him and put him to death.[36] From the ashes of the Titans struck down by the lightning of Zeus, arose mankind, a race guilty without having sinned because of the deicide of its ancestors. But, since the Titans had incorporated part of the god, men also inherited a spark from the murdered child, the divine child whose game is the metaphor of the ages: "Aion is a child who plays checkers: the sovereignty of a child!"[37]

### (iii) The Phantasmic Eros and the Appeasement of Desire

Wherever Eros is at issue, so is desire. Where desire is at issue, so is its appeasement.

That applies to Dr. Freud as much as to the theoreticians of love in the Middle Ages and the Renaissance, with one exception: the latter, sometimes revealing amazing knowledge through their freedom and candor with regard to human sexuality, nevertheless grant the existence of other forms of satisfaction of desire. Indeed, Eros, being by nature spiritual, hence located at an intermediate level between the soul and the body, the intelligential world and the sensory world, it can lean toward one or the other of those cosmic regions. But, given that desire is the pursuit of a phantasm and that the phantasm itself belongs to a world, the imaginary world—the *mundus imaginalis* whose loftiness Henry Corbin has so well described without dealing with its penumbra—there is also a third possibility, namely that Eros burns away altogether in a phantasmic sphere.

The spiritual Eros functioning anagogically: that is what Dante propounds, as R. Klein has so well demonstrated;[38] the natural love that descends to the body: that is the experience of many writers of the school of Boccaccio, rediscovered in Freudian psychoanalysis with the stubborn intent of reducing to a single factor the multitudinous manifestations of Eros. It goes without saying that those two traditions have one point in common: the recognition, if not of the nature of Eros, at least of its phantasmic techniques. For all parties, the preliminaries of desire consist in setting up a phantasm within the subject. For some, this phantasm will have the capacity to awaken their allayed desire, to propel and accompany them on their trip through the intelligential cosmos. This will become a heroic passion ending in an ecstatic fusion of the hunter and the object of his hunt—according to an image employed by Ficino and later revived by Giordano Bruno. For others, the phantasm will only point to a painful and urgent need for a physical release which increases in proportion as its fulfillment is postponed.

In this case there will be a fundamental contradiction between the medical concept of a phantasmic Eros that disturbs the equilibrium of the organism and demands prompt assuagement to restore this equilibrium, and the concept of the "faithful," a complete denial of the former, finding expression through a semantic inversion valorizing the disequilibrium in terms of a plenary spiritual experience. This will to distort, first brought to bear on medical matters of the period, subsequently provoked much ribaldry directed against believers in mystical love whose ideas, bereft of sense, are to become synonymous with an erotic strategy in which the purely verbal idealization of woman is merely an expedient to silence her resistance as quickly as possible.

The conflict between those two important traditions also signifies the relative dependence of the one on the other. Erotic mysticism becomes distinct by contrast to the naturalistic trend, whereas the latter defines its positions in controversy, explicit or implicit, with the idealism and the intellectualism of the faithful.

A third trend, as meek and obscure as the others were famous and persistent, almost passed unobserved or was close to being assimilated by the two others. Indeed, there can exist phantasms unrelated to a real object, but, thanks to the quality of their images, there can be no phan-

FɪɢURE 2. Bacchanalian revels. From Francesco Colonna, *Discours du Songe de Poliphile [Hypnerotomachia]* (Paris, 1554). Courtesy of the Wing Foundation, The Newberry Library, Chicago.

tasms without physical support of one kind or another. That is why a story about phantasms is always interpretable: we can see it either as the symbol of adventures in the intelligential cosmos or as the allegory of actual events.

Unfortunately, although there are many theoreticians of phantasmic Eros, the number of writers who have tried to describe phantasms at work is very limited. One of them surely is the respectable monk from Treviso, Francesco Colonna, who, having become sacristan of the monastery of St. John and St. Paul in Padua, died in 1527 at the age of ninety-four.[39] He is the author of a work almost unique of its kind, the *Hypnerotomachia Poliphili*, which, as the author points out in the book's explicit, had been finished May 1, 1467, but was not published until 1499 by Aldo Manuzio; it was paid for by a magistrate of Verona, called Leonardo Crasso.[40]

The contents of the *Hypnerotomachia* tally with the date 1467. Indeed, the work is external to the current of ideas circulated by Marsilio Ficino

FIGURE 3. "Two wretched damsels, naked and disheveled." From Francesco Colonna, *Discours du Songe de Poliphile [Hypnerotomachia]* (Paris, 1554). Courtesy of the Wing Foundation, The Newberry Library, Chicago.

beginning more or less in 1463.[41] From our point of view, the fact that it escapes Ficino's influence is invaluable. Even when expressing a personal point of view on love, which rarely happens, Pico della Mirandola, Pietro Bembo, Baldesar Castiglione, Leo the Hebrew, and Melanchthon bear the indelible mark of Ficino's thought. On the contrary, Colonna (though he, too, treats of the phantasmic Eros) is original and inimitable, less in his ideas—a common heritage of the period, of which Ficino is to become the systematic organizer—than in the literary and didactic quality of his work.

### (iv) Phantasms at Work

Let us make the acquaintance of phantasms.

Taken literally, the title *Hypnerotomachia* means a "love fight during sleep." This leads us to expect that a person dreams of phantasms involved in an erotic fight, perhaps his own erotic phantasm. That is precisely what happens: two phantasms, that of the dreamer—Poliphilus—and that of the girl he loves—Polia—are at the center of the scenario.

The tale is not constructed so as to be easily understood. It is an *enigma* whose solution is given only at the end. The reader is informed that Poliphilus seeks Polia, but does not know why or how. Of the 311 pages of the Guégan-Kerver edition, the first part takes up 250 whereas the second, which provides indispensable explanations, takes up only 60. The first part tells of the endless roaming of Poliphilus amid the ruins of antiquity, of triumphs, emblems and *impresae,* each with its own secret meaning. As Yates observed, it could be a matter of mnemotechnics "escaped from control and degenerated into wild imaginings."[42] In any case, such oneirico-archeologico-mnemotechnics, however fascinating, will not preoccupy us here. In the end, Poliphilus finds Polia, and the lovers plead their case before the heavenly tribunal of Venus. The second part, which contains two monologues, is therefore *a tale within a tale,* and the end is destined to complicate the enigma still more: we learn that everything that happened was only Poliphilus's dream, so that the search for Polia and the appeasement of desire were but adventures in phantasy.[43]

Neither mystical love nor vulgar love, Poliphilus's dream represents the trite story of phantasmic desire that finds fulfillment.

The tale is saved from platitude and indecency by its *phantasmic* quality: desire, provoked by a phantasm, is appeased by the phantasm, after a period of erotico-mnemotechnic tribulations.

## (v) The Depth Psychology of Ficino
### DESCENT OF THE SOUL

Souls descend into the bodies of the Milky Way through the constellation of Cancer, enveloping themselves in a celestial and luminous veil which they put on to enter terrestrial bodies. For nature demands that the very pure soul be united with the very impure body only through the intermediary of a pure veil, which, being less pure than the soul and purer than the body, is considered by the Platonists to be a very convenient means of uniting the soul with the terrestrial body. It is due to that descent that the souls and bodies of the Planets confirm and reinforce, in our Souls and our bodies respectively, the seven original gifts bestowed upon us by God. The same function is performed by the [seven] categories of demons, intermediaries between the celestial gods and men. The gift of contemplation is strengthened by Saturn by means of the Saturnian Demons. The power of the government and empire is strengthened by Jupiter through the ministry of the Jovian Demons; similarly, Mars through the Martians fosters the soul's courage. The Sun, with the help of the Solar De-

FIGURE 4. The ithyphallic god Pan. From Francesco Colonna, *Discours du Songe de Poliphile [Hypnerotomachia]* (Paris, 1554). Courtesy of the Wing Foundation, The Newberry Library, Chicago.

mons, fosters the clarity of the senses and opinions that makes divination possible; Venus, through the Venereans, incites Love. Mercury, through the Mercurials, awakens the capacity for interpretation and expression. Finally, the Moon, through the lunar demons, increases procreation. (*Amore*, VI, 4)

Except for the idea that the planets exert their respective influences on the soul and the human body through the intermediacy of demons, this passage from Ficino is inspired by the *Commentary on the Dream of Scipio* by the Latin Neoplatonist Macrobius, who must have had as his source a treatise by Porphyry.[44] Macrobius's work had been circulated in the Middle Ages, and it is possible that Ficino was acquainted with a commentary attributed to William of Conches, one of whose fourteenth-century manuscripts is in the National Library in Florence.[45] The author of *Philosophia mundi*, in dealing with procreation, divided the womb into seven compartments retaining sperm in which "the human form is imprinted like a coin."[46] It is very likely that the seven divisions correspond to the planets, whose influence on the development of the embryo would thus have been prepared in advance through divine wisdom permeating nature.

Those "seals" that mold the human form, the *cellulae impressione humanae formae signatae*, recur in Ficino at the level not of the maternal womb but of the heavenly one. Indeed, the process of cosmization of the soul, of its entry into the physical universe, can be compared with the gestation and growth of the embryo. On the one hand, there is the soul-child, which inclines downward and descends into the cosmic womb formed by the seven planets; on the other, there is the child's body preparing to receive the soul. In William of Conches the parallelism is total, for the human womb is in the image of the cosmos.

That parallelism also exists in Ficino in the framework of a depth psychology that the author does not try to make too complicated. Its basis is the concept of a *stamped impression* or planetary *form* combined with a rather peculiar theory, unconfirmed by an astrological treatise, concerning the influence of the stars on various erotic groupings. Ficino states (*Amore*, VI, 5) that certain planetary types—Jovian, Solar, Martian and Venerean—are more apt than others to receive the arrows of love and that they give preference to a person belonging to their own type—the Jovian to a Jovian, etc.

To explain the profound and unconscious attraction between persons, he gives an example that serves as model for the entire foregoing series. Let us suppose that a soul descends into the body at the time Jupiter reigns in the zodiac; it will bring into itself a Jovian image that will also be imprinted on its pneumatic medium. Another form of the same kind is impressed on the sperm, which, to receive it, must have certain qualities at its disposal. If it does not, Jupiter's traits can only be transmitted more weakly, resulting in a certain disharmony of the body. The moment this uncouth Jovian meets a Jovian who has had the good luck to receive proper sperm, he will be captivated by the other's beauty, unaware that the deep cause of his affection resides in the attraction to the same planetary prototype, especially when it has been better incarnated in a terrestrial body.

> Those born under the same star are so disposed that the image of the most beautiful among them, entering through the eyes into the soul of the other, conforms absolutely to a certain [preexistent] image, impressed at the beginning of procreation onto the celestial veil of the soul, as well as on the soul itself. (*Amore*, VI, 6)

The two original images are copies of the same planetary prototype, even though one is less perfect than the other. A *profound recognition* will take place, and a wish to emulate will seize the form of the weaker Jovian, who will tend to perfect himself according to the model furnished by the other.

Ficino emphatically states that this unconscious impression stamped on the soul is not a phantasm. On the contrary, it is a matrix conditioning the phantasmic process to the extent it imperiously commands the phantasms received to conform to a prenatal prototype.

This theory of the *facies* or preexistential image of the individual stems from a stratum of very archaic beliefs also found among so-called "primitive" peoples. The later Neoplatonists gave it a philosophical foundation. Later, the cabalistic *Zōhār*, by Moses of León, again took up the idea of an eternal impression stamped on the soul:

> During the nuptial mating on earth, the Saint, etc., sends a human form which bears the imprint of the divine seal. This form is present at the mating, and, if we were allowed to see it, we would observe above our heads an image that resembles a human face. It is in this image that we are formed. (*Zōhār*, III, 104a–b)

Through Neoplatonist doctrine, Ficino means to provide a transcendental basis for the empirical psychology of Eros. This field is bounded by the completely unconscious choice made by the soul from among the phantasms capable of becoming the object of love.

MELANCHOLY AND SATURN

Of all the planetary types, the Saturnian has special importance in Ficino's thought. This is probably a plea *pro domo sua*, for Ficino called himself a Saturnian because, on the day of his birth (October 19, 1433), Saturn entered the sign of Aquarius.[47] The "esthetic recluse," prey to periodic attacks of elation and depression, catatonic and *pessime complexionatus*, but also gifted for contemplation of the highest aspects of the human being, is only the description of the result of introspection directed by Ficino upon himself.

It goes without saying that Ficino's explanation of the syndrome of melancholy comes from the mold of a culture that is no longer ours. But insofar as the semiology of that morbid affliction is still under consideration in our treatises of psychiatry or psychoanalysis, there are also perceptible connections between Ficino's observations and those of our modern observers such as Freud or Binswanger.[48]

The question of Saturnian melancholy has been dealt with in detail by E. Panofsky and F. Saxl in their famous analysis of the *Melencholia I* by Dürer.[49] We refer to it here only to add some particulars.

The psychology of antiquity was founded on a very interesting quaternary classification, which deduced the principal temperaments from the predominance in the organism of one of the four humors: yellow bile, phlegm, blood, and black bile, *atra bilis,* in Greek *melaina cholos,* hence the word "melancholy." The four elements, the cardinal points, the divisions of the day and of human life correspond to those four liquids of the organism. The series of *yellow bile* comprises fire, the wind Eurus, summer, high noon, and maturity; that of *phlegm* water, the Auster, winter, night, old age; that of *blood* air, the Zephyr, spring, morning, youth; that of *black bile* the earth, the wind Boreas, autumn, evening, and the age of sixty. The predominance of one of the humors determines the four temperaments: choleric or bilious, sanguine, phlegmatic, and melancholic. Somatic traits, or *complexion* (in Latin, "mixture of humors"), bear a close relationship to character.[50]

Melancholics are, in general, *pessime complexionati:* thin and gloomy, they are, into the bargain, clumsy, sordid, drab, apathetic, cowardly, irreverent, drowsy, lazy—in short, people without religion or self-control who lack respect for human relations. The symbol of the atrabilious temperament is an old miser lying on the bare ground.

This unflattering description of the most unfortunate of the four fundamental psychosomatic types corresponded, in astrology, to the traditional description of the pet aversion among the planets: Saturn, the lord of Capricorn and of Aquarius.

A systematic description of the characteristics of the planets and of the signs of the zodiac has been given us by the iatro-mathematician Johannes of Hasfurt, admirer of Ficino, in his *De cognoscendis et medendis morbis ex corporum coelestium positione.*

> Saturn is cold and dry.[51] The Saturnian individual has a broad and ugly face, small eyes downcast, one larger than the other and having a spot or a deformity; thin nostrils and lips, connecting eyebrows, bristly black hair, shaggy and slightly wavy, uneven teeth. His beard, if he has one, is sparse, but his body—especially his chest—is hairy. He is nervous. His skin is fine-grained and dry, his legs are long, his hands and feet deformed with a cleft heel. The body is not too big, honey-colored, smelling like a goat. . . . In his complexion coldness and dampness prevail.[52]

The psychic qualities granted by Saturn are hardly more attractive: the Saturnian man is apt to ponder advice given him by well-disposed people but, being misanthropic, does not take it.

It rarely happens, but if he takes a fancy to someone, he is passionate, just as he is passionate in his hatred. He is prone to anger, but he can control himself for a long time. A glutton, he is usually fat and slow-moving. Miser, impostor, crook, thief, sorcerer or magician, you have no doubt met in your life this silent type, of the profession of usurer, farmer, revolutionary, perpetrator of treason. In conclusion, the Saturnian is sad and solitary, without faith in God or his fellow men.[53]

The sign of Capricorn, dominated by Saturn, "is inordinately cold and dry, destructive of plants, trees and seeds. . . . It is a feminine sign, nocturnal, heart of the South, solstitial, hibernal, changeable, underhand, grubby, and melancholic."[54]

The two most unfortunate psychosomatic types, whose natures are so similar they end by intermingling, nevertheless each have an extraordinary compensation.

Theophrastus early differentiates between two kinds of melancholy; this was later reiterated by Aristotle.[55] One kind, produced by cold black bile, answers to the above-mentioned characteristics, whereas the other, caused by the predominance of the *hot* humor, confers upon the subject a psychic lability and instability that goes with genius. The following symptoms are apparent in "hot" melancholy, according to Aristotle: "fits of gaiety, ecstasy, lability, inspiration." The eccentricities disappear from the behavior of the melancholic of genius, without disturbing his extraordinary faculties, if the temperature of the bile is modified.[56]

What are these exceptional tendencies of the melancholic? According to Albert the Great,[57] hot melancholy, or *melancholia fumosa*, has two extremely important effects on the phantasmic activity of the subject. The first consists in the *mobility* of the phantasms within the subtle organism: the second, in the great capacity of phantasms to stay *impressed* upon the pneuma. This brings with it, besides a prodigious memory, an extraordinary capacity for analysis. That is why, Ficino tells us, "all the great men who have ever excelled in an art have been melancholic, either because they were born so or became so through assiduous meditation."[58] However, Henry of Ghent, who recognized in melancholics a special aptitude for the arts due to their highly developed phantasmagoric faculty, denied them any leanings toward abstract thought. Ficino corrected that injustice by identifying the melancholic with the Saturnian. If the former had been traditionally regarded as a labile genius, the latter also revealed a fundamental ambiguity, having been forced by his ruling planet into a solitude characterized either by perversity or by the highest contemplative aptitude: "Saturn does not lay down a law concerning the quality and destiny of mortals, but makes a man distinct from others, divine or bestial, happy, or oppressed by extreme misery."[59]

That Saturn should, in addition to the aforementioned disagreeable characteristics, endow its subjects with an exceptional propensity toward metaphysical contemplation and abstract reasoning (without objective support, albeit with a minimum of phantasmic activity) is an idea as old as Hellenistic astrology. Being the planet farthest from Earth, Saturn occupies, in the Aristotelian-Ptolemaic-Thomistic system, the nearest position to the sphere of fixed planets and hence to the Empyrean, a privileged position inconsonant with the exclusively negative qualities attributed to it in Babylonian astrology. This ambiguity holds regarding the doctrine of the descent of the soul on earth: Macrobius and Proclus attribute to Saturn the contemplative faculty (*theōretikon*) and the faculty of reason (*logistikon*), whereas Servius attributes to it torpor and moodiness, the hermetic *Poimandres* the lie, and the commentary on Macrobius in the Florentine Codex nothing less than *tristicia*, synonymous, in the Middle Ages with *acidia* or melancholy. Ficino himself, as we have already said, endorses Macrobius and Proclus.

Klibansky, Panofsky, Saxl, and Wind have demonstrated that the fusion of the syndrome of melancholy and "Saturnism" was achieved by Ficino. More recently, Giorgio Agamben, having misunderstood that Ficino's originality consisted not in expressing new concepts but in combining existing ones in a new way, has countered these scholars with the idea that the ambiguity of melancholy was already well known in the

Christian Middle Ages.[60] Indeed, the ambiguity of Saturn was no more foreign to the Middle Ages than to antiquity, but Ficino should probably be credited with having superimposed the two faces of "Saturnism" upon the two faces—the bestial one and the face of genius—belonging to melancholy. Through this identification, the melancholic obtained from Saturn that which in principle he had always been denied: the aptitude for metaphysics; and the Saturnian, too, could pride himself on having the faculty of imagination and of prophecy bestowed on him by melancholy: "The star of misfortune is also the star of the genius: imperiously he detaches the soul from appearances, he opens to it the secrets of the universe; through the trials of melancholy he brings to bear a more penetrating sensitivity, *ad secretiora et altiora contemplanda conducit.*"[61]

Agrippa of Nettesheim, who inspired Albrecht Dürer's *Melencholia I,* reiterated Ficino's ideas without taking account of the traditional divisions. In his classification, the number I, recapitulated in the title of Dürer's famous engraving, referred to the Saturnians whose *imagination predominates over reason*—the great artists and artisans—which formerly would have been a contradiction in terms, since Saturn's strong point was, precisely, the faculty of reason and not of phantasy. Solely Ficino's identification of melancholy with the Saturnian enabled Agrippa to mix the characteristics of those two types otherwise distinct from one another.

Neither Ficino nor Agrippa laid claim to anything new when they asserted that melancholy, being a kind of *vacatio,* separation of soul from body, bestowed the gift of clairvoyance and premonition. In the classifications of the Middle Ages, melancholy was included among the seven forms of *vacatio,* along with sleep, fainting, and solitude.[62] The state of *vacatio* is characterized by a labile link between soul and body which makes the soul more independent with regard to the sensible world and allows it to neglect its physical matrix in order, in some way, better to attend to its own business. When it gains awareness of its freedom, the soul devotes itself to contemplation of the intelligential world. But when it is merely roaming about between worlds, it has nevertheless the faculty of noting events occurring far away, in space as well as in time. For we can say, in simplifying a question that is neither easy nor univocally soluble, that time, in the intelligential world, is not *deployed:* past, present, and future are not separate and distinct, everything is there *sub specie aeternitatis.* That is why the soul that casts a glance into the eternal archetype of time can obtain, about past and future, knowledge that does not come from sensory experience. Obviously, these things occur

only if the pneumatic casing protecting the soul is sufficiently transparent to permit it to *see*, and this can be either a natural gift or an
acquired or accidental quality.[63]

That pneumatic *sagacity* of melancholics has been well expressed by a
Calabrian monk of the Reformation period, Tommaso Campanella, author of the treatise *De sensu rerum ac magia*, in the chapter entitled "Of
the sagacity of melancholics pure and impure and of demonoplasty and
consent of the air." In the Aristotelian tradition, Campanella differentiates between "hot" melancholy (pure) and "cold" melancholy (impure).
The second

> according to the learned Origen . . . is the seat of elfish spir-
> its and of the devil. The latter sees that the corporeal spirit is
> infected by [melancholic] vapors whose oppressiveness
> forces the reasoning faculty to be inactive and then, being
> impure and heavy, delights in that sort [which befogs the
> spirit] and enters and uses [the spirit] to horrify and restrain
> reasoning and enjoys the strange place it has entered.[64]

Pure melancholy, on the other hand,

> is hot and a sign of sagacious spirits but not their cause; the
> cause is the subtlety and facility of spirits. That is why melan-
> cholics are determinedly solitary, for all movement troubles
> them; they withdraw and think a lot, because their discern-
> ment is very sharpened. More than other men, the melan-
> cholic has aptitude for premonition through dreams, because
> his spirit is more subtle and more gifted than the spirit that is
> too thick to receive the almost imperceptible movements of
> the air.

Now we already know that pneumatic waves, causing pressure on the
surrounding air, are apt to be picked up by another spirit. If the latter is
adequately trained, it will succeed in noting not only the waves whose
length coincides with the capacities of his sensory organs (sight, sound),
but also the imperceptible pneumatic movements such as those of
thought, for example. It is simply a matter of having a phantasmic apparatus sufficiently "pure" (that is, *clean*) to be able to vibrate to the wave-
lengths below the threshold of perception. "Thus," Campanella tells us,
"when they see a person, they quickly guess his thoughts by picking up
the imperceptible movement his spirit imparts to the air in the act of
thinking, and they are also capable of learning everything quickly."[65]

We have to pay for everything in this world, and those with supranor-
mal faculties must pay most dearly. Capable of extrasensory perception,

Ficino's melancholic is an abulic, a borderline case, often tempted by suicide, which he is dissuaded from carrying out—as in the famous instance of Porphyry lectured by Plotinus. The cause of his difficulty in adapting to his mortal condition is an intense nostalgia for his celestial country, for the intelligential world, nostalgia for a "lost object" that is later manifest in Freud's description of the syndrome of melancholy.[66] In this interpretation, Ficino's Neoplatonist and Christian heritages commingle. Indeed, the contrast between "cold" or "impure" melancholy and "hot" or "pure" melancholy was transformed, in the Middle Ages, into an antithesis between a *tristitia mortifera*, or *diabolica*, or yet again *tristitia saeculi*, which induces the religious person to seek secular distractions (instead of the profound boredom which, according to William of Auvergne, all theological questions instill in him), and the *tristitia salutifera* or *utilis*, or, yet again, *tristitia secundum Deum*, which stems from the feeling of being deprived of God.[67] This is why, William of Auvergne goes on to say, many *piissimi ac reliogiosissimi* men of his time burned with desire to be seized by the melancholic sickness, that they might increase their nostalgia for God.[68]

When the idea of the lost country atrophies, only the baneful symptoms of melancholy remain. Kierkegaard, that "intimate confidant of melancholy," has given us a masterly description in his *Diapsalmata:*

> I wish for nothing. I do not wish to ride horseback, it is too strenuous; I do not wish to walk, it is too tiring; I do not wish to lie down, because then either I should have to lie down constantly, and I do not wish to do so, or I should have to get up, and I do not wish to do that either. *Summa summarum:* I do not wish for anything.[69]

According to André Chastel, the concept of the romantic genius who is variable, catatonic, prey to sudden fits of enthusiasm that disturb his abulia, is disclosed to the modern world through Ficino: "The genius who is familiar with the alternations of inspiration and of distress, afflicted by *furor* and then bereft of his inner force, belongs to no conventional type: he is of interest because of the dramatic intensity of his experience."[70] Whether or not it bestows genius, melancholy is primarily a pathological syndrome that became known through the *Corpus hippocraticus* and Aristotle as well as through Sigmund Freud. This evil, like the plague, has struck our continent repeatedly. Aristotle mentioned some melancholics—Hercules, Bellerophon, Heraclitus, Democritus, the poet Maracos—and Ficino adds others: Sappho, Socrates, and Lucretius.[71] The medieval cloisters were decimated by *acedia* and the castles of the eleventh to the thirteenth centuries resounded with the chants and atrabilious verses of the troubadours and love's faithful, men suffering from the lethal syndrome of *amor hereos,* itself a kind of heady melancholy. In the fifteenth and sixteenth centuries the fashion of black bile reaped a rich harvest of victims including Ficino, Michelangelo, Dürer, and Pontormo. England had its share, such as the poets John Donne and Richard Crashaw. In the nineteenth century, dandyism was an infantile camouflage for the wounds of melancholy, a sickness that attacked Baudelaire as well as Kierkegaard, De Quincey, Coleridge, Nerval, Huysmans, and Strindberg.

It is very likely that this melancholic epidemic can be explained also by a secret solidarity between the patient and the sickness, since the yearning for "useful suffering" is not limited to contemporaries of William of Auvergne but affects all those who, for one reason or another, were not satisfied with what earthly existence can offer. They had bumped against its confines: everything is *thus* and cannot be otherwise.

Ontologically justifiable, this state of unemployed boredom or lethargy is a consequence, for Ficino, of a phenomenology of daily life that anticipates Pascal and Heidegger.

Man, exiled (*exul*) in the world, lives in a permanent state of torpor or sadness (*maeror*) whose origin remains mysterious. Unable to live alone, he always seeks the company of others, trying, through diversions (*oblectamenta*), to forget his anxiety. He plunges into a kind of delirium that imparts to his life the unreal quality of the dream.[72]

This analysis, to be sure, lacks the emotional quality of Pascal's work, but Pascal's concept closely resembles that of Ficino:

> Men have a hidden instinct that prompts them to seek diversion and occupation from without, stemming from resentment at their unceasing misery. And they have another secret instinct remaining from the grandeur of their primary nature which makes them aware that happiness resides only in tranquillity. And from those two contrary instincts is formed a confused plan hidden from sight at the bottom of their soul that leads them to reach for tranquillity through agitation and always to imagine that the satisfaction they lack will come to them if, by surmounting certain obstacles they face, they can thus open the doors to peace and tranquillity. . . . So that in considering them seriously, man is more to be pitied for being able to amuse himself with such low and frivolous things than for being afflicted by real misery; and his diversions make much less sense than his boredom. (*Pensées,* 26)

# 3| Dangerous Liaisons

### (i) Pico della Mirandola, Continuator of Ficino

The perfect understanding between Ficino and Pico della Mirandola, in which they lavished each other with more or less sincere compliments, did not last long. Apart from the fact that both were of the Saturnian type, suited to penetrating contemplation of theological truths, it is difficult to imagine two people more dissimilar.

The son of Cosimo de' Medici's physician, Ficino was instructed by his protector to translate Plato's works into Latin. In youth he is attracted to Augustinianism but loses no time in submitting to Scholasticism, of which he is to become undoubtedly the most valuable representative in the Renaissance. Burdened by defects, physical and psychic, he was hunchbacked, had a slight stammer,[1] and often fell into fits of melancholic despair, so grievous that he once almost died of starvation. Aside from that, he was head of the Academy of Careggi and also a priest, which did not permit him to give up the public obligations devolving on him. He resigned himself to leading a healthy and frugal life, to avoiding melancholy by means of diet, walking, music, some ritual manipulations, and astrological magic.

The opposite of Ficino, Pico della Mirandola, a prodigious philologist and theologian, had the advantage of youth, noble birth, and wealth. More or less of an extremist, though not lacking in diplomacy, he had his adventures and misadventures. The end of his short life coincided with his conversion to the puritan ideal of Savonarola. After many tribulations that went on until the death of Innocent VIII, he was pardoned by Pope Alexander VI, but the services he rendered the Church were limited to a long refutation of astrology. His life ended at the age when others are just beginning their activities. Can one assume that, when the time came, he would have abandoned Savonarola? He lacked the versatility of Ficino, who was capable of all sorts of political turnabouts but had certainly shown goodwill equaled only by that of the pope.

In principle, difference in character does not always make collaboration between equals impossible. The young Pico is, on the one hand, sufficiently admiring of the Florentine Platonist that a considerable por-tion of his work is strongly influenced by him, in spirit as well as in the letter; but, on the other hand, he often allows himself to adopt a polemical tone, admixed with sarcasm to stigmatize Ficino's "vulgarity" in the most serious philosophical matters. As for the Platonist from Careggi, who probably saw Pico as merely an exceptionally gifted disciple, a *mirandus iuvenis* very worthy of his academy, he addresses him in terms whose almost imperceptible irony ends by negating their extreme courtesy. In the long run, Pico must have found Ficino's paternalism unbearable, and his rebellion regarding the interpretation of love is proof of that state of irritated dependency.

It is a matter of *discordia concors* rather than *concordia discors*, for, while wishing to give Ficino a lesson in Platonism, Pico, probably unbeknownst to himself, remains nevertheless under his influence. In his excellent book on Pico della Mirandola, Henri de Lubac emphasizes the circumstances of the writing of *Commento sopra una Canzona de Amore* of 1486,[2] pointing out, among the reasons moving Pico not to publish it, a concern not to wound Ficino, "whose interpretations the *Commento* criticized more than once."[3] Ficino, whom mutual friends had doubtless informed of the young man's impertinence regarding him, thought it wise to write to Germain de Ganay that, with regard to publishing the *Commento*, Pico's last wish—repudiating this writing, which dated from his adolescence—should be respected.[4]

Ficino's diplomacy, whose purpose is probably to save appearances, perplexes Girolamo Benivieni. The *Commento* was included in 1519, through the good office of Biagio Buonaccorsi, among the works of Benivieni himself, who, in an introduction, blames a third party for its publication, keeping his distance from it by noting that Pico, as well as himself, had written *come Platonico, et non come Christiano*.[5] The least respectful passages about Ficino were carefully deleted in the 1519 edition, and the *Works* of Pico della Mirandola published by his nephew Giovan Francesco contain this expurgated version of the *Commento*. Another letter from Benivieni addressed to Luca della Robbia, which appears in an appendix to the *Works*, again deplores the publication of those *ineptie puerili*.[6]

Pico's embarrassment, Benivieni's perplexity, Ficino's indignation, and Buonaccorsi's salutary censorship all make us suspect a serious ideological breach, in 1486, between the impetuous young count and the level-headed cathedral canon. What was it about?

On reading the unexpurgated version of the document, published in 1942 by E. Garin, we are astonished by the violence of Pico's attack on Ficino:[7] a mind unworthy of his difficult task in annotating Plato's *Sym-*

*posium,* "our Marsilio" is accused of defiling the subject of love on which he is working. While granting that Ficino's systematic mind—a scholastic heritage that Pico himself shares—can often irritate his reader, his young rival's aggressiveness can only be explained by personal resentment, since the "lesson" he thinks he is giving Ficino can be summed up as an almost literal repetition of Ficino's ideas and turns of phrase. By removing from it the "purpose to distort," which mostly affects marginal questions without bearing on Ficino's total vision, we arrive at a general account that would have elicited the enthusiastic approval of the Florentine Plato had it not contained the foregoing invective.

Since Eros is the tool that helps to traverse the intelligential stages separating God from his creatures, it would be unthinkable to treat the subject of love without first dealing with ontology. Moreover, because humans occupy the most privileged position of all creatures, they are the only ones to contain within themselves all levels of the cosmos, from God to matter. That is why they are also the only beings capable of climbing to the top of the ladder of creaturehood into invisible worlds. This system of successive links of being which goes to descending levels is called the "Alexandrine schema" and is inherited by Plotinus from the gnostic systems he attacks.[8] The thinking of the first Neoplatonist comprises an *apostrophē* (in Latin, *processio*), or estrangement from the essence of being, which humans alone can make good by the opposite process of *epistrophē* (*conversio*) or return to being.

As for Ficino, the degrees of progression are as follows: God, the angelic or universal intellect, Reason, Soul, Nature, and Body.[9] Through its intermediary position the soul, like two-faced Janus,[10] has some of the characteristics both of the intelligential world and of the sensory world. That is why it is called *copula mundi* or *nodus mundi,*[11] whereas man-microcosm, *parvus mundus,* is *vicarius Dei in terra,* vicar of God on earth.[12]

Pico della Mirandola repeats Ficino's expressions literally and the stages of development of the human being: man is *vincolo et nodo del mondo,*[13] he is the hyphen between the World of angels and Nature. He has, of course, two bodies: one, called by the Platonists the "heavenly vehicle," is the imperishable wrapping around the rational soul; the other, composed of the four elements, is subject to the laws of growth and decay.[14] Man is also equipped with two organs of sight: one directed toward the sensory world and the other toward the intelligential world, the latter corresponding to Ficino's *oculus spiritalis.* The descent of souls into bodies is faithfully summed up by Pico according to Ficino's commentary on the *Symposium:* "Among human souls, some have Saturn's nature, others the nature of Jupiter and so on. And by that the Platonists mean that a soul can be more closely related and in conformity to the soul of Saturn's sky than to the soul of the sky of Jupiter, or vice versa."[15] We have the impression that Pico is at pains to avoid the unorthodox consequences of that theory, for he makes clear that the sole intrinsic cause of those differences resides in God Himself, the unique producer of souls. But right after speaking of the "soul's wrappings" he rashly adds that "the rational soul descends from its star," which seems to contradict the protestation of faith of the preceding article. Since ecclesiastical censure, which was also to affect Ficino, had already paid too much attention to his own person, we have the impression that Pico here exerts self-censure. This naive cleverness, which induces him to present only partially a subject that Ficino had expertly presented fully and openly regardless of possible reprimands, will not spare Pico the troubles he feared.

We might well see here a prelude to the antiastrological polemic contained in the *Disputationes adversus Astrologiam divinatricem*. But, in this case, the hypothesis that this document was conceived with the purpose of obtaining from the Curia the pardon necessary to enter the Dominican order and to put on the cardinalate purple seems not without foundation.[16] All the more so since the *Commento* repeats the whole story of incorporation that Ficino got from Macrobius, with the descent of the soul through the door of Cancer, the acquisition of the astral wrappings, and the soul's reascent through the door of Capricorn,[17] adding that its astrological physiognomy is justified by the fact that the terrestrial body is formed by the soul.[18] Now, if Ficino accepts the truth of that doctrine—which he himself, in a phrase worthy of his duplicity, had characterized in his *Theologia* as a "Platonist fable"—it is hard to see how he can refute wholesale all the claims of astrology. To be sure, between 1486, the date of the *Commento,* and 1494, the date of his death, which left his *Disputations* unfinished, Pico had been struck by the thunderbolts of the Curia, subsequently to find peace with the preacher Savonarola. His conversion, however genuine it might be, poses the question of a split between the writings of his youth and the *Disputations against Astrology*. After the death of Innocent VIII, Pico was pardoned by the new pope. Having reached the age of reason, should he not try to redeem himself definitively in the eyes of Rome? Lacking the petty mentality of Ficino, who, in 1490, "found out the birth date of Innocent VIII . . . in order to prepare a remedy for him in gratitude (this is the limit!) for having refused to condemn him for astrology,"[19] Pico writes, to mark the end of the errors of his youth, a huge treatise against astrology, even though it gains him the enmity of Ficino and his adherents. Strangely enough, this time Pico spares the old master whom he had not hesitated to discredit in his *Commento:* "He had . . . enough discrimination not to confuse the great apologist, whose apostolic purpose was the same as his own, with all the men he believed to be enemies of the Christian faith."[20] But Lubac does not fail to point out the solidarity between Pico and Ficino that resulted from the condemnation to which the trilogy *De vita* had been subjected in 1489–90, "and by those very people who had fought Pico two years earlier."[21]

As for the rest of the *Commento,* we cannot but be surprised anew by the violence of Pico's attacks on Ficino (had he lost his judgment?). Did they not both agree that the essence of love is spiritual and that its object passes through the eyes to the inner sense located in the heart?[22] Had they not both been engaged in describing the deleterious effects of *amor hereos,*[23] the phantasmic sickness "so plague-stricken and venomous that it has been able to cause almost incurable weakness in the most perfect and the strongest souls"?

If this *discordia concors* between Pico and Ficino could not produce, in the former, any strikingly new interpretation of love, it is nevertheless to his stubborn will to distort that we own one of the most interesting and persistent themes in the theory of Eros in the sixteenth century: the *mors osculi,* or death from love. This theme has a dual origin: its point of departure is Ficino's phenomenology with the process of alienation of the subject who desperately seeks a place to locate his "subjectness". It was a syndrome closely resembling *amor hereos,* which Francesco Colonna was able to describe without recourse to Ficino's system. As in most of his interpretations, Pico takes exception to Ficino's "vulgar" hermeneutics. Rejecting the intersubjective exegesis, he deals exclusively with the death from love as a moment of the dialectic of the mystical Eros. For that purpose he adopts the symbolism of the caballa which reveals to us the secondary source of the theme.

The *binsica, mors osculi,* or *morte di bacio* that Pico describes in four columns[24] is a corporal extinction accompanied by intellectual ecstasy. No one can rise to intelligential life without having first renounced sensory life. But when the soul has left the mortal remains of the body, it will be called to a new form of existence through spiritual regeneration, like Alcestis, who, not refusing to die of love, could rise again by the will of the gods.[25] Making use of the Christian and cabbalistic interpretation of *Shir ha-Shirim,* Pico asserts that the lover is the symbol of the soul, the beloved is the intelligence, and the kiss is the ecstatic union. The oral kiss, *bacio,* among all the postures of corporal love, is the last and the most advanced that can appear as a symbol of ecstatic love:[26] *"Binsica* or *morte di bacio* signifies the intellectual *raptus,* during which the soul is so firmly united with the things from which it has been separated that, on leaving the body, it abandons it completely." Such was the experience of "Abraham, Isaac, Jacob, Moses, Aaron, Mary (or Elijah), and others."[27]

What was this mysterious *mors osculi?* Pico and his successors give other details which help us to define the scope of this mystic phenomenon. It is a terrifying vision of the intelligential world that Pico rediscovers, through allegorical interpretation, in the fable of Tiresias as told by Callimachus: because he saw Diana naked, "which means nothing other than ideal Beauty, source of all true wisdom," Tiresias went blind, lost the use of corporeal sight, but received the gift of prophecy, incorporeal sight. The same thing happened to Homer when in the throes of the inspiration that made him contemplate the mysteries of intellect. And Paul too, after his journey to the third heaven, went blind.[28] The *morte di bacio,* the full and complete contemplation of angelic Intelligences, is rapture in heaven, a *vacatio* during which the body remains in a state of catalepsy, as Celio Agostino Curione seems to inform us in the appendix to the *Hieroglyphica* of Pierio Valeriano.[29] After very few variations, the description of *binsica* reappears in Baldesar Castiglione, Egidio da Viterbo, Francesco Giorgio Veneto, Celio Calcagnini, Leo the Hebrew (*Dialoghi d'amore*), and Giordano Bruno (*Heroici furori*).[30]

With Bruno, we enter the unfathomable arcana of Eros in which the pure theory of the Florentine Platonists leads to several quite mysterious conclusions. One of these, at least, relates to the dangerous liaisons that Bruno was inclined to maintain all his life, until his death at the stake, to which he consented in order not to contradict his own illusions, brought him ultimate freedom. The smoke had hardly dissipated when Giordano Bruno was almost unanimously proclaimed a "symbol of democracy." A strange paradox that crowned the posthumous fate of the man who was "probably the most antidemocratic of all philosophers."[31]

### (ii) The Ambiguous Gods of Eros

GIORDANO BRUNO, A MAN OF THE PHANTASMIC PAST

Imprisoned in Venice before being handed over to the Roman Inquisition, Giordano Bruno in his interrogation of May 30, 1592, relates that, after delivering an extraordinary lecture in Paris,

> I gained such fame that King Henry III sent for me one day to ask if my memory was natural or magical. I satisfied him by answering and proving that it was not magical but scientific, of which he himself was convinced. Afterward, I had printed

a memoir entitled *De umbris idearum* that I dedicated to His Majesty, who therefore made me lecturer extraordinary with a stipend, and I continued to lecture in that city . . . for perhaps five years, after which I resigned because of the civil riots and, recommended by the king himself, went to England to His Majesty's ambassador called seigneur de Mauvissière, Castelnau by name.[32]

Bruno's natural memory being unequal to his artificial memory, he is mistaken about the length of his first stay in Paris, beginning in 1581 and ending in June 1583, after which, under the protection of Michel de Castelnau, he moved to London, where he remained until October 1583.[33]

By a strange optical illusion, Giordano Bruno has been envisaged as the herald of the future, freemason and liberal, whereas this unfrocked Neapolitan monk was, wherever he went, merely one of the last impassioned defenders of the culture of the phantasmic era. This explains his rebuffs in Protestant circles, where he soon found himself worse off than in the bosom of the Church he had been rash enough to abandon:[34]

Neither in London, nor in Marburg, neither in Wittenberg nor in Helmstädt, nor even in Frankfurt had he met with the liberal and expansive welcome of his dreams. Calvinists and Peripatetics had hunted him down mercilessly. He was no more successful with the Lutherans, who should have been influenced to adopt a more hospitable flexibility by virtue of Melanchthon's doctrine.[35]

Only the iconoclasm of youth, which brought down upon Bruno the first conflicts with Church authority, remotely resembles Protestantism. On the other hand, all his culture, of which he was so proud and for which he was somewhat renowned, was in the sphere of the past, of the phantasmic, of mental acrobatics: in sum, in the realm of the grotesque, like Giulio Camillo's theater. To understand something about his works, posterity, interested in them because of his martyrdom, was obliged to eliminate eight-tenths of them: all the mnemotechnic and magical tracts. Posterity claimed to be satisfied, for Bruno had been a defender of Copernicus and even the first to connect the idea of the infinity of the universe with heliocentrism. Yet a huge gulf separates this Neoplatonic pantheist from rationalists like Spinoza. Grasping how uninteresting Bruno's work was to the modern age, Hegel, who found his doctrine involved and repulsive, termed his philosophy "bacchantic," probably an excuse for being unable to read him. All of which proves that, far from being the man of the future misunderstood in his own time, Bruno was misunderstood precisely because fundamentally he belonged to a past too subtle, too complicated for the new spirit of rationalism: he was the descendant of those who proclaimed the least accessible arcana of the era of phantasms: mnemotechnics and magic.

SCANDAL IN LONDON

In London, Bruno soon found himself at the center of one if not two scandals. As early as 1584, in the dedication to Sir Philip Sidney of the *Spaccio della Bestia trionfante*, he shows himself so sensitive to the "wounding and painful discourtesies" of which he was the object that he considers leaving the country. It is certain that Sidney, and perhaps also Bruno's old friend Fulke Greville (Folco Grivello, as he called him), played an important part in keeping him there until autumn of the following year.

The first scandal was caused by an unfortunate debate with two Oxford doctors that Bruno decided to immortalize in his tract *La Cena de le ceneri*, dedicated to Michel de Castelnau. The two parties indulged in a rivalry cruelly wanting in tact. The Southerner, to be sure, was wrong to count too heavily on respect for the laws of hospitality, whereas the barbarian inhabitants of that island *toto orbe divisa* were only concerned with their dignity and independence. Bruno's contempt for the two Oxonians was expressed in such a way—"imbued with Greek, but also with beer"—that he ended by alienating the sincere friendship of Fulke Greville, whose name was distressingly implicated in that unprecedented offense not only against the worthy scholars and the chauvinistic commoner, but also against British lack of civility in general.

The scene of the debate is a memorable one: having cleverly replied to one harmless doctor, "a domestic ass," Bruno was taken over by another, "whose ignorance equaled his presumptuousness." The Neapolitan did not spare this "wild ass," "a rude pig without manners," whose academic chain should have been replaced by a halter.

"Look, be still, and learn," this imposing beast of burden tells him, "I shall teach you about Ptolemy and Copernicus." Of course Bruno loses his temper, especially as the man seeks to persuade him, while admonishing him to be silent, that the earth of Copernicus occupied a place where in reality there was nothing but a point of the compass.

All this must seem very strange if we reflect that England was the first country in which heliocentrism had met with success. In 1576, Thomas Digges, a protégé of the learned John Dee, published a *Perfit Description of the Caelestiall Orbes according to the most annsiente doctrine of the Pythago-reans, lately revived by Copernicus,* in which, according to S. K. Henninger, through an astonishing leap of imagination he takes the daring position of postulating a universe that is infinite.[36] In fact, Digges does not ap-pear to have defended the same ideas as Bruno; for him, only the Em-pyrean heaven, habitation of God, was without limits, which does not assume the unlimited multiplication of worlds.[37]

As chance would have it, the very year Bruno arrived in London, John Dee, the only person who could have understood and appreciated him, left the country. Dee was, moreover, so unpopular that the mob took the opportunity to wreck his house right after his departure for Poland.[38] The missed meeting with Digges also meant a lost opportunity to know Digges's family. He had to be satisfied with the two Oxford doctors, which brought about the troublesome scandal we have mentioned. We are told that Bruno acted here as a messenger of scientific truth, but the "truth" of Copernicus and of Bruno in no way corresponds to the pic-ture we have made of it. If Bruno concedes to that "German" a certain perception and wisdom—not forgetting, however, to declare that he himself "saw neither with the eyes of Copernicus nor with the eyes of Ptolemy, but with his own"[39]—it is for the same Pythagorean reasons that had led Copernicus to replace geocentrism by his heliostatic con-cept. In that, Bruno follows in the steps of the "divine Cusanus,"[40] whose arguments he merely repeats, implementing them with his own polemical passion.

Let us not forget that, at the beginning of the sixteenth century, Cath-olic thinkers like the cardinal of Bérulle and Father Mersenne, who was not even a believer in the heliocentric concept, grasped the enormous importance the Copernican system might have had for theological imag-ination. If their appeal found few listeners, it was mainly because of the Puritan attitude, which, through its rigidity in interpreting Scripture, forced the Catholic Church into an equal rigidity in the defense of Thomism. Bruno's cause, which was also that of the cardinals Nicholas of Cusa and of Bérulle, was similarly lost on the Puritans, who saw things only from a utilitarian point of view. The Bible is good, their rep-resentative Smitho tells us in the *Cena de le ceneri,* because it gives us rules, and

> the purpose of rules is not to seek primarily the truth of
> things and of speculations but the good effects of its practices
> on civilization, understanding between peoples and ease of

human intercourse, the maintenance of peace and national progress. Often, and in many respects, it is more stupid and ignorant to say things according to truth than according to the occasion and the opportunity.

The man of the future was not Giordano Bruno but Smitho, the Puritan.

The argument about heliocentrism, which had great repercussions, has long eclipsed another controversy Bruno had with the Puritans, in many ways a more important one: the debate about the Art of Memory.

Hardly had Bruno arrived in England than he hastened to dedicate to Michel de Castelnau a number of mnemonic writings printed by John Charlewood. The French ambassador must have received this gift with some embarrassment: he had been welcomed in Puritan circles as the translator of a work by Petrus Ramus, a victim of the massacre of St. Bartholomew in 1572. This pedagogue, whose reputation as a Huguenot brought him a warm welcome in England, was the implacable enemy of the old mnemotechnics.

Ramus, who turned up his nose at academic scholastic psychology, did not believe in the primacy of phantasm over speech, nor in the phantasmic essence of intellect. The first condition for memory, conversion into phantasm, was abolished. Thenceforth, gigantic constructions of inner phantasms crumbled: they were replaced by an arrangement of the subject into "dialectical order," memorizable because of its "natural" character.[41]

Ramus's main argument against inner phantasmagoria is, however, a religious one, the biblical decree not to worship images. The Art of Memory is condemned for its idolatrous nature.[42] It is easy to understand why the Puritans were ready to make use of that instrument of antiecclesiastical battle, which gave the finishing touch to their external iconoclasm by means of an inner iconoclasm.[43] The ancient Art of Memory was therefore associated with the Catholic Church, whereas Ramus's memory without images was adopted by Calvinistic theology.[44]

In London, where Ramus was the man of the day and of the rationalistic future, Bruno, representing an obsolete past, could not expect a favorable reception, especially since other personalities with strong influence in England, such as Erasmus and Melanchthon, had also come out against the Art of Memory.[45]

If Bruno succeeded nevertheless in winning a disciple and the tacit approval of Sir Philip Sidney, he owed that in great measure to the memory of John Dee.[46] Dee had been professor of philosophy to Sidney, Greville, and Edward Dyer, which perhaps explains why Greville became close to Bruno, and why the latter unceasingly dedicated writings infested with the Art of Memory to Sidney in the hope of converting him to his opinions.

Conflict broke out in 1584, but Bruno did not take part in it personally. His disciple, Alexander Dicson, who had published a treatise, *De umbris rationis,* inspired by Bruno's mnemonic writings, was repeatedly attacked by the Reverend William Perkins of Cambridge, a supporter of Ramus. Dicson—under the pseudonym Heius Scepsius, which comes from Metrodorus of Scepsis, originator of the mnemonic system based on the zodiac and also used by Bruno—wrote a reply, his *Defensio pro Alexandro Dicsono.*[47] The prophetic voice of Perkins was raised again in a scurrilous satire, *A Warning against the Idolatrie of the Last Times,* in which these dreadful words occur during the Puritan funeral service for the Art of Memory: "A thing conceived in the mind by the imagination is an idol."[48] The minister's hair stands on end when he reflects that some practitioners of memory like Peter of Ravenna had no qualms about recommending the use of lustful images capable of arousing unhealthy passions. Perkins made a point of banishing that perverse Art from England forever, acting in behalf of every pious individual.[49]

There would be nothing strange about this controversy if Dicson, who belonged to Sidney's coterie, had not had his two treatises published by Thomas Vautrollier, the Calvinist who had published Petrus Ramus's first works in England. Furthermore, although Paris is the place inscribed on the title page of the two works that Bruno dedicated to Sidney in 1584 and 1585, they were certainly printed in London.[50] Sidney was reputed to be a follower of Ramus, and it was to him that Sir William Temple, also in 1584, dedicated his edition of Petrus Ramus's *Dialecticae libri duo.*

How should we interpret this charade? Frances Yates thinks that if Sidney had been a Puritan and a true believer in Ramus, he would not have been able to write the *Defence of Poetrie,* the Renaissance manifesto in England, a fervent defense of the imagination against the moral scruples of a Perkins.[51] Taking advantage of his indecision, the two warring factions must have tried to win him over; time was short because the knight died in 1586, perhaps not before discreetly revealing his preference for the Bruno and Dicson faction.

The humiliating setback described in *Cena* was useful to Bruno. Quickly he grasped the situation and submitted to a dialogue with the Puritans. The two works he dedicated to Sidney bear the stamp of that wise decision.

The second of these, *De gl'heroici furori,* the one that interests us here, cannot be understood without a foray into Bruno's mnemonical kitchen. Without having any immediate connection with the system employed in the *Heroic Furors* the *Spaccio* will be of considerable help to us in grasping Bruno's technique and his attempt to adjust to English usage.

The *Spaccio* propounds an artificial memory in which the place and arrangement, according to the earlier structure of Metrodorus of Scepsis, are in the form of the zodiac, not in the version of the twelve signs or thirty-six decans, but in the version borrowed from Hyginus (*Astronomica,* Venice 1482) of the forty-eight constellations, already employed by Johan Romberch in his *Congestorium.* Responding, however, to doubts which might be forthcoming from Sidney and other readers of his treatise, Bruno notifies them immediately that he does not want to support the foolish system of the constellations: on the contrary, it is a matter of a *Spaccio,* of an *expulsion* of the animals that the absurd imagination of the ancients elevated to the skies. In the form of a satire on astrology and classical mythology, a satire that could only please the taste of his English public, the *Spaccio* tries to pay respect to the fundamental principles of mnemonics.

The forty-eight constellations, set in forty-six sectors, are taken over by a retinue of gods—personifications of the psychic faculties—with Jupiter as their patron "representing each one of us," who replace them by a cohort of moral entities, positive and negative, varying in number from sector to sector, which entails a rather complicated circular configuration in space. On this, another structure is superimposed, which circulates freely in all fields: it is formed by Fortune, Wealth, Poverty, and their innumerable fields (*Spaccio,* II, 2s).

Bruno himself explains that there are other possible mnemonic fields, and he outlines two of them, which he uses elsewhere. The first, that of the *Sigillus sigillorum* of 1583, resembling the theater of Giulio Camillo, entails the arrangement of forms in seven planetary fields (*Spaccio,* III, 2). The other, which he calls cabbalistic and might correspond to the *ars combinatoria,* presages a multiplication according to rather sophisticated reasoning, yielding the following series of fields: 1 (First Principle), 4, 12, 72, 144, etc.

Having taken the precaution of mocking the fables of the ancients and exalting virtues, he could now preemptively counter the attacks of any Perkins without giving up his Art. This procedure, moreover, was tantamount to a semiconversion to Ramus's point of view, since all the phantasms that formerly peopled the zodiac had been painstakingly banished: only virtues and vices remained.

MNEMONIC PHANTASMS

After that diplomatic tour de force, Bruno must have felt encouraged in his enterprise. It was customary for the person to whom a book was dedicated to pay the printing costs, and Sir Philip Sidney surely did not infringe that rule. In concealing his own name, the printer avoided the responsibility of having published the work of a foreigner who had scandalized London, and Sidney's silence on the subject of Bruno (less surprising than that of Michel de Castelnau), on the same grounds of expediency, does not mean that the knight had contempt for the *Spaccio*. On the contrary, some discreet sign of appreciation must have shown Bruno that he was on the right track. History is silent on the subject, but without Sidney's encouragement and generosity it is inconceivable that the impulsive Neapolitan would not have kept his promise to leave the country and would have dedicated his next book to him also, *De gl'heroici furori*.

In the *Heroic Furors*, mnemonics are at the disposal of Eros. The method is already outlined in the second part of the third dialogue of the *Spaccio*, where Bruno gives a literal translation of the famous passage in the hermetic *Asclepius* concerning Egyptian statues, "full of life, full of intelligence and spirit, capable of many important functions. Those statues foresee the future, cause infirmities, and produce the remedies, joy and sorrow, according to the merits [of each], in human affectivity or body."[52]

This time, the material used by Bruno is made up of phantasmic emblems whose prestige also derives from the hermetic statues. Are not those spiritual constructions, in the final analysis, forms used by magic itself? It is true that their use here comes down to memorizing the stages of Eros, but is not Eros itself an anagogic force which produces the ecstatic union of the soul with God?

At first glance, *De gl'heroici furori* is a series of sonnets with commentary, of the type of Dante's *Vita nova*. Like Pico della Mirandola, from whom he borrowed many of the themes of the *Commento*, Bruno does not hesitate to copy certain poems which, according to F. Fiorentino, belong to Tansillo of Venosa, the main character and Bruno's spokesman in the dialogue. But most of the sonnets are the creation of the author himself, whether they be commentaries in verse on the representations of Eros or poetic expressions of the "heroic furors."

In the *Sigillus sigillorum*, Bruno had already explained the deep reason for *ut pictura poesis*, the equivalence between painting and poetry. Zeuxis is the painter of internal images in the memory, who excels in *phantastica virtus,* imaginative power. In turn, the poet possesses powers of thought out of the ordinary whose source is also spiritual. "It follows that philosophers are also painters and poets, poets are painters and philosophers, and painters are philosophers and poets."[53] Indeed, since intellect is phantasmic by nature, the philosopher must be able to manage phantasms, to be a great painter of the spirit. Did not Aristotle say that "to comprehend means to observe phantasms?"[54] The place where phantasms are reflected, as we already know, is the mirror of the pneuma.

Philosophy, poetry, painting: these are the contents of *De gl'heroici furori.* These three stages of phantasmic speculation are so inextricably intertwined that it is impossible to separate them without destroying the unity of the subject. Unfortunately, being incapable, since the triumph of rationalism, of understanding the phantasmagoric of the great artists of Memory, we shall have to make a sharp dichotomy between what is possible to grasp with our mere logical, historical, and comparative methods and that which, to avoid being drawn into the revived mnemonics, we must leave aside after a concise description.

The fifth dialogue in part 1 is a course in the Art of Memory applied to intellectual processes, in fifteen chapters. The *impresae* symbolizing the stages of love's sophistry are explained in sonnets, which, in turn, are the subject matter of the prose commentary. To give an idea of the processes utilized by the painter Zeuxis, it is enough to mention the third mnemonic image appearing on the escutcheon of the "heroic furor":

> the third door on his escutcheon bears a nude adolescent, stretched out on a green meadow, his head leaning on his arm, his eyes looking up at the sky where, above the clouds, there are edifices comprising rooms, towers, gardens and orchards; there is also a castle made of fire; and in the middle there is an inscription: *Mutuo fulcimur.*

Or the seventh of the escutcheons, "a sun with a circle inside and another outside it, with the *motto: Circuit,*" etc.

Other *impresae,* twelve in number, are commented on in the first dialogue of part 2. One of them opens a dialogue containing the most important substance of Bruno's treatise.

It was to images of this kind that the abbot Pluche referred when he wrote in 1748:

> Since a picture is only intended to show me what I am not told, it is absurd that efforts should be required in order to understand it. . . . And as a rule when I have succeeded in guessing the intent of those mysterious figures, I have found

that what I have been taught was not worth the price of the wrapping.[55]

Let us admit that our mentality would incline us to agree that the abbot Pluche was in the right rather than the Renaissance philosophers of symbolic forms. The effort to code and decipher those complicated messages, the *ludus serius* whose meaning was found in the mysterious combination of spiritual processes having the purpose of enriching knowledge of the soul, lacks meaning from the time we no longer believe in either the principles or the conclusions of that knowledge. Not only has the wrapping become too expensive, but the parcel itself is never going to arrive. For those images of artificial memory must be understood in their proper mental context, which was spiritual and phantasmic. Otherwise there is too great a risk that they be considered a sort of crossword puzzle, a game lacking in seriousness, which, if the modern researcher obliges, may be transformed into an endless labryinth where all sense and meaning are lost.

AMBIGUITY OF EROS

An Italian scholar recently thought he glimpsed in the title *Heroici furori* an allusion to the medieval syndrome *amor hereos* or *heroycus*.[56] Now, even if Bruno was aware of that kind of melancholy, as he probably was, he had in mind something else when he wrote his treatise on ethics.

In Bruno, heroic love is defined as the antithesis, on the one hand, of "natural" love and, on the other, of the passive anticipation of grace characteristic of a certain kind of mysticism.

First of all, the heroic Eros establishes its positive existence in contrast to the natural Eros, "which attracts toward procreation." Its object is a woman; the object of the other kind is God. The same dichotomy separates it from the melancholic state of mind: "It is not an atrabilious frenzy . . . but heat generated in the soul by the intelligential sun, and a divine impetus (*impeto*) that makes it grow wings" (II, pp. 333–34)—an allusion to the myth of *Phaedrus* and to the wings of the soul, which, damaged by the catastrophic event of our entry into the world, could only be recovered by a few chosen people, in particular, philosophers.[57] In sum, this form of erotic enthusiasm "has as its main goal grace of spirit and control of passion, not corporeal beauty" (II, p. 330).

But with what kind of grace are we concerned? It is not a gift passively awaited and received but rather the result of active contemplation. Bruno readily makes fun of the saint who, without any personal effort, is transformed into *vas electionis*. The hero (or even the demon) he contrasts him with is not a vase but the artisan who makes it. Likewise, the saint is compared to an ass who carries the sacrament, the hero to the sacred things themselves. In the former we can contemplate the "work of the Divine," in the latter, the "excellence of humanity" (II, pp. 332–33). In Bruno's concept of heroic frenzy, commentators have seen "the idea of the universal immanence of the divine that leads . . . to a universally coherent conclusion concerning the human will and capacity for awareness."[58] "The feat of the *Heroic Furors* is the changing of man into God, the *homoiōsis theō*," E. Garin[59] tells us, and G. Gentile speaks of "the sublimation of reason in the progress of truth."[60] All of that, as P. O. Kristeller has recognized, makes Bruno a worthy representative of Renaissance Platonism, a disciple of the Florentine school of which Marsilio Ficino had been the leader. Yet Bruno's originality and genuineness, hard to classify, explode in joyous fireworks from the opening pages.

This time Bruno's victim is Petrarch, representative of the shameful and degrading passion of love. "This vernacular poet who sighed for a girl of Valchiusa . . . , lacking the intelligence to apply himself to better things, cultivated his melancholy assiduously, thereby yielding to the tyranny of base, idiotic and filthy bestiality" (II, p. 293). And Petrarch's work is described as the result of this obsessional contemplation of an unworthy object, as the wasted suffering of a sick imagination, against whose pernicious influence Bruno fights with all his might:

> Here we find, written down, bound in books, displayed to the eyes, intoned to the ears, a noise, a bawling, a buzzing of charades, of tales, of puns, insinuations, epistles, sonnets, epigrams, books, prolix documents, violent sweats, lives wasted away with gnashings of teeth to deafen the stars, lamentations resounding in the caverns of hell, woes that stun the souls of the living, sighs to cause the merciful gods to faint, all that for the sake of these eyes, these ears, this blush, this tongue, this tooth, this hair, this dress, this coat, this little shoe . . . , this sun in eclipse, this crazy person, this slut, this stench, this deathbed, this privy, this mensturation, this corpse . . . which, by means of a superficial appearance, a shadow, a phantasm, a dream, a Circe-like charm in the service of procreation, deceives us by taking the form of beauty. (II, p. 289)

This extreme misogny, as Bruno very frankly informs us in his dedication to Philip Sidney, is not caused by impotence. On the contrary, he says, without boasting: he has eaten of the forbidden fruit without ever being satiated, for the snows of the Caucasus and of the Rif would not suffice to cool the heat of his veins. But the realm of physical love must be separated from the realm of divine contemplation with a clarity that Petrarch, the repressed sensualist, lacked.

The anti-Petrarchism[61] of Bruno represents, fundamentally, an attempt to relegate to the sphere of pure consciousness the turbid self-satisfactions of the subconscious, which, in Petrarch's work, are systematically raised to a level of intellectual dignity that from the point of view of the Nolan they do not deserve. In Bruno's ethics there is no room for the phantasms of a degenerate imagination.

An attitude not without ambiguities: first, because he accepts woman as an object of utility, provided that her use be not accompanied by phantasy; second, because he himself does not hesitate to hypostasize woman while taking care to keep his distance from Dante, whom he envisages only as a companion of the unfortunate Petrarch.

Bruno's feminine hypostasis is not Beatrice, in whom Dante was not able to separate the sphere of the profane from that of the divine. Bruno's unknown precursor seems, in this sense, to be a misogynous mystic on the order of Sanā'ī, for whom the feminine hypostasis of the Intelligence has no actual reference.

This comparison, though somewhat pertinent, tells us nothing about the historical context influencing Bruno. We must remember that we are in the middle of the Reformation and that puritanism—in the timeless meaning of the word—is growing harsher on the Protestant as well as the Catholic side. To be sure, that a former monk should make no effort to hide his carnal relations is a very serious matter for all concerned. All the same, his attitude is forgivable if he acknowledges the truth of that principle sacrosanct to witch hunting and enunciated by the tragic manifesto of puritanism, the *Malleus maleficarum* of the inquisitors Institoris and Sprenger: "Woman is a bane of nature clothed in bright colors."[62] Bruno's misogyny is a legacy from his era, combined with the very practical mnemonics of the ex-Dominican which permitted him to exercise almost complete control over the phantasms of the subconscious. *In this sense, this "knight of the infinite" epitomizes the most perfect, hence the least human, product of the age of phantasms: a person capable of free will untrammeled by the turgid forces of his nature, which he has learned to dominate.*

Like Ibn 'Arabī's prologue to the *Dīwān*, Bruno's dedicating his book to Sidney is a protestation of innocence, which, in his case, finally arouses suspicion. Against what did he have to defend himself, since no one had accused him of having thought of an actual woman, someone to whom his love poems were addressed? Nevertheless, Bruno refutes this hypothesis so forcefully that he seems to prepare the ground for biographers who, not wishing to be duped by his too vehement pronouncements, will play the easy game of discovering some Beatrice, Petra, or Laura unintentionally responsible for the Nolan's sighs.

Bruno first intended, he tells us, to entitle his manuscript *Canticle*, but he changed his mind to avoid being accused of drawing his inspiration from an "ordinary" (that is, "natural," sexual) love for a person of flesh and blood.

These various matters aroused the suspicions, fundamentally sound but absurd in their consequences, of A. Sarno, who, in a 1920 article,[63] tried to show that the inspirer of Bruno's love poems was none less than Queen Elizabeth of England and that it was only later, *post festum*, that the author transformed them into lyrical metaphysics by means of philosophical commentary. In fact, if Bruno rejects as a terrible insult the idea that the *Heroic Furors* should have been interpreted as poetic confessions of love for a *woman*, he immediately excludes from the concept "woman" (which, alas, he finds degrading) all female inhabitants of the British Isles, *toto orbe divisa*, who are nymphs and not women (II, p. 293). As a matter of fact, *toto orbe divisa* means "separated from the continent" not only in a spatial sense but also in an ontological one: England is of an alien race with regard to Europe (we have already seen the ambiguity to which this apparent compliment lends itself in Bruno's designs, since he was far from being an admirer of British civilization of the sixteenth century). Among those nymphs the peerless, the "unique Diana"—Queen Elizabeth—shines like the sun amidst the planets:

> . . . l'unica Diana
> Qual'è tra voi quel che tra gli astri il sole.
> (Iscusazion del Nolano alle più virtuose e leggiadre dame,
>                                                 (II, p. 306; cf. p. 302)

Though not inspired by a woman, Bruno's poems according to him were inspired by a goddess, a mistress of nymphs, Diana, who is partly identifiable with Queen Elizabeth. This is all undeniable, but the conclusion reached by A. Sarno and F. Flora is, ultimately, quite platitudinous. While they think they are cutting a Gordian knot to reach the truth, which essentially must be simple, those two scholars do not realize that they are at the center of a network of very complicated meanings at the very heart of Bruno's philosophy as well as of the spirit of his era.

AT THE HEART OF BRUNO'S DOCTRINE

Central to Bruno's moral doctrine is Ficino's thesis of the dispossessing of the subject, of the loss and the transfer of its "subjectness" into the object. To be sure, that applies exclusively, as with Pico della Mirandola, to the state of mystic love, whose object is the Deity. Hence the *mors osculi*, as we shall see, as well as the story of the nine blind men, which, though a revival, literal in places, of the eclogue *Cecaria* of the Neapolitan Marco Antonio Epicuro, takes its inspiration equally from Pico's theory of prophetic blindness as formulated in his *Commento*.

On the chessboard of this artificial erotic memory, the "statue" of Diana is by far the most important chessman: the Queen, literally and figuratively. But this phantasm's function is more than a representation of a distinguished person, in this instance Queen Elizabeth. The symbolism of the English court was welcomed all the more enthusiastically by Bruno because it concurred with his own metaphysics, wherein a female being called Amphitrite, of whom Diana is the manifest hypostasis, plays a primary role. With the characteristics of a queen, Diana transcends not only the phenomenology of the phantasmic Eros but also the realm of the entire human imagination. Her presence is not the sign of a nonreciprocable love—the love of a poor foreign clerk for the first lady of a strange country—but the symbol of spiritual adventures as well as metaphysical entities.

Bruno is perfectly familiar with Ficino's theory of love and also with Pico della Mirandola's *Commento*. Part of the *Heroic Furors* (II, p. 3) is made up of an exchange of questions and answers between heart and eyes, pneumatic organs with a familiar role in the psychology of Eros. However, the new scholasticism of which Ficino had been the most famous representative is ridiculed by Bruno in his comedy *Candelaio*, published in Paris in 1582.[64] The character Scaramuré, a charlatan magician and astrologer, recites this passage taken almost literally from Ficino's works:

> Fascination is produced by virtue of a shiny and rarefied spirit, generated by the heart from the purest blood which, sent out in the form of rays from open eyes . . . , wounds the thing beheld, touching the heart, and goes on to contaminate the body and spirit of the other person. (III, pp. 48–49)

Elsewhere as well, Bruno reveals that Ficino's ideas do not satisfy him. In the pro-prologue of the comedy (III, p. 27) he makes fun of contemplative melancholics and their exceptional powers (*quelli . . . a quai Saturno ha pisciato il giudizio in testa*).

Without saying so explicitly, Bruno scorns Ficino for his pedantry. That can be explained by the phantasmic essence of Bruno's culture stemming from Ficino's preaching. But, while Ficino's writings comprised very exact and often tedious descriptions of phantasmic mechanisms, Bruno's are *living descriptions of inner scenarios*. Ficino's distinctive peculiarity is scholastic, the use of locutions chosen to express fixed concepts; that of Bruno is mnenotechnic, a very careful and often tedious presentation of phantasms of the artificial memory. The ground on which Bruno and Ficino meet is the *style*, very precious in both, Bruno having a marked predilection for oxymoron, quite common in the sixteenth century. Like St. John of the Cross, Bruno uses terms of mystical love, for example: *In viva morte morta vita vivo* (II, p. 327).

The explanation for this turn of phrase brings us back to Ficino's theory of transforming subjectivity: "one [the subject] is not dead, because one lives in the object; one is not alive, because one is dead within oneself" (ibid.). Another expression applying to this wasting away from love is, of course, the death kiss, the *binsica* of Pico della Mirandola, "in which the soul languishes by being dead in itself and living in the object" (II, p. 351).

Bruno would not be a true artist of memory if he did not use "statues" and an appropriate scenario to illustrate this crucial moment in the dialectic of mystical love of the loss of subjectness. The myth that seems to him most suitable is that of Actaeon, the young hunter who, having surprised Diana bathing naked in a spring, was changed into a stag by the goddess and devoured by his dogs. The fable of Actaeon has always been used in many ways. Poor Ovid, who relates it in his *Metamorphoses*, complains in the *Tristia* of having suffered the fate of Actaeon although the dismemberment has been replaced by exile to the Black Sea. Surely he must have noticed something unseemly about the love affairs of a goddess, very likely the daughter of Augustus. In Bruno's time, the story was as well known as in the time of Ovid. The writer who here supplies us with the material to illustrate it is a gentleman from Poitiers, Jacques du Fouilloux (1519–80), originally from Gâtine, a precursor of Casanova and also—though confining himself to mistreating his own wife—of the marquis de Sade. Du Fouilloux wrote a treatise on hunting, famous in his time, called *La Vénerie*, printed—followed by the erotic poem *Adolescence*—by "De Marnefz et Bouchetz frères" at Poitiers in 1561.[65]

Du Fouilloux was adept at stag hunting, which earned him a *Stag's Lament* in verse by Guillaume Bouchet published at the end of the 1561 edition.[66] The stag pleads his case against the hunter and pronounces this final malediction:

> But if you remain zealous in your evil,
> Despising the power and wrath of the gods,
> May you meet Diana of Cynthus,

FIGURE 5. Capture of the stag. From Jacques du Fouilloux, *La Vénerie* (Paris, 1606). Courtesy of The Newberry Library, Chicago.

Bathing naked in some fountain,
And, like Actaeon, turned into a stag like me,
Crying under your dog stretched out on you,
Who will suck your blood [fig. 5], until it makes sense
This cruel pain does equal your offense.

It is to this story of the hunter hunted that Bruno's famous sonnet of the *Heroic Furors* (I, p. 4) is dedicated. Here we render it in an almost literal translation:

> Young Actaeon, when destiny directs his hesitant and rash deeds, sets free his mastiffs and his greyhounds in the woods, on the scent of game. He sees in water the most beautiful bust and face it has ever been granted a mortal or even a god to see, made of purple and alabaster and fine gold; and thus the great hunter in turn becomes the game.
> The large and numerous dogs quickly devoured the stag who used to go with long, light leaps to inaccessible places. Just so am I, who in my thoughts take aim at prey high up, but they turn against me, killing me with their cruel and greedy bites.

In Bruno's poem it is not the narrative that matters but the characters. Now, these characters are *statues of the artificial memory*. We must envisage the scene as being a little like a Flemish engraving in the Antwerp edition of the *Metamorphoses* (1591, pp. 84–85): a goddess emerging half naked from the water and a hunter changed into a stag and devoured by his own dogs. Goddess, hunter, and dogs are the phantasmic supports of the mnemonic contents described by Bruno in his commentary. Diana is seen as having a complexion of alabaster, lips (or breasts) of purple, and hair of fine gold. Only her bust emerges from the water, which means that she is endowed with one part that is visible and another that is hidden. The water symbolizes the sensory world created in the image of the intelligential world. The visible part of Diana represents "the extreme power and performance that mortals or gods can see through the nature and the act of intellectual contemplation." The alabaster of her complexion is symbolic of divine beauty, the purple of active power, and the gold of divine wisdom.

The dogs are divided into mastiffs and greyhounds, which is not at all accidental. The mastiffs represent the subject's will; the greyhounds, discursive intellect, the *dianoia*. The game, pursued by hunter and dogs, represents "the intelligential kinds of ideal concepts which are occult, pursued by few people, captured by still fewer, and not available to all who seek it."

Bruno's poem must be interpreted as a *picture* painted while we watch, a picture recorded forever in the archives of artificial memory. It represents, in a way, the quintessence of intellective processes, whose object, the Truth which is also Beauty, is also the object of Eros.

As in the engraving of the *Metamorphoses*, the statue of Actaeon, as conceived by the memory, must have the head of a stag to indicate the process of transformation of subject into object. Why and how does the hunter become the game? "Through workings of the intellect, which helps to change into itself things learned. . . . Because it forms intelligential species in its own way and adjusts them according to its capacities, for they are received according to the capacity of the receiver, *ad modum recipientis.*" It is only because of the limits of the intellect that the subject cannot embrace the whole splendor of divine truth; indeed, this phantasmic recipient compels the intelligential world to reveal itself in the form of phantasms. It is not a kind of knowledge *facie ad faciem* of the soul but, on the contrary, an indirect, pneumatic knowledge.

It is here that the matter of ecstatic union arises: as he advances on the chessboard of knowledge, the helpless pawn suddenly finds himself changed into a queen, Diana, the object of his quest. The intellect is annihilated, thunderstruck: the hunt continues only "through will power which transforms the subject into the object . . . , for love *transforms and changes into the thing that is loved.*" It is a matter of a hidden ritual of transition from one existential state to another, symbolized by the image of devouring, of dismemberment: "Thus it is that *large and numerous dogs put him to death:* thus it is that his life in the mad, sensual, blind, and phantasmic world ends, and he begins to live intellectually, to live the life of a god, to nourish himself on ambrosia and become intoxicated on nectar" (II, p. 352).[67]

If painter and poet have had the upper hand hitherto, the philosopher will take his revenge from now on, endowing the allegory of Actaeon with an explanation so clear that it is surprising it has always been so poorly interpreted:

> It is not possible to see the sun, the universal Apollo, pure light in its best and highest form. It is possible, however, to see his shadow, his Diana, the world, the universe, nature which is inside things, which is the light within the opacity of matter, shining in the darkness. Of the many who traverse the paths of this deserted forest, there are very few who proceed to Diana's spring. There are many who are satisfied to hunt wild and less renowned beasts, while most of them do not know what to do with themselves, having set their course conventionally and consequently finding only flies. Actaeons

are very rare who have the good luck to look upon Diana
naked, to fall so much in love with the beauty of the body of
nature . . . , that they are changed . . . from hunters into
game. For the final goal of the science of hunting is to come
upon this rare and wild beast who transformed the hunter
into the object of his hunt: in every other kind of hunt in
which the object is special things, the hunter seizes the
things, he absorbs them through the mouth of his own intelligence; whereas in the case of a divine and universal ven-
ison, he opens his heart so widely to knowledge that he is
assimilated to it, absorbed by it, integrated with it. From
being commonplace, ordinary, civilized, and social as he had
been before, he becomes wild as the stag and the desert
dweller. In this vast forest, he lives in the lairs of the caver-
nous mountains, *lairs which do not belong to the artificial memory*
[*stanze non artifiose*], in which he admires the sources of great
rivers, vegetates in purity, far from the contamination of ordinary desires.

The two fragments that explain the subject's rites of passage to the
intellectual state are at pains to state precisely that this passage consists
in *outstripping phantasmic knowledge*. In the sensory world, man is condemned to acquire knowledge only through phantasms. On the other
hand, Bruno's great original approach, which pertained to the intelligible world, gains knowledge without the intermediary of phantasms, *facie ad faciem*, without requiring spiritual mediation between body and
soul, since man only lives in and through the soul. It is, of course, a
paradoxical state whose strangeness and peculiarity Bruno does not attempt to conceal:

> So it is that the dogs, that is to say, the thoughts about divine
> things, devour this Actaeon, *killing him in his aspect of social
> and common man* [*facendolo morto al volgo, alla moltitudine*], free-
> ing him from the ties of the perturbed senses,[68] from the car-
> nal prison of matter; so it is that he will no longer see his
> Diana as if through holes and windows, but, having demol-
> ished the high defensive walls, *he will have become* a single eye
> looking at the whole horizon. In this way, he contemplates it
> all as being one thing, he no longer sees distinctions and
> numbers according to the diversity of the senses. . . . He sees
> Amphitrite, origin of all numbers, all species, all causes, who
> is the *monad*, true essence of all being. And if he cannot see
> her in her essence in pure light, he sees her nevertheless
> through her progeniture, which is similar to his, having been

made in her image: since this monad—nature, the universe, the world—derives from the other monad, which is divinity. The latter is reflected and beheld in the former, like the sun in the moon. . . . *This one is Diana*, the One, the entity, the truth, intelligential nature in which the sun and the splendor of higher nature shine.

### ACTAEON

The mnemonic "statue" of Actaeon is the phantasm of the subject in search of truth, a search in which he uses all the irrational and rational resources of his soul. Like every man, Actaeon is endowed with sensibility and with phantasy, the two means of learning about the external world of nature and the internal world of the soul. Moreover, Actaeon is a *social man*, who takes part in public life with its limitations, its twaddle, and its prejudices.

The contemplation of the nude goddess is tantamount to the death of Actaeon: he loses all the attributes of the human condition—sociability, sensibility, and phantasy. But death is only the terrible side of an initiation, of a rite of passage toward the subject's intellectual state. This is marked by *direct knowledge* of the intelligential world, transcending public opinion, sensory information, and pneumatic phantasmagoria.

Actaeon, the subject, will henceforth be a "dead man alive," a being whose existence is paradoxical since it no longer has existence according to the preestablished states of his species. Fundamentally, the traumatic experience he has undergone has transformed him into the object of his own quest, into the divinity itself. Actaeon is no longer a man, he has become a god. That is why the continuation of his social existence among men who are no longer his like is a paradox. That is why the symbols of *coincidentia oppositorum* abound in Bruno's work: because he actually envisages the possibility of existence of a man who, emptied of his humanity, can fill himself with divinity without thereby exiling himself completely from his terrestrial abode. Like the subject who loses his subjectness, he is dead; but, like him, he regains existence insofar as, and only insofar as, he is loved by the object who becomes thus transformed into himself. In the traumatic process undergone by Actaeon when he surprises the naked Diana bathing in the spring, the goddess really *gives herself*, lets herself be possessed, but in the only way possible: by changing Actaeon into a stag, a familiar animal, someone who has left the level of his old existence to attain a form of existence in which he can enjoy his companion, the naked goddess.

We can already understand Bruno's *presumptions* (let us confine ourselves to the etymological meaning of this word): he states that he himself is this "dead man alive," this man liberated from the confines of the human species. He considers himself a religious *leader* who, like St. Thomas, Zoroaster, St. Paul, etc., has opened the "seal of seals," who has been loved by the virgin goddess, the unattainable Diana.[69]

In this framework it is easy to understand that the Inquisition sent him to the stake. Should he not, in principle, have been capable of a small miracle to save himself? And was not the wise and wily Inquisition sure that no one had been able to perform such a miracle? In every witchcraft trial—and I believe Bruno's was one—the passion of Jesus was repeated: had he not been asked to save himself if he could? Certainly, one of the deepest meanings of Christian truth resides in the fact that Jesus bends to the will of his Father, who decides, rather than save him, to change him into a sacrificial victim to expiate the sins of humanity (*felix culpa, quia tamen ac tantum meruit habere Redemptorem . . .* ).

It is not impossible that Bruno envisaged being burned at the stake as the final act of a process which had developed within himself long before: the rejection of his humanity, the transition to a state of divinity. Do not his last words, which have always been misinterpreted, bear witness to this? *Maiori forsan cum timore sententiam in me fertis, quam ego accipiam,* "You feel more fear, yourselves, in convicting me than I do, in receiving your sentence of death."

If he sought to be the apostle of a new religion, Bruno no doubt accomplished that wish. His name influenced the spirit and the voice of many a freemason, freethinker, revolutionary, materialist, or anarchist of the nineteenth century, and the place where Bruno's statue now stands, in front of the palace of the Papal chancellery, on the Campo de' Fiori, the site of his stake, has remained by tradition the rendezvous of the anarchists of Rome. Unfortunately, all those who transformed him into the champion of their social and political cause misunderstood his work and his personality, only recalling his martyrdom in the struggle against the Church. Bruno, indeed, has become the prophet of a religion of which he would never have approved, whose ideals were, on the contrary, diametrically opposed to his own. He, the most antidemocratic of thinkers, winds up as a symbol of democracy!

It is now possible to reconstruct and to understand what Bruno wanted. Far from being a champion of progress, democracy, technology, or ecology, Bruno was merely a thinker who tried to reinfuse vitality into the most sophisticated values, the most amazing in the Western Middle Ages. An attempt which, ending in bloody defeat, would—had it not been for the atrocious end of its protagonist—have remained buried forever amongst the oddities of history, along with the productions of a Giulio Camillo, a Peter of Ravenna, or a Fabio Paolini.

DIANA

While the statue of Actaeon was simple and univocal, the statue of Diana presents multiple aspects which, though forming an indissoluble unity, are nevertheless capable of being analyzed one by one. Thus Diana is simultaneously *nature*, the *moon*, and also the *queen*, Elizabeth of England.

*a. Nature*

When changed into a stag, Actaeon actually experiences a *revelation:* he surveys the goddess naked.

Now, Diana, who is "nature, the universe, the world," is the daughter, that is to say, the image, of Amphitrite, "origin of all numbers, of all species, of all causes." Here is the most complete definition of Diana: "Diana is one, the entity itself, the entity that is truth itself, truth which is intelligential nature in which the sun and splendor of higher nature shine, according to the distinction of unity between the generated and the generator, or the producer and the product."

We must not conclude, hastily, that this vision of nature corresponds mainly to Bruno's works on magic, or that these works are quite different from the philosophic doctrine set forth in the dialogue *De la Causa, Principio, et Uno.* While agreeing that there are, perhaps, differences in vocabulary between Bruno's treatises on magic and the philosophic work, there is no essential difference in principle and in method.

To Bruno, matter is the substratum of the cosmos, and the cosmos is animate matter. The universe without the world's soul, corporeal substance without incorporeal substance, are inconceivable. The only thing that changes is accidental form, external and material, whereas matter itself and substantial form, the soul, are "indissoluble and indestructible." The same matter, however, receives various "beings" (modalities of existence). Matter in its unity, like the Platonic *chora,* is only perceptible intellectually. Its powers are active and passive; action, unique and limited, does not coincide with power with regard to specific beings. Action and power are only identical in the first principle, which alone is *everything that can be.*

The universe (Diana), which appears as a *simulacrum* of primary nature (Amphitrite), is all that can be, since it contains all matter, but it is not all that can be because of the differences between the forms assumed by individual beings. It is only the *shadow* of the first action and power;

in it, action and power are not the same thing, not being the same in its parts. The universe is "deployed" (*explicato*), supported, distinct, whereas the first principle is "entangled" (*complicato*), uniform, one. Corruption, death, vice, the monstruous, stem from the shortcomings and impotence of things which are obliged to be many things simultaneously, trying to attain being through their power to be, which exceeds action and is thereby realized only imperfectly. But, since it is absurd that something be several things at a time, the individual being only succeeds in exchanging his being for another being.

So it happens that the universe, Diana, is the shadow of the universal soul, of Amphitrite: a shadow that swarms with beings but nevertheless can be envisaged as an indistinct unity. To surprise Diana naked is to perceive this shadow, to allow oneself to be absorbed by it, giving up the limitations belonging to a particular state of being. Actaeon, who thought he had a separate existence, finally realizes—while he is still able—that he is only the shadow of a shadow: at one with the whole.

*b. The Moon*

Not only the poet Ovid has called the moon *nocturna forma Dianae* (*Met.*, XV, 196) but also the other Romans.[70] Insofar as Diana, who is the universe, also reveals lunar behavior, Bruno seems to share this belief.

Now, let us remember that in *Heroic Furors* Diana is the daughter of Amphitrite: "for the monad that is the divinity produces this other monad, which is nature, the universe, the world, where she contemplates herself and is reflected, like the sun in the moon." In the system of this comparison, which does not claim to describe the exact structure of reality, Amphitrite plays the role of the sun (= the intelligential world), whereas Diana plays the role of the moon (= sensory world), the nocturnal planet that reflects the sun's light.

Amphitrite, a sea nymph raised to the rank of goddess of the sea through her marriage to Poseidon, is another very important figure in Bruno's artificial memory. Amphitrite has two faces, according to the kind of discourse in which she is encompassed: in the metaphysical discourse, she represents the intelligential world; in the political, she is Queen Elizabeth.[71]

The first face of Amphitrite is further illuminated in *La Cabala del cavallo Pegaseo* (1585). Here, the goddess is a source of *spirit*, of *pneuma*: "All spirits come from Amphitrite, who is spirit, and all return there." The amusing story of Onorio, the donkey, which carries on the main idea of the dialogue *Spaccio de la Bestia trionfante*, is freely inspired by the moral works of Plutarch.

Onorio came from the environs of Thebes. He was a glutton, and one day a common plant tempted him. In trying to get it, he fell into a gully and broke his bones. As he lay dying, he realized that his mind was no different from that of other living creatures, such as man. When his body was buried, the soul of Onorio, the equal of all other souls, flew to the zenith. Reaching the river Lethe, it pretended to quench its thirst but actually kept intact the memory of its ecstatic adventures.

Is it possible to identify Bruno's Amphitrite with Plutarch's lunar Persephone, who is also queen of souls?[72] There is probably a connection between them, but Bruno's Amphitrite does not appear to assume too explicitly lunar a character except in the case where, to represent the Queen of England, she finally becomes identified with her own child, Diana.

## c. The Queen

Ficino's theory of the externalization of love through the eyes, barbarously imitated by French literature in the sixteenth century,[73] had a strange and unexpected result. Given that the image of woman is of her who *wounds* the lover's heart, "warlike images" and "bellicose vocabulary" are typical of the female.[74] In Philippe Desportes, turns of phrase such as "this beautiful murderess," "my warrior," "my beautiful man-killer" abound.[75] The other tradition, abundantly illustrated by Du Bellay, Ronsard, Grévin, Pontus de Tyard, and Brantôme, transforms woman into "goddess," "divine," "sweet unearthly person," etc.[76] Of course, the two traditions often converge as in Desportes's verses:

> This beautiful goddess, ah! not only beauteous:
> A warrior, like Bellone, has surmounted me.[77]

The exaltation of the regal concept has reached its height. Du Bellay calls François I and Henri II "Gallic Hercules" and "great monarchs of the world," "eldest children of the Gods." Henri II is Jupiter, Catherine de' Medici is the "great" Juno, his companion.[78] Brantôme takes pleasure in the same kind of images when describing the appearance of a princess: "The most beautiful, superb, and ample figure that can be seen with such majestic carriage that she will always be taken for a goddess from the heavens rather than a princess here on earth," or again: "A princess . . . superhuman and celestial, and in every way perfect and accomplished."[79]

This fairytale atmosphere surrounds everything to do with royalty. At the time of Henri II, "the Louvre, rather than the king's house, is a sanctuary where courtesans, poets, and artists worship their deity according to a rite which we shall see take shape increasingly with time."[80]

England, which in the person of Queen Elizabeth sees all the ideals of universal monarchy revivified, creates according to the French model, her own royal cult, formed partly of common elements but also of individual elements derived from her personal situation. Elizabeth cannot, of course, be called the "British Hercules." Another comparison is almost self-evident: since she is unmarried, tantamount in public opinion to a vocation of perpetual virginity and chastity, the Queen is comparable to every famous Virgin, be it Astraea, [81] a Vestal Virgin,[82] Ariana,[83] the constellation of the Virgin,[84] the Virgin Mary (playing also on the phonetic similarity between *Beta* and *Beata* Maria).[85] The preferred comparison and, so to say, the most perfect, is the one that changes her into the goddess of the hunt, Diana, also known as Cynthia and Belphoebe.[86]

This choice, which is only too justified by the character both bellicose and virginal of Diana, raises no question except on one point: we well know that Diana (Cynthia, Belphoebe, etc.) is a lunar goddess. Now, what does Queen Elizabeth have to do with the moon? Ancient symbolism supplies a marvelous solution to this: whereas the sun had traditionally been associated with the Papacy, the moon was the symbol of Empire[87] (and vice versa, according to convention). In conformity with this doctrine, the Queen of England, who is confused with the goddess Diana, becomes the object of a lunar cult developed by a school of poetry called the "School of Night," of which Sir Walter Raleigh and George Chapman were the most famous representatives.[88]

Giordano Bruno, a fanatic believer in world empire, becomes, in London, a fervent adherent of the obscure cult of the goddess Diana. But the symbolism he adopts so promptly has a metaphysical value for him that probably escaped Raleigh and Chapman, also adherents. With unbelievable audacity, Bruno, who always remains a great specialist and professor of the Art of Memory, addresses his chosen public in language that was all too familiar to everyone. The "statue" of artificial memory that dominates the dialogues written in England is of Diana. Sidney and Greville, not to speak of persons in the know such as Raleigh and Chapman, associate Diana with Queen Elizabeth or, what amounts to the same thing, *had the ability to represent Diana without any special effort since, in their phantasy, she spontaneously assumed the features of the revered queen.* Bruno's allegory, designed to introduce metaphysical ideas and mnemonical personal techniques, also had the advantage of gaining for its author a very good reputation in the eyes of her who had been exalted—the Queen herself. Unfortunately, complicated political considerations, or rather Sir Philip Sidney's disgrace, compelled Bruno to leave the English court without having had time to garner the vainly awaited fruits of his praise.

THE PARABLE OF THE NINE BLIND MEN

The presence of Diana in Bruno's theater of phantasy is not the only sign of British influence. Through the intermediary of the French ambassador, who had taken part in it, Bruno was probably familiar with the allegory staged in Woodstock in 1575 by Sir Henry Lee in honor of the Queen, related in English, Latin, Italian, and French by George Gascoine in a pamphlet that appeared at the end of the same year. Henry Lee, the best man-at-arms in Elizabeth's time and a friend of Philip Sidney's, gave an "entertainment" featuring the story of the hermit Hemetes, who, having lost his sight, regained it as soon as he arrived in the best and most wisely governed country in the world.[89]

This transparent allegory, which he had probably read and partly memorized, awakened in Bruno an adolescent memory: the pastoral eclogue *Dialogo di tre ciechi* or *Cecaria* of the Neapolitan Marco Antonio Epicuro. In the last dialogues of the second part of the *Heroic Furors*, he freely imitates Epicuro's eclogue, also having in mind Pico's interpretation of the prophet's blindness.

The actors in Bruno's parable are nine blind men, mnemonic "statues" representing the nine species of love, which, through internal or external failure, predispose to sensuality, including the classic syndrome of *amor hereos* according to Pico della Mirandola's description.

The first is born blind; the second has been "bitten by the serpent of jealousy"; the third, on emerging from darkness is struck blind by intelligential light; the fourth lost his sight for having looked upon that light only; the fifth for having wept too much thus preventing the visual ray from coming out of the pupils; the fifth for having wasted all his vitreous humour in tears, so rendering opaque his ocular membranes thus no longer able to reflect visual rays; the seventh suffers from the same ailment caused by the terrible beat of his heart; the eyes of the eighth were damaged by the arrows of love shot by some "beautiful murderess"; finally, the blindness of the ninth was brought about through lack of self-confidence.

What had happened?

The nine young men, full of vitality, implore heaven to help them find love: "Oh, may it please heaven to cause to appear now, as in previous happier centuries, some sorceress like Circe, who, by means of plants, minerals, poisons, and charms, had the power almost to restrain nature itself!" Their prayer is answered, and a wonderful castle appears on Circe's mountain. They enter and find themselves in the presence of Circe, daughter of the Sun, *dives Solis filia* (*Aen.*, VII, 11), who strikes them blind. The nine men travel ten years until they arrive on the island of

Britain, at the river "Tamesi" (Thames), where they encounter native nymphs and explain their situation. Circe gave them a precious vase which is only to be opened when they have attained "exalted wisdom, noble chastity, and beauty combined." A nymph opens the "fatal vase," and the nine men regain their sight and begin to dance happily in a ring (a *ridda*). Their song is a hymn of thanks to kind destiny, which revolves eternally: "The wheel changes direction, over there it is high up, down here it jolts; day follows night, always." Another hymn then celebrates the source of the tides of the divine infant Anadyomene, welcomed to the heavens by Jupiter. This oceanic Venus is another "statue" of the Queen of England, alluded to in the sixth book of Spenser's *Faerie Queene* (1596), a more or less transparent reference to the same English court with its "nymphs" and its mistress, the *faire one*.

CIRCE

Another statue of Bruno's artificial memory closes the series opened by Actaeon: the statue of Circe the sorceress, herself daughter of the Sun and a lunar deity. Moreover, she represents the terrible aspect of the Great Goddess of nature, Diana: Circe binds, Diana unties; Circe blinds, Diana cures.

Giovanni Gentile believed that Bruno saw Circe as symbolizing the Catholic Church,[90] under whose yoke the philosopher had entered "into the beautiful region of Campania" and from which he would only be loosened in the land of the British nymphs, where, so to speak, he had regained his sight.[91] In Gentile's time, very little was known about the Art of Memory, and everyone envisaged Bruno merely as the champion of antiecclesiasticism. Circe, however, could not be the Catholic Church, since she is only a "statue"—a very important one—in Bruno's mnemonic system. It is she who keeps the "seal of seals," it is she who presides over magical memory and makes possible various processes through the intermediary of the planetary demons.[92]

Whereas Diana represents the universe in its unity, Circe is the mistress of magical processes, whose purpose is, precisely, to reunite the parts of the world, to place them in relationship to each other. Without Circe, there would be no Diana: the remedy would not exist without the poison.

# II  The Great Manipulator

*Vinculum quippe vinculorum amor est.*

Giordano Bruno

# 4| Eros and Magic

## (i) Identity of Substance, Identity of Process

Ficino is father of the equation Eros = magic, whose terms can doubtless be reversed.[1] It is he who points out, for the first time, the substantial identity of the two techniques for manipulation of phantasms as well as their operational procedures.

Love is, to be sure, a magician—the creation of this formula is also Ficino's (*Amore*, VI, 10, p. 106). That is because

> the whole power of Magic is founded on Eros. The way Magic works is to bring things together through their inherent similarity. The parts of this world, like the limbs [that is to say, the organs—Trans] of the same animal, all depend on Eros, which is one; they relate to each other because of their common nature. Similarly, in our body the brain, the lungs, the heart, liver, and other organs interact, favor each other, intercommunicate and feel reciprocal pain. From this relationship is born Eros, which is common to them all; from this Eros is born their mutual rapprochement, wherein resides true Magic. (Ibid.)

This is tantamount to saying that, since the substance in which the processes of Eros and of magic occur is unique—the universal pneuma (see chap. 5 below)—those two techniques are closely related, indeed identical. Moreover, Eros, presiding over all spiritual activities, is what ensures the collaboration of the sectors of the universe, from the stars to the humblest blade of grass. Love is the name given to the power that ensures the continuity of the uninterrupted chain of beings; pneuma is the name given to the common and unique substance that places these beings in mutual relationship. Because of Eros, and through it, all of nature is turned into a great sorceress (ibid., p. 107).

If magic is love, the opposite is no less true. Mathematical equations are always reciprocal and transitive. Philosophic equations do not follow the same rule. But, in this case, the substantial identity that makes it possible to equate these two terms is also accompanied by an operational identity that permits their reversal: love is, in turn, magic, since its processes are identical to magic processes. Indeed, what does the lover do by means of his deeds, words, services, and gifts other than create a magic *web* around the object of his love (ibid.)? All his means of persuasion are also *magic* means, whose goal is to bind the other to him. Ficino himself, to define this process, uses the word *rete*, meaning "net" or "web." To put it simply: the lover and the magician both do the same thing: they cast their "nets" to capture certain objects, to attract and draw them to them.

Later (chap. 6) we shall have the opportunity to analyze the vocabulary of magic: Ficino's word *rete* only repeats other accredited vocables such as *illex*, *illecebra*, or *esca*, which mean "bait," "decoy." Like a hunter, the lover and the magician—who is in love with nature, with Diana, Giordano Bruno would say—cast their nets and put out their phantasmic bait and traps in order to take possession of their precious game. It goes without saying that the quality and dimensions of the game vary. The lover uses his talents to gain control of the pneumatic mechanism of the beloved.[2] As for the magician, he can either directly influence objects, individuals, and human society or invoke the presence of powerful invisible beings, demons, and heroes[3] from whom he hopes to profit. In order to do so he must gather knowledge of the nets and bait that he must put out in order to gain the desired result. This procedure is called by Bruno to "bind" (*vincire*) and its processes bear the generic name of –'chains" (*vincula*). The doctrine of the identity of love and magic, already outlined by Ficino, is only carried to its logical conclusions by Giordano Bruno.

Since the first part of this work has been devoted to the phantasms of Eros and, to a certain extent, to artificial memory, the subject of *erotic magic* seems to me the most appropriate to ensure the continuity of my account. I take it up here with the reservation that it can only be explored in more depth after the mechanism and origins of pneumatic magic have been explored (chap. 5). The principle underlying the way it works has been mentioned in passing in the foregoing pages. In order to enhance comprehension that is still peripheral to what will follow, the reader is requested always to keep in mind that *magic is a phantasmic process that makes use of the continuity of the individual pneuma and of the universal pneuma.* We shall see in due course how this continuity is ensured and by what means magicians hope to attract the collaboration of supernatural presences. Beyond this presupposition common to all magic, erotic magic reveals other aspects, disconcertingly modern, requiring separate treatment. Bruno is the first to exploit the concept of magic to its ultimate conclusions, envisaging this "science" as an infallible psychological instrument for manipulating the masses as well as the individual human being. Awareness of the appropriate "chains" (*vincula*) enables the magician to realize his dream of universal Master: to control nature and human society. This undertaking, however, encounters almost insuperable difficulties.

### (ii) Manipulation of Masses and of Individuals

*De vinculis in genere* ("Of bonds in general") by Giordano Bruno is one of those little-known works whose importance in the history of ideas far outstrips that of more famous ones. In its frankness, indeed the cynicism of the analysis of its contents, it might be compared to Machiavelli's *The Prince*, especially as the subject matter of the two works is connected: Bruno deals with psychological manipulation in general, Machiavelli with political manipulation. But how colorless and ridiculous the Machiavellian prince-adventurer now seems, compared to Bruno's magician-psychologist! The popularity of *The Prince* gained for it the respect of succeeding centuries and has recently even led to the theory of the modern "Prince"—the Communist party—advanced by Antonio Gramsci. Unpublished until late, little read and always misunderstood, *De vinculis in genere* is nevertheless the written work that deserves to have the real and unique place of honor among theories of manipulation of the masses. Without being aware of it, the brain trusts that dominate the world have been inspired by it, have put Bruno's own ideas to practical use. A continuity surely might exist, for Bruno seems to have exerted a certain influence on the ideological movement at the beginning of the seventeenth century, the Rosicrucian movement, which had great repercussions.[4] But to our knowledge there has never been, either before or after Bruno, any writer who has treated this subject empirically, free from any ethical, religious, or social considerations. For no one would have dreamed of attacking such a subject *from the point of view of the manipulator himself* without first positing, as the fundamental principle of his research, some intangible human or divine right in whose name the manipulation would be condemned.

In the nineteenth century, of course, we find ideologues like Karl Marx and Frederick Engels who believe that religion is the "opium of the people." Therein they only repeat Bruno's statement in *De vinculis*, where religion is seen merely as a powerful tool for manipulating the masses. But, while Marx and Engels have humanitarian and utopian ideals, Bruno shows little concern for safeguarding human dignity; the only right he envisages belongs neither to God nor to man but to the *manipulator* himself.

Toward the end of the nineteenth century, Gustave Le Bon laid the foundations of the discipline called "mass psychology" (*The Crowd*, published in 1895) later developed by Sigmund Freud, whose *Mass Psychology and the Analysis of the Ego* (1921) excited much interest. But the purpose of Le Bon and of Freud is to determine the psychological mechanisms operating within a crowd that influence its makeup, not to teach *how to control a crowd*. Science, because of moral scruples, refuses to adopt a point of view it prefers to allocate to the political man, Adolf Hitler, author of *Mein Kampf*. The Prince is allowed to keep what is his, even if it entails protesting—as in the case of Freud—against the abuses of a Stalin and the "new order" set up in the Soviet Union.

All mankind has heard of Machiavelli's *The Prince*, and many politicians have hastened to emulate his example. But only today can we appreciate how much *De vinculis* outstrips *The Prince* in depth, in timeliness, and in importance—today, when no head of state of the Western world would any longer dream of acting like the Prince but would use, on the other hand, methods of persuasion and manipulation as subtle as those the brain trusts are able to place at his or her disposal. In order to understand and show to advantage the timeliness of *De vinculis*, we ought to know about the activities of those trusts, those ministries of propaganda; we should be able to glance at the manuals of schools of espionage, from which we may glean something of what happens outside the corridors of those organizations whose *ideal* goal is to guarantee order and the common welfare, where it exists.

Machiavelli's Prince is the forebear of the political adventurer, a type that is disappearing. On the other hand, the magician of *De vinculis* is the prototype of the impersonal systems of mass media, indirect censorship, global manipulation, and the brain trusts that exercise their occult control over the Western masses. He is not, doubtless, the type followed by Soviet propaganda, for he by no means lacks subtlety. On the contrary, Bruno's magician is altogether aware that, to gain the following of the masses, like the loyalty of an individual, it is necessary to take account of all the complexity of the subjects' expectations, to create the total illusion of giving *unicuique suum*. That is why Bruno's manipulation demands perfect knowledge of the subject and his wishes, without which there can be no "bond," no *vinculum*. That is why Bruno himself also asserts that it is an extremely difficult maneuver, only to be accomplished by the use of intelligence, perspicacity, and intuition equal to the task. The complexity of the task is not diminished, for the illusion must be perfect to satisfy the many expectations it proposes to fulfill. The greater the manipulator's knowledge of those he must "enchain," the greater is his chance of success, since he will know how to choose the right means of creating the *vinculum*.

We see that the goal of Bruno's erotic magic is to enable a manipulator to control both individuals and crowds. Its fundamental presupposition is that a big tool for manipulation exists—Eros in the most general sense of the word: *that which we love*, from physical pleasure to things probably unsuspected, in passing, by wealth, power, etc. Everything is defined in relation to Eros, since aversion and hatred merely represent the negative side of the same universal attraction:

> All affections and bonds of the will are reduced to two, namely aversion and desire, or hatred and love. Yet hatred itself is reduced to love, whence it follows that the will's only bond is Eros. It has been proved that all other mental states are absolutely, fundamentally, and originally nothing other than love itself. For instance, envy is love of someone for oneself, tolerating neither superiority nor equality in the other person; the same thing applies to emulation. Indignation is love of virtue . . . ; modesty and fear [*verecundia, timor*] are none other than love of decency and of that which one fears. We can say the same of the other mental states. Hatred, therefore, is none other than love of the opposite kind, of the bad; likewise, anger is only a kind of love. As regards all those who are dedicated to philosophy or magic, it is fully apparent that *the highest bond, the most important and the most general* [*vinculum summum, praecipium et generalissimum*], belongs to Eros: and that is why the Platonists called love the Great Demon, *daemon magnus*.[5]

Magic action occurs through indirect *contact* (*virtualem seu potentialem*), through *sounds* and *images* which exert their power over the senses of sight and hearing (*Theses de Magia*, XV, vol. III, p. 466). Passing through the openings of the senses, they impress on the imagination certain mental states of attraction or aversion, of joy or revulsion (ibid.).

Sounds and images are not chosen at random; they stem from the occult language of the universal spirit (ibid., p. 411). With regard to sounds, the manipulator should know that tragic harmonies give rise to more passions than comic ones (ibid., p. 433), being able to act on souls in doubt (ibid., p. 411). There, too, it is necessary to take account of the subject's personality for, though there are some people easily influenced there are others who react in an unexpected way to the magic of sound, like that barbaric emperor who, on listening to a very sophisticated musical instrument, thought that it was the neighing of horses (ibid., p. 433).

In turn, *images* are capable of giving rise to friendship or to hatred, to loss (*pernicies*) or dissoluteness (ibid., p. 411). This artificial phenomenon can, moreover, be verified daily by virtue of the fact that individuals and things seen inspire in us spontaneously sympathy or antipathy, aversion or attraction (ibid., p. 447).

Sight and hearing are only secondary gateways through which the "hunter of souls" (*animarum venator*), the magician, can introduce "chains" and lures (*De vinculis in genere*, III, p. 669). The main entrance (*porta et praecipuus aditus*) for all magic processes is phantasy (*De Magia*, III, p. 452), the only gateway (*sola porta*) for internal mental states and the "chain of chains" (*vinculum vinculorum*) (ibid, p. 453). The power of the imaginary is increased by intervention of the cogitative faculty: that is the thing that is capable of subjugating the soul (ibid.). Therefore the "chain" has to pass through phantasy, for "there is nothing in the intellect that was not previously perceived by the senses [*quod prius non fuerit in sensu*], and there is nothing which, coming from the senses, can reach the intellect without the intermediary of phantasy" (*De Magia*, XLIII, vol. III, p. 481).

According to the abstraction drawn by the manipulator himself, who is supposed to exert total control over his own imagination (theoretically, at least), the majority of mortals are subject to uncontrolled phantasies. There are only particular professions that demand the *voluntary* application of imagination (the poet, the artist); as for the rest of them, the realm of imagination is settled by external causes. In this case, we must distinguish between phantasies caused by voluntary action (but of another kind) of the subject himself, and the phantasies whose origin lies elsewhere. The latter, in turn, can be caused by demons or induced by human will (*De Magia*, III, p. 449).

Implicated here is the will of the manipulator, which must be of an altogether special kind. Indeed, Bruno warns every manipulator of phantasms—in the event, the artist of memory—to regulate and control his emotions and his phantasies lest, believing himself to be their master, he nevertheless becomes dominated by them. "Be careful not to change yourself from manipulator into the tool of phantasms": that is the most serious danger confronting the disciple (*Sigillus sigillorum*, II, 2, p. 193). The real magic manipulator must be able "to arrange, to correct, and to provide phantasy, *to create the different kinds at will*" (*De Magia*, XLVIII, vol. III, p. 485).

It seems that man is endowed with a hypercomplex brain that has no special capacity to analyze stimuli according to their provenance: in short, he is not capable of differentiating directly between dreamlike data and those transmitted by the senses, between the imaginary and the tangible.[6] Bruno demands of the manipulator a superhuman task: first he must accurately and immediately classify data according to their provenance, and then he must render himself completely immune to any emotion prompted by external causes. In short, he is supposed *no longer to react* to any stimulus from without. He must not allow himself to be moved either by compassion, or by love of the good and the true, or by anything at all, in order to avoid being "enchained" himself. In order to exercise control over others, it is first essential to be safe from control by others (*De Magia*, XLVIII).

With incomparable lucidity, Bruno draws a clear distinction between theology (with fundamentals of morality, which, let us remember, was an exclusively theological discipline) and "the mental view of the laity" (*civilis speculatio*), whose representative he considers himself to be. For theology, there is a true religion and false beliefs, there is good and evil which are largely ideological in nature. There can be no question of the *manipulation* of individuals and masses, but simply of a mission with the goal of converting to the one and only truth. On the contrary, for Bruno, there is only one sacrosanct principle, only one truth, and that is: *everything is manipulable*, there is *absolutely no one who can escape intersubjective relationships*, whether these involve a manipulator, a manipulated person, or a tool (*De vinculis*, III, p. 654). Theology itself, the Christian faith, and all other faiths are only beliefs of the masses set up by magic processes.

For a magic process to succeed—as Bruno never tires of repeating—it is essential that the performer and the subjects be equally convinced of its efficacity. *Faith* is the prior condition for magic: "There is no operator—magician, doctor, or prophet—who can accomplish anything without the subject's having faith beforehand" (*De Magia*, III, p. 452), whence Hippocrates' remark: "The most effective doctor is the one in whom many people have faith" (ibid., p. 453). "It is generally agreed . . . that not only must we be credulous, we who act upon them, but the patients must be also. That is the essential condition, without which nothing can be achieved" (*De Magia mathematica*, VI, vol. III, p. 495). "Faith is the strongest bond, the chain of chains [*vinculum vinculorum*] of which all others are, so to speak, the progeny: hope, love, religion, piety, fear, patience, pleasure . . . , indignation, hatred, anger, contempt, and so on . . . " (*De Magia*, LIII, vol. III, p. 490). "It is essential

that the performer (of magic) have an active faith and the subject a passive faith. Especially is the latter important because without it no operator, either rational or divine, can accomplish anything" (ibid.).

It is obvious that the ignorant are more readily won over by the phantasms of theology and medicine:

> It is all the easier to enchain (*vincire*) people who have less
> knowledge. In them, the soul opens in such a way that it
> makes room for the passage of impressions aroused by the
> performer's techniques, opening wide windows which, in
> others, are always closed. The performer has means at his
> disposal to forge all the chains he wants: hope, compassion,
> fear, love, hate, indignation, anger, joy, patience, disdain for
> life and death, for fortune. (*De Magia*, III, pp. 453–54)

It is not by chance that the prophet is mentioned alongside the magician
and the doctor. The most obvious result of Bruno's thought is that all
religion is a form of mass manipulation. By using effective techniques,
the founders of religions were able, in a lasting way, to influence the
imagination of the ignorant masses, to channel their emotions and make
use of them to arouse feelings of abnegation and self-sacrifice they
would not have experienced naturally.

Statements of this kind can be easily misunderstood, giving credence
to the belief that here Bruno is making a sociological criticism of religion.
This is far from the case, for he does not try "to show it up" but only to
look at it from a wider angle from the point of view of the manipulator.
Bruno does not condemn religion in the name of humanitarian principles which are completely foreign to him. Moreover, he is not interested
in religion per se but rather in the way in which any religion can be
established if it finds the masses predisposed to accept it and a message
suitable for their conversion. As regards the manipulator himself, he
will be persuasive and unshakable in his faith and power to convince the
more he has succeeded in smothering in himself and others *philautia*,
self-love, egotism (*De vinculis*, III, p. 652, 675). Everything is manipulable, Bruno teaches us; but the manipulator has no right to use his power
over the masses for selfish ends. On the other hand, it seems that self-
love in the subject facilitates in some way the creation of "bonds."

In general, it is easier to exert a lasting influence over the masses than
over a single individual. Concerning the masses, the *vincula* used are of
a more general kind. In the case of an individual, it is first necessary to
be very familiar with his pleasures and his phobias, with what arouses
his interest and what leaves him indifferent: "It is, indeed, easier to

manipulate (*vincire*) several persons than one only" (ibid., p. 688). "That which is difficult, I believe, is not to bind or to liberate [*vincire et solvere*], but to find the right bond among all the bonds, the choice being arbitrary rather than controlled by nature or manipulative technique" (ibid., p. 686).

There are, no doubt, categories of age, physiognomy, etc., into which each individual can be placed, but, in general, the variety of individual differences, as well as the variety of "bonds" (*vincula*) applicable to them, must be accounted for. Two individuals never correspond to one another completely (ibid., p. 646).

Different individuals are manipulable according to different criteria: the beauty that subjugates Socrates does not subjugate Plato, the multitude has other preferences than do the elite, males have different tastes than females, some men have a predilection for virgins, others for promiscuous women (ibid., p. 639). In all of the above, the constant is the quality of the "chain of chains," the *vinculum vinculorum*, which is Eros (or sensual pleasure and, sometimes, phantasy, which amounts to the same thing).

**(iii) Vinculum Vinculorum**

The phrase, *vinculum vinculorum*, "chain of chains," as we have seen, is applied by Bruno to three separate things: Eros, phantasy, and faith. We already know, of course, that Eros is a phantasmic process which reduces the number of terms to two. Then we learn that the ground on which faith can be formed and can prosper is the imagination, which amounts to saying that, fundamentally, the *vinculum vinculorum* is the synthesizer, receiver, and producer of phantasms.

However, Bruno uses this expression most often to describe the extraordinary power of Eros, *daemon magnus*, which presides over all magic activities. These are only a deft exploitation of individual propensities and attitudes in order to create lasting bonds with the purpose of subjugating the individual or the group to the will of the manipulator.

The assumption is that no one can escape the magic circle: everyone is either manipulated or a manipulator. Having attained extraordinary domination over his own phantasy, and having also got rid of the ballast of vanity that made him vulnerable to the praise or blame of others, the manipulator, in order to use his techniques, applies himself to knowing and fathoming through intuition the characteristics, reactions, and emotions of the subject to be bound to him. Like a spy wanting to procure material for future erotic blackmail, the magician must collect all the indices that permit him to file his subject under some classification or other. A difficult task which, once accomplished, sets off to motions of the *vinculum*, four in number: the first is fastening the bond or chain (*iniectio seu invectio*), the second is the actual bond itself (*ligatio seu vinculum*), the third is the attraction resulting from it (*attractio*), and the fourth is the enjoyment of the object that gave rise to the whole process (*copulatio quae fruitio dicitur*). At issue, of course, is an erotic bond, which wastes away "through all the senses by means of which the attachment was created. . . . This is why the lover wishes to transform himself entirely into the beloved: through tongue, mouth, eyes, etc." (*De vinculis*, p. 642). The chain reaches the subject "through knowledge, binds through affection, and acts through enjoyment, generally speaking" (ibid., p. 641).

What is the purpose of this description of the *vinculum cupidinis*, the libidinal bond? This question is more difficult than it seems, for Bruno's treatise is far from explicit on many points. Since I have already answered it, I must justify my response.

A first possibility might be that Bruno, treating of love as a natural bond, aims his phenomenology not at goals of manipulation but simply to establish a paradigm of every other artificial and magic bond. Indeed, he never says *expressis verbis* that the purpose of the manipulator is to exploit "human weaknesses," the natural inclinations of the libido. This hypothesis is countered by several factors, some of which we have mentioned but the most important are yet to be clarified. Indeed, the verb *vincire*, "to enchain," is used in contexts where its active, operational meaning leaves no shadow of a doubt: "He who is in possession of the universal cause, or at least the nature, the tendency, the attitude, the use, and the finality of this particular thing he must enchain, that person will know how to enchain [*vincire ergo novit*]" (ibid, p. 659; cf. also p. 638). Furthermore, this passage seems to give us the key to Bruno's treatise—for what is it if not an analysis of the nature and tendencies of the "things to be enchained," of the *particulares res vinciendae?*

A second hypothesis, even more tenuous, would be that Bruno is simply describing the phenomenology of Eros, like Ficino and Pico della Mirandola. In contrast to this is the fundamental idea of the treatise already evident in its title: we are not dealing with abstract mechanisms of Eros but with *vincula*, the *production* of attachments, which is considerably simplified by virtue of the fact that all the "chains" are reduced to the erotic *vinculum*. It is therefore true that the phenomenology of Eros is a paradigm of the *vincula in genere;* but these are *magic* chains used by the manipulator to manipulate individuals or associations of individuals.

A third hypothesis, which does not implicate the idea of manipulation, is that knowledge of the erotic phenomenology is useful to the manipulator not only for exerting his influence on the external world but also for obtaining a perfect immunity to "bonds" of all kinds. That is altogether probable and amounts to saying that Bruno's manipulator is the man who knows all about love, *in order to learn not to love*. For it is the person who loves who is enchained. "The love of the lover is passive, it is a chain, a *vinculum*. Active love is something else, it is power active in things and it is this that enchains [*est ille qui vincit*]" (ibid., p. 649).

A fourth and final hypothesis, which also does not involve the capability of the manipulator either to forge the chains of love or to ward them off, is that Bruno might be concerned, among other things, with supplying his disciple-reader with *medical* knowledge enabling him to consider erotic questions without prejudice, to "unbind" and break the imaginary *vincula* that attach his patients to him. In some cases that is very probable and is confirmed by the use of the verb *exsolvere*, antonym of *vincire*, which appears next to it (ibid., p. 675). The passage is interesting for it shows that the subject's state of receptivity is very important *ad quomodolibet vinciendum et exsolvendum*, "to enchain and release from bonds in every way." It is therefore clear that the manipulator's activity consists not only in the exercise of a magic influence but also in the opposite, namely the breaking of the *vincula* from which a patient suffers.

In conclusion, the treatise *De vinculis in genere* should be interpreted as a practical manual for the magician, teaching him to manipulate individuals according to their emotional natures and to keep himself at a distance from the dangerous influence of Eros, to cure patients in the grip of a powerful erotic spell.

The fundamental idea of the treatise is that "love rules the world," that "the strongest chain is that of Venus" (ibid., p. 696): Eros "is lord of the world: he pushes, directs, controls and appeases everyone. All other bonds are reduced to that one, as we see in the animal kingdom where no female and no male tolerates rivals, even forgetting to eat and drink, even at the risk of life itself" (ibid.). In conclusion, *vinculum quippe vinculorum amor est*, "indeed the chain of chains is love." And again, "All bonds relate to the bond of love, either because they depend on it or because they are reduced to it." "Love is the foundation of all emotions. He who loves nothing has nothing to fear, to hope, to boast of, to dare, to scorn, to accuse, to excuse himself for, to humiliate himself for, to rival, to lose his temper over. In short, he cannot be affected in any way" (ibid., p. 684). This individual is, of course, the manipulator himself, who, exercising absolute control over the sphere of Eros, knows how to keep himself away from all *vincula*, from all the traps that love has set for him.

What is this *vinculum?*

It is, of course, beauty in its widest sense. But this beauty-that-en-chains does not consist in a prescribed proportion of the limbs.[7] It has an "incorporeal reason for being," which differs according to the nature of each individual. It can happen that a perfectly beautiful young girl is less attractive than another, who is theoretically less beautiful. That can be explained by a secret *communication* (ibid., p. 641) between the lover and the object of his love.

How does the *vinculum* function?

It is caused by phantasy, of course, which has its own autonomy and reality: "Phantasy is true, it operates in actuality, it can really influence the object" (ibid., p. 683). It also invades the subject through the "door of the imagination." It reaches the cogitative faculty, it determines emo-tions and incites the subject to pleasure (ibid., p. 641). Sight plays an essential role in this, and often the lover perishes for want of seeing the object of his love (ibid., p. 648).

The most interesting part of Bruno's thesis is dedicated to the kinds of *vincula*. They are very numerous for the emotion that each person dem-onstrates is differentiated according to the recipient: "It is with a differ-ent bond that we embrace sons, father, sister, wife, a woman, the libertine, and a friend" (ibid., p. 646). "Semen is of many kinds, Venus is of many kinds, love is of many kinds, bonds are of many kinds" (*Mul-tiplex semen, multiplex Venus, multiplex amor, multiplex vinculum;* ibid., p. 651). "The female becomes attached to a female, the child to a child, the male to a male, the male to a female, the man to his superiors, to his equals, to his inferiors, to natural things, to artificial things. Things be-come attached to other things" (ibid.). In principle, man is freer than beast in the choice of "chains": a mare has no difficulty in giving herself to any horse; on the other hand, a woman does not give herself to every man (ibid., p. 648).

Though it is almost impossible to determine precisely the nature of the "bonds" capable of enchaining one person or another, there are nev-ertheless some general rules according to which the subjects can be clas-sified in groups of age, temperament, physiognomy and social position. Those classifications facilitate the choice of the *genus* of "bonds" but do not suffice to establish the particular species.

For instance, the child is less subject to erotic attractions. Only after his fourteenth year is he capable of responding to erotic stimuli. The most vulnerable are mature people since their genital powers are more developed—and among them adolescents especially, for to them Eros represents a new and long awaited experience and because, the genital passage being smaller, the erotic pleasure is more intense (ibid., pp. 676–77).

Of the four temperaments, melancholics are most inclined to experience the seductiveness of sensual pleasure since they are endowed with intense phantasy life capable of imagining all sorts of erotic delights. But this propensity for speculation and contemplation makes them more unstable emotionally. Furthermore, melancholics pursue sensual pleasure for its own sake; they do not consider the propagation of the species (ibid., p. 677).

Physiognomy also helps the manipulator to place the subject in an erotic classification. For instance, people with weak and sinewy shinbones, a prominent curved nose, altogether resembling a billy goat, are like satyrs, tending toward venereal pleasures. Their emotions are not lasting and their passion is quickly assuaged (ibid., p. 678).

People of a higher social class like to be honored and flattered. Their sycophants have an easy time of it, provided they do not exaggerate. It is enough for them "to enlarge mediocre virtues, to diminish vices, to excuse the inexcusable, and to change faults into qualities" in order to "enchain" their benefactor (ibid., pp. 646, 666).

Finally, there are psychic pleasures or physical pleasures, or both simultaneously (ibid., p. 645); there is natural love and abstract love practiced by the *heremita masturbans* (ibid., p. 644). Along with those generalizations, Bruno also states some very cryptic rules for controlling sexuality, rules we shall now try to interpret.

### (iv) Ejaculation and Retention of Semen

Some passages of *De vinculis* are especially interesting because they seem to show that the practice of *coitus* reservatus was not foreign to Bruno's magic. We know that this was practiced by Taoists in China[8] and the tantric yogis in India and Tibet.[9]

Bruno's remarks are so concise, however, that great care is needed to define their meaning without misrepresentation. Since only a few sentences are involved, we can make an exception to the general rule observed in this book so that readers can consult the Latin text as well as the translation:

> *Iactu seminis vincula relaxantur, retentione vero intenduntur; taliter debet affectus qui vincire vult, qualiter qui vincire debet. Propterea in conviviis et post convivia inspirare introducitur in ossibus ignem Cupido. Vide. Continentia est principium vinculi, abstinen-*

*tia praecurrit famem, haec melius cibum attrahit. (De vinc.,* p. 645:
Ejaculation of semen releases the bonds, whereas its retention strengthens them. He who wishes to enchain is obliged
to develop the same emotions as he who must be bound.
That is why, when we are overheated at banquets or after
banquets, Cupid invades us. Look: continence is the beginning of the bondage, abstinence precedes hunger, and hunger leads to victuals.)

*Vinculum fit ex prolifico semine quod ad actum suum rapitur,
nititur atque rapit; ideo hos emissum secundum partem, perit secundum partem vinculi vis. (Ibid.,* p. 663: There is a bond by means
of prolific semen, which is attracted, strives, and approaches
its act. That is why, if it has been partially emitted, the
strength of the bond is also partially dissipated.)

*Cupidinis vincula, quae ante coitum intensa erant, modico seminis
iactu sunt remissa et ignes temperati, obiecto pulchro nihilominus
eodem permanente. (Ibid.:* Cupid's bonds, which were strong
before the mating, were dissipated after the moderate ejaculation of semen, and the ardor was diminished even though
the attractive object did not cease to be.)

Let us agree that Bruno's notes, concise to the point of unintelligibil-
ity, can give rise to several interpretations. We have already stated a first
hypothesis: that he deals with the practice of retention of sperm, of
*coitus reservatus.* We know that by means of such a practice, along with
exercises of "embryonic breathing," the Taoists sought vitality and longevity, whereas the Tantrics, within the framework of a subtle and
much more sophisticated physiology, were supposed, through the *mai-
thuna,* to reawaken dormant cosmic energies and to channel them to the
"Lotus of a thousand leaves" at the top of the head, entering a state of
ecstasy. In both cases, *coitus reservatus* represents one of the indispensable methods to reach the goal.

Since, in a treatise on erotic magic, Bruno speaks of the retention of
sperm, we may ask whether he does not have in mind a practice of the
same kind.

We soon discover he is not thinking of that. What interests him, as we
know, is the way we can seduce, create bonds and attachments. Now,
he observes that once pleasure has been had, the bonds dissolve. That is
why, to maintain the strength of a bond, it must not be enjoyed.

But to whom does this refer: to the manipulator or to the subject to be
bewitched by Eros? If he were speaking of the manipulator, we already

know that he must be free of any attachment, and therefore it would be more fitting for him to emit semen in order to dissolve the bond. On the other hand, it is to his interest that the subject not assuage his desire, for enjoyment leads to the destruction of the "bond."

So far we have not got to the heart of Bruno's message. Among the cryptic passages we have translated there is one that could lead us in the right direction: "There is a bond by means of prolific semen, which is attracted, strives, and approaches its act." That probably means that the person who ardently *desires* has the power to attract into his orbit the object of his desire. On the other hand, if he emits the semen, the strength of his desire diminishes, and consequently, the strength of the "bond" is also reduced. That is why the manipulator is supposed to *strengthen the bond*, retain the sperm, for "he who wishes to bind is obliged to develop the same emotions as he who must be bound." That is the *transitive result* of magic: to arouse an emotion the manipulator must develop it in himself, whence it will not fail to be transmitted to the phantasmic mechanism of his victim.

What Bruno wishes to say has no connection with the practices of coitus reservatus: he simply recommends that the manipulator be *continent* and, at the same time, *ardently desire* the subject. Does he not assert, moreover, that the "more saintly one is, the greater one's ability to bind [others]" (ibid., p. 651)? He must, indeed, cultivate assiduously the same passion he wishes to arouse in his victim, taking care, however, not to be possessed by his own phantasms and never to aspire to the assuagement of desire, else the strength of the bonds disappears.

The tenet of a connection between the continence of the manipulator and his magic or visionary abilities is a very old, prestigious one, taking many forms. We have seen that a close connection had been established, through the medicine of antiquity, between the five senses, the production of the voice, and the secretion of sperm. The last two are closely allied in Renaissance medicine, since they represent the only two modalities through which the spirit leaves the body *in an observable way*.[10] It goes without saying that too abundant a loss of sperm will affect not only the voice but also the other spiritual activities of the subject and that, reciprocally, speaking too much will produce the same result.[11] The opposite of pneumatorrhea is the accumulation of the pneuma, which is gained, for one thing, through sexual continence.

All those ideas are concentrated in a treatise that appeared in 1657, *Alphabeti vere naturalis Hebraici brevissima Delineatio*, by Franciscus Mercurius van Helmont (1614–98), son of the famous Paracelsian iatrochemist Ioannes Baptista van Helmont (1577–1644):[12] "If semen is not emitted, it is changed into a spiritual force that preserves its capacities to reproduce sperm and invigorates breath emitted in speech."[13]

In his *De vinculis*, Giordano Bruno probably refers to a similar tenet exalting continence for its ability to create *vincula*, magic bonds. It is remarkable that only *physical* continence is at issue, since, on the psychic level, Bruno recommends producing voluptuous phantasms whose purpose is to influence the subject's internal consciousness.

To sum up: Bruno's manipulator has to perform two contrary actions: on the one hand, he must carefully avoid letting himself be seduced and so must eradicate in himself any remnants of love, including self-love; on the other hand, he is not immune to passions. On the contrary, he is even supposed to kindle in his phantasmic mechanism formidable passions, provided they be sterile and that he be detached from them. For there is no way to bewitch other than by experimenting in himself with what he wishes to produce in his victim.

It is a strange and almost unbelievable method, which, however, well explains the concise passages translated above and is also confirmed by the advice Bruno gives to the artists of memory in his *Sigillus sigillorum:* He tells them almost literally: "Be excited; those people who are most inclined toward erotic pleasures and hatred are the most active" (*Sig. sig.*, 22, vol. II, 2, p. 166). There is no artificial memory without very strong affectivity, emotionally charged images. And there can be no superior intelligence and contemplation without passing through the gateway of emotional images (ibid., 22–23, pp. 166–67).

It is easy to guess how much discernment on the part of the manipulator was required by Bruno's method. He was simultaneously required to be "hot" and "cold," intoxicated with love and totally indifferent to all passion, continent as well as debauche. That explains the abundant oxymoron in his poetry, the contiguity of contradictory images and symbols. Most of the time he describes his state of soul as a mixture of fire and ice, which we can understand all too well, having studied his magic practices.[14]

### (v) Of Magic as General Psychosociology

Bruno's erotic magic, though unorthodox, has allowed us a close view of the extreme conclusions to which identity of substance and manipulation between Eros and magic could lead.

We must reverse our tracks and ask ourselves again about the relationship between Eros and magic, namely: Where does Eros end, where does magic begin? The answer seems very simple: at the very moment

Eros is made manifest, so is magic also. That is why erotic magic, at bottom, represents the starting point of all magic.

We still have to go deeper into the definition of magic as a *spiritual manipulation*. In any case it is a question of a transitive assumption making it possible to say that every other spiritual manipulation is at the same time a magical one. Now, the simplest *natural* pneumatic activity involved in any intersubjective process is Eros, which implies that all erotic phenomena are simultaneously magic phenomena in which the individual plays the role either of manipulator or of the manipulated or of the instrument of manipulation.

For a subject to take part in magic practices it is not necessary that the idea of magic itself cross the threshold of his consciousness. In fact, since there is no act which does not involve the pneuma in one way or another, we can even say that the whole existence of an individual lies in the sphere of natural magic. And since the relations between individuals are controlled by "erotic" criteria in the widest sense of that adjective, human society at all levels is itself only magic at work. Without even being conscious of it, all beings who, by reason of the way the world is constructed, find themselves in an intersubjective intermediate place, participate in a magic process. The manipulator is the only one who, having understood the ensemble of that mechanism, is first an observer of intersubjective relations while simultaneously gaining knowledge from which he means subsequently to profit.

All of the foregoing bears a strange resemblance to the concept of the "transference process" according to Jacques Lacan, for whom the world itself is but a huge apparatus of intersubjective exchanges in which each individual takes in turn the role of patient or of analyst.

The magician has greater possibilities: those of the doctor are relatively limited. Take two individuals A and B and the relationship between them, which we shall call Y. Let us then suppose that A loves B and that B does not respond: Y, their relationship, is defined in those terms. It is the magician's task to modify Y: placing himself at the service of A, he will obtain for him the favors of B. But let us suppose that A's family has a stake in having A give up his mad passion for B: placing himself at his service, the manipulator changes Y and "cures" A. That is the task of the doctor. Let us suppose that A is a manipulator of magic and that he wants to obtain favors from B. He is a magician, not a doctor. Third case, involving two of actual magic and one of medicine. What, exactly, is the borderline between those two disciplines? It is easy to realize that the powers of the doctor are legally limited to the cases in which A's disease conflicts with the interests of society, which amounts to saying it is out of the range of normality. On the other hand, the practitioner of erotic magic in general can utilize his talents against society itself and against the will of an individual.

Let us suppose that A is a multiple individual, a crowd with uniform reactions. B is a prophet, the founder of a religion, or a political leader, who, using magic techniques of persuasion, subjugates A. His techniques, like those of the physician, are equally admissible since, by gaining the social consensus, our manipulator himself dictates the rules of society.

Three hypostases: magician, physician, prophet. They are indissolubly bound together and have no precise line of demarcation. The "psychoanalyst" is also a member of the group, his sphere of action being confined to the illicit and the superhuman.

Along with specialization and delimitation of skills, we would tend to say that the two other practitioners of Bruno's magic, the actual magician and the prophet, have now vanished. More probably, however, they have simply been camouflaged in sober and legal guises, the analyst being one of them and, after all, not the most important. Nowadays the magician busies himself with public relations, propaganda, market research, sociological surveys, publicity, information, counterinformation and misinformation, censorship, espionage, and even cryptography—a science which in the sixteenth century was a branch of magic. This key figure of our society is simply an extension of Bruno's manipulator, continuing to follow his principles and taking care to give them a technical and impersonal turn of phrase. Historians have been wrong in concluding that magic disappeared with the advent of "quantitative science." The latter has simply substituted itself for a part of magic while extending its dreams and its goals by means of technology. Electricity, rapid transport, radio and television, the airplane, and the computer have merely carried into effect the promises first formulated by magic, resulting from the supernatural processes of the magician: to produce light, to move instantaneously from one point in space to another, to communicate with faraway regions of space, to fly through the air, and to have an infallible memory at one's disposal. Technology, it can be said, is a democratic magic that allows everyone to enjoy the extraordinary capabilities of which the magician used to boast.

On the other hand, nothing has replaced magic on its own terrain, that of intersubjective relationships. To the extent they have an operational aspect, sociology, psychology, and applied psychosociology represent, in our time, indirect continuations of magic revived.

What could be hoped for through knowledge of intersubjective relationships?

A homogeneous society, ideologically healthy and governable. Bruno's total manipulator takes upon himself the task of dispensing to subjects a suitable education and religion: "Above all it is necessary to exercise extreme care concerning the place and the way in which someone is educated, has pursued his studies, under which pedagogies, which religion, which cult, with which books and writers. For all of that generates, by itself, and *not by accident*, all the subject's qualities" (*De Magia*, LII). Supervision and selection are the pillars of order. It is not necessary to be endowed with imagination to understand that the function of Bruno's manipulator has been taken into account by the State and that this new "integral magician" has been instructed to produce the necessary ideological instruments with the view of obtaining a uniform society.

Is the Western State, in our time, a true magician, or is it a sorcerer's apprentice who sets in motion dark and uncontrollable forces?

That is very hard to say. In any case, the magician State—unless it involves vulgar conjurers—is vastly preferable to the police State, to the State which, in order to defend its own out-of-date "culture," does not hesitate to repress all liberties and the illusion of liberties, changing itself into a prison where all hope is lost. Too much subtlety and too much flexibility are the main faults of the magician State, which can degenerate and change into a sorcerer-State; a total lack of subtlety and of flexibility are the main defects of the police State, which has abased itself to the status of jailer State. But the essential difference between the two, the one which works altogether in favor of the first, is that magic is a science of metamorphoses with the capacity to change, to adapt to all circumstances, to improve, whereas the police always remains just what it is: in this case, the defender to the death of out-of-date values, of a political oligarchy useless and pernicious to the life of nations. The system of restraints is bound to perish, for what it defends is merely an accumulation of slogans without any vitality. The magician State, on the other hand, only expects to develop new possibilities and new tactics, and it is precisely excess of vitality which impedes its good running order. Certainly, it too can only take advantage of an infinitesimal part of its magic resources. But we surmise that these are so extraordinarily rich, that, in principle, they should have no difficulty in uprooting the decayed tree of police ideology. Why does that not happen? Because the subtlety of those internal forces at play exhausts the attention of the magician State, which reveals itself ill prepared to attack the question of a fundamental and effective magic in its external relationships. This monster of intelligence finds itself without weapons when long-term operations are involved or when it ought to create a "charming" image in international relations. Its pragmatism, lacking in ceremony and in circumspection, results in an image which, however false, is nevertheless repugnant in its partners' eyes, and this absence of promises and of Byzantine speeches, when all is said and done, proves as counterproductive as its obvious excesses of intelligence and its well-known incapacity to propose radical solutions.

If we can be surprised by the fact that the police-State can still function, we can just as well ask why the magician State, with boundless resources, functions so badly that it seems daily to lose ground vis-à-vis the ideological and territorial strides made by the other one.

The conclusion is ineluctable: it is that the magician State exhausts its intelligence in creating internal changes, showing itself incapable of working out a long-term magic to neutralize the hypnosis induced by the advancing cohorts of police. Yet the future seems to belong to it anyway, and even the provisional victory of the police State would leave no doubt concerning this point: coercion by the use of force will have to yield to the subtle processes of magic, science of the past, of the present and of the future.

# 5| Pneumatic Magic

### (i) The Starting Point of Magic

The inception of magic is represented by Eros: this gives rise to the construction of an erotic magic—a form of intersubjective magic—functioning by virtue of the law of pneumatic interaction between individuals. It goes without saying that this interaction, in Ficino's theory, is predetermined by prenatal circumstances of an astrological kind. They play a less important role in the theories of Giordano Bruno.

From Ficino to Bruno, the doctrine of erotic magic undergoes transformations analogous to those of the concept of "transference" from Freud to Lacan. For Freud, transference is a complex phenomenon limited to the relations between analyst and patient; to Lacan, the entire world of mankind is merely a transference function of gigantic proportions in which everyone, in turn, plays the parts of analyst and of patient. In the same way, Eros, to Marsilio Ficino, means the relationship between two individuals, the lover and the beloved; to Giordano Bruno, Eros is the driving power of intersubjective relationships in general, group phenomena included.

Another essential transformation undergone by Eros from Ficino to Bruno concerns the role assigned to the manipulator in the production or reduction of erotic relationships. Though aware of the syndrome *amor hereos* and its fatal consequences and of the physician's importance in curing it, Ficino neglects the aspect of the *production* of Eros, whose causes he considers transcendental. On the other hand, Bruno concerns himself particularly with the possibility of erotic manipulation of the individual and the masses.

Ficino describes the phenomenon of hypnosis that occurs spontaneously during the *natural* manifestation of the emotion of love; Bruno concerns himself particularly with *directed* hypnosis, active and voluntary, *upon* an individual or collective subject--hypnosis whose rules of production trace those of spontaneous love. It involves profound awareness and intuition, a close examination of the subject's unconscious (or subconscious) to extract shameful "weaknesses": the means by which the subject may be "bound," manipulated, hypnotized, put in a state of manageability. This "psychic" method is used not only in magic but also in medicine, whose success depends primarily not on the efficacy of remedies but rather on the patient's confidence in the healer.

So also is religion a phenomenon of collective hypnosis practiced by a prophet on a group of individuals. The founder of a religion is, in a way, a transcendent instrument, for he does not act in pursuit of egotistical ends. The condition for his success lies in creating an atmosphere in which his collective subject becomes manageable, a subject he renders capable of total self-sacrifice. A religion once instituted, can endure only by the active control it exercises over the education of individuals, a control that must also be repressive in order to prevent the individual from losing his state of depersonalization or becoming capable of being reprogrammed. The same criterion, of course, applies to the promotion of an individual in the religious hierarchy.

From Ficino's love involving two people, representing the starting point of Eros as well as of magic, we have now come to phenomena of unheard-of complexity. The psychosociology of the couple is transformed, in Bruno's thinking, into *general psychosociology:* an interdisciplinary science disconcertingly modern, whose far-reaching implications neither "classical" psychology nor sociology was capable of envisaging and whose "use value" neither could appreciate.

For if, in our day, anything has a use value that may even outstrip technology value, it is precisely general psychosociology, the science of the forming of the individual within and according to a preexistent context, the science of manipulation and of intersubjective relationships. Its importance must not be judged by its still deficient representation in the academic world, which has, by definition, a greater force of inertia than that of any social system in motion. Nevertheless, in existing institutional frameworks, the principles of psychosociology have long been known. The forerunner of this discipline of the present and the future is, most probably, the erotic magic of Giordano Bruno.

### (ii) "Subjective" Magic and "Transitive" Magic

Everyone knows that magic claims to act not only on individuals endowed with a pneumatic body but also on the inanimate world and on lower forms of life. There is nothing wrong with this popular idea, but, to explain the wide range of magic outside intersubjective relationships, there must be another principle that supports it.

The English scholar D. P. Walker has suggested classifying magic into "subjective" (which works on the subject himself) and "transitive" (working on the surroundings). What he means by *transitive magic* should be called instead, as we have done, "intersubjective magic":

The use of transitive magic aimed at living beings coincides in part with practical psychology. This form of magic purports to monitor and direct the emotions of other people by altering their imagination in a specific and permanent way. These magic techniques show a marked tendency to be founded on sexual drives whose power and special importance were probably recognized and also because they are, indeed, more closely linked to the imagination than any other natural appetite. The treatises on witchcraft became almost pornographic; and Bruno (*De vinculis in genere*) made a remarkable attempt to evolve a technique, explicitly based on sexual attraction, for global emotional control.[1]

In light of the preceding discussion, Walker's schema is revealed to be simplistic. Insofar as it is a form of transitive magic, intersubjective magic differs from other functions by the quality of the object on which it is supposed to act: indeed, its object is itself a subject whose structure is analogous to that of its performer. This partly applies to animals, they too being endowed with a pneumatic synthesizer, but does not apply at all to plants or to inanimate substances. The principles of subjective and intersubjective magic do not function in the lower realms of nature because these are not capable of producing phantasms and therefore cannot be directly influenced by the imagination of the manipulator.

According to Walker's methods of classification, the schema of forms of magic should be relatively uncomplicated. Indeed, subjective magic is a preliminary form of all magic, since it is directed toward changing the individual pneuma in such a way as to render it capable of carrying out magic functions. Besides, subjective magic is itself "intersubjective" except that the influences it exerts turn back onto the manipulator himself, he being his own patient in the literal sense of the word. It follows that all magic is, essentially, *transitive,* even in the event that it takes place in a closed circle.

According to Giordano Bruno, we must then differentiate between actual magic and medicine, a form of spiritual healing that presupposes a subject whose psychosomatic functions are altered, and to differentiate the two from religion, a form of (altruistic) magic that works on a collective subject. Finally, intersubjective magic could not produce changes in the lower realms unless, through correction of its fundamental principles, those realms could be encompassed in a general theory of magic. In any case, given the lack of phantasmic production in lower forms of life and in inanimate substances, the difference between intersubjective magic and general magic would still exist.

These conclusions lead to a classification of forms of magic very different from Walker's:

*General magic,* which is a function essentially *transitive,* is subdivided into: (1) *intersubjective magic,* which presupposes an identity or analogy of pneumatic structure between the manipulator and the patient; (2) *extrasubjective magic,* whose action is directed toward beings of a lower order, or at least, does not stem from pneumatic interaction between two subjects.

In turn, *intersubjective magic* is aware of a special case, that of *intrasubjective magic* (called subjective by Walker), where the performer is his own patient.

Finally, when intersubjective magic is applied to the cure of a deranged psychophysical organism, it is called *medicine,* whereas if applied to a collective subject, propounding a general orientation of existence and special rules of conduct, it becomes identical with *religion.*

In general, magic represents a technique for manipulating "nature." For us, the term "nature" signifies a rigidly determined organization in which there are, however, margins of chance, especially in complex microsystems such as the atom. The word "chance" is also applied (fortuitously) to dependent systems, such as that of animal or vegetable species, which reveal a rather broad capacity for adaptation and ecological changes. That has permitted the frequent claim that natural selection is due to "chance," which is doubtless valid within a category such as *species* but no longer makes sense when applied to the general determinism of nature.

In Renaissance thought, the concept of "nature" is much broader than our own, since it also includes all sorts of nonquantifiable existences— from the gods, heroes, and demons of Neoplatonism to the "rudimentary beings" of Paracelsus—which we know nothing about for want of ever having met or observed them. Certainly our concept of "nature" has been scrupulously expurgated of those entities. On the other hand, "nature" in the Renaissance was overpopulated with them, and magic prided itself on turning their exceptional qualities to account.

In the second place, natural determinism, in Renaissance thought, did not concede any margin of chance. Everything bore the rigid and implacable stamp of destiny, free will itself being a mere invention of theologians which must be blindly endorsed. In our day we believe our encounters and our feelings are due to chance; on the other hand, a man of the Renaissance would show us, horoscope in hand, that they were predetermined by the position of the planets in the zodiac on the day of our birth and the day of our encounter. He might even do more, helping our will to realize its secret or public inclinations. When someone finds himself poor while wishing to be rich, to be in love with a person who despises him, to have powerful enemies who destroy his plans, or when the weather is good when it should have rained, or vice versa, he resorts to magic. Now, the performer of magic, who is an expert in natural determinism, also knows that there are gaps in natural determinism, that there are propitious times for his will to produce changes in the events of the universe. The human condition has its limits, which the magician can transcend. For instance, he can move about in time and space without the usual restrictions; he can influence people or meteorological conditions, etc. Is X plotting something against Y? This can be found out. Does X want to do away with Y? It can be done. Does X want news of Y, who is far away? Nothing could be easier. Does X want to be loved by Y? There is nothing to prevent it. Does he wish for rain or for good weather? Done; and so on.

Medicine is also a special branch of magic. When natural determinism has struck the psychophysical organism of the patient, the practitioner's will—once the diagnosis is made—can effectively intervene to put things back in order.

What are the "remedies" of magic? One cannot understand them without having studied natural determinism as a whole.

### (iii) The Conspiracy of Things

The doctrine of macro- and microcosmic homology in Western culture has an amazing history. It is rare for a Greek philosopher or a Christian theologian not to have been deeply influenced by it, and Henri de Lubac has shown that it is no more foreign to western medieval thought than to that of the Renaissance.[2] It goes without saying that it is impossible to retrace all its vicissitudes here.

As early as the period of Hellenism the doctrine took two forms, of relatively equal importance in its later evolution. Both are found in Renaissance thinkers.

It is likely, as Anders Olerud has shown,[3] that Plato, when establishing the homoly between humans and the universe, was inspired by the Hippocratic corpus. However, his theoretical proof for that doctrine as a whole derives from his own theory of ideas. According to this theory, the sensory world has a preexistent prototype, stable and eternal: the intellectual or noetic world. In turn, the human, who is composed of soul and body, combines those two worlds within himself; his soul is a compendium of the world of ideas. Since the noetic cosmos encloses in its essential matrices all that is made sensory in the lower world, it follows that the reasoning part of the human soul contains no less than the intelligential model of creation.

The Platonist postulate does not directly take over the theory of magic, whose principles remain more or less identical from Late Antiquity to the Renaissance. It is Stoic pneumatics that constitutes the point of departure for all those speculations about practical magic.

For the Stoics, the cosmos was conceived as a living organism, endowed with the faculty of reason, able to engender rational microcosms: *Animans est igitur mundus composque rationis*.[4] The doctrine of universal sympathy was formulated by Zeno of Citium and developed by Cleanthes of Assos and his successor, Chrysippus. Like the model of man who possesses a hegemonikon or "Principal" (the cardiac synthesizer), the macrocosm is also equipped with a hegemonikon, located in the sun, the heart of the world.[5] "The harmony between human psychology and the psychology of the cosmos is therefore complete: just as the psychic pneuma animates our whole organism, so also the cosmic pneuma enters even the most remote extremities of this great organism called the world."[6]

Chrysippus, author of two books on soothsaying,[7] uses the theory of the continuity of the pneuma to prove prognostic phenomena. The attention paid to this subject[8] by Cicero seems to indicate that the Stoic philosophers practiced the prediction of future events through dreams. During sleep, Cicero informs us, the soul is detached "from contact with the body," *a contagione corporis*, to move about in time, learning things past or to come. To judge from the result, this function performed by dreams differs in no way from that performed by prophets in a state of wakefulness: *Nam quae vigilantibus accidunt vatibus, eadem nobis dormientibus*.[9] To deliver oracular responses, the *vates* make use of external stimuli, especially of certain fumes (*anhelitus*) from the earth,[10] in which may be found the "soothsaying pneuma," the spirit of prophecy mentioned by Plutarch of Chaeronea.[11]

From soothsaying activity to real magic there is only one step. Whereas soothsaying actually represents the ability to make use of the natural flights of the pneuma, the magic of the papyri of Late Antiquity is none other than a series of practical methods to attract, nourish, and accumulate or store up the divine spirit. In most cases, the pneuma is contained in a material object made for this purpose or in an animal. With this reservoir of spiritual energy within his grasp, the magician counts either on obtaining either knowledge of the future or on achieving some practical purpose.[12]

Credit for having synthesized in an original fashion the Platonic, Aristotelian, and Stoic elements that make up the theoretical basis for Renaissance magic is due to Synesius of Cyrene, who, having been the disciple of the Neoplatonist martyr, Hypatia of Alexandria (d. 415), ended by converting to Christianity and becoming a bishop.[13]

For the Stoics, the functional relationship between the cardiac synthesizer (hegemonikon) and the pneuma was clearly determined: the hegemonikon "is like a receiving post to which all impressions received by the senses are communicated."[14] On the other hand, the Stoic philosophers also develop a theory of phantasms produced by the hegemonikon. For Chrysippus, the clear representation of the sensory object formed in the cardiac synthesizer is called *phantasia kataleptikē* or "comprehensive representation" and leads naturally to rational adhesion (*synkatasthesis*).[15] The main difference between Aristotle and the Stoics consists in the fact that the latter think *the pneuma is the soul itself,* whereas the former believe it to be only a kind of ethereal intermediary between the soul and the physical body. That is why the Stoics conceive of fantasy, according to Zeno and Cleanthes, as a "stamp upon the soul," a *typosis en psychē.*

Later, Epictetus is to state that phantasms are influenced by the state of the pneuma that receives or conceives them. He resorts to a comparison: "Just as houses at the edge of a body of clear water are reflected in its limpid surface, so also are external objects reflected in our psychic pneuma, with the obvious result that they are influenced by the present state of the pneuma."[16] In order that the images reflected in the mirror of the pneuma may be precise and faithful to their subject, the pneuma itself must be tranquil and pure.[17] So it is that Epictetus, continuing and developing the moral preoccupations of the Stoics, combines them with the doctrine of spirit: to have a clean pneuma, a well-polished cardiac mirror, becomes the equivalent of being virtuous. Here Stoicism finds itself in the company of the whole Platonic tradition, whose most important practical outcome is to obtain, by a suitable technique, the separation of the soul from the body so that the former may not be sullied by the latter. Beginning in the second century A.D., a technique of this kind is known as theurgy, which primarily designates a purification of the soul for purposes of soothsaying and benefic exalted magic but also for pursuit of a better posthumous destiny. That is why the theurgic preliminary to any process classified among the practices of spiritual magic will be "cleansing one's pneuma" or hegemonikon, or "cleansing one's heart."

These are the theoretical givens that make it possible to understand a number of mystico-magic Oriental techniques that place much importance on the tranparency, purity, and brilliance of the "seat of the heart," such as Taoism, Yoga, Sufism, and Hesychasm. Whether or not it is designated by the vocables *hsin*, *ākāśā hṛdaya*, *qalb*, or *kardía*, this "cardiac space" always represents the phantasmic synthesizer whose cleanliness is the condition essential to all manifestation of divinity.

While theurgy assumes the place of honor as far as Iamblichus is concerned, Synesius holds the pneumatic synthesizer responsible for soothsaying and magic. The synthesis he achieves in his treatise *De insomniis* (its title is sometimes quoted as *De somniis*, which means exactly the same thing), translated into Latin by Ficino in 1489, is to be revived in Ficino's theory of magic expounded in the treatise *De vita coelitus comparanda*.[18]

According to Platonic dogma, the soul contains intellective marks of sensory objects.[19] Knowledge is achieved through comparison: the object is recognized by the soul through the preexistent information it contains. Now, in order to recognize an object, first it is necessary to perceive it, which can only be done by the synthesizer. It plays the role of a *mirror*, but a *double-faced mirror* that reflects both what is above (the eternal prototypes of the soul) and what is below (information from the sensory organs).[20] The synthesizer, of course, is by nature pneumatic: it is formed by the "phantasmal spirit [*phantastikon pneuma*] which is the primary body of the soul in which visions and images are formed.[21] It resides in the interior [of the body] and controls the living being as from the summit of a fortress [*akropolis*]. For nature has, indeed, built it, within the surrounding structure of the head."[22]

In contradistinction to Stoic tradition, Synesius places the synthesizer not in the heart but in the head. It is not Galen he means to follow but Plato himself (from whom he borrowed the metaphor of the fortress), who endowed the head of man-microcosm with a much higher value than the heart.[23]

We have already seen that Epictetus compared the pneuma to a basin filled with water, a liquid mirror. Plutarch of Chaeronea is the first to speak of a *pure mirror*, nothing more.[24] For Synesius, this double-faced mirror provides the opportunity for two parallel surfaces to meet on neutral territory. Insofar as it is the intermediary between the intelligential world and the sensory world, this mirror, if perfectly clear, will make it possible for inner judgment to contemplate the world above epitomized by the reasoning part of the soul, and will give the latter the opportunity to perceive and to judge the sensory objects whose image is transmitted to common sense through the external senses. *The pneumatic synthesizer becomes, for Synesius, the preeminent terrain of soothsaying and magic.* In order that some result may be obtained, it is essential that the pneuma be pure, that nothing carnal obscure the clarity of the mirror.[25] Soothsaying through dreams, of which we have already heard from Cicero, is justified by virtue of the same principle: the events of the noetic world, which is stable and eternal, that is, not subject to the dimension of time, are reflected in the pure pneuma and form veracious dream images that one can recall when awake. "And I know not whether this sense," says Synesius in his praise of the pneumatic synthesizer,

> is not more saintly than others. For it is because of it that we can communicate with the gods, either through sight, through conversation, or by other means. It is not to be wondered at if dreams are, for some men, their most precious treasure; because, for example, if someone sleeps tranquilly and, during sleep, speaks to the Muses and listens to what they have to say, he can [on awakening] become, quite unexpectedly, a very elegant poet. As for me, all of that does not seem mad,[26]

the Archbishop of Ptolemaïs concludes.

But there is much more to it. Since the phantasmic synthesizer affords the possibility of an encounter with a world peopled with divine powers, and since, according to Platonic dogma, this world is homologous to the intelligential world, there is a way of acting upon the synthesizer to invoke numerous presences. This invocation, resulting in the company of gods and demons, can be carried out by using certain substances, forms, and colors to which the higher beings are sensitive.

Before becoming aware of his own possibilities, man-microcosm finds himself in a universe in which the parties, both low and high, *cooperate* with each other without his knowledge. At the time he grasps the structure of that cooperation, the correspondences between the visible universe and its invisible prototype, he will be able to make use of them in the service of capturing the unknown presences that lurk on the threshold between the two worlds, the demons and even the most celestial gods. That is the doctrine of the *signatures* of things, the cosmic homologies which Michel Foucault has brilliantly analyzed.[27] And that is also Synesius's definition of magic:

> The parts of this universe that sympathize and *cooperate* with man must be joined together by some means. . . . And per-

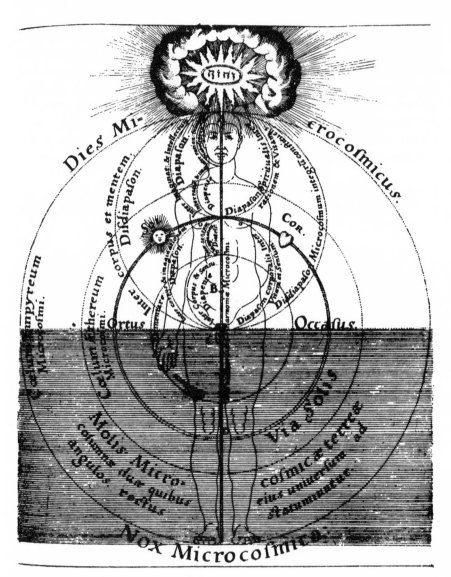

FIGURE 6. Man-microcosm. From Robert Fludd, *Utriusque cosmi . . . historia* (1617–21), II, a, 1, p. 275.

haps magic incantations provide such means, for they are not limited to conveying meaning but they also *invoke*. He who understands the relationship of the parts of the universe is truly wise: he can derive profit from the higher beings by capturing, by means of sounds [*phonas*], substances [*hylas*], and forms [*schēmata*], the presence of those who are far away.[28]

Besides this more sophisticated expression of the relation between humans and the world, Synesius also utilizes traditional Platonic theory according to which "the human intellect contains within itself the forms of all the things that exist."[29] A thousand years after Synesius, Cardinal Nicholas of Cusa is still convinced that the intellect of man-microcosm (*parvus mundus*) "is the living description of eternal and infinite wisdom. . . . Through the activity of our intellective life we are able to find within ourselves the object of our search."[30]

With regard to Ficino, we find a Platonist doubling as a magician:

> Plato is right in his concept of the world as a machine constructed in such a way that celestial things have, on earth, a terrestrial state, and likewise that terrestrial things have, in the heavens, a celestial dignity. In the secret life of the world and in the mind (*mens*), queen of the world [*regina mundi*], there are celestial things endowed with vital and intellective attributes and with excellence. Moreover, that confirms the principle of magic, which enables men to attract to themselves celestial presences by means of inferior things utilized at opportune moments and corresponding to higher things [*per inferiora . . . superioribus consentanea posse ad homines temporibus opportunis caelestia quodammodo trahi*].[31]

It is difficult to state more clearly the fundamental principle of magic. But we are still far from suspecting how complex the study of "inferior things" proves to be, as well as "opportune moments" and the many "celestial gifts" which magic is supposed to deliver.

### (iv) The Theory of Radiations

Study of the magical papyri of Late Antiquity would take us outside the scope of this book. Some observations must be made, however: the recent research done on the *Papyrus Grecae Magicae* published by Preisendanz,[32] of which Hans Dieter Betz has edited the first complete translation into a Western language, reveals that magic represents a very ancient tradition with *unitary* characteristics.[33] Underground currents beginning in Late Antiquity reach Byzantium at the time of Michael Psellus and, through Arab channels, go west in the twelfth century. This indicates an uninterrupted continuity of the methods of practical magic, which goes on perfecting its principles and its instruments especially in connection with the only exact "science" of the time, astrology. Renaissance magic, while more sophisticated because imbued with Neoplatonist theosophy and anthroposophy, realizes the debt it owes to its venerable medieval predecessors such as Roger Bacon and Albert the Great. They, in turn, are indebted to Arab magic, of which the two fundamental works must be mentioned: the *Picatrix* by Pseudo-Madjritī and the treatise *De radiis* by al-Kindī.

*Picatrix* is the title of the Latin translation, done in 1256 at the court of Alphonso the Wise, king of Castille, of the pseudo-epigraphic work *Ghāyat al-Hakīm fi'l-sihr* or *End of the Sages by means of Magic* attributed to the Andalusian mathematician al-Madjritī (d. ca. 1004–7).[34] It would be hard fo deny the influence of *Picatrix* on Renaissance magic.[35] It must also be pointed out, however, that this influence is primarily practical and cannot justify the importance given by Ficino or Giordano Bruno to the purely theoretical side of magic.

The *Picatrix* itself, of course, is aware of the distinction between "theory"—astrology—and "practice"—the manufacture of talismans (I, 2, p. 256, Matton). But, the authors of books about magic in the Renaissance are not satisfied with so little: they think astrology has an ontological foundation and justification, whose explanation must be sought in Neoplatonism on the one hand and, on the other, in the much more incisive work of al-Kindī.

Having stated the general principle of work in magic, which is the faith of the operator (I, 4, p. 261), a principle that is repeated incessantly (p. 293, etc.), the *Picatrix* confines itself to giving advice for the making of talismans based on the position of planets in the zodiac, and to formulating the text of "planetary prayers" to be addressed to the personified planets. Interspersed in these lists are commonplaces of a philosophical kind such as the homology of the macrocosm and the microcosm (pp. 297 sq.). Regarding talismans, they are supposed to produce many results, some of which are mentioned in the first two books of the *Picatrix:* arousing (lasting) love or union between two people, obtaining the protection of the great or the respect of servants, increasing wealth and commerce, bringing good luck to a city, destroying an enemy or a city, preventing construction of a building, releasing a prisoner from his prison, evicting a man from his home, separating friends, causing someone to incur the king's wrath, assuring fishermen a good catch, putting scorpions to flight, healing wounds, ensuring the (financial) success of a doctor, increasing harvests and plants, curing many diseases, etc.

Ficino's astrological magic derives much from the *Picatrix*, but the influence is primarily quantitative, not qualitative. The imposing structure of the spiritual magic of the Renaissance is not comparable to the mediocre pile of empirical procedures that make up the *Picatrix*. However, since it befell the philologists to have the easy task of discovering in Ficino whole passages borrowed from the *Picatrix*, they were too easily satisfied with a genetic explanation of a very general kind, according to which the Arab treatise translated into Latin would be one of the Florentine Platonist's principal sources.

The inadequacy of this kind of *Quellenforshung*, which seeks exclusively the literal stamp made upon a work by an earlier one, is easy to demonstrate. Let us suppose there is a scholar who, engaged in emphasizing the artistic influence upon a monument of Christian architecture, and knowing that it was built on the ruins of an old Mithras temple, should undertake to establish an exhaustive inventory of the stones of the pagan temple used to construct the new basilica. Having stated, for instance, that 60 percent of the stones of the Christian structure come from the pagan monument, he would have to conclude—according to the principles of *Quellenforschung*—that the basilica is 60 percent a Mithraic temple, which the reality would contradict all too quickly, the two buildings having nothing in common except their raw material, a minor factor. As soon as it came to establishing the difference of style and function between the two works, the *Quellenforschung* would prove entirely unable to serve our purpose, since, by a strange optical illusion, it is incapable of perceiving the two in their unity. Similarly, the large number of passages from the *Picatrix* that were used almost literally in Ficino's magic are not enough to prove a deep influence of the first over the second.

On the other hand, though Ficino, like Roger Bacon, has high regard for al-Kindī's treatise on stellar rays, he rarely borrowed literal expressions from it, which should suffice, for the *Quellenforschung*, to remove al-Kindī from the list of Ficino's principal sources. Nevertheless, it is easy to note that Ficino's magic, the science of the occult correspondences in nature, is largely inspired by al-Kindī's theory of universal radiations. There is, of course, a major difference between the two writers. Ficino, faithful to the Platonic tradition, bestows on al-Kindī's radiations the generic name of Eros, and it is from this concept that Giordano Bruno develops the erotic magic taken up in the preceding chapter to which we shall return later.

The treatise *De radiis*, by the famous astrologer and philosopher Abū Yūsuf Yaqūb ibn Ishaq al-Kindī (d. ca. 873), has come down to us in an anonymous Latin translation of the twelfth century.[36] The fundamental idea of this work, only one among the 270 that the historiographer an-Nadīm attributes to its author, is that each star has its own nature, which it communicates to the surrounding world by means of *rays*. Now the influence of stellar radiations upon terrestrial objects changes as a function of the mutual *aspects* that the stars and the objects produce. Besides,

*prejacent* substances receive the qualities of rays in different ways according to their intrinsic properties, which are *hereditary* (whence it is apparent, for instance, that the son of a king will have a natural disposition to
rule and the son of a laborer to follow his father's calling).

Except for the highly technical vocabulary, there has been no essential
difference between al-Kindī's and any other treatise on astrological magic, including the later *Picatrix*. But al-Kindī soon emerges from the nar-
row framework of this concept. He believes that not only the stars emit
rays but also the *elements*: "Everything that actually exists in the world of
elements emits rays in all directions, which in their own way fill the
entire rudimentary world" (III, p. 88). Since the material world in its
entirety represents a combination of the four elements, that too is the
reason why the rays of the *elementary compounds* are differentiated from
each other, no two of them being alike.

According to al-Kindī, we find ourselves in the midst of an invisible
network of rays coming from the stars as well as from all earthly objects.
The entire universe, from the most distant stars to the humblest blade of
grass, makes its presence known by its radiations at every point in
space, at every moment in time; and its presence, of course, varies according to the intensity and mutual influence of the rays of the universe,
so that there cannot be two things truly identical to one another. Besides
the psychic emotions (joy, sorrow, hope, fear) are also transmitted to the
surrounding world in the form of invisible radiations, which also mark
their changes, according to the arrangement of every prejacent
substance.

> Man . . . due to his balanced temperament, resembles the
> world. Thus he is a microcosm, and that explains why he
> receives, as does the world, a power to induce, by his own
> efforts, movements within an equivalent substance, always
> provided that imagination, intention, and faith be previously
> formed in the human soul. Indeed, the man who wishes to
> perform something first imagines the form of the thing he
> wishes to impress by action in a given manner; having con-
> ceived the image of the thing, after he has judged this thing
> to be useful or useless, he either wishes to have it or feels
> contempt for it in his soul. And if he has judged the thing to
> be worthy of his desire, he longs for accidents to occur, in
> consequence of which, according to the opinion he has
> reached, the thing may actually come to pass.
>
> Now the passions of the soul are accidents that contribute
> to produce a momentum. And concerning them we say that
> human imagination and intelligence gain resemblance to the

world so long as the species of worldly things are transmitted into action due to the functioning of the senses. This is because the *spiritus ymaginarius* [the *phantastikon pneuma* of Synesius—author's note] has rays conforming to the world's rays; thereby, too, they gain the power to move, by their own rays, external things, just as the world, both higher and lower, stirs up the rays of things according to various momenta.

Besides, when man conceives of a material thing through imagination, this thing acquires an actual existence according to the species in the phantasmic spirit (*spiritus ymaginarius*). Also this spirit emits rays which move external things just as does the thing whose image it is. Therefore, the image conceived in the spirit corresponds in kind with the thing produced in deed on the model of the image through voluntary or natural work, or both simultaneously. This is why there is no cause for surprise if the theme of birth (*constellatio*), which produces an image in the spirit of man, produces the same image in another subject, since the one does not differ from the other, except only in substance. (V, pp. 95–97)

The preliminary faith of the performers is the condition essential to the success of his magic act: "Certainly, the first and principal accident necessary to generate a thing through the model of the mental images is the wish of the man who imagines that the thing can be done" (ibid, p. 97). Magic manipulation takes place through sound (prayers, incantations) and through gestures:

There are two kinds of actions by which, when they are carried out properly, a thing conceived in spirit comes true in action: namely, verbal expression and the working of the hand. There are indeed certain speeches which, coming from the mouth of man—while expressing imagination, faith, and desire—actualize in the world motions within individual beings. (Ibid., pp. 98–99)

Sounds produced in action emit rays like everything else in action, and . . . , through their rays in the world, work upon the elements similarly to the other individual things. And as there exist innumerable varieties of sound, each sound produced in action has its effect on other elementary things, and this effect differs from the effect of others. Now sounds, as well as grasses and other things, have received from the celestial harmony their own effect, and similarly a quality of effect very different in different things. (VI, p. 100).

All of the foregoing demonstrates that al-Kindī was largely inspired by the spiritual magic of Synesius, who recommends the use of sounds (*phonai*), substances (*hylai*) and figures (*schēmata*) through which "the true wise man, knowledgeable in the relations between the parts of the universe, can exert influences" on some subject or object.[37]

To revert to the magic of sounds: there are two kinds of magic sounds, according to their *astrological* correspondence (according to the star, the purpose of process, and the position of the sky) or *elementary* correspondence; these have an influence on the elements and the compounds of elements, like the bodies of plants and animals. "Furthermore, for a result to be obtained, there must exist in the manipulator mental application and representation of the form he wishes to see actualized by the emission of sounds" (ibid., p. 101). This magic of sounds is subordinate to a theory of the natural origin of languages. Every sound was formed, according to its purpose, by the celestial harmony. The meaning of words is not arbitrary, but their intended purpose may not coincide with the meaning that man has attributed to them. "On the other hand, when in a sound the meaning created by harmony and that created by man coincide, the power of the meaning of the sound is doubled" (ibid., p. 103). We recognize here the origin of later cabbalistic theories of the "natural language," which is Hebrew, "since Hebrew, being the language of Creation, was the natural language in which the words indicated that essential natures of the things they had first produced and then represented."[38]

Of course, al-Kindī's magic of sounds utilizes comprehensible turns of phrase, in artificial language, as well as incomprehensible ones which, by being pronounced in "natural language," increases the effectiveness of the process.

What can we obtain through the use of magic sounds? Almost everything: prognostications, telekinesis, psychosomatic effects on animals and on man, the casting of a spell on a human being that consists in changing the direction of his will, and, finally, paradoxical phenomena such as making heavy objects float on water or rise into the air, producing rain, lightning and other atmospheric phenomena, extinguishing distant fires, etc. (ibid., pp. 104–9). The most effective turns of phrase are *optative*, since they stem from the *heart*, which is the center of man-microcosm (ibid., p. 111).

With regard to magic shapes and characters, their functional properties and faculties closely resemble those of sounds (ibid., pp. 119–23). Al-Kindī's treatise ends in an extremely interesting theory of sacrifices

(IX, p. 123). The animal is envisaged as a microcosm whose violent death produces a breach in the macrocosm: through this breach the will of the manipulator enters, capable of changing circumstances and things. The sacrificial animal is, of course, in harmony with the goal to be attained.

We shall have opportunity to recognize the extent of Ficino's debt to al-Kindī. Suffice it to say here that al-Kindī's universe, akin to that of modern physics, is composed of two states of energy: the elementary state and the state of radiation. In turn, the elements combine to form aggregates, whose radiations will have new properties. Every object in the world is at the center of a universal transference of radiations, whose field varies according to the position of the object in space and in time, such that there can never be two objects that have perfectly identical behavior concerning the emanation and reception of rays. The Italian writer Dino Buzzati, feeling that the dying of a mere cockroach crushed inadvertently has consequences of a cosmic order, seems to be completely transposed into the mind and spirit of al-Kindī, for whom every event, even the most insignificant, has a universal influence (especially intense in the case of violent death). Magic draws from this very principle its possibility for existence, which consists in emitting radiations the length of whose wave can reach the receiving posts sighted by the performer. The addressees of the message will be forced to react to it according to the intention impressed into the radiation. We must not lose sight of the fact that al-Kindī's rays are *pneumatic* in nature, that his magic is a spiritual magic which is simply a continuation of the magic of Synesius of Cyrene. This means that a human, endowed with a phantasmic synthesizer, can produce mental states and send them out in pneumatic space to the receiving spirit of another individual of the same species. The effectiveness of this intersubjective magic is ensured by the constitution of the human aggregate and by the performer's faith.

In our day, when a belief of this kind emerges from religious establishments and reappears in subjects convinced that their own emotions are transitive, that they can act on other individuals or on the physical world, it is generally agreed that such persons suffer from a form of insanity called "schizophrenia." According to Pierre Janet's definition, which was used by Carl Gustav Jung and then became a classic one, schizophrenia is characterized by a "lowering of the mental level" and, consequently, by a short circuit between oneiric and diurnal existence, the world of our inner phantasms and the real world. If we give credence to Edgard Morin, it is not difficult for this short circuit to be produced, since the human brain, with all its hypercomplexity, has at its disposal no special instrument enabling it to differentiate dreaming from the waking state.[39]

Having established the resemblances between magic behavior and schizophrenic behavior Géza Roheim, the Hungarian-born anthropologist, opened the way to the interpretation of magic as "institutionalized schizophrenia."

To be sure, there is a remote analogy between magic methods and the mental illness called schizophrenia. The two, however, cannot be confused with each other. True, the magician must be convinced of his capacity to transmit his own emotions to another subject or to perform other transitive actions of that kind, but he never ceases to be aware that the phantasmagoria he has produced function exclusively on the terrain belonging to phantasms, namely the human imagination. This seems to be all the more true since there are cases, very rare, in which the performer suffers obvious symptoms of schizophrenia, which differentiates him at once from the mass of other magicians, who are completely sane. In a schizophrenic performer of magic, the inner phantasmagoria finally gain the upper hand, like a foreign presence (see later the example of M. Berbiguier and his goblins). Now, let us remember that Giordano Bruno never ceased to alert the manipulator of phantasms to the dangers involved in his activity, which, collectively, amounted to the loss of mental health. Thus it seems that the magician must not be regarded as schizophrenic *in principle*, nor magic as "institutionalized schizophrenia." On the contrary, there are analogies between certain types of magic and psychoanalysis itself, whose method permits, within limits, a comparison with the method of Giordano Bruno's "healers."

When the dream is envisaged as a phantasmic production stemming from the unconscious, and schizophrenia as a state of confusion between oneiric context and sensory content, we no longer need marvel at the correspondence between the phantasms of schizophrenics and the phantasms brought into play by magicians. After all, they have the same provenance, except that in the case of the magician the phantasms are produced voluntarily and directed by the performance, whereas in the case of the sick person they appear to him as strange realities, they "possess" him. Jung's hypothesis of "archetypes," which are performative categories of phantasmic production, rests largely on analogies between the phantasies of patients and the mythico-magic repertory of mankind. How are these things looked upon from the point of view of anthropology, which is not directly called upon to give its verdict on the mental health of its subjects?

*Ecstatic Religion,* a book by the Scottish anthropologist Ian M. Lewis, answers this question.[40]

Lewis outlines a quite instructive typology of the "manipulator of spirits" (supernatural entities), coming to the conclusion that there are three classes: (a) *the participant in ecstatic cults* (like the Dionysian in ancient Greece or the *zar* in North Africa), who is involuntarily possessed by "spirits"; (b) *the shaman,* who, after being mastered by spirits, becomes, in turn, their master (a *wounded surgeon,* in T. S. Eliot's phrase); (c) *the sorcerer,* who, mastering spirits by his will, directs them against the passive subject, who will be possessed by them against his will.

What are "spirits"? Are they beings endowed with an objective existence or are they phantasms, productions objectified on the plane of the imagination, stemming from the unconscious?

My next chapter, devoted to the demons and demonomagic of the Renaissance, will give many details on this subject. Spirits are phantasms that acquire an autonomous existence through a practice of visualization resembling first and last the Art of Memory. However, it is not unusual for them to reveal themselves without being invoked in that way—for example, in the use of hallucinogenic drugs by sorcerers, or in mental illnesses. Of course, Lewis is wrong in stating that sorcerers dominate familiar spirits at will, for that is not true of Western sorcery, where the relationship between sorcerers and spirits is more problematic. Likewise, it is difficult to differentiate between shamans and sorcerers, since the latter do not learn how to dominate their spirits until these have revealed themselves spontaneously to them. In other words, we can essentially make a distinction between two classes of individuals who have to do with spirits: one class invokes spirits while inventing them; the other receives them but can make use of them only after conscious organization.

There is no doubt at all that the spirits that make their presence felt stem from the unconscious; but the others, those that are "invented," where do they come from? Their source is the same, since their models, transmitted through tradition, have already sprung up in the fantasy of another manipulator. The Renaissance magician or sorcerer learns of their existence through manuals of higher magic such as the *Steganography* of the Abbot Trithemius (although this is only, for the most part, a treatise or cryptography) or the *Occult Philosophy* of his disciple Henricus Cornelius Agrippa, or through manuals about low magic such as those catalogued in the *Antipalus maleficiorum* of the same Trithemius, a very learned occultist (see below, chap. 7).

In conclusion, there are only two kinds of manipulators of phantasms:

those imbued with unconscious production, having only succeeded with great difficulty in putting it into some kind of order; and those whose activity was entirely conscious, consisting in inventing mnemonical phantasms, which they endowed with autonomous existence. Only manipulators of the first sort are comparable to schizophrenics, except that for better or worse they learned to find a modus vivendi with their unconscious productions, elicited, in most cases, by the use of hallucinogens. Among them—this is verifiable—there are also genuine schizophrenics such as M. Berbiguier at the beginning of the nineteenth century or Dr. Ludwig Staudenmaier at the beginning of the twentieth, who utilize magic beliefs and techniques to try to organize their seriously disturbed mental processes. In this case, far from considering magic to be "institutionalized schizophrenia," we should, on the contrary, look at it as a remedy—and a very potent one—*against* the devastating invasion of mental illness. *Magic is not a factor of disorder; on the contrary, it is a means to reestablish a peaceful coexistence between the conscious and the unconscious* where this coexistence is under attack, either by mental illness or by the voluntary use of chemical substances with psychedelic effects. The magician is an analyst who can only practice his profession after being analyzed himself. But access to the unconscious can be left open to him in two different ways: by "invasion," either pathological or brought about by external means, or by assimilation of the tradition. In the second instance, no analogy with schizophrenia is admissible—any more than it would be in the case of anyone who learns anything, including the scientist.

These thoughts, which we shall develop later (see below, chap. 7), are a preamble to the account of intersubjective magic from al-Kindī to Giordano Bruno. The concept of "radiation," fundamental to al-Kindī, is gradually replaced by the concept of Eros. Pneumatic harmony of the universe is the general assumption from Ficino to Bruno and its instrument is Eros. Through Eros the universe knows a certain *concentus*, which is order, harmony, integration, and whose most disturbing formulation is found in one of Ficino's epistles:[41] "I believe that there is of necessity a law and a certain harmony [*concento*] and consonance between the world's elements, in the humors of animals, in the life of beasts, and even in the society of brigands since they could not associate with one another if there were not a certain order in all of that." This is far removed from theories of the self-destruction of evil. On the contrary, even in evil there is order, for otherwise outlaws could not stay together.

This general harmony, of which Eros is the main instrument, Ficino does not place in as large a framework as that of al-Kindī. Only Giordano Bruno restores things to their true complexity in his vision of a universe in which each individual and even each object is connected to all others by invisible erotic links. The expression *vinculum vinculorum amor est* is substituted for an analogous expression that we can ascribe to al-Kindī without risk of distorting his ideas: *vinculum vinculorum radium est,* "the bond of bonds is *the ray.*"

The energetics of al-Kindī adds to the psychologism of Bruno, for whom things do not emanate from cold, sterile, and almost inert radiations but from living rays, colored by passions, by their very existence prompting sympathy or antipathy, love or hate. Contrasted to the objective transference of al-Kindī is the highly subjective transference of Giordano Bruno; from universal magic the concept of *intersubjective magic* is clarified and takes shape.

## (v) Pneumatic Magic

The spiritual magic of the Renaissance—Marsilio Ficino being its first and most influential representative—is built on the principle of universal pneumatic sympathy. The first corollary of this principle is that man, endowed with a hegemonikon located, generally speaking, in the heart, the organ corresponding to the sun in the cosmos, has the capacity to impart voluntary changes to his own phantasy. These changes, due to the continuity of the pneuma, are transmitted to the objects aimed at by the manipulator.

This phenomenon is natural, produced without conscious manipulation on the part of either the sender and/or the receiver of the pneumatic current, and its starting point is self-consciousness, which is Eros. The latter establishes links between individuals according to the transcendental information that the pneumatic conveyances of their souls have accumulated during their descent through the planetary heavens.

As for magic proper, it represents knowledge permitting the performer to exploit the pneumatic currents which establish occult relations between the world's parts. Now these relations are regular and can be classified into seven great planetary series, such that all nature, with its mineral, vegetable, and animal kingdoms—including the human species—is linked to the seven wandering heavenly bodies and to the other stars by invisible bonds. The magician has, in the first place, expert knowledge of these bonds; he is able to classify every object in the world according to the appropriate series and, thereby, to attract benefits from the star in charge of the particular series.

The fact that there are many representatives of Renaissance magic should not hide from the investigator the main lines of its development, which prove to be relatively simple. Its point of depature is Ficino's treatise *De vita coelitus comparanda* (1489), which specifically states the following principles: just as the soul of the world is concentrated in the sun, whence it radiates to all parts of the universe through the *quinta essentia* (which is the ether, or the pneuma), the human soul is concentrated in the heart and enters the body through the spirit. Things have a varying degree of craving for the *quinta essentia*, which means that certain things have a pneumatic capacity superior to others.

What is the *quinta essentia?* It is the cosmic spirit, which fulfills the same function of intermediary between the soul and the body of the world as does the human spirit between the individual soul and body. This source of all generation and growth "we can call either heaven or *quinta essentia*" (chap. III).

> Through it the Platonists [that is, Arab astrologers and magicians—author's note] by adapting our spirit to the spirit of the world by means of the magic of talismans [*ars physica*] and emotion [*affectum*], try to direct our soul and our body toward the blessings of heaven. That causes the strengthening of our spirit by means of the world's spirit, through the action of the stellar rays acting beneficently upon our spirit, which is of the same kind as these rays; this lets it attract to itself celestial things.[42]

Ficino is a Synesius who, in so far as the theory of the vehicle of the soul is concerned, is corrected later by Proclus and Macrobius and, concerning the doctrine of universal correspondences, by al-Kindī's theory of radiations and by his astrological magic and that of the *Picatrix*.

As we have demonstrated elsewhere,[43] Ficino's spiritual magic does not call for fewer maneuvers through the intermediary of demons, but demonology properly so called was only developed by Trithemius, an enigmatic individual to whom I devote part of an ensuing chapter. A combination of Ficino's magic and Trithemius's demonomagic is to be found in the three books of Agrippa's not very original but very influential *Occult Philosophy*. Giordano Bruno's magic is inspired in the first place by Ficino, utilizing as complementary sources Albert the Great, Trithemius and Agrippa. With respect to Tommaso Campanella, a dissident Calabrian monk at the beginning of the seventeenth century, whose political utopia seems to have exerted a decisive influence on the group of German friends who produced the "farce" (*ludibrium*) of the Rosicrucians,[44] he too cultivated a pneumatic magic deriving from

Ficino, with (inoffensive) rituals that were greatly appreciated by Pope Urban.[45]

From Ficino to Campanella, a number of writers know about Ficino's theory of the pneuma without always making use of its magic side. Among them we mention Pico della Mirandola, Francesco Cattani da Diacceto, Ludovic Lazzarelli, J. Gohory, Pomponazzi, Francesco Giorgi, Pontus de Tyard, Guy Lefèvre de la Boderie, and others.[46]

# 6| Intersubjective Magic

## (i) Intrasubjective Magic

Since all magic that does not presuppose the intervention of demons is intersubjective, it is possible that the performer's action is directed to himself, in which case we have to deal with an *intrasubjective* magic.

This branch of magic is particularly important, representing, to some extent, the propaedeutics of all the more advanced activities of the pneumatic art.

Just as magic phenomena exist in nature (attraction by the magnet, to mention only the most common example) and in human society (the attraction of lovers), so also do born manipulators of magic exist, even though their field of action is reduced and not subject to control by the will. As a rule, however, with or without a natural gift, the magician *becomes*. And just as the student of psychoanalysis cannot practice without having first been analyzed himself, so the magician able to practice his art has first practiced it on himself.

Since magic in general is a spiritual function, the individual who practices it must have certain qualities lacking in most mortals. Indeed, insofar as mortals are concerned, the ethereal body, originally transparent and pure, has become opaque and thick through contact with the body. All the filth of matter has become encrusted on it, jeopardizing its primordial luminosity and flexibility. Now, since spirit is the vehicle of the soul and the soul is the medium of liaison between the intellect and the natural world, this miraculous contact is broken as soon as the vehicle has become too slow to let the soul travel or too dirty for the phantasmic messages transmitted by the soul to reach the inner sense.

The pneuma is a mirror with two faces, one of which reflects perceptions coming from the external senses and the other the phantasmagoria of the soul. If the surface turned toward the soul is not sufficiently clean, the individual is reduced to a lower, almost bestial state. What can be done to remedy this situation common to most mortals? Well, nothing could be simpler: it is just a matter of polishing the mirror, removing its impurities—acquired, not congenital—restoring to the clouded spirit its original transparency as well as its purity, flexibility, and hardness.

> For spirit is the intermediary between the gross body of the world and the soul. In it and through it there are stars and demons. . . . Man draws from it through his own spirit, which conforms to the other by virtue of its nature. But that can be done mainly if this spirit, thanks to art, is made more compatible with the spirit of the world, namely, more heavenly. It becomes heavenly if it is scrupulously purged of its filth and everything tainted by it—purged of everything dissimilar to its heavenly essence.[1] It must be taken into consideration not only that food entering the viscera dirties the spirit but that the stains are often caused by the soul, by the skin, by clothing, lodgings, and the surrounding air. (*Vita coel.*, IV)

It is easy to comprehend that Ficino's novice must submit to rigorous discipline to keep his distance from all that could contaminate and infect his pneuma. He is required not only to observe a very strict diet but also to practice purifications; to be careful of the cleanliness of his person, his clothing, and his house; to choose the route for his walks, the people he sees, the things he talks to them about; and, of course, to cultivate virtues. All of these procedures, whose purpose is the *expurgatio a sordibus*, "the purging of filth," are accompanied by more specific external methods:

> First, the spirit must be purified by sufficient medicines to remove the vapors that becloud it. Second, its luminosity must be restored by shiny things. Third, it must be treated in such a way as to make it more subtle and harder. And it will become celestial to the highest degree . . . if it is much exposed to the influence of rays and above all to the influence of the Sun, which is dominant among celestial things. (ibid.)

Among the seven planets of the so-called "Chaldean" series (Moon, Mercury, Venus, Sun, Mars, Jupiter, Saturn), there are those which are especially beneficent (Sun, Jupiter, Venus), called by Ficino "the Three Graces." Their influences, as well as the influence of Mercury, are fundamentally important to the purging of the pneuma.

We already know that there are series of objects classified according to their planetary affiliation. When it is impossible to expose oneself directly to the rays of the beneficent planets, it will suffice to make use of them. To acquire the "solarization" of the spirit, for instance, one must observe a healthy diet, take walks in *loci amoeni*, in pure and mild air filled with light and the perfume of plants, but also to use substances such as wine and sugar (ibid., I), plants, metals, and precious solar or Jovian stones.

> When our spirit has been carefully prepared and purged by natural things, it is able to receive many gifts through stellar rays, from the spirit of cosmic life. Cosmic life is visibly propagated in grasses and trees, which are like the hair of the body of earth; it is also revealed in stones and metals, which are like the teeth and bones of this body; it circulates in the living shells of the earth, which adhere to stones. By making frequent use of plants and other living beings it is possible to gain a great deal from the spirit of the world. (ibid., XI)

Precious stones, transformed into potions or worn as talismans, impress on the human spirit the qualities of the planets, protecting the organism from the plague and the effect of poisons, etc. (ibid., XI–XII; XIV).

It can be said that pneumatic purging is one of the themes constantly taken up by Synesius, but the bishop of Cyrene does not go, in depth, into the theurgic procedures through which the purification is supposed to take place. These procedures can be found in a different context, that of the *Chaldean Oracles* edited by Julian the Theurgist, son of Julian called the Chaldean, in the second half of the second century A.D., partially preserved and commentated by the Neoplatonists and by the learned Byzantine Michael Psellus. "Telesmatic science," Psellus tells us in his *Commentary*, "is that which, so to speak, initiates the soul through the power of substances from here below. . . . According to the Chaldean . . . we can only rise to God by strengthening the vehicle of the soul through material rites. Indeed, in his opinion, the soul is purified by stones, by herbs, by incantations and this works well to bring about its ascension."[2] The allusion to the vehicle of the soul does not refer to the authentic doctrine of the *Oracles*. Psellus must have come upon it when frequenting Neoplatonist commentators. On the other hand, the ritual procedures for purifying the soul to make possible its theurgic elevation are truly expounded in the *Oracles*.[3]

As we have seen, the theme of pneumatic purifications was already manifest in late Stoicism. The Stoics, taking their cue from Sicilian medicine, had worked out a rather complex animology, through which they tried to give an empirical basis for their deep moral preoccupations. Hence, according to Epictetus, to be virtuous means having a calm pneuma, pure and transparent; and, vice versa, the attainment of this clean and limpid "cardiac mirror" depends entirely on the individual's moral life.

The "purification of the heart" through virtuous practices, as well as by use of efficacious sounds and other more or less "magical" procedures, represents a very ancient preoccupation in the Orient. The *Upanishads* develop a subtle physiology based on the role of a cardiac synthesizer called *manas* whose existence was never in doubt according to any school of Indian philosophy—except, perhaps, for a few materialists. During sleep, the energies, or *prānas*, withdraw into the *manas*, or inner sense (a phenomenon called "telescoping of *prānas*"); in the waking state, they circulate in the subtle body. In mystic practices, the "cavity of the heart" or "ethereal cavity" (*ākāśā hṛdaya*) plays an essential part:

> The little space in the heart is as big as this great universe. The heavens and the earth are there, the sun, the moon, and the stars, fire and lightning and winds are there also; and all that exists now and all that exists no longer: for the whole universe is in Him and He lives in our heart. (*Chāṇḍogya Upaniṣad*, VIII, 1)

It goes without saying that it is incumbent on the transparency of the *ākāśā hṛdaya* to recognize in the heart the presence of the divinity or of the intellect; a number of mystical practices, including the preliminary stages of yoga, have as their goal the purification of the subtle organism, the restoration of its original purity.

The *hsin* or heart is no less important in Taoism and in Ch'an Buddhism. Even when it is not named, it is understood that the Taoist finds the gods within a cavity of his own subtle organism which answers to *ākāśā hṛdaya*. The procedures of visualization employed by the Taoist are analogous to those of Yoga and of the Western art of memory.

As for the Sufi mystic in Iran, he makes use of a number of procedures to obtain the "cleansing of the heart" (*qalb*), the most important being the use of ritual formulas (*zekr*) or Persian mantras.

In turn, the Hesychastic mystic in Oriental Christianity is using a technique called "cardioscopy," which consists in visualizing the space of the heart (*kardía*) and in trying to restore to it all of its purity and transparency. He too makes use of one or more formulas and increasingly slow breathing rhythms, like the yogin and the Taoist.

We shall not dwell on those generalizations, for even a rough analysis of these basic problems of the history of religions would take up more space than can be given here. Can the conclusion be drawn that Indian philosophy is the source of all mystical speculations and techniques dealing with the "heart"? Though it cannot be excluded, such a conclusion is most unlikely.

Humans react to external stimuli through emotions producing immediate secretions of adrenaline. Every external stimulus is accompanied
by an internal impulse, which is experienced in the "heart's space." The
earliest "language," the "verb," is a corporeal expression, and verbal
schemata "are the referentiality of all possible actions of *Homo sapiens*."[4]
Let us take some random verbal schemata relating to the heart: a person
incapable of being touched by the suffering of another reveals "hardness of heart," has "a heart of stone"; on the other hand, someone who
reacts appropriately to his emotions has "a kind heart," and he who has
no evil intent in his social behavior, imagining that others have none
either, has a"pure heart." Another person has his heart in his mouth,
wears it on his sleeve, has a heart of gold, but may also be heavy-heart-
ed, faint-hearted, or sick at heart. It is possible to do things light-heart-
edly or even whole-heartedly, but it may happen that we lack the heart
to do anything. When we have set our heart on something, we want to
clear the matter up, and youthfulness of heart means a fickle heart. As to
love affairs, they lead us to offer or to refuse our heart, and so on. There
must surely be an extralinguistic truth in all these expressions, a truth
which asserts that the heart is the seat of sensibility, of all emotional
reactions, and is the preeminent moral (or immoral) organ.

If the Englishman thinks with his head, there are people like the Man-
churians who "think [*gun 'imb'i*] with the heart [*gun'in*]."[5] They are ill
when their heart "is shadowy" [*gun'in bur 'imb'i*], whereas healthy people have "a transparent heart." S. M. Shirokogoroff finds nothing
strange in these concepts:

> It must be recognized that the emotional perception of the
> "shadowed being" is altogether admissible and that the con-
> cept of the heart as organ of the process of thought is entirely
> positivist, for thought, in its emotional manifestations, is per-
> ceived by the heart. (According to the positivist point of view
> of Europeans, an effort is made to localize "thought" in par-
> ticular sections of the brain, a naive conception of positivism
> based on various hypotheses that all depend on the idea of an
> abstract brain. Seen in this light, the European "positivist"
> point of view is not too far removed from that of the Man-
> churians, who have the right to speak of the localization of
> the thought process within the heart, because they *feel* it so.)[6]

Aristotle denied that it was possible to think without phantasms. Now
phantasms are colored emotionally, and, though they are able to occupy
any space, the place that suits them best is the "heart," for it is *the heart
that feels emotions*. This bodily given, the *real* manifestation of emotional

reactions *in the space of the heart,* includes the fact that several peoples of antiquity separately constructed analogous theories such as that of the manas in India and of the hegemonikon in Greece.

Since it is impossible to deny that emotions have a concrete nature, it is also impossible to deny the existence of a place where they are made manifest, a place which corresponds more or less to the anatomical localization of the heart. In this localization there must lie the anthropological explanation of the genesis of the *subtle* organ called heart, which must be older than that of the discovery of the anatomical organ of the same name.

As a screen for projection of internal phantasmagoria, the "heart" must very early have obsessed the human spirit. By identifying bodily energies with emotions, Indian philosophy and Greek medicine transformed the heart into a depository for both, into the principal organ of life and of communication with the outside world. As for visionary activity, it is easy to agree that it could only be localized where phantasms have a predilection for manifesting themselves, namely in the very center of the subtle organism.

What about the "head"? We can still rely on the huge documentation put together by Richard Broxton Onians[7] and by Anders Olerud[8] to form an idea about it. It seems that the dignity Plato confers on the human head in *Timaeus* (44d, 90a) rests on an intricate archaic problem differentiating two organs of consciousness: the "heart" (*kēr* or *kradiē*), seat of the vegetative soul (*thymos*), and the "head," seat of the *psychē*. To Onians, *thymos* is the "blood-soul" and *psychē* the "breath-soul," but the original difference between the two concepts must not have been noteworthy, since the word *thymos* is itself related to Indo-European vocables indicating vapor or breath (Latin *fumus*, Sanscrit *dhūmah*, Slavonic *dymu* and *duchu*). As to the *psychē*, like the Latin *animus*, it too is preeminently a "breath" since it derives from the verb *psychein* ("to breathe"), but its exclusive localization in the head is moot.[9] On the contrary, in a whole complex of beliefs, the *psychē* represents *all* bodily respiration, being linked to the *sperma*, which is a "genital respiration."[10]

It is in Platonic ontology and anthropology that there appears a precise differentiation between "head" and "heart," plainly favoring the former. "The human head, resembling a sphere, is in the image of the cosmos. The head is the outstanding microcosm, the body and its limbs are an appendage, or, as Plato himself says, the body is a subordinate servant. In *Timaeus* (44d) he emphasizes that the soul lives in the head in exactly the same way as the soul of the world lives in the spherical cosmos."[11] Plato adds, also in *Timaeus:* "For we are a plant, not earthly but celestial. And, indeed, it is from the top, the side where the original birth of the soul took place, that God suspended our head, which is like a root, and, in the same way, he gave our whole body erect posture."[12] It is on account of this ontological polarization expressed in terms relating to space ("top"-vs.-"bottom"), which is simultaneously a *moral* polarization ("good"-vs-"bad"), that Plato postulates the doctrine of a tripartite soul to which corresponds the tripartition of the human body into "head" (rational soul), "breast" or "heart" (irrational soul), and "belly" (appetitive soul) (*Timaeus*, 69b sq.). Considered by Plato to be entirely subordinate to the "head," the "heart" is the seat of the emotions, but it is not predominantly the visionary organ, that role being attributed, rather unexpectedly, to the *liver*.[13] Not until the Stoics were the relations between "head" and "heart" posited in a new way so that virtues became associated with "purity of heart." Renaissance magic derived from this concept, making the "cleansing of the heart" one of its main pursuits.

The word "theurgy" sometimes designates purifications whose purpose is to restore to the pneuma its original transparency, fineness, and flexibility.

Ficino's image of the theurgist, the practitioner of intrasubjective magic, did not amount to enough to run counter to the customs of the time. Far from evoking the spirits of the dead like the necromancer described by Benvenuto Cellini, far from flying up into the air and casting a spell on men and beasts like traditional witches, even far from applying himself to pyrotechnics like Henricus Cornelius Agrippa, or to cryptography like Father Trithemius, Ficino's magician is an innocuous individual whose habits are neither reprehensible nor shocking in the eyes of a good Christian.

We can be sure that if we look him up—unless he does not consider our company to be respectable, which is very likely—he will suggest that we accompany him on his daily walk. He will lead us surreptitiously, to avoid undesirable encounters, to an enchanted garden, a pleasant place where sunlight, in the fresh air, comes in contact only with the scent of flowers and pneumatic waves emanating from bird song. Our theurgist, in his white wool gown of exemplary cleanliness, will perhaps apply himself to inhaling and exhaling air rhythmically, then, having noticed a cloud, will anxiously go home, afraid of catching cold. He will play the lyre to attract the beneficent influence of Apollo and the other divine Graces, after which he will sit down to a frugal repast of some cooked vegetables and lettuce leaves, two rooster hearts to strengthen his own heart, and a sheep's brain to strengthen his own brain. The only luxury he will allow himself will be a few spoonfuls of white sugar and a glass of good wine—though on close examination this is mixed with an insoluble powder in which we can discern a ground amethyst, sure to draw upon him the favors of Venus. We shall notice that his house is as clean as his clothing and that our theurgist will wash himself systematically once or twice a day, in contrast to most of his compatriots, who do not have his good habits.

We shall not be surprised that this individual, intent on bothering no one and who, into the bargain, was as clean as a cat, never aroused the anger of any authority, secular or religious. He was tolerated in proportion to his own tolerance or, rather, indifference toward his less advanced fellows, whose pneuma was never as transparent as his own.

## (ii) Intersubjective Magic

Intrasubjective magic is only a special case of intersubjective magic, which functions according to the principle of the continuity of the universal pneuma.

Wording of this principle changes little from Synesius to Ficino. Let us listen to this:

> No one should think that, through the use of certain earthly substances, it is possible to attract the presence of numinous entities that appear immediately. On the contrary, what is attracted are demons, or rather [*potius*] gifts of the animate world and of the living stars. May it not be thought, either, that it is possible to bewitch [*allici*] the soul by means of material things. For it is the universal soul itself that makes the bait [*escas*] that suits the soul and with which it can be bewitched, and it stays there willingly. For there is nothing in the living world that is so deformed as not to possess a soul or, likewise, its gifts. Zoroaster designated these affinities of forms to the reasoning faculty of the universal soul by the term "divine enticements" [*divinas illices*], and Synesius corroborated their quality of magic charms [*magicas illecebras*]. (*Vita coel.*, I)

> Many people aver that magic is a [technique that allows] *men to attract, at favorable times, celestial presences through lower things corresponding to higher things.* (ibid., XV)

These two passages require some clarification.

Ficino states that the universal soul is itself the source of all magic because, in its freedom, it has chosen to create affinities between the higher and the lower worlds. By virtue of this principle, there are certain objects with which it is possible to invoke higher presences, and tradition has named them baits, decoys, lures, enticements, charms, seductions, etc. (thus it is possible to translate the words *esca, illex, illecebra*). The soul itself, in its goodness, has created the possibility, in certain circumstances, of surrendering itself to the wise man who is aware of the use of these objects. Nature exists so that man may use it: it is as though the fish itself, by wishing to feed man, taught him how to make the fish hook.

Ficino's definition of magic is concise and clear: the purpose of magical maneuvers is to obtain far-off results by means of immediate causes, especially action upon higher things by the lower things that are their affinity (*per inferiora consentanea*) and that serve as "lures" (*escae, illices, illecebrae*), "enticing" them (*allici*) at favorable times (*temporibus opportunis*).

He speaks, to be more precise, of a transitive mechanism which, at first, puts in motion physical causes in order to obtain hyperphysical results. In turn, the results are changed into new causes, which produce new results of a physical kind.

In order to form a clear idea of these maneuvers, we must analyze the meaning of the three components that constitute the operation of magic "seduction" (*allici*): the higher presences (*superiora*); the lower things that are their affinities or "get on well with them" (*inferiora consentanea*), or "lures" (*escae, illices, illecebrae*); and the "suitable times" (*tempora opportuna*).

HIGHER PRESENCES

"What is attracted are demons or, rather, gifts of the animate world and of the living stars" (*sed daemones potius animatique mundi munera stellarumque viventium*), says Ficino in the first chapter of his treatise *De vita coelitus comparanda*. A synthetic but exhaustive turn of phrase to describe the kind of aids the magician expects to obtain.

The next chapter of this book will, in large part, be devoted to the various categories of demons, pneumatic beings between the worlds. It remains for us to define here "gifts of the animate world" and "gifts of the living stars."

The "gifts of the animate world" are the natural recipients of pneuma, which have the property of feeding the human spirit by virtue of the law of pneumatic solidarity of cosmic parts.

> We can incorporate more and more of *quinta essentia* by knowing how to isolate the alimentary compounds of which it is a part or by making frequent use of those things that abound

mostly in spirit of a high degree of purity, such as noble wine, sugar, balsam, gold, precious stones, myrobolan, the things that have the sweetest perfumes and things that are shiny. (*Vita coel.*, I)

In the same way, through frequent use of plants and other living things, it is possible to draw a great deal from the cosmic spirit. (Ibid., XI)

If one desires that a food take hold of the brain [*rapiat prae ceteris formam cerebri tui:* that is, that it have influence upon the brain, etc.], the liver, and the stomach, one must eat as much as one can of the brain, liver, and stomach of animals that are not far removed from human nature (mammals, probably, but not exclusively). (Ibid., I)

But the main part of Ficino's work is devoted to the description of "gifts from the living stars" (*munera stellarum viventium*). We shall confine ourselves to expounding the fundamental principles of astromagic without going into detail.

Astrologers, called "Platonic philosophers" by Ficino out of respect for tradition, have established celestial universal figures, which, in their parts, contain the varieties of all lower things. There are twelve signs and thirty-six decans in the zodiac, making a total of forty-eight *universales figurae*, to which are added three hundred and sixty more, according to the number of degrees in the zodiacal circle (ibid., I). These *figurae* make up the space in which the seven planets revolve, determining their aspects. The "gifts of living stars" are the properties peculiar to the planets according to their respective positions, in other words, according to "propitious times" (*tempora opportuna*).

Since the human body is an image of the physical cosmos, each of the seven planets has a particular influence. These affinities, called *astral melothesia*, form the nucleus of the doctrine expounded in the *iatromathematica* attributed to Hermes Trismegistus:[14]

> *Soli oculus dexter, Lunae sinister.*
> *Saturno auditus, auresque, Iovi cerebrum.*
> *Cruor, sanguisque Marti, Veneri olfactus, gustusque.*
> *Mercurio lingua, et gurgulio.*[15]

This is the theoretical principle underlying the construction of *homines phlebotomici* or the images which show exactly the influence of the planets, the signs, and the decans on the human body. In reality, since planets, signs, and decans sometimes form very complicated combinations, it is necessary to draw up a new list of affinities for almost every planetary position and to construct a new phlebotomic man.[16] The remedies of iatromathematics entirely depend on the exact composition of the above to determine, by reason of the planets and signs that govern a certain part of the body at a certain time, the use of the appropriate medicinal herbs.

> In order to know the fate of a sick person, if not to cure him, strange calculating machines are still used, deriving from astrological data; for example, the one from the "sphere of Petosiris," invented in the first century A.D., according to Boll. In order to treat the person, it is essential to remember that, according to the Greek principle of melothesia, his anatomy and his physiology are governed by the stars: each sign of the zodiac rules a part of the body; each planet reigns over an organ. A surgeon cannot operate on a diseased limb if the Moon is in the sign of the zodiac responsible for that limb, or else the humidity of the planet would cause the most serious complications to ensue at once.[17]

In the fifth chapter of his *Vita coelitus comparanda*, Ficino describes the doctrine of astral melothesia, and, in the sixth and tenth chapters he deals with the principle of phlebotomic man, but without going into detail.[18] Comparing the space he gives this subject with the learned constructs of a real iatromethematician like Johannes of Hasfurt,[19] we can conclude that it is a marginal though indispensable element in the sum total of Ficino's magic. Indeed, Ficino is most preoccupied not with curing body illnesses but with the purification of the spirit and the spiritual advantages that the practitioner can draw from the position of the planets.

Let us remember that three of the seven planets that Ficino calls "the Three Graces" (the Sun, Jupiter, and Venus), are beneficent, Mars and Saturn are malefic, whereas Mercury veers between one group and the other. How can the qualities of the beneficent planets be drawn to the individual pneuma?

> If you wish to imbue your body and spirit with the qualities of one of the members of the cosmos [the word *membrum* means, to Ficino, "organ"], for example, of the Sun, look for things that are preeminently solar among metals and stones, and more among plants, and even more among animals, and most of all among men. [There follows a list of solar metals, stones, plants, animals, and men.] Likewise, if you wish to impregnate your body with the virtue of Jupiter, move your

body to the day and the hour of Jupiter, under the domination of Jupiter, squeeze yourself between all things that belong to Jupiter. [A list follows.] As to the qualities of Venus,
they can be attracted by turtledoves, pigeons, and wagtails
and also by other things that modesty forbids us to reveal.
(*Vita coel.*, I)[20]

Depending on the kind of activity to be stimulated, all the planets are
equally important: Saturn has charge of higher philosophy and occultism; Jupiter of natural philosophy and politics; Mars of virile *cer-
tamina*; the Sun and Mercury of eloquence, music, and glory; Venus of
festivities; and the Moon of nourishment (ibid., II). The influence of the
planets over the parts of our body determines the kind of astrological
remedies that should be applied depending on the case (ibid., VI). Pharmacology, moreover, is one of the most important branches of magic
(ibid., XI, XIII, XV). To summarize all the above concisely: *Res naturales
atque etiam artificiosae habent virtutes a stellis occultas: per quas spiritum
nostrum stellis eisdem exponunt* (ibid., XII)—"Natural things as well as
artificial things have occult qualities conferred upon them by the stars:
through these things our spirit attracts the influence of the respective
stars."

THE LURES

The purpose of Ficino's pneumatic magic is to improve the spiritual,
physical, psychic, and social conditions of the magician himself, or his
client. Theurgy and medicine are the magician's principal activities.
Plants, stones, metals, and the various other substances used according
to the position of the planets in the zodiac exert a positive influence
upon the spirit of the theurgist and upon an invalid's health. Amulets,
talismans and images, depending on the case, can have a prophylactic
or curative effect. It goes without saying that the same remedies can be
used to obtain results of a different kind: social success, learning facility,
practicing a profession, harmony in intersubjective relations, etc. It is
easy to imagine that, for every undertaking, there is a lucky position of
the stars and a method of making use of it. As for Ficino himself, his
main interest is directed toward theurgy and iatromathematics.

The arsenal of magic is made up of a series of substances which are in
touch with the planets in a certain way. Their use can be direct or indirect. In the first instance, it can be a matter of simple potions or talismans. In the second, a matter of more complex objects produced
according to "propitious times" to store up the beneficent influence of a

certain configuration of the chart of the heavens. "One attributes a quality of a sometimes miraculous kind to the astrological images made of metals and stones" (*Vita coel.*, XII.

> The use of talismans does not contravene free will. Albert the Great, in his *Speculum*, says that free will is not limited by choice of a propitious time; but, rather, by holding in contempt the choice of a propitious time for beginning great ventures, one gives no proof of freedom: on the contrary, one only overturns free will. (Ibid.)

> Ptolemy says in his *Centiloquium* that the images of lower things are exposed to many celestial images. That is why the wise men of antiquity were accustomed to fabricating certain images when the planets entered constellations which were almost the model of terrestrial things. (Ibid., XIII)

We shall not here take up the doctrine of images expounded by Ficino according to hermetic, Neoplatonic, and Arab sources. We already know that each planet is attached to a whole series of things on earth (ibid., XIV, XV). These make up the primary matter for the manufacture of astrological talismans. In any case, Ficino attributes to them qualities inferior to those of remedies and ointments (ibid., XV, ad finem).

PROPITIOUS TIMES

The *tempora opportuna* for picking a medicinal herb or for making a potion or a talisman depend entirely on the position of the planets in the zodiac and in the celestial "houses." The preparations for these astrological maneuvers are of a degree of complexity varying according to the case. From the most simple (chaps. IV, VI, XV) to the most sophisticated (chap. XVIII), they all correspond to the same principle enunciated above. One example will suffice:

> To gain a long life, they fabricated the image of the aged Saturn in stone of *pheyrizech,* that is to say, sapphire,[21] at the time of Saturn ascending and in propitious relation to the rest of the sky. The form it took was thus: an old man seated on a raised throne or on a dragon, his head covered with a cloth of dark-colored linen, his arm upraised, fish or a weight in his hand and dressed in a tunic also dark in color. (Chap. XVIII)

Images of this kind are mostly borrowed from the *Picatrix.* They correspond to planets and to personified entities of the zodiac (signs, decans, stages), whose invention the *Picatrix* attributes to the Indians.[22] Again, one example will suffice to show the affinities between the two kinds of depiction: "In the first aspect of Aries a man rises, with red eyes, a big long beard draped in white linen, walking with huge strides, girded with a red sash on a red costume, standing on one foot as though looking at what lies before him."[23]

These descriptions were probably meant to be incorporated into the magician's phantasy when he prayed to the planets. The "planetary orations" in the *Picatrix*, moreover, contain an enumeration of qualities attributed to the respective planets undoubtedly delivered by the magician with his eyes fixed on the internal image of the sidereal divinity:

> O Master, whose name is hallowed and whose power is great, supreme Master, O Master Saturn, thou the Cold, the Sterile, the bleak and the baleful; thou whose life is sincere and whose word is truth, thou the Wise and the Solitary, thou the Impenetrable; thou who keepest promises; thou who art weak and weary, thou who hast more cares than anyone, thou who knowest neither pleasure nor joy; sly old man who knowest all ruses, thou who art deceiver, wise and sensible, who bringest prosperity or ruin and who makest man happy or miserable! I beg you, O Supreme Father, through thy great benevolence and generous goodness, do this and that for me.[24]

It is easy to judge how closely related were magic properly so-called, the Art of Memory and glyptics. Talismans were supposed to represent personified entities of the zodiac that the magician had memorized and impressed on his phantasy to be directed toward all useful ends. Every invocation of these entities was to be accompanied by instantaneous visualization of them. Endowed with autonomous existence and *actually* appearing in the pneumatic apparatus of the trained magician, in the last analysis these strange personages are none other than the renowned *demons* inhabiting all zones of the cosmos.

# 7| Demonomagic

### (i) Some Concepts of Demonology

Who is not acquainted with those cohorts of demons of Christianity whose most benign activity was continually to exert natural constraints (drowsiness, hunger, erotic desire) upon people conceited enough to think themselves above them? Doubtless, demons were equally capable of producing alarming kinetic phenomena, which got the better of more than one saint and were certainly more than mere hallucinations.

The art of the Middle Ages and the Renaissance endows demons with the strangest and most repulsive forms borrowed from the animal kingdom: beetles, brachyurous decapoda, crawling batrachian sea slugs, the oxyrhynch fish or the armored Saurians, not forgetting ophidians, bats, and even avian reptiles which in a way anticipate the discoveries of paleontology.[1]

The disciples of the *Chaldean Oracles* could cause numinous entities to appear, especially the goddess Hecate and the souls of Greek heroes and famous philosophers such as Plato.

The invocation of the gods was often followed by their appearances (*autophaneia*).[2] The apparition of Hecate is very typical:

> After this invocation, you will behold either a fire which, like a child, advances by leaps and bounds toward the current of air; or else a great light which winds around the earth, humming; or a horse even more resplendent than the light, or yet again a child mounted on a horse's swift back, illuminated, or covered with gold or, on the contrary, naked, or yet again, bow in hand, standing up on the horse's back.

In their magic practices, the theurgists made use of a gold disk (*strophalos*) encrusted with magic graphic symbols with a sapphire at the center. It could be turned by means of a leather headband while the theurgist intoned magic phrases and occasionally emitted inarticulate sounds imitating the squeals of animals to frighten away evil spirits. The instrument, still used by Proclus, one of the last Neoplatonists, was called "Iynx" after a sort of fire bird which was supposed to transmit messages between the world of intellect and the perceptible world.[4]

Using an "Iynx," Proclus was able to produce rain, like Julian the Chaldean, author of the *Oracles*, who boasted of having done this in the year 174 when he was a soldier fighting under Marcus Aurelius. (Unfortunately, it is difficult to establish precisely who performed this wonder because the Christian fighters of the Thundering Legion, the pagans, and an anonymous Egyptian magician all claimed credit for it.[5]

In any case, the theurgists' disk was studded with magic symbols—the same ones reappear on Chaldean talismans—representing, probably in graphic form, the same symbols which, having been "scattered" in the world by the supreme intellect, could also be expressed in solemn formulas (*synthēma*).[6] In certain cases, these forms were supposed to reproduce the *symbol* inscribed "in the heart," that is, in the human soul, consisting of a combination of semicircles and the Greek letter X. Many Greek heroes had a psychic diagram and a mystic name which permitted theurgists to conjure them up. Michael Psellus, the Byzantine Platonist, reports that Julian the Chaldean invoked the soul of Plato, asking him a number of questions. According to Hans Lewy, one of the most authoritative interpreters of the *Oracles*, the soul of Plato appeared as a luminous geometric shape. The idea that the human soul is made of semicircles and of the letter X derives from Plato's *Timaeus* (34b, 36b), where the cosmic soul is described as composed of two axes in the form of X, bent into a semicircle and joined at the ends. The Christians, according to Justin the Martyr, maintained that this figure imitated the cross of Moses' serpent of brass (*Numbers*, 21:9).[7]

Besides gods, heroes, and great men like Plato, there were other entities which, according to the Chaldeans, peopled the world of the surreal, sometimes becoming visible to the human eye. These were demons, who were good or evil. The Platonists Plutarch of Chaeronea and Apuleius of Madaura, as well as the Neoplatonists Porphyry and Iamblichus, distinguished between two classes of demons: those residing permanently in the supraterrestrial zones and the disembodied human souls who were transformed into demons for a thousand years, later to return in the cycle of metensomatosis.

The world of nature (*physis*), in other words, the sublunar zone, was peopled with aerial, aquatic, and terrestrial demons who produced cosmic calamities and individual passions. They took the form of animals—preferably dogs: "From the bosom of earth, chthonian dogs leap up, which never show a truthful sign to mortal man."[8] The leader of the evil demons was Pluto: attempts were made to defeat his diabolical cohorts through sacrifices of stones (such as the *mnizouris* stone) and of plants, such as were used for purification of the vehicle of the soul. Use was also made of amulets, phylacteries, and apotropaic statuettes, and evil spirits were chased away by clanging bronze instruments.[9]

All the principal sources of Neoplatonist demonology were translated into Latin by Marsilio Ficino. These are treatises by Porphyry (*On Sacrifices, Gods and Demons, Opera*, II, p. 1934 sq.), by Iamblichus (*On Mysteries* II, p. 1873 sq.), by Proclus (*On Soul and Demon*, fragment of Proclus's commentary on *Alcibiades* I, II, p. 1908 sq.; *On Sacrifice and Magic*, p. 1928 sq.), and by Michael Psellus (*On Demons*, II, p. 1939 sq.).

Porphyry informs us that, according to Plato, there is a multitude of demons, some the objects of a public cult similar to that of the gods, others the object of a secret cult. Still others, those that mortals neglect, can easily seek vengeance.

How do we go about obtaining benefits from demons? Through prayers and sacrifices, which prove to be extremely useful because good demons, who reside in the heights of sublunar space, can grant us favors in the whole sphere of social existence. As for evil demons, residing near the ground, we must at least gain their indifference, since they can be extremely obnoxious when crossed. Indeed, they are endowed with a spiritual body that is mortal and needs to be fed. When frustrated, they stop at no spiteful act, provoking pernicious passions in the phantasy of man as well as phenomena such as earthquakes or the destruction of harvests. What do they feed on? Since their body is a sort of vapor, they find delectable the smell of meat, of fumigation, and of blood. That is why they appear en masse at animal sacrifices. The wise man, knowing that where there is bleeding flesh there are also evil demons, will prefer a vegetarian diet to one containing meat, in imitation of the proverbial abstemiousness of the Essenes.

Iamblichus gives us still more valuable information about supraterrestrial beings, which he divides into several categories: on high there are hypercelestial gods and the souls of stars of celestial gods; there follow archangels, angels, demons, principalities, heroes, and human disembodied souls.[10]

The function of demons is to place souls into earthly bodies; on the other hand, the function of heroes is to vivify, to impart reasoning powers, to tend the herd of souls and free them from their bodies.

It is remarkable that Iamblichus's text informs us that "all the higher presences can be invoked and reveal themselves in variable aspects" according to their category. The Neoplatonist endeavors to describe minutely the manifestations of the beings of the invisible world. The gods, archangels, and angels have simple and uniform aspects. The demons, principalities, heroes, and human souls have varied and complex appearances. The impressions they give are just as varied: the gods are majestic and helpful, the archangels terrible but tender, the angels sweet, the demons frightening, the heroes less awe-inspiring, the principalities shiny, the princes obnoxious and hostile, the souls similar to the heroes.

Apparitions of gods, archangels, and angels cause no disturbance of any kind. Demons, on the other hand, upset order and inspire fear. Principalities are majestic and stable. Heroes are on the move and in a hurry. Princes stir up commotion. Souls resemble heroes but are less orderly and stable.

Gods, archangels, and angels are of miraculous and incomparable beauty. Demons are beautiful by nature, heroes are beautiful in the expression of their courage, the principalities' beauty is their main quality, whereas the beauty of princes is artificial and elaborate. Souls partake of demonic and heroic beauty.

The speed and effectiveness of their respective actions decrease according to the hierarchy of these beings. In particular, principalities act with authority and strength whereas princes have a grandiloquence which outstrips actual results.

Manifestations of the gods fill the whole sky, a sight too dazzling for mortal eyes. Archangels occupy only part of the world, are very resplendent, and bear symbols. Angels are neither as gleaming nor as large. Demons are smaller and less perceptible, and the light emanating from them is more bearable. Heroes have less imposing dimensions and magnanimous aspect; principalities are very big; princes are self-important, haughty, and insolent; souls vary in their dimensions but are smaller than heroes.

There are, of course, also evil demons. It is true, Proclus informs us, that heroes, demons, and angels are higher beings who profit from the vision of intelligential beauty. But there are also evil demons, and these are all the more dangerous because they can masquerade as beneficent demons to confuse the sacrificer (II, pp. 1909–10).

Having been acquainted with the qualities and powers of demons, whom they can invoke with the aid of natural substances, magicians have the faculty of interrogating them about the categories of higher divinities. In turn, the demons profit from direct acquaintance with the gods and can pass this on to their disciples. What good luck for a magician, through the intermediary of demons, to have access to the gods and goddesses! (II, p. 1929).

The Neoplatonists differentiated between beneficent demons, inhabiting the higher spheres, and malevolent demons, living close to earth.

The Christian Platonist, Michael Psellus, considered all demons evil. Like angels, they have a very tenuous pneumatic body. But, while angels' bodies are aglow, those of demons are dim.

Psellus tells us that he received instruction in the rather strange doctrine of demons from the hermit Mark of Chersonesus. He maintained that demons are able to ejaculate semen and to be born in the bodies of animals. They have limbs, and, since they eat, they also defecate. Their food consists of spirit and body fluids, which they inhale and absorb like sponges. Mark, a specialist in demonology, knows several kinds of demons, for they are suprisingly numerous: "all the air above and around us, the whole earth, the sea and the bowels of the earth are full of demons" (II, p. 1940). There are six categories: those who live in the fire that borders upon the higher zone of air, "calling themselves, in barbaric parlance, *Leliureon,* which means igneous" (sublunary demons); demons that are aerial, terrestrial, aquatic, subterranean, and, finally demons of a kind "who flee the light, who are invisible, wholly dark, violently causing destruction by cold passions" (II, p. 1941). Although all these demons are maleficent, the last three categories are particularly dangerous. Indeed, the activities of sublunar, aerial, and terrestrial demons are exclusively spiritual, whereas those of the others can be directly materialistic. The former are confined "to depraving the soul by means of phantasies and cogitations" (in particular, the aerial and terrestrial ones provoke erotic phantasies). All of that is easy to explain, since demons, having a pneumatic essence, can assume all the forms and colors they wish, revealing themselves to the human spirit in deceptive forms.

> Taking those disguises, they can inspire many deeds and decisions and give us much advice. They evoke in us the memory of past sensual pleasures, frequently stimulating, while we are in a state of slumber or of wakefulness, semblances of passions, even exciting us in the inguinal zone and arousing us; they are a party to unwholesome couplings, especially if we are inclined to them by our own hot and humid body fluids. (*Ibid.*)

### (ii) Demons and Eros

This doctrine of succuba and incuba will, until the eighteenth century, spark debates specific enough to warrant closer study here.

While admitting that demons can feign to possess male sex organs, the hermit Mark of Chersonesus believes nevertheless that all demons are by nature feminine and lacking in definite shape and able, at will, to assume any deceptive appearance.

Specialists in witchcraft from the fifteenth until the end of the seventeenth century are not all convinced that demons can ejaculate semen and procreate, though semiofficial treatises such as the *Malleus maleficarum* of 1486 and the summa of the Jesuit Del Rio at the end of the sixteenth century are of that opinion.

The most widespread opinion, perhaps, expressed by Jean Vineti, inquisitor at Carcassonne, in his *Treatise Against Those Who Invoke Demons* (ca. 1450), is that demons are transsexual. Functioning as succuba with a man, they gather sperm and later deposit it in the vagina of a woman with whom they act as incuba.[11] It is a moderate position shared, among others, by Father Alphonso da Spina in his *Fortalitium fidei* written around 1460. According to Da Spina, nuns who have intercourse with incuba wake up "as defiled as if they had made love with a man."[12]

Pierre Naudé, author of a *Déclamation contre l'Erreur exécrable des Malificiers, Sorciers . . . à ce que recherche et punition d'iceux soit faicte* (Paris, 1578), is convinced that nearly all witches have incuba, and sorcerers succuba, and also that they have intercourse with corpses animated by their household devils.[13] Jean Bodin, in his *Démonomanie des Sorciers* (Paris, 1580), informs us that in Valois and Picardy succuba are called *coche-mares*.[14]

Jordanes de Bergamo (*Quaestio de Strigis*, manuscript, c. 1470) relates that the bishop of Verona, the famous humanist Ermolao Barbaro, reported to him the case of a man who, for fifteen years, had a succubus as mistress,[15] and stories of this kind abound in tales of witchcraft.

Johannes Henricus Pott, at the end of the seventeenth century (Jena, 1689), in his *Specimen Juridicum de Nefando Lamiarum cum Diabolo Coitu, in quo abstrusissima haec materia delucide explicatur, quaestiones inde emergentes curata resolvuntur, variisque non injucundis exemplis illustratur*, takes the same position as *Malleus* and Del Rio, adding "droll examples" such as the following: since incuba take the form of animals, there have been women who, as a result of their bestial relations with demons, gave birth to all sorts of animals (lion, cat, dog, etc.) or to monsters. The most interesting case, which he quotes Philip-Ludwig Elich as having given him (*Daemonomagia*, Frankfurt, 1607), is that of a woman who, having probably coupled with a demon in the guise of a rooster, laid eggs every day.[16]

The question of the procreation of demons was still of interest in the eighteenth century, for Johann Klein's academic dissertation of November 19, 1698 (in Rostock), was reprinted in 1731 under the title *Examen juridicum judicialis Lamiarum Confessionis se ex nefando cum Satana coitu prolem suscipisse humanam.* Klein, on the authority of *Malleus* and Del Rio, believes that demons can beget children with the unfortunate women they seduce:

> We can read in judiciary proceedings the confessions of witches: they derived more pleasure from the indecent organs of Satan, having abominable intercourse with that most impure spirit, than from permissible cohabitation with their legitimate husbands, albeit they were not always delighted by the consequences of those detestable depravities. It has often occurred that from this odious and sodomitic copulation they have given birth to live children.[17]

Ludovicus Maria Sinistrari de Ameno, whose treatise *De Daemonialitate et Incubis et Succubis,* written toward the end of the seventeenth century, was translated into French by Isidore Lisieux and printed in Paris in 1875, is much more original. He believes that the incuba and succuba are not demons but beings called *follets* in French, *folletti* in Italian, and *duendes* in Spanish (in English, elfish spirits). They are not spirits hostile to the Christian religion, but they take a wild delight in violating chastity, *contra castitatem.* Sinistrati de Ameno has a theory opposite to the idea of the transsexuality of *follets.* They are capable of ejaculating semen; after all, they are creatures, human in appearance, endowed with a soul that can be saved or damned and a tenuous body with greater longevity than that of man. They can enlarge or shrink their bodies at will, moving through chinks in matter; they form organized societies, with governments and cities.[18]

The apologists of the Inquisition do not fail to inform us in detail of the sexual relations between sorcerers of both sexes and the demon. One of the greatest authorities of the sixteenth century on this subject is Nicolas Remy, poet and privy councillor of the duke of Lorraine, author of the *Daemonolatria, ex judiciis capitalibus nongentorum plus minus hominum qui sortilegii crimen intra annos quindecim in Lotharingia capite luerunt* (Lyon, 1595). The treatise ends with a poem in French in which Remy takes pleasure in describing outrageous forms of tortures of which he has long experience, and concludes:

> Judges, do not fear to be relentless
> In arrests you make to punish witches;
> . . . Every age will praise those acts of justice.

While admiring his enviable assurance, I must point out that, fortunately, Remy was mistaken. In any case, having made a fifteen-year study of some nine hundred trials for witchcraft, he gives us one of the most lively, interesting, and authoritative descriptions of demonophily that one could wish for:

> All those who have had sexual intercourse with incuba and succuba unanimously declare that it is difficult to imagine or describe anything more repulsive or unrewarding. Pétrone Armentaire states that, no sooner had he strangled his Abrahel, than all his limbs became rigid. And Hennezel asserts that his Scuatzebourg (those were the names of succuba) gave him the impression of having a frozen hole (instead of a vagina) and that he had to withdraw before having an orgasm. As to witches, they declare that the virile organs of demons are so thick and hard that it is impossible to be penetrated by them without dreadful pain. Alice Drigée compared her demon's erect penis with a kitchen tool she pointed out to the assembly and gave the information that the former lacked scrotum and testicles. As to Claudine Fellée, she knew how to avoid the piercing pain of such intercourse by a rotary movement she often performed in order to introduce that erect mass, which no woman, of no matter what capacity, could have contained. . . . Those unfortunates often complain that their demon smothers them but they have never been able to put an end to the situation. . . . And nevertheless, there are some who reach orgasm in this cold and loathsome embrace.[19]

South of the Pyrenees the demon behaves violently on the sabbath: grasping a witch, *con su mano yzquierda (a la vista de todos) la tendia en el suelo boca abaxo, o la arrimaba contra un arbol, y allà la conocia somaticamente.*[20] The intercourse is no less painful (*El Demonio la tratò carnalmente por ambas partes, y la desflorò y padecia mucho dolor*[21]), but it also has the peculiarity of plunging the unhappy woman into the mortal sin of sodomy.

We see the kind of havoc, moral and physical, the incuba and succuba were supposed to wreak. We have still to examine the social havoc they wrought as well as the origin of these evil pneumatic beings.

### (iii) Witches and Demoniacs

The activity of demons is especially intense in the sphere of illicit Eros, but it is not limited to that, contrary to the opinion of the optimist (or the "minimalist") Sinistrari de Ameno. There is no need to refer to *Malleus* or the summa of Del Rio to see that witches were also blamed for crimes other than those they committed through the intermediary of demons.

Johannes Nider, author of *Formicarius: De Visionibus et Revelationibus,*
written in 1435–37 at the time of the Council of Basel, pointed out seven
ways for *malefici* or sorcerers of either sex to inflict injury upon human
society: by arousing love or hate; by causing impotence, sickness, insanity; by causing death; and by destroying the property of others.[22]
Now Nider is not part of the radical trend which, a few years later, will
recommend the death penalty for sorcerers and witches and eventually,
in 1468, will change the crime of witchcraft into *crimen exceptum,* opening
the door to all possible judiciary abuses.[23] On the contrary, Nider recognizes the authenticity of an old document called *Canon* or *Capitulum Episcopi,* dug up by the ecclesiastical writer Reginon of Prüm (*De Ecclesias-
ticis Disciplinis,* ca. 906; lib. II, ca. 364) of the alleged acts of a "Council of
Ancyra" where this document is not mentioned. Bishop Burchard of
Worms and Gratian persist in the same fanciful attribution, as well as St.
Thomas, who cites a Council of Aquileia which did not produce any
writing of this kind either. Reason enough for H. C. Lea to believe it is a
fake, made up by Reginon himself at the beginning of the tenth
century.[24]

Be that as it may, the *Canon Episcopi* expresses the Church's position
until its displacement by the *Malleus maleficarum* and even beyond, every
time a clergyman or a layman has the courage to contest its assertions.

The *Canon Episcopi* did not deny the existence of the devil or of witches. But it had the peculiarity of considering that the exploits of witchcraft
(witches' sabbath, magical flight) accomplished by "evil women perverted by the devil" were "demoniacal illusions and phantasms." In
other words, the *Canon* denied that there was any physical reality in the
hallucinations of witches: "Who is so stupid and rash as to believe that
all these things that only take place in the mind actually occur in the
body?"[25] Besides Burchard and Gratian, a very influential work of the
twelfth century, the *Liber de Spiritu et Anima,* attributed to St. Augustine,
reinforces the unquestionable authority of the *Canon Episcopi,* calling the
witches *quaedam mulierculae post Satanam conversae, daemonum illusionibus
et fantasmatibus seductae.*[26] St. Thomas Aquinas, more formally, puts it
thus: "It is said that these women attend [the sabbath] in spirit; now,
this is not that spirit which, insofar as it is the substance of the soul, acts
outside the body. No, hallucinations [*visa*] of this kind are formed in the
spirit, which is the fantasy of the soul [*in phantastico animae*]."[27]

A story told for the first time by Nider in his *Formicarius,* and often
repeated, gives us all the data we need for understanding how witches
obtain their visions of flight and of the sabbath. Nider relates that a
Dominican, having met one of these *mulierculae* who laid claim to having

flown on the sabbath with the followers of Diana, asked for permission to witness her exploit. The woman *smeared her body with an ointment,* recited a set phrase, and at once sank into such a disturbed sleep that she fell out of bed and knocked her skull on the floor. Convinced she had visited distant countries, she was astonished when the monk informed her that she had not left her room.[28]

The names *pixidariae* and *baculariae* that are attached to witches attest to the importance, in their practices, of the box of ointment and the broomstick.[29] Jordanes de Bergamo states explicitly that they rode horseback on a stick smeared with ointment or that they used their unguent *on their armpits.*[30] Examining the recipes for unguents, we understand immediately the reason for these customs.

Several recipes are known,[31] which contain, besides various other ingredients whose role should be carefully studied, certain active components extracted from plants that belong mostly to the same family as the nightshade, such as *Datura stramonium, Hyoscyamus niger, Atropa belladonna,* Aconite, *Solanum nigrum, Physalis somnifera, Helleborus niger,* or *Cannabis indica,* used separately or in combinations of two or three. Among these powerful narcotics and hallucinogens, those used most often were *Datura,* also called the "Magicians' weed" or the "Sorcerers' weed" or the "Devil's weed," and *Solanum nigrum* ("Magicians' herb," "Verjus du Diable").[32]

The Church was aware of the causal relationship between the use of unguents made of plant extracts and the phenomenon of sorcery. In 1528, the provincial Council of Bourges decided to prosecute the plant gatherers. In 1557, de Mouluc, bishop of Valence and of Die, forbade priests to serve them communion, and the same law was promulgated in 1618 by means of the synodal statutes of the bishop-governor of Cahors, and subsequently by St. Francis of Sales and d'Aranton d'Alex, bishops of Geneva, by Le Camus, bishop of Grenoble, and by Joly, bishop of Agen.[33]

In all witchcraft the importance of the broomstick cannot be overlooked. Many sources inform us that it was smeared with ointment, and many sixteenth-century engravings portray *naked* witches taking off on their broomstick. Now, the extracts of the nightshade plant have just this peculiarity of being absorbed through the skin, entering the organism where they immediately become active.[34] The most sensitive zones of the body are, precisely, the vulva in women and the armpits, which explains the apparently incongruous use of the *baculariae.*[35] The hypothesis that the "classic" sorcerers, whose existence has been authenticated at least since the tenth century, were merely a combination of empirical pharmacists and drug addicts is not new. Present-day pharmacology has raised it to the rank of fact, and anthropologists have at least accepted it almost unanimously.[36] Of course, the uniformity of means does not suffice to explain the uniformity of witches' hallucinations.

For the present, here is a point won: the "classic" sorcerers were borderline cases of both sexes who, through the use of hallucinogens, induced access to the unconscious. What they experienced under the influence of drugs, they took for reality, imagining they had performed certain stereotypical acts. Constant use of drugs definitely resulted in eliminating the rather labile and problematical boundaries between the states of dream and waking. The sorcerers lived surrounded by their own phantasms, which must, for them, have assumed real and personal characteristics. It is not strange that they had sexual intercourse with them, or that it occurred in the grotesque way described by Nicolas Remy and others.

"The sleep of the faculty of reason produces monsters." Hallucinogens prove to be one of the most powerful means of arousing phantasms to invoke demons. It takes only one more step to endow them with real forms and attributes.

A second method for invoking demons—this one altogether artificial—is to imagine them through mnemotechnical processes.

A third circumstance in which demons are revealed, this time without being called, is mental illness.

The case of Alexis Vincent Charles Berbiguier de Terreneuve de Thym, a rich gentleman born in Carpentras during the second half of the seventeenth century, is very instructive.[37] He himself describes it in the three volumes of his autobiography published in Paris in 1821, entitled *Les Farfadets, ou tous les démons ne sont pas de l'autre monde*.

From 1813 to 1817, Berbiguier lived at the Hotel Mazarin, 54 rue Mazarine in Paris, where the "hobgoblins" did not cease to persecute him. He, in turn, made a speciality of capturing them, which earned him the title of "Scourge of Hobgoblins," triumphantly inscribed by him above his own portrait.

It is probable that the signs of Berbiguier's mental illness were already apparent before his sojourn in Paris. In Avignon, he went to see a Doctor Nicolas, who had to apply mesmeric passes to frighten them away. In Paris, he went to consult clairvoyants and the magician Moreau, who was himself only a powerful representative of the hobgoblins. But it seems there was no crisis until a soothsaying session with tarot cards, arranged for him by two clairvoyants, Jeanneton la Valette and Le Mançot, who, conniving with his hidden enemies, placed Berbiguier "under the influence of a bad planet." From that time on, the valiant router of demons knew never a moment of peace. The hobgoblins spied on him in his room, pursued him onto the Pont-Neuf, into the church of Saint-Roch, and as far as the confessional in Notre-Dame. We are not surprised that he decided to visit Professor Pinel, a doctor at the Salpêtrière, who lived at 12 rue des Postes, near the Estrapade. Imagine his anguish on observing that Dr. Pinel had himself been changed into a hobgoblin, whom Berbiguier recognized as the representative of Satan (the other doctor, Nicolas of Avignon, was proclaimed the representative of Moloch). Pinel was not satisfied to receive our hero at home but also paid him an inopportune call in his hotel room, which he entered through a hole in the chimney. And it was Pinel who, with a premeditated blow, killed poor Coco, Berbiguier's faithful squirrel.

Pinel's heinous desertion was not the only disillusionment in the existence of this unfortunate man, who determined to defend himself at all cost from the attacks of demons. He obtained hobgoblin-killing plants, needles, sulphur, and other substances and embarked on a merciless pursuit of hobgoblins, which he imprisoned by the thousand in an ordinary glass bottle.

Worried by the attacks of the inflexible Berbiguier, the hobgoblins dispatched a centurion called Rhotomago, who made him an honorable proposition: to join them. Our hero rejected it with dignity; thereupon the assemblages of hobgoblins increased. Pinel appeared among them in person, armed with a pitchfork, and so did Étienne Prieur, a law student, disguised as a pig, and so forth. (Étienne Prieur must have been the son of Prieur, the druggist, representing Lilith.) The attempt to resist his enemies obliged Berbiguier to carry out spectacular fumigations which alarmed the whole neighborhood and resulted in a visit from an evil fire captain.

One proof that mental illness does not pick and choose its victims: our second case regards a scientist of considerable culture. This was the doctor Ludwig Staudenmaier,[38] who, after graduating from a Bavarian *Gymnasium* in 1884, pursued his studies for four years in a Catholic academy of philosophy and theology. Soon afterward, he enrolled at the university and, in 1895, obtained his doctorate in zoology and chemistry at Munich, where he was made an assistant. In 1896, he became titular professor of experimental chemistry at the Royal *Gymnasium* of Freising, where he remained until retirement.

In 1912, Staudenmaier published a very interesting book entitled *Die Magie als experimentelle Naturwissenschaft*. In it, he carefully described an experience somewhat analogous to Berbiguier's, but the German scholar approached it in a totally scientific spirit. Staudenmaier, without being alarmed about it, had begun to hear voices, to perceive disturbing presences. He spent his whole life establishing friendly relations with the beings who visited him, making their acquaintance, calling them by name. He began to practice a sort of yoga and, having retired, took advantage of his savings to expatriate himself to Italy, a country with a pleasanter climate. He died in Rome, August 20, 1933, in a hospital belonging to a religious order, in which he was carrying out a respiratory experiment to "revive the vital heat."

Berbiguier and Staudenmaier are harmless mental cases with the leisure to hand very valuable documents down to posterity. In both cases we learn that foreign presences foist themselves upon the sick man, entering into more or less odd relations, which enables us to state that the principal source of demons is the unconscious, capable, in certain circumstances, of invading the subject's zone of consciousness.

Sorcery employs hallucinogens to induce experience of a reality other than the everyday kind; the mental patient is transported despite himself into the midst of his phantasms. Only the magician utilizes altogether conscious techniques to invoke and command his helpful spirits. In his case, the *invention* of a demon is equivalent to its coming to life.

### (iv) Demonomagic from Ficino to Giordano Bruno
CLASSIFICATIONS OF MAGIC

Modern scholars are convinced that there are two kinds of magic, Ficino's "spiritual" or "natural" magic and the "demonomagic" of Trithemius.

This distinction is arbitrary and rests on no solid foundation. Since demons themselves are spirits without a body, they form the object of *spiritual* magic, like the "gifts of the animate world" and the "gifts of living stars." Ficino is himself a demonologist and deals with planetary demons in his *Commentary on the Symposium*, and, if he does not go deeply into the subject of demonology, it is because he fears for his life.

As to the "natural" quality of Ficino's magic, it goes without saying, except that there is yet another kind of natural magic, that of Giambattista della Porta—a sort of repertoire of odd phenomena and popular recipes—which is not at all "spiritual." And, in the same way, Trithemius's magic is performed through the intermediary of planetary demons without being spiritual either.

We arrive at the conclusion that there are several forms of magic that can be simultaneously spiritual and demoniac, which makes that dichotomy irrelevant.

Of the categories of magic in the Renaissance, the most interesting is undoubtedly that of Giordano Bruno. He lists nine categories: *sapientia, magia naturalis* (*medicina, chymia*), *praestigiatoria,* a second form of natural magic, *mathematica* or *occulta philosophia,* a *magia desperatorum,* which is demonomagic, also called *transnaturalis seu metaphysica* or *theourgía, necromantia, maleficium* (of which *veneficium* is a subcategory) and *divinatio* or *phophetia* (*De Magia,* III, pp. 397–400). Although the criteria for this classification are not always clear, it seems that Bruno had in mind primarily the kind of auxiliaries that the magician expects to obtain and the method he utilizes for that. The outline, furthermore, can be simplified: the first four kinds of magic make use of *natural* means; mathematical magic—which Bruno prefers—is intermediary; the last four kinds employ *extra-, supra-,* or *transnatural* means:

> The methods of the fifth kind of magic are words, charms, the reasons of numbers and times, images, forms, seals, symbols, or letters. This magic is intermediary between natural magic and extra- or supranatural magic. The most suitable name for it is *mathematical magic* or, rather, *occult philosophy.*
>
> The sixth kind is achieved by means of the cult or invocation of external or superior intelligences or agents, through prayers, incantations, fumigations, sacrifices as well as certain customs and ceremonies directed toward the gods, demons, and heroes. The result is to contract the spirit into itself in such a way that the spirit is changed into receiver and instrument and appears endowed with the wisdom of things but this wisdom can easly be withdrawn, at the same time as the spirit, by means of sufficient remedies. This is the *magic of the hopeless,* who become recipients of evil demons caught with the help of the Art [*Ars notoria*]. Its purpose is to command the lower demons through the authority of the higher demons; the latter, one cultivates and attracts; the former, one exorcises and controls. This form of magic is *transnatural* or *metaphysical* and is called *theourgia.* (Ibid., p. 398)

At first we have the impression that Bruno is careful to draw the line between "natural" forms of magic, toward which the Church had shown itself to be more tolerant, and the forms of magic acting through the intermediary of demons, which the Church had condemned. His outline with nine headings would then immediately be transformed into a hierarchy of intolerance in which the forms that occupy the highest positions should be the most condemnable. That is true up to the eighth level—evil spells and magic poisonings—but is invalidated at one stroke by the ninth, divination. Now divination is practiced by soothsayers (*di-

*vini*), and it is to them that Bruno ascribes all forms of supernatural magic which he qualifies as *divine*. Things become more and more complicated when we learn that the nine species enumerated above are of three kinds: *magia physica*, *mathematica*, and *divina*, of which the first and the third are always beneficent whereas the second, mathematical magic, can be beneficent or evil, depending on the case (ibid., p. 400; cf. *Theses de Magia*, II, p. 455). We must deduce either that Bruno dropped the idea of counting the magic of the hopeless, necromancy, and evil magic among the admissible kinds of magic or else that he includes them, this time, among the broader possibilities of mathematical magic.

Only the fundamentally *polemical* nature of all of Bruno's works yields the key to this enigma. Indeed, in *De Magia*, Bruno does not fail to let fly an arrow at the obscurantism of the *Malleus maleficarum:*

> Recently, the words "magician" and "magic" have been denigrated: we have not taken this into consideration at all. The magician has been called a stupid and evil sorcerer who has obtained, through dealings and a pact with the evil demon, the faculty to do harm or to enjoy certain things. This opinion is not shared by wise men or philologists [*apud grammaticos*], but it is taken up by the hooded ones [*bardocuculli;* that is, monks] such as the author of *Malleus maleficarum*. In our day, this definition has been reassumed by all sorts or writers, as we can observe by reading the catechisms for the ignorant and for drowsy priests. (*De Magia*, III, p. 400)

At the same time, Bruno is on his guard against future attacks by the clergy by condemning some forms of magic acting through the intermediary of demons. One of these, namely necromancy, is a form of soothsaying accomplished by means of exorcisms and incantations addressed to the souls of the deceased (ibid., p. 398). It is easy to understand why necromancy should make up part of the three kinds of magic that Bruno himself considered reprehensible. But, since the magic he calls *divina* amounts, when all is said and done, to soothsaying, why does he not recognize that, like mathematical magic, it can be of two kinds—beneficent and maleficent? The answer is, on the one hand, that Bruno seems determined not to include necromancy and maleficent magic in his boiled-down classification of the varieties of magic, and, on the other hand, that he transfers to the category of mathematical magic a considerable part of the processes performed through the intermediary of demons. Can we understand the motivation for this rather intricate strategy? Yes, if we refer to a semiofficial document (such as the *Malleus*), the *Treatise on Magic Spells* by Paul Grillandi, written about 1525 and published in Lyon in 1536 under the title *Tractatus de Haereticis et Sortilegiis*. Here Grillandi states that invocations of the demon by *modum imperii*, those that Bruno earmarks for small demons, are not heretical but only sacrilegious. On the other hand, foretelling the future *is always heretical*.[39]

Now Bruno was a person of dazzling culture for his period, and it is unusual for even his most insignificant writings not to contain certain allusions whose source must be known in order for their meaning to be deciphered. In the last part of this book I shall analyze the polemical scope of one of Bruno's theses that has always been deemed original, that of the ass and of "asinity" (*asinitas*) as saintly qualities. Suffice it to say here that the whole theory of saintliness and heroism is developed by Bruno in direct polemic with one of the writings of the reformed period of Cornelius Agrippa, a writer Bruno held in high regard. It is therefore not out of the question that in *De Magia* he should implicitly take issue with Grillandi, demonstrating that, far from being maleficent, the highest form of divination is always beneficent. But that does not prevent Bruno, in the classification of the three kinds and nine species of magic, from being dependent on semiofficial writings such as the *Tractatus de Sortilegiis*. Indeed, Grillandi himself draws up a "hierarchy of intolerance" of the Church directed at the forms of magic in which, exactly as with Bruno, soothsaying is at the bottom of the list as being the most condemnable of all. That easily explains Bruno's classification, which is inspired by a treatise *against* magic such as Grillandi's, while proposing other criteria for determining the degree of culpability of magic disciplines. Among other things, he disagrees with Grillandi on the subject of divination and seems inclined to reject demonomagic more than Grillandi himself, even if it takes place *per modum imperii*. But he rescinds this at once, since the mathematical magic he himself seems to cultivate is not extraneous to the processes employed through the intermediary of demons. At this point he is obliged to accept Grillandi's precept, which he had implicitly disputed two pages before. He recognizes that mathematical magic can be maleficent, but he hopes, very probably, that if judged according to Grillandi's criteria it will only be sacrilegious and not heretical.

All these doctrinal subtleties are peculiar not only to Bruno but to all those writers who, while dealing with magic in the sixteenth century, are nevertheless trying to save appearances. Among them Bruno seems the most naive. Though unusually perceptive, Bruno handles his own impulsiveness badly—and this character trait is to prove fatal. On the other hand, Father Trithemius, who also has friends in high places, is a model of shrewdness. Where does Bruno err tactically? By never being able to agree with anybody; he could have stayed out of trouble if he had made it clear at the beginning that he shared the other person's views up to a certain point but differed on the details—which was often the case. But, Bruno proceeds in the very opposite way: he begins by attacking someone only to make it clear later that what is at issue is basically a question of detail.

If we have taken the right view of this—and the classification of *De Magia* is either by Grillandi or another writer of treatises *against* magic and sorcery—then we must agree that Bruno's entire procedure is very strange: what he borrows from implicitly incriminating sources is much more important than what he rejects. And he avoids saying so explicitly merely to save appearances.

In the sixteenth century, none of the Christian churches was a democratic institution and none showed any sympathy for magic. Since Bruno had studied the *Malleus*, the later works of Agrippa, which stem from a very strong Protestant influence, and also, in all probability, treatises such as that of Grillandi, we are surprised that he did not form a more accurate judgment of the climate of intolerance in his era before experiencing the consequences in his own life. This is because, more or less openly, he saw himself as a prophet and was not averse to martyrdom. He says so himself in the *Sigillus sigillorum:* "I would never be inclined to believe that anyone who fears physical sufferings has ever had intimate knowledge of the divine. He who is truly wise and virtuous will never feel pain, and he is perfectly happy—as perfectly as the condition of our present life permits" (*Op. lat.*, II, 2, p. 193).

But let us return to Bruno's magic. We shall see later that his *magia mathematica* is nothing but a demonomagic compilation whose principal sources are Trithemius and Agrippa. As to his natural magic, that simply amounts to Ficino's spiritual magic, whose ultimate consequences regarding Eros are set forth in the two editions of the treatise *De vinculis in genere*. Proof that he meant to profit from Grillandi's leniency in distinguishing between merely sacrilegious magic and heretical magic is the fact that, in his *De Magia*, he presents a doctrine of demons which, though inspired by Psellus's work translated into Latin by Ficino, is not completely lacking in originality.

Demons are invisible spirits who have the ability to act upon the intelligence and judgment. They produce visual and auditory hallucinations, sometimes simultaneously. Bruno differentiates five categories of demons. The first, who correspond to Psellus's subterranean and aquatic demons, are *bruta animalia* and have no sense. The second, who inhabit ruins and prisons, are "timid, suspicious and credulous." They can be invoked, since they are capable of hearing and understanding spoken language. The third are of "a more prudent kind." They inhabit the air and are especially redoubtable since they lead man astray through imagination and false promises. The fourth, who inhabit the airy regions, are beneficent and resplendent. The fifth, who inhabit the stellar light, are sometimes called gods or heroes but in reality they are only agents of the one and only God. The cabbalists call them Fissim, Seraphim, Cherubim, etc. (*De Magia*, III, pp. 427–28).

"Each variety of spirits has its own chiefs, princes, herdsmen, commanders, rectors, and ranks. Those who are wiser and more powerful rule and command those who are stupider and more uncouth" (ibid., p. 429). They live everywhere and are invisible except for the first groups— the aquatic and terrestrial demons—whose bodies are coarser (*crassiores*) and can make themselves visible in certain circumstances. They cause illnesses that some individuals have the gift to cure, such as King Cyrus, "who cured those with a diseased spleen by touching them with his finger," or the King of France, who cured the scrofulous in the same way (ibid., pp. 430–32).

We shall have occasion to return later to Bruno's demonomagic. Here we are concerned merely with examining the validity of the categories of magic. We have seen that, although the distinction between "spiritual" magic and "demonic" magic does not hold up, it corresponds, nevertheless, to an ancient tradition. At the time of the Renaissance, this distinction answered to the need felt by officialdom, as well as by their potential victims, to establish a boundary between lawful and illicit magic.

Since sorcery was a *crimen exceptum* after 1468 and dealings with the evil demons of Satan's hordes were ascribed to sorcerers, it followed naturally that any form of magic invoking demons was held to be suspect and was persecuted. This is why Marsilio Ficino, who had to endure the attacks of the Church for his treatise *De vita coelitus comparanda*—which the pope finally judged to be inoffensive—did not know what precautions to take to demonstrate that the "natural" magic he practiced was not demonic. Probably he was right only in the sense that the magician was able to restrict his own processes, but that did not prevent demonomagic, in certain if not all cases, from being a form of spiritual magic.

In the same way, the dichotomy between *natural* and *transnatural* magic is an artificial one, but officialdom seems to accept it to the extent that it uses a scale of measurement for the "culpability" of the various forms of magic. In his classification, Giordano Bruno utilizes the classic sources of occultism but also seems to take inspiration from one of these "hierarchies of intolerance" which he cannot totally disapprove of because he uses it himself.

In conclusion, the distinction between a "natural" magic and a "transnatural" or demonic magic, while being false on a strictly conceptual plane, is nevertheless accredited by a long historic tradition in which the potential culprits are in almost complete agreement with their accusers.

### TRITHEMIUS OF WÜRZBURG

In reply to eight questions put to him by Emperor Maximilian in 1508, Abbot Trithemius at once launched an attack on witches according to the doctrine of the *Malleus maleficarum*:[40] "Witches [*maleficae*] are very pernicious; they make pacts with demons and by solemn profession of faith, become vassals of the demons, whom they worship everlastingly." He concludes: "They must not be tolerated but, rather, exterminated wherever found, for God, creator of all things, commands it: 'Thou shalt not allow sorcerers to live'" (*Exodus*, 22; *Deuteronomy*, 18).

In October of the same year, when finishing the *Antipalus maleficiorum*,[41] Trithemius was, if possible, even more emphatic, proclaiming his concern over the reduced number of inquisitors and judges to deal with such numerous and serious crimes of witchcraft.

Who was this monk who, not content to demand capital punishment for *maleficae* and necromancers, exorted the Church to greater watchfulness?

It is certainly surprising to learn that this pillar of the establishment was considered one of the greatest—if not the greatest—sorcerer of the sixteenth century, an authority equal to Hermes and King Solomon.

First, the legend. Amazing stories were current in his lifetime and were to proliferate after his death, as well as the pseudo-epigraphic writings attributed to him.[42]

It is Augustin Lercheimer of Steinfelden who seems best informed about the wonders worked by Trithemius. He possessed an auxiliary spirit who took a motherly interest in seeing that his master not suffer from hunger or cold. During a trip to France an imperial German councillor, jealous and amazed, was able to see how the spirit brought him a hot meal and a bottle of wine in an inn "where there was nothing good to eat."

But that was nothing compared to the other performances by the abbot, who excelled in necromancy. Indeed, Lercheimer tells us, Emperor Maximilian, who was mourning the death of his wife, daughter of

Charles of Burgundy, begged Trithemius to invoke her ghost so that he might see her one last time. The abbot yielded to persuasion, and, before their eyes and the eyes of a third witness, "Maria appeared, like the ghost of Samuel to Saul, and walked before them, so resembling the real Maria that there was no difference between them."[43]

This tale was known to Luther,[44] who adds quite interesting details: the emperor was not limited to the pleasure of a fleeting glimpse of his wife but also received visits from other famous ghosts, such as those of Alexander and Julius Caesar. The story was confirmed by the doctor Johannes Wier, or Weyer, who does not mention the name of Trithemius but gives many details about ghosts that a great sorcerer attendant at court produced before Emperor Maximilian. This time the phantasms were those of Hector, Achilles, and the prophet David.[45]

The first person to give a very plausible explanation for these optical phenomena was a Swede, Georg Willin, in 1728,[46] followed by our contemporaries Will-Erich Peuckert and Kurt Baschwitz.[47] In essence, the abbot made use either of a *camera obscura* or of tricks with mirrors, which enabled him to delude the onlookers. Judging by the *Antipalus maleficiorum*, Trithemius knew the principle of a darkroom and could construct one. His disciple, Henricus Cornelius Agrippa, also tells in detail how he was able to produce optical illusions with the help of mirrors—a phenomenon, at that time, stemming from natural magic, in which Trithemius may have been a major specialist.[48]

This is why Bartholomeus Korndorff seems to be right in saying there was *nichts mit teuflischem Werk gemischt gewesen*, that no demonic work was entailed, even though he, as well as his contemporaries, understood nothing about it. This time, it was a matter of two "unquenchable lights" that Trithemius, according to his old servant Servatius Hochel, had prepared for the emperor. The two candles were still burning in the same place twenty years later.[49] It was a "miracle" of the same kind as that attributed by the authors of the Rosicrucian manifestos to Father Christian Rosenkreuz, whose tomb, opened 120 years after his death, revealed, among other things, "mirrors with many peculiar characteristics, hand-bells, lighted lamps . . ."[50]

Who was Trithemius? History holds two quite contradictory images of him. The first is that of the sorcerer, author of an abstruse work entitled *Steganography*, or "secret writing," the presumed author of a great many astounding pseudo-epigraphs and the subject of a popular tradition calling him a particularly able necromancer and magician; the second portrays "a famous poet, an original orator, a very clever philosopher, an ingenious mathematician, a perfect historian, and a great theologian"[51]—according to the phraseology of his biographer Wolfgang Ernest Heidel of Worms, who wrote a defense and apology for him in 1676.

Indeed, the abbot of Sponheim and subsequently of the monastery of St. Jakob of Würzburg was the protégé of Emperor Maxilian I himself and of two elector princes, and his *Steganography* was dedicated to one of them, Philip, count of the Palatinate and duke of Bavaria.[52] His other writings—some ninety compilations and pamphlets, exclusive of many epistles—treat of various subjects.[53] Considerable space is devoted to sorcery and vulgar superstitions—the abbot distinguishing himself through his remarkable zeal in the Church's fight against the sect of *maleficae*. There is, however, reason to believe that Trithemius practiced a certain duplicity with regard to sorcery. Indeed, Peuckert has noted that, in his *Antipalus*, the abbot does not hesitate to recommend, for use against spells, traditional remedies from the paraphernalia of medieval magic.[54] Trithemius is surely one of the great scholars of occultism in the sixteenth century. Far from confining himself to studying it in order to fight it as befitted his ecclesiastical duties, the abbot himself—a tactless remark betrayed it—was a very active occultist. Analysis of the parts of the *Steganography* still extant does not invalidate this hypothesis.

Not only the beginnings of his career but everything he did, as Trithemius himself said, resulted from close collaboration with supernatural forces.

Born in Trittenheim February 1, 1462, the future abbot was called Heidenberg (De Monte gentili, "of the pagan mountain") after his father, who died when the boy was a year old. His mother remarried, and the child and his brother had to take their stepfather's name (Zell or Cell), which he refused to use because of the perpetual quarrels he had with his stepfather until the age of fifteen. Johannes wanted to study, whereas the head of the family, lacking the funds to fulfill the overambitious wishes of the adolescent boy, tried to dissuade him by means which must have exceeded the purely verbal. For Johannes the only recourse was to the extreme methods of all oppressed people: fasting and prayer. After a regimen of harsh mortifications he had a nocturnal vision rather closely resembling the dreams reported by Dante in his *Vita Nova:* a young man in white—probably an angel—shows him two tablets, one covered with writing, the other with painted figures. He instructs him: *Elige ex his duabus tabulis unam, quam volueris,* "choose the one of these two tablets you desire." It can be assumed that by choosing the painted tablet Trithemius would become a great performer of mnemotechnics, like Giordano Bruno. But he chose the tablet with the writing on it, and the young man told him: *Ecce Deus orationes tuas exaudivit, dabitque tibi utrumque quod postulasti, et quidem plus, quam petere potuisti* ("God has granted your prayers and will give you both the things you have asked for and even more than you were in a position to ask for").[55] His first wish was to learn Holy Scripture, but the second was never made public. Klaus Arnold must, however, be right in supposing that it was "to know all that can be known in the world,"[56] which seems to be confirmed by the project of the *Steganography* as well as by his insatiable thirst for knowledge, taking the form of intensive reading.

The day after this vision he had the opportunity to learn the alphabet at the house of a neighbor's son. In one month he read German perfectly. Having noticed his efforts, his paternal uncle, Peter Heidenberg, paid for lessons from the priest of Trittenheim, from whom he probably learned Latin. Later he pursued studies sporadically at Trier, in Holland, and finally at Heidelberg. He learned Greek but never obtained an academic degree.

In January 1482, after he had visited the convent of Sponheim with a friend, a snowstorm obliged the two to remain there for a week, which decided Johann Zell to stay. He became a novice on March 21 and made his profession of faith on November 21. On July 29, 1483, at the age of twenty-three, he was elected abbot of Sponheim. This rapid career is astonishing, the more so because Heidel's apology does not reveal the real motives for his choice.

Sponheim was one of the poorest monasteries in the Palatinate. Avoided by everyone, shortly before the young man's arrival it only had five inhabitants, who must have been the most refractory of monks, attracted by the prospect of complete freedom, the only compensation for the destitution of the place. It is not surprising that the sole preoccupation of every abbot was to leave as soon as possible for a more hospitable and prosperous monastery. This explains the motivation of the monks, who hasten to choose the youngest among them as abbot, counting on his lack of experience to pursue their own leisure-time activities.

Trithemius does not lose his nerve even when faced with the lamentable condition of the buildings, his predecessors' debts, and the obvious disobedience of the monks. He proves to be an excellent administrator and puts Sponheim's affairs in order until 1491. After that date he even undertakes the complete reconstruction of the monastery; he does not stop at ostentation, decorating the walls of his apartment with quatrains by the humanist Konrad Celtis and himself, and the walls of the refectory with the coats of arms of the twenty-five abbots who had preceded him, as well as his own, a bunch of grapes.

The new building is somewhat surprising, but its main attraction is the library, unparalleled at the beginning of the sixteenth century. Trithemius buys or exchanges rare books and manuscripts and puts the monks to work feverishly copying and binding. If the monastery owned forty-eight volumes in 1483, it had 1,646 in the inventory of 1502 and, in 1505, before the abbot's departure, nearly 2,000. As early as 1495 the Dutch composer Matthaeus Herbenus, rector of St. Servatius in Maastricht, expressed amazement at the quantity of books in a letter to Jodocus Beissel. A few years later, Sponheim had become an obligatory place of pilgrimage for all humanists passing through Germany: "Just as no distinguished foreigner at the beginning of the nineteenth century omitted to pay his respects to Goethe in Weimar, so it was good form in the Germany of circa 1500 to have called on Trithemius at Sponheim."[57]

The exhausting activity of copyists and bookbinders as well as the exorbitant expenditures for the library must have caused the monks to protest.[58] That must be the reason for Trithemius's regretful departure from his abbey. The mutineers chose a new abbot, while the former one, beginning in 1506, had to be satisfied with the little monastery of St. Jakob in Würzburg. The library at Sponheim was almost inaccessible for him (he revisited it only twice, in 1508 and 1515) but the pro-Trithemius faction, which continued to function, outnumbered but still effective, prevented its destruction until the former abbot's death in 1516. Trithemius himself proposed that he buy back the books in Greek and Hebrew that the monks wished to sell, but he seems to have given up the idea of assembling a library at Würzburg comparable to that of Sponheim. He was quite ill, needed rest, and probably lacked the strength to give the little monastery of St. Jakob the splendor of the one he had to leave.

In his praise of his famous library, Trithemius himself gives us some important information in a Latin that needs no translation: *Nec vidi in tota Germania, neque esse audivi tam raram, tamque mirandam Bibliothecam, licet plures viderim, in qua sit librorum tanta copia non vulgarium, neque communium, sed rarorum, abditorum, secretorum mirandorumque et talium, quales alibi vix reperiantur.*[59] On the other hand, it was certainly easy for the abbot to buy rare books in Benedictine or other monasteries in the event that "the monks who possessed them feared that to own them imperiled observance of monastic rules."[60] The 1502 catalogue of the library was lost during the abbot's lifetime, and there exists no source that can tell us the titles of all books and manuscripts in the collection. However, it is not impossible that the rare and "dangerous" writings included all sorts of works on occultism. When editing his *Antipalus*, Trithemius gives us an admirably exact description of a number of books "opposed to religion." Now we know what he had revisited Sponheim precisely in 1508: this corresponds to the date of the *Antipalus* (October 10, 1508). It is very likely that, to refresh his memory on the subject of occultism, Trithemius once again made use of his priceless library. If this hypothesis is correct, it contained at that time the following works, among others, sometimes in several editions: The *Calvicula Salomonis*, the *Book of Offices*, the *Picatrix*, the *Sepher Raziel*, the *Book of Hermes*, the *Book of God's Purities*, the *Book on the Perfection of Saturn*, a book on demonomagic attributed to St. Cyprian, the *Calculation Art of Virgilius*, the *Book of Simon the Magician*, a treatise on necromancy attributed to Rupert of Lombardy in various versions, a book on the seven climates attributed to Aristotle, the *Flower of Flowers*, the book *Almadel* attributed to King Solomon, the book of *Enoch*, a book on astromagic attributed to Marsala, *The Four Rings of Salomon*, *The Mirror of Joseph*, *The Mirror of Alexander the Great*, the *Book of Secrets of Hermes of Spain*, a pamphlet on magic by one Ganel of Hungarian or Bulgarian descent, a demonomagic treatise by Michael Scot, two treatises on magic attributed to Albert the Great, the *Elucidarium* by Pietro d'Abano, the *Secret of the Philosophers*, the *Schemhamphoras*, the book *Lamene* by Solomon, the anonymous book *On the Composition of the Names and Characters of the Evil Spirits*, the demonomagic treatise *Rubeus*, another pseudo-epigraph attributed to Albert, *On the Office of the Spirits*, attributed to Solomon, *The Bonds of the Spirits* and the *Pentacles of Salomon*, several works attributed to Tozgrec—Solomon's disciple whose name varies in Trithemius's transcriptions (Torzigeus, Totz Graecus, Tozigaeus, Thoczgraecus, etc.)—other books attributed to Mohammed, to Hermes, to Ptolemy, works of Arab, Western, or anonymous writers, etc.[61]

In 1508, Trithemius had read all these pamphlets, which he summarizes accurately. In most instances they deal with the seven planetary spirits, their physiognomies, their names, the graphic symbols needed to invoke them. Others—like the *Speculum Joseph*, whose *incipit* goes: *Si cupis videre omnia* (If you wish to see all that is)—contain tricks for catoptromancy or divination "through the personal mirror." The book attributed to Michael Scot, one of the great translators from the Arabic in the thirteenth century, reputed to be a formidable magician, instructs on the means to procure a familiar spirit. Solomon's book *Lamene*, or *Lamem*, deals with prediction of the future through the intermediary of demons, etc.

Trithemius might be thought of as a sort of sixteenth-century Sir James Frazer, a man who acquired remarkable erudition regarding popular and learned superstitions with the sole purpose of exposing their foolishness. It is certain, however, that the abbot did not confine himself to exposing magic but practiced it himself, while proclaiming his innocence at every opportunity.

The day after Palm Sunday 1499, Trithemius sent a letter to his friend Arnoldus Bostius, a Carmelite of Ghent, head of a "Fraternity of Joachim" founded about 1497, whose purpose was to defend the idea of St. Anne's immaculate conception of the Virgin and who counted the abbot of Sponheim among his most faithful members, along with Sebastian Brant and others. Unfortunately, when the letter arrived in Gand—shortly after Easter—Bostius had already departed for a better world and the prior of his monastery thought he had the right to read Trithemius's message and even to show it to the inquisitive. That was the beginning of the legend of Trithemius the sorcerer.

In fact, the letter was more sensational than compromising. Trithemius informed his friend of the projected work whose first book would be entitled *Steganography* (in our day it would be called cryptography), "which, when published, will astonish everyone." This first outline comprised four volumes (not five, as Klaus Arnold believes), the first two of which dealt with cryptography and writings in encaustic, the third of an accelerated method of learning a foreign language, and the fourth of cryptographical methods as well as occult subjects "which cannot be advanced in public."[62] Trithemius asserts, to be sure, that nothing he professes is transnatural, but on hearing him boast that according to his method the common man could master Latin *in two hours*, we are tempted to suspect that such a feat is impossible without the intervention of a very powerful spirit. This steganographic Art had come to its author through nocturnal revelation and had brought to fruition, no doubt, the promise that supernatural entities had made him at age fifteen: "to know all that there is in the world," not in an indirect sense (to accumulate bookish knowledge about everything), but in the most direct sense possible: that of knowing, every minute, what is going on elsewhere, and perhaps even in the future.

Later, Trithemius was rash enough to show the incomplete manuscript of the *Steganography* to the Picard Charles Bouelles, who in 1504 paid him a two-week courtesy visit. Bouelles riffled through the book for two hours and formed a very unfavorable opinion of it, which he conveyed to Germain de Ganay, bishop of Cahors, in a letter dated, according to Klaus Arnold, March 8, 1509[63] (Peuckert dates it 1506). According to Bouelles, the *Steganography* was nothing but dreadful hodgepodge of demonic incantations. When these accusations became publicly known, Trithemius had to defend himself against them in a writing now lost but whose bitter tone recurs in the preface to his *Polygraphia* dedicated to Emperor Maximilian.[64] He decided never to have the *Steganography* printed and even, according to some reports, burned the manuscript at Heidelberg, which might be true of the second part of this incomplete work.

To understand the first two books of the *Steganography* which Bouelles had glanced through, we have to consider time and insight. Now, Bouelles, in two hours, could only form an idea very far from the truth. This first part of the work is a *ludibrium,* a farce intended to mislead the reader; otherwise everyone would have at his disposal the keys to the cryptography and no one could make use of it in safety. If it was time that Bouelles was short of, it was insight that was lacking on the part of Johannes Wier, disciple of Agrippa, who had ample opportunity to read the manuscript at the latter's house. Without understanding anything about it, Wier corroborated Bouelles's accusations and devoted a very malicious chapter to Trithemius in his famous book *De Praestigiis Daemonum.*[65] The learned Jesuit Del Rio took possession of this version, and his influence sufficed to include the *Steganography,* beginning in 1609, in the *Index librorum prohibitorum.* But, after the first edition of 1606, defenses were written: it is enough to cite here those of Adam Tanner,[66] the abbot Sigismond Dullinger of Seeon,[67] Gustav Selenus,[68] Juan Caramuel y Lobkowitz,[69] Jean d'Espières,[70] and finally, those of Athanasius Kircher,[71] Wolfgang Ernest Heidel,[72] and Gaspar Schott.[73] The most interesting of these are, without any doubt, those of Caramuel and Heidel.

Caramuel is the first important interpreter of Trithemius's cryptography, which he recognizes as such and absolves from demonomagic. Caramuel indicates that demonic "incantations" are only encoded texts whereas the names of demons represent the code of messages.

Caramuel had analyzed only the first book of the *Steganography.* Heidel, who often contradicts and outstrips his predecessor, applies this method to the first two books, recognizing, moreover, that what remains of the third contains methods of an entirely different kind.

The first book of the *Steganography,* finished on March 27, 1500, offers the reader several ways to encode a seemingly incongruous message. From the demonic name heading the message, the receiver will be able to discern the code, which means removing all the letters that have no significance and selecting those that do. Here is an example of a "demonic incantation" in which should be read only the even letters of the even words, that is, the letters that occupy the positions 2, 4, 6, etc., in words also located in positions 2, 4, 6, etc.:

> parmesiel oShUrMi delmuson ThAfLoIn peano ChArUsTrEa melani LiAmUmTo colchan PaRoIs madin MoErLaI bulre aTlEoR don mElCoUe peloin, IbUtSiL meon mIsBrEaTh alini DrIaCo person. TrIsOlNaI lemom AsoSlE midar iCoRiEl pean ThAlMo, asophiel IlNoTrEoN baniel oCrImOs estenor NaElMa besrona ThUlAoMoR fronian bElDoDrAiN bon oTaLmEsGo merofas ElNaThIn bosramoth.

All that is required to obtain the following message is to extract the significant letters and divide them into segments:

SUM TALI CAUTELA UT PRIME LITERE CUIUSLIBET DICTIONIS SECRETAM INTENCIONEM TUAM REDDANT LEGENTI.

The second book, finished a month later, contains twenty-four series of alphabetical permutations, organized according to the "spirits" that govern the twenty-four hours of the day and the night. Spirits, of course, have nothing to do with it, and the permutations are carried out according to a very simple rule that consists of placing two alphabetical series next to each other, the first remaining in a fixed position:

A
B = A
C / B
etc.

In the same way, B = A, C = B, etc., until A = Z. Of course, the twenty-four permutations are not the only possible ones.

On March 21, 1508, Trithemius finishes his *Polygraphy*, which is to be dedicated to Emperor Maximilian on June 8 of the same year. This is a work of cryptography and shorthand, this time containing 384 alphabetical series in which a Latin word is substituted for each letter. Here Trithemius merely takes to its ultimate conclusion a method he has already used in his *Steganography*. The encoded text has the harmless form of a long prayer in Latin. By substituting a letter for each word we obtain the real enciphered message. The *Polygraphy* aroused public interest, as revealed by the fact it was translated into French by Gabriel de Collange in 1561. Trithemius did not know that, long before, the Roman curia had commissioned Leon Battista Alberti to provide them with a tract on cryptography and that the Florentine humanist had done so in 1472. The idea of circular permutations of the letters of the alphabet stems from exercises of Christian cabbala going as far back as Ramon Llull. Under the title of *Ars inveniendi* or *Ars combinatoria*, Llull had composed figures consisting of two or more superimposed and shifting circles, by displacing which it was possible to obtain all desired alphabetical substitutions. We can still see these figures, often rather complicated, in Giordano Bruno's commentaries. Trithemius's cryptography only avails itself of the "profane" aspect of this method of cabbalistic combinations—a sort of Christian *temurah*.

Though he does not deserve the title "father of cryptography," Trithemius must nonetheless be considered the "father of modern cryptography" as the author of the first work of major importance in this field.[74]

Returning to the *Steganography*: the first two books do not contain any demonic incantation whatever, and the names of spirits are, as Heidel accurately observed, *ficta et pro beneplacito assumpta*, fictitious and arbitrary.[75] It is really a farce with the purpose of confusing the public so that cryptography, having come to light, might not lose its efficacy. If everyone is able to read an encoded message, we might as well give up the benefits of this art. Trithemius succeeded brilliantly in carrying out his purpose: with the exception of Caramuel and Heidel, early scholars as well as their modern counterparts have continued to regard the *Steganography* as one of the most abstruse works of practical cabbala and occultism.

Whoever has read the first two books of the *Steganography* can only agree with Caramuel and Heidel. But the most interesting part of this unique work undoubtedly remains the fragment of the third book, which is not subject to their interpretation, brilliant as well as veracious and inoffensive.

Trithemius has had many apologists whose inability to understand the last book of the *Steganography* is easily explained. They are uncomfortable when speaking of it, willing to use the least likely hypotheses in justifying its existence. Thus, for example, Klaus Arnold, author of an excellent biography of Trithemius: "The third book remains incomplete, either because its author never mastered his aim of sending messages without graphic symbols or messenger, wishing to hide [this failure] by fragmentary and obscure clues, or because—though it seems unlikely—this part [of his work] can no longer be considered authentic."[76] Arnold cites, as representing this last hypothesis, the English scholar D. P.

Walker, who, however, never formulated it. And how could he have done so when Agrippa, who had met Trithemius, assured us he practiced this method and *that this method worked?* We shall take up his evidence later. For the time being it suffices to conclude that the five lines Arnold devotes to the magic part of the *Steganography* include no less than three errors: no one has dared to maintain—and certainly not the late D. P. Walker, a specialist on magic—that Trithemius was not the originator of this strange method; the reason the third book remained incomplete cannot be attributed to the ineffectiveness of its tricks, which, according to Agrippa, were infallible; Trithemius's directions are perhaps shocking but not in the least obscure, and their fragmentary nature results from the incomplete editing of the work, *from its condition at the time Trithemius himself allowed it to be put in circulation.*

Let the reader make up his own mind.

In *De septem secundeis* or *Chronologia mystica*[77] written in 1508, Trithemius reveals the secrets of the universe to Emperor Maximilian. The abbot avers, in a way that reminds us of Ficino, that God rules the cosmos through seven "secondary intelligences" (*intelligentiae sive spiritus orbes post Deum moventes*), none other than the planetary spirits: Orifiel, angel of Saturn, Anael, angel of Venus, Zachariel, angel of Jupiter, Raphael, angel of Mercury, Samael, angel of Mars, Gabriel, angel of the Moon, and Michael angel of the Sun. The third book of the *Steganography* takes this as its point of departure except that here the spirits are given a more distinct identity. In fact, they can be invoked by tracing their physiognomy and adding turns of phrase. The method is reminiscent of the art of symbols and shows striking analogies to mnemotechnics, with the difference that in our example the magician is changed into a painter in the most concrete sense of the word: he has to model in wax or draw on paper a form meant to represent a planetary angel, endowed with his attributes. This *creation* of the spirit is also meant to *invoke* its presence, assigning it a task which, in the example in question, relates to long-distance communications.

Other knowledge is necessary: the forms and names of all the spirits representing the zodiacal entities and also an astrological calculation.[78] Let us suppose that the performer wishes to send a long-distance message through the intermediary of Saturn's angel, Oriphiel. Here is what he must do.

> Make an image in wax or draw on a blank piece of paper the form of Orifiel in the guise of a nude, bearded man, standing on a multicolored bull, holding a book in his right hand and a pen in his left. After you have done this, say: "Let this image of the great Orifiel be honest, perfect, and qualified to trans-

mit my secret thoughts safely, faithfully and completely to my friend N., son of N. Amen. [Here another image must be drawn, representing the addressee.] Write on the forehead your name in encaustic made of diluted oil of roses [*temperato*] and on its chest the name of your absent friend, while saying: "This is the image of N., son of N., to whom this drawing conceived by my thoughts must be announced by Orifiel, angel of Saturn. Amen." Write on the forehead of your image MENDRION and on his chest THROESDE, and then unite the two images, saying: "Hear me, Orifiel, prince of the star of Saturn; by virtue of all-powerful God, obey me. I order you and send you, by means of this image, to transmit to N., son of N., the following message [compose this message] in a safe, secret and faithful way, without omitting anything I wish him to know and that I have charged you with. In the name of the Father, the Son and the Holy Ghost, Amen." After that, wrap up the two images, which have been joined together in a piece of clean material, washed in white water, and place them in one of the receptacles that the Indian wise men call *pharnat alronda*. Cover all that carefully with bark shaved off a tree and place the whole thing in the entrance of a closed house, wherever you wish. [This is a literal translation of the passage; actually we should expect to see the performer place it under the doorstep.] Without any doubt, your wish will be fulfilled within twenty-four hours.

The spirit can also be used by the addressee to send a message in the opposite direction.

After twenty-four hours, remove the images from the place you have put them and put them aside, for you can use them to work through the intermediary of Orifiel at any time, to transmit messages not only to the same friend but to anyone, merely having changed the name of the friend.[79]

By this method, the supernatural presences had revealed to Trithemius, in a dream, what must have been the wish closest to his heart: to know everything that was happening in the world. He says so himself, *using capital letters* on the next to last page of what remains of his *Steganography:*

ET OMNIA, QUAE FIUNT IN MUNDO, CONSTELLATIONE OBSERVATA PER HANC ARTEM SCIRE POTERIS.

In the very last passages of the fragment of the third book, Trithemius informs us that, by similar procedures, it is possible to learn everything about anything at all. Why does he stop there?

The most plausible hypothesis is that Trimethius, by means of the cooperation of the powerful planetary demons, also believed himself capable of predicting future events. Once again, Paul Grillandi gives us an indirect explanation of the reason Trithemius never finished this third book or—which is still more likely—why he burned it at Heidelberg. According to Grillandi,[80] all the magical procedures invoking the help of a demon *ad modum imperii* are not heretical but merely sacrilegious. On the other hand, foretelling the future *is always heretical*. Differentiations of this kind must have been current in Trithemius's time, and as an expert in occultism he must have been aware of them. In order to avoid committing the sin of heresy, he destroyed the final part of the autographic manuscript of the *Steganography*, which must, logically, have pertained to soothsaying. But he could not bear to destroy this part, which, albeit sacrilegious, he nonetheless considered to be one of the most useful methods of long-distance communication. This explains, moreover, why the *Steganography*, from 1609 until the nineteenth century, was listed in the *Index librorum prohibitorum*.[81]

The reader is invited to try out Trithemius's method for himself in order to judge of its effectiveness. While prevaricating about the "natural" character of this maneuver, Agrippa nevertheless praised its merits:

> It is possible in a natural way, removed from superstition and without the intercession of any spirit, for a man to transmit his trend of thought to another man at no matter what distance and location, in a very short time. It is not possible to estimate exactly the time it takes, but all that takes place within twenty-four hours. I knew how to do it myself, and I have often done it. Abbot Trithemius also knew how and used to do it. (*Occ. phil.*, I, 6, p. ix)

There are also sound reasons to doubt Agrippa's dogmatic statement. On reading the hopeless messages he so often sent to correspondents in no hurry to reply, I sometimes wonder why this occultist did not employ Trithemius's infallible method. Many episodes in Agrippa's biography show us that he was unable to obtain the friendly help of any spirit. On the other hand, in order to find out why he fell into the disfavor of Louise of Savoy, he does not hesitate to have recourse to biblical spells (which, moreover give him the answer), that he might have dispensed with had he profited from the assistance of a powerful planetary demon.[82]

Agrippa's remarks are valuable, however, for they confirm the authenticity of Trithemius's method. With regard to its effectiveness,

Agrippa's letter of November 19, 1527, to Brother Aurelio d'Aquapen-
dente seems to warrant some skepticism on the part of modern readers:
"As a humble mortal," Agrippa avers,

> consecrated knight in the blood of battle, courtier for almost a
> lifetime, attached by the bonds of the flesh to a beloved wife, a
> toy of the caprices of fortune, a slave to the world and to
> domestic cares, I could not claim to have the sublime gifts of
> the immortal gods. I do not have them at all. I only present
> myself as a sentinel at attention at the gate to point out the way
> to others [*velut indicem qui ipse semper prae foribus manens*].[83]

# III End Game

The Renaissance is a rebirth of the "occult sciences" and not, as taught in schools, the resurrection of classical philology and a forgotten vocabulary.

Will-Erich Peuckert

# 8| 1484

### (i)  A Wingless Fly

The historian too often tends to endow "facts" and the chronology of events with fundamental importance, forgetting that the causes of these "facts" are very complex and cannot be reduced to a denominator of an economic nature.

I do not intend to take up here what I have explained elsewhere in more detail.[1] The present study centers on the rise of modern science. Having established that modern science presupposes a very different mentality from that of the "sciences" of the Renaissance, the historian of ideas has not only the right but the duty to inquire into *the causes that have produced the tremendous change in human imagination* that has led to the transformation of the methods and goals of the natural sciences.

There are, of course, many superficial replies to this question fundamental to the history of our culture. Without the telescope, they say, Galileo could not have contributed to a more precise picture of the solar systems. Nevertheless, without using any optical instrument, Copernicus had long before envisaged a heliocentric (or heliostatic) universe according to a Pythagorean model. And, long before Copernicus, Nicholas of Cusa had postulated the infinitude of the universe, an outgrowth of ideas deriving from his personal metaphysics. This easily demonstrates that technical advances have played a marginal role in forming the spirit of modern science.

Another hypothesis, just as superficial, states that Renaissance sciences had amply demonstrated that they lacked utility. It was natural that they should have been replaced by sciences whose practical results—modern technology—compelled recognition due to their pragmatic "usefulness." The postulate of this thesis is that their very method put a check on the Renaissance sciences such as astrology, medicine, alchemy, and magic. We cannot deny that in quite numerous cases these "sciences" had failed. There is absolutely no reason, however, to doubt the confidence placed in them in their time.

Astrology was not infallible, but many of its predictions turned out to be more or less accurate or were adjusted in retrospect so that they seemed to pertain to recent events. Just as individual errors did not lower the prestige of an astrologer, so his correct or nearly correct predictions were capable of earning him an undeserved reputation. Whether truth or legend, the English astrologer John of Eschenden claims to have foreseen the plague epidemic of 1347–1348; the German astrologer Lichtenberger the birth and career of Luther; and another astrologer of the sixteenth century, Carion, said to have made many mistakes, seems to have predicted accurately the French Revolution of 1789. Far from being a fading science, sixteenth-century astrology inspired a general confidence which must have outstripped by far its *real* utility. However, it is only a posteriori that we can judge it; for people in the Renaissance the utility of astrology was esteemed as highly as the theory of radioactivity or of relativity is in our day.

With regard to astrological medicine—a very complicated and rigorous science—though it may have been founded on infantile premises, its natural remedies were to prove effective in some cases, which implies that its practical value was no less than that of astrology. The doctors themselves having no reason to scorn their own theoretical and practical knowledge, there is no cause to doubt they had the same assurance and self-possession as their modern colleagues, which, in less serious cases, must have sufficed to cure the patients. The patients themselves were usually so ignorant that they cared little about the doctor's methods provided they had personal confidence in him. In our day the situation has not much changed from this point of view, and if, by some miracle, all our doctors were supplanted by iatromathematicians or iatrochemists, most patients would not even notice it.

Of all the Renaissance sciences, alchemy experienced the most failures. Since, however, it had an important role to play in iatrochemical remedies and even in those of astrological medicine, we cannot altogether deny its utility. To the extent that it was closely connected with sciences whose effectiveness was accepted by most people, alchemy had no reason to believe itself fundamentally threatened. The great number of charlatans discredited it, of course; but Newton's application of alchemy shows us that it had not lost interest for the most enlightened minds of the seventeenth century. Some historians of science still wonder why, if alchemy was of basic importance to Newton, he published everything except his alchemical experiments.[2] The answer is so simple that it is surprising it has been avoided or distorted so systematically. Newton lived in an era marked by the victory of Puritanism on the political level. Puritanism despised occult sciences because they did not conform to the spirit of the Bible. Newton did not make his alchemical experiments public because he had his head on his shoulders and preferred to have it stay there. For the psychological and even physical restraints imposed by the Church's reform—Protestant as well as Catholic—were no less than those imposed by the French Revolution at its height or—mutatis mutandis—by the Soviet revolution.

With regard to magic, there is no doubt that it was as useful at the time of the Renaissance as was astrology. Let us not forget that, under the rubric of "natural magic," very varied kinds of technical knowledge were in circulation—from the manufacture of animal and vegetable dyes to pyrotechnics and optical procedures—as well as theurgic and medical procedures, methods of cryptography, of stenography, and telecommunication. Let us also not forget the techniques for manipulation of the individual and the masses which have only been fully applied in our day. As for the Art of Memory, it worked so well that it is astonishing that it fell into disuse in the seventeenth century.

It is quite obvious that the Renaissance sciences, whatever their *real* value may have been, did not lack *relative use value*. All contemporary evidence to the contrary is suspicious, since it stems from writers seeking easy influence over their public. Giordano Bruno, a firm believer, did not hesitate, in his comedy *Il Candelaio*, to satirize Ficino's theory of mind and spirit but he put it in the mouth of an unscrupulous charlatan. The conclusions based on passages of this type borrowed from the Italian writers[3] are irrelevant, like judging Socrates' personality in the light of Aristophanes' plays. When all is said and done, the minorities during the Renaissance who enjoyed the satires on contemporary sciences must have been much less numerous and powerful than the organized groups who, in our time, protest against the use of modern technology.

Another realm in which a very mistaken picture of the Renaissance prevails is the teaching and transmission of knowledge. There were famous universities at the time, proud of their tradition, which conferred prized degrees. These degrees affected the practice of a profession to such an extent that we see Agrippa of Nettesheim, in order to obtain a position, assume false titles which, even with the royal privilege that seemingly made them unnecessary, he definitely needed. There is no doubt that a degree from the Sorbonne or the University of Padua represented a guarantee, for these institutions of higher learning were reputed to convey infallible knowledge whose usefulness in a given social context it would be idle to dispute, just as it would be idle to dispute in this instance their *absolute* value of a practical nature.

The mistake in principle made by most cultural historians amounts to denying the validity, *nowadays*, of that knowledge and those degrees. It is obvious that no university in the world would agree to grant the chair of theoretical physics or medical semiology to a graduate of the Sorbonne of 1500. But this strange reasoning does not carry the conviction that, since the knowledge of a graduate in the year 1500 is rejected in our time, it was also rejected by its contemporaries—without taking into account the existence of disciplines in the humanities wherein we could place far more faith in a degree from the sixteenth century than in one dated 1987.

Renaissance society reveals few signs of decadence: it is not in a state of crisis and has very superficial doubts concerning its own institutions and ideological and practical truths. The hypothesis that the developing sciences lacked practicality must be discarded. It is merely an a posteriori explanation of the transformation of the scientific spirit and, as such, must be discarded as untrue.

On the other hand, if we wish to understand anything about that historical enigma the rise of modern science—which occurred just when *it was not needed*—we must first go to the heart of the Renaissance sciences, of which astrology, because of its universality, was the most important (magic, medicine, and even alchemy can be regarded, in a way, as astrological disciplines). Another fundamental factor of Renaissance ideology is Christian doctrine and the Church, which never altogether accepts the message of "science": revealed truth has hegemony over all temporal truth, which can only be relative to the former.

Modern science emerges from an interaction of very complex ideological forces by a process resembling the natural selection of species. Now we know that this is not determined by a providential law but rather by environmental accidents, accidents which Jacques Monod has, perhaps erroneously, called "chance."

What chance has a wingless fly to obtain food in our climate? None, because, not having means to move quickly and without a reliable shelter like subterranean worms, it will easily fall prey to birds. This genetic mutant will be eliminated by natural selection. However, this is the same selection which, on a very windy island in the Galapagos archipelago, wiped out the "normal" population of flies equipped with wings, which are incapable of fighting the wind. Only wingless flies were spared, because they move on the ground and birds find it hard to catch them.

A wingless fly is, by definition, a "sick" fly, that particular mutation depriving it of the ability to survive. In a certain ecological niche, however, it is only these mutations, these aberrant products of nature, that have the good fortune to be preserved.

This is exactly what happened to the modern scientific spirit, the spirit

of experimentation that abandons broad assumptions in order to construct purely inductive arguments. It was no bird of paradise, hatched
all at once by Providence or the (nonexistent) laws of the triumphant
history of the Hegelian spirit to replace the Renaissance sciences, worth-
less and henceforth without appeal. On the contrary, our modern scientific spirit was born like a wingless fly which, in the fierce whirlwinds of
the history of the sixteenth century, had the good luck to remain unobserved and not to be eliminated by harsh natural selection. The latter
struck Renaissance sciences so hard that they could never right themselves again.

Let us examine more closely the situation in which our wingless fly
becomes able to procreate. The witch-burning stakes covered Europe;
the Reformation would have preferred that the only book surviving on
earth be the Bible, but in any case it was not inclined to tolerate either
Eros or magic or the contiguous "sciences" of the Renaissance. A magic
invocation or an alchemical experiment could cost a man his head. Fear
justified everything, and that is why people gave up astrology, magic,
and alchemy or retired into cautious silence, as did Newton, on matters
of an occult nature. The Catholic Church not only called for a change in
morals but also undertook the zealous defense of what it considered
most previous, Thomism. Galileo brushed against the stake not because
he was a representative of "modern science" (which he surely was not),
but because he dared to oppose Thomism. Bruno was consumed by
flames because he was an unrepentant magician, not because he defended the ideas of the cardinal of Cusa. Everywhere people engaged in
less offensive occupations, which could not run counter to the image of
the world and of human society that conformed with one or another of
the Christian churches. They were coerced into expressing themselves
cautiously, into carefully hiding their goals. Some enthusiastic Pythago-
reans remained, a Galileo or a Kepler, but their kind was being stamped
out. There were Descartes and Bacon, still strongly suspected of having
sympathized with the farce of the Rosicrucians and whose real inten-
tions it is not easy to decipher. Were they the representatives of a new
world? If so, they certainly did not represent the forthcoming world any
more than their philosophy was a "modern philosophy."

At a given moment, censorship transformed personality: people had
lost the habit of using their imagination and thinking in terms of "qualities," for it was no longer permitted. Loss of the faculty of active imagination naturally entailed strict observation of the material world
revealed by an attitude of respect for all quantitative data and suspicion
for every "qualitative" statement.

In a certain sense it can be said that flies that fly have a completely different image of the world than that of flies that crawl, lacking wings. But this comparison seems to imply a value judgment it does not wish to make. Renaissance man and present-day man may have the same external form, but the latter is a psychological mutation of the former, within the same species. Those who contend that people of the Renaissance felt, thought and acted like us are greatly mistaken. On the contrary, we have the time-honored custom of seeking within ourselves the world image of the Renaissance person, to such an extent that he is confused with our own "unconscious," with what we have learned to uproot and mutilate within ourselves. He is a sickly colleague that we still harbor within ourselves because we cannot rid ourselves of him. If he is a caricature of ourselves—since he collects all our most infantile and absurd traits—let us put ourselves in his place for a moment: of course, it is most likely that he has no more flattering an image of us than we have of him. But any communication is impossible, for the barriers of the era do not give way. And there is even less hope that this disturbing visitor from our depths may disappear forever.

For lack of reaching a friendly understanding, we must learn to gaze at him without too much condescension. For we have lost that which he had and he lacks what we have mastered. When all is said and done, these quantities are equal. And, if we have accomplished some of the most burning wishes of his imagination, we must not forget that we have destroyed just as many others, which may prove to be irretrievable.

### (ii) Why Was the Year 1484 So Formidable?

In the kind of history popular with our contemporaries, emphasis is placed on events which, for the people of the Renaissance, were only of secondary importance. On the other hand, we obviously overlook what in their view was crucial.

If we look at its chronology, the year 1484 is not particularly interesting: Columbus had not yet left, the Turks were not forcing the gates to the West any more than usual, the Neapolitan war had not yet broken out causing the spreading of syphilis throughout Europe, the Reformation was still far away. The only event attributable to that year is the birth of Luther, although modern writers prefer to date it 1483, Luther himself inclining sometimes toward one date, sometimes toward the other.

It is therefore surprising to learn that the astrologers of the period attributed tremendous importance to the year 1484. At least this time no a posteriori revision occurred, since those who expected something visible and tangible to happen in 1484 were all too disappointed.

Al-Kindī, whose theory of stellar radiations is already known to us, had also formulated a theory of the general conjunctions of planets and their influence on the fate of religions. The general conjunctions depend on the periodic conjunctions of the higher planets, Jupiter and Saturn, since they advance the slowest. According to al-Kindī, there were "little conjunctions of planets occurring every twenty years and finally greater ones every 960 years. The latter exert a crucial influence not only on observable nature but also on political and religious deeds; every great conjunction inaugurated a new era in history."[4] The Christian Middle Ages knew of this theory through the *Liber magnarum coniunctionum* by Albumasar, a disciple of al-Kindī. Roger Bacon applies it to the birth of great personalities in history and to real (or false) prophets at intervals of 320 years. In his list we find first Alexander the Great, then Jesus, Mani, and Mohammed.[5]

In fact, a *coniunctio magna* had occurred, in 7–6 B.C., in the signs of the Fish and the Ram. Kepler, who had carefully studied the *coniunctio magna* of 1604 (in Sagittarius), wrote two treatises (*De stella nova* and *De Vero anno*) in which he deals with the "true date" of the Savior's birth.

At the time of the conjunction of 1604, a *nova* appeared in the sky "at the very place where the three [higher] planets had converged."[6] This is why Kepler believes that a new star had also announced the birth of Jesus—and that it was the star of the Magi:

> This effect of the great conjunctions cannot be adequately explained by nature; God himself had to arrange it in some way: experience bears witness that he placed in the sky these great conjunctions with miraculous stars *extra ordinari* or other admirable works of His providence. This is why he decided to place the birth of His son, Christ, our Savior, at the very moment of the great conjunction of the signs of the Fish and the Ram, *circa punctum equinoctialem,* by emphasizing this dual fact, the event that occurred on earth and the conjunctions revealed in the sky through the appearance of a new star; by means of this He guided the Magi from the East to Palestine, to the important village of Bethlehem and the stable where the King of the Jews was born.[7]

Kepler was not alone in following the conjunction of 1604; the editors of Rosicrucian manifestos also speculated on it, for they date the death of Christian Rosenkreuz in 1484 and the date of discovery of his tomb in 1604, representing the exact interval between two great conjunctions.[8] We must not be surprised that the "farce" of the Rosicrucians fired the great minds of the Europe of those times with enthusiasm: the dates

perfectly coincided with the astrological data, and a new world was expected after 1604. The disclosure of the secret order founded by Christian Rosenkreuz could only gratify to the full the hope aroused by the
event whose importance is emphasized by Kepler. When Johann Valentin Andreae, who was one of the principal authors, characterized the
Rosicrucian manifestos as *ludibrium*—which they actually were—no one
wished to believe him. And Frances A. Yates explains many facets of
Descartes's existence by a stubborn pursuit of the Rosicrucians, whose
tracks, in a sense, he rediscovered.[9]

Kepler was neither the first nor the last to busy himself with the horoscope of Jesus Christ. Cardinal Pierre d'Ailly (1350–1425) had set the
fashion that was followed during the Renaissance by the great astrologer
Luca Gaurico and the equally famous Girolamo Cardan. The horoscope
projected by Pierre d'Ailly and taken up by Cardan was the basis for all
ensuing efforts of this kind, such as that of Ebenezer Sibly (*A Complete
Illustration of the Occult Sciences*, 1790). What could be read in Jesus' horoscope? His divine paternity, the birth of a royal house, the Virgin birth,
his humility, his death sentence, and his crucifixion,[10] in short, the
whole history of his human life and death. Of course, the fact that a
cardinal and a bishop (Gaurico) dealt with this signifies that the enterprise, though neither commonplace nor safe, was nevertheless possible
within certain limits. Indeed, if we grant the thesis of Jesus' two natures—divine and human—it is not absurd to apply to the *man* the limitations of astral destiny. To be sure, the Church did not look well upon
these efforts or upon astrology as a whole.

D'Ailly, Gaurico, and Cardan had treated the subject of Jesus' birth
according to conventional data; Kepler computed it for the spring of 6
B.C., and Sibly, we know not why, for December 25, A.D. 45. Of them
all, Kepler, influenced by the astrological events of the year 1604, is the
cleverest, because he establishes a relationship between the birth of the
Savior, a *coniunctio magna*, and the appearance of a nova.

The doctrine of conjunctions, derived from al-Kindī and Albumasar,
was linked to various theories of cosmic cycles formulated by Roger
Bacon, Peter of Abano, the abbot Trithemius, Adam Nachemoser, Kepler, and others. There is no perfect agreement among them, but they all
stem from al-Kindī's data, which Peuckert sums up thus:

> The conjunction of the higher planets repeats every 20 years;
> it changes 4 times in succession between the signs of a tri-
> angle; finally, at the end of 240 years, it passes over to the
> triangle following in the order of signs and repeats its cycle;
> likewise in the 3d and 4th triangles. After 4 times 240 years

(960), it is at its point of departure, the first sign of the 1st triangle, at the same degree as at the beginning, and in passing over to the next degree, it begins a new cycle. There are, therefore, three principal periods or cycles:

1. The small cycle, of 20 years duration, between two conjunctions;
2. The medium cycle, of 240 years duration, from one triangle to the other;
3. The large cycle, of 960 years duration, lasting until the return of the conjunction to the same place in the zodiac.

The last, which is almost a millennium, marks a complete renewal of the world; that involves in particular a new religion. The medium one confines itself to great political upheavals, changes of government, etc. Finally, the small cycle generally indicates important events, royal successions, revolutions, and other crises of the State.[11]

If we took these numbers literally, the years 1484 and 1604 would be excluded from the list of all the conjunctions. Now, very important conjunctions occurred in 1345 in Aquarius, in 1484 in Scorpio, and in 1604 in Sagittarius. In December 1348, in his *Summa iudicialis de accidentibus mundi*, the English astrologer John of Eschenden wrote, apropos of the plague that had just ravaged Europe:

> It is exactly what I had written in the year 1345. For all that I had written then concerning the events of which I have just spoken corresponded to the opinion of many astronomers. The disasters I predicted occurred just after 1345 and on a grand scale. The mortality in 1347 and 1348 was such that the whole world seemed to be in a state of revolution and in many countries towns and villages were deserted; rare survivors fled those places, leaving their houses and their household goods behind; no one dared even to visit the sick or bury the dead for fear of contagion.[12]

Since John of Eschenden was referring in 1348, to an earlier prophecy that we do not have, we might conclude that he only formulated it after the event. On the other hand, we know that in Italy, in the fifteenth century, people awaited the coming of a prophet[13] who was supposed to be born or reveal himself in 1484. In October 1484, the Dutchman Paul of Middelburg, bishop of Urbino, wrote his *Prognostica ad viginti annos duratura*, in which he tried to spread out the birth of the prophet in the belief that the results of the conjunction would extend over a period of twenty years. Consequently, the "little prophet" should have been born in 1503 and should have been active for nineteen years.[14] Paul of Middelburg complained of having been plagiarised by the German, Johannes de Clara Monte (Lichtenberger), in his *Practica*; Middelburg's complaint, written in 1492, was contained in his *Invectiva in superstitiosum quemdam astrologum*, which did not later prevent Lichtenberger's prophecies from creating a great stir in northern Europe since they were envisaged as having most strangely presaged the coming of Luther. Here is what Lichtenberger predicted about the conjunction of Jupiter and Saturn in Scorpio, November 25, 1484:

> This remarkable constellation and concordance of the planets shows that a little prophet will be born who will give an excellent interpretation of the Scriptures and will also furnish responses with great respect for the divine Being and will rally human souls to Him. For astrologers call little prophets those who bring about changes in the laws or create new ceremonies or a different interpretation to the word considered by men to be divine. . . .
>
> I say that in the land under the sign of Scorpio [Germany] a prophet will be born, and beforehand the strangest and most extraordinary things will be seen in the heavens, but it is not possible to say at which end of the earth, the south or the north, since such numerous divergences exist in the opinions of scholars. Albumazar thinks it will be in Aquarius, and toward the south. But most astrologers think it will occur toward the north. Be that as it may, says Messahala, he will be born in a country moderately warm and humid. . . .
>
> A monk is seen wearing a white robe with the devil standing on his shoulders. He wears a full-length greatcoat with wide sleeves and a young monk follows him. . . .
>
> He will have a very quick mind, know many things, and possess great wisdom; however, he will often lie and have a heretical conscience. And, like a Scorpion, for that conjunction occurs in the House of Mars and its shadows, he will often emit a venomous sting from his tail. And he will be the cause of great bloodlettings. And since Mars will announce him, it seems he will confirm the beliefs of the Chaldeans, as evinced by Messahala.[15]

Luther was probably born November 10, 1483, but Philipp Melanchthon, who firmly believed in astrology, connects his birth with the prophecies of Lichtenberger so that alternative dates appear, notably October 22 and November 23, 1484. The most fashionable astrologer of the time, Luca Gaurico, calculated Luther's horoscope based on October 22 at ten minutes past one in the morning; it clearly revealed the substance and destiny of a heretic. On the other hand, the German astrologers Carion and Reinhold, both in favor of the Reformation, calculated it for the same date but at nine in the morning, which yielded an entirely different result.

All of the above stems from the astrologers' sympathies for one or the other party. What could not be in doubt was that in Italy and northern Europe the coming of a "little prophet" was expected in 1484 because of the conjunction of Saturn and Jupiter in the triangle of Aquarius: the testimony of Paul of Middelburg and of Johannes Lichtenberger is explicit.

The results of the conjunction, however, were to include another realm as well. This time the explanation could only be a posteriori, which did not preclude its having been generally accepted. We know that, if the plague wreaked havoc in the fourteenth century, syphilis—which was regarded as a form of plague—did no less between the sixteenth and nineteenth centures. Imported from America, the "French disease" developed into a terrible epidemic during the campaigns of Charles VIII in Naples (1495).[16] At the beginning of the sixteenth century, Joseph Grünpeck, astrologer at the court of Maximilian of Austria, gave an astrological explanation for this phenomenon in his *Tractatus de Pestilentiali Siorra sive Mala de Frantzos, Originem Remediaque Ejusdem Continens. Compilatus a venerabili viro Magistro Joseph Grünpeck de Burckhausen super Carmina quaedam Sebastiani Brant utriusque Juris Professoris.*[17] This is what Grünpeck wrote: "Brought down upon the world is this cruel disease, unheard of and unbelievable, the French disease that the conjunction [of 1484] caused to cross over from France into Northern Italy and thence into Germany; that is brought about, as we have seen, because Jupiter rules over France; now [Jupiter] is a hot and humid planet."[18] The same interpretation is resumed and explored in depth by the astrologer Astruc (1684–1765) in his treatise *De morbis venereis* of 1736.[19]

It is remarkable that the local treatment with mercury—which is still used in our time, not ineffectually—was originally nothing but an astrological and alchemical remedy for the *malum de Frantzos*.[20]

The epidemic of syphilis and the birth of Luther, the reformer, were only the tangible results subsequently attributed to the conjunction of November 25, 1484. Its intangible results were, however, of much greater importance. Although the great European witch craze did not start before the second half of the sixteenth century, historians are in agreement that the signal for the witch hunt was the papal bull *Summis de-siderantes affectibus*. The date it was promulgated is striking: December 5, 1484, right after the conjunction of 25 November!

We know that Innocent VIII would become a formidable adversary of cabbala; he would persecute Pico della Mirandola and threaten the canon Marsilio Ficino. That implies that he constantly received information about the occult sciences. An event as important as the conjunction of 1484, which he could read about in the rather worrisome work by Paul de Middelburg, took place in time to magnify his fears. If he had waited a few years, Lichtenberger's pamphlet would have shown him that the "little prophet" he would have to defend himself against was a monk dressed in white . . .

It is more than probable that the treatise of Paul of Middelburg called the attention of the pope to what was happening in Germany. But the bull, recommending extreme repression of the cult of witchcraft in Germany, represented the immediate consequence of an encounter between Innocent and Henry Institoris, Inquisitor for Upper Germany and the brain behind the *Malleus maleficarum* (1486). Institoris was a crank; bull in hand, he went from place to place, arousing the sincere hatred of all local bishops. Fanatics like him or the inquisitor Pedro Arbues of Zaragoza would usually meet a sudden death at that time. Only a miracle may have saved Institoris, who died, as it seems, *of natural causes* between 1501 and 1503.

The action taken by the German inquisitor is just an isolated case at the end of the fifteenth century. The prosecution of witches grows more intense in the sixteenth century as a result of the Reformation.

Systematic witch hunting did not start until the end of the sixteenth century (1589 in Germany), a time when the Holy Inquisition was no longer active in Northern Europe, at least in Protestant Germany. Even the great trial of 1589 in Bavaria was instituted by the lay authorities. One can legitimately conclude that the 1484 bull was indeed the signal for the witch craze, but the Church subsequently withdrew from actual prosecution during the sixteenth century; John Tedeschi has brilliantly confirmed this (see Bibliography).

Joseph Hansen and, more recently, Jeffrey Burton Russell have shown that the great witch burnings took place in the richest European countries: France (including Lombardy under French jurisdiction), the Rhineland, and the Netherlands. In none of these territories did the Inquisition conduct the prosecutions and trials. Though obvious for the Protestant countries, this statement might seem surprising with respect to France; but the outstanding work of Robert Mandrou has demonstrated that, until 1682, when the *ordonnance royale* of Louis XIV dismissed witches' trials as irrelevant to justice itself, it was the local lay authorities who burned witches.

One can assert without any doubt that there is an immediate connection between the witch craze and the European Reformation. In a sense, the witch craze was the social counterpart of the destruction of religious images: in both cases, the victim was human fantasy. The idea behind the *Malleus* is to stop the social disorder caused by the exercice of magic. This book became an ally of the Reformation and Counterreformation in the sixteenth century, prefiguring the spirit of those movements.

# 9| Censoring Phantasy

### (i) Abolition of the Phantasmic

It is probably due to the influence of liberal Protestants that some history books still maintain that the Reformation was a movement of emancipation, whose aim was to free people from the repressive tutelage of the Catholic Church. Considering the multiplicity of Protestant sects, this idea might not be totally wrong, but it surely does not correspond to the original purposes of the Reformation, or to the ideologies of the main reformed denominations, Lutheranism and Calvinism.

In leafing through history textbooks, we often come across this explanation of the Reformation: at the beginning of the sixteenth century there was a rich Church, organized into a powerful State and acting as such; the clergy and monks, for the most part, were also occupied with worldly things; trade in religious articles prospered; Luther came to end this situation through *liberal reform:* he granted the clergy the right to marry, he rescinded dealings in indulgences and the cult of images, he reduced to a minimum the external forms of ritual in order to concentrate on inward religious experience.

This is an explanation that takes results for causes and is satisfied with a moralistic point of view which, though useful in principle, is nevertheless dangerous in application. On the contrary, a breath of liberal air had been circulating in the Renaissance Church, which, through the cleavage between the modern mentality of the clergy and Christian morality, had led to many abuses. It was at this point that Luther arrived on the scene to reestablish the purity of the Christian message.

Far from appearing as a liberal movement, the Reformation represented, on the contrary, a radical-conservative movement within the bosom of the Church, where it had several precursors (of whom it will suffice to mention here the preacher Savonarola in Florence).

The Reformation did not claim to "emancipate" the individual; on the other hand it aimed to reestablish in the world a *Christian order* it believed the Catholic Church—which in its view had become a temporal institution—was unable to maintain.

This is why the reformers consider the Church to be a supererogation which does not answer to the spirit of Christianity, and, by returning to the Bible, they intend not only to refute Catholicism but also *to reestablish the original purity of the Christian community.*

The revival of interest in eschatology, iconoclasm, rejection of traditional ecclesiastical practices, general participation in the creed, acceptance of marriage of the clergy as a *malum necessarium* permitted by St. Paul, are only a few aspects of the Reformation. Its most important result which, under the influence of Melanchthon, will in the final analysis be less apparent in the Lutheran Church than in that of John Calvin in Geneva and among the English Puritans, is the *total rejection of the "pagan" culture of the Renaissance, of which the sole substitute is the study of the Bible.* To attain this goal, the Protestant denominations do not hesitate to launch an intolerance which at first exceeded the intolerance of the Catholic Church, made more indulgent by the experience of the Renaissance.

Characteristic of the Reformation is the fact that, recognizing no cultural reference other than the Bible, it repeated a situation in the history of primitive Christianity that corresponded to a phase of its birth: a Jewish sect engaging, rather hesitantly, in a dialogue with the Gentiles. Far from abrogating the Torah, the sect accepts the Old Testament as a whole, except to state that the life of the Christian is located not under the sign of the Law but under the sign of Grace. Now the Jewish religion is distinctive because, drawing its originality from the reaction against the Canaanitic cults, it has no graven images and it attempts to give a *historical* meaning to that which was represented by the neighboring peoples as periodical fertility cults.[1]

Hence, one of the most important goals of the Reformation is to root out the cult of idols from the Church. The results of this iconoclasm are tremendous if we consider the controversies about the Art of Memory aroused by Bruno in England: ultimately, the Reformation leads to *a total censorship of the imaginary, since phantasms are none other than idols conceived by the inner sense.*

Renaissance culture was a culture of the phantasmic. It lent tremendous weight to the phantasms evoked by inner sense and had developed to the utmost the human faculty of *working actively upon and with phantasms.* It had created a whole dialectic of Eros in which phantasms, which at first foisted themselves upon inner sense, ended by being manipulated at will. It had a firm belief in the power of phantasms, which were transmitted by the phantasmic apparatus of the transmittor to that of the receiver. It also believed that inner sense was preeminently the locale for manifestations of transnatural forces—demons and the gods.

By asserting the idolatrous and impious nature of phantasms, the Reformation abolished at one stroke the culture of the Renaissance. And, since all the Renaissance "sciences" were structures built on phantasms, they too had to be overpowered by the weight of the Reformation.

But, we ask, what was the reaction of the Catholic Church? At bottom, outside the obvious drawbacks of an internal division, the spirit of the Reformation could only suit it very well. In response to Luther and to Puritanism, the Church embarked on its own reform (which historians usually call the Counterreformation). Far from consolidating the positions assumed by Catholicism during the Renaissance, this movement severed itself completely from them and went in the same directions as protestantism. It was along the lines of *severity and harshness* that the Reformation developed, from the Protestant as well as the Catholic side.

The Counterreformation, however, has its own important characteristics. At the Council of Trent, which took place in the second half of the sixteenth century, the Church made clear its new style of behavior. It decided to assign the instrument of the Inquisition, which had been created in the twelfth century at the time of the anti-Cathar campaigns and had traditionally been in the hands of the Dominicans to a new, rigorous order dating from the sixteenth century: the Society of Jesus, founded by Ignatius of Loyola. Henceforth, the name of the Holy Inquisition is intertwined with that of the Jesuits.

In the spiritual practices of the Jesuits, the phantasmic culture of the Renaissance is revealed in all its power for the last time. Indeed, education of the imagination represents the teaching method of Ignatius of Loyola in his *Spiritual Exercises*, printed in 1596. The disciple is called upon to practice a sort of Art of Memory. During these exercises he must imagine the atrocious tortures of Hell, the sufferings of humanity before the incarnation of Christ, the birth and childhood of the Lord, his preaching at Jerusalem—while Satan, from his dwelling place in Babylon, launches attacks by his demons throughout the world—and, finally, Calvary, the crucifixion and resurrection of Christ. It is a question not of pure meditation but of an internal phantasmic theater in which the practitioner must imagine himself in a role of spectator. He is not only to record what happens but to observe the actors through the senses of sight, hearing, and touch (*Secunda Hebdomada, dies* I–VII). Introjected in his own phantasmic apparatus, the phantasm of the practitioner is to participate—in a more or less active way—in the development of the scenario.

Loyola's exercises obviously derive from the great achievements of the Renaissance in the manipulation of phantasms. But here these phantasms are placed at the service of faith, to accomplish the reform of the Church, which amounts to saying that *they are actively in opposition to the legacy of the Renaissance.*

In Loyola, we find that the culture of the phantasmic directs its weapons against itself. At the end of several decades, this process of self-destruction will be almost complete.

### (ii) Some Historic Paradoxes

I intend here to go beyond generalizations. The nature and progress of the Reformation, on both the Protestant and the Catholic sides, will be illustrated by some examples chosen at random. I have not tried to trace the history or the phenomenology of the Reformation. This book attempts, in fact, to record the concepts of a phantasmic era, their rise and fall. The Reformation interests me only to the extent that it produced censorship of the phantasmic and, consequently, a profound change in human imagination.

In contrast to the first two parts of this book, part 3 does not subject the culture of the Reformation to rigorous analysis. That culture will be touched upon here only inasmuch as it still harbors vague recollections of the *mundus imaginalis* of the Renaissance, which it attempts by all possible means to exorcise and to annihilate. During the sixteenth century we witness a very typical phenomenon, the *ambivalence* of the culture of individuals such as Cornelius Agrippa or Giorando Bruno. The representatives of the phantasmic Renaissance are no less subject to the profound influence of Protestantism. Sometimes those two irreconcilable directions of the mind remain side by side without mixing: this is the case with Agrippa, not only one of the most famous writers on occultism but also one of its most savage opponents! But there are also tenuous conciliatory measures, such as the one attempted by Bruno, which proved to be impracticable and which resulted, for its originator, in a bloody defeat.

In the seventeenth century we observe two curious phenomena: the Reformation comes to fruition, and people begin to think, to speak, to act, and to dress in an entirely new way, but this occurs in the Protestant faction as well as in the Catholic, so that, despite the *external* differences between the Churches, the difference between the *spirit* of the Protestant Reformation and the *spirit* of the Catholic one are reduced to empty questions, such as the dispensing of communion, the confession of sins, and marriage of the clergy. A process of *normalization* occurs now, finding expression in the appearance of a new culture with more or less unitary traits from London to Seville and from Amsterdam to Wittenberg, Paris, and Geneva. At the very time the Christian sects born of the schism in the West finally recognize their deep-seated antagonisms, those antagonisms end up by limiting themselves to matters of internal organization which have nothing to do with the fundamental question of the essence of Christianity. Without abandoning its millenary traditions, the Catholic Church moves towards Protestantism; for its part, Protestantism, without giving up the reforms for which it had done victorious battle on the local front, becomes consolidated in big institutions which more and more resemble the Catholic Church. The Catholic faith and the Protestant denominations have drawn as close together as possible without being aware of it. Henceforth it is no longer a question of Reformation and Counterreformation. Ever unwilling to recognize it, the principal Western faiths no longer fight alone. Side by side, they build a common edifice: modern Western culture. Individuals can still harbor deep suspicions regarding those who, they think, are on the other side of the barricades. In their total adhesion to their party, to their institution, they do not even perceive that those they consider adversaries resemble them and that the conflict at issue is no longer the essence of Christianity but merely a few matters of internal organization. The pagan culture of the Renaissance has been vanquished. To that result Catholics and Protestants contributed equally, unaware that, far from fighting among themselves, they had done battle against a common enemy.

All of this seems quite simple without necessarily being so. The Reformation, at its inception, draws into its orbit—even though it disavows them almost immediately—an extremely varied series of movements of the "left," on a scale that goes from liberalism to libertinism, from utopianism to the spirit of revolution, from antiauthoritarianism to egalitarianism. These movements had appeared as a direct result of the Renaissance and, in their most useful manifestations, worked in conformity with the spirit and "sciences" of the Renaissance.

At the beginning of the seventeenth century, a liberal and utopian Catholicism still exists, represented by Brother Tommaso Campanella, who, after more than twenty years of persecution, nevertheless finds a pope in need of his knowledge of spiritual magic. In his reclusion, Campanella is visited by one of Johann Valentin Andreae's group of friends. The influence of the Calabrian monk on the liberal Protestant movement concealed behind the "farce" of the Rosicrucians cannot be ignored. The singularity of the great thinkers who gravitate around this movement—a Robert Fludd, a Kepler, a Descartes, or a Bacon—is that they refuse to subject themselves entirely to the reformed religion and continue to seek their sources of inspiration in the culture of the Renaissance. We are at the beginnings of modern science, which represent a continuation of the Renaissance insofar as the great discoveries of the seventeenth century still derive from the postulate of analogies between microcosm and macrocosm and from a complex of Pythagorean ideas about the harmony of the world; we are also at the beginnings of a negation of the Renaissance, insofar as the spirit of the Reformation produces a substantial modification of the human imagination.

As for the liberal and utopian movements, persecuted by the official churches—in a Europe rigorously moralistic and divided between two powers which, though enemies in principle, have the same essential spirit—they will finally gain an enormous underground influence in the form of secret societies.

The progress of the spirit of liberal institutions represents another of history's enigmas, outside the province of this book. In the beginning, Protestantism—be it Luther's conservative movement in Germany or the Calvinist terror in Geneva or the Puritan terror in England—was certainly no more liberal than the Jesuits. Nevertheless, we see in England the appearance of democratic institutions, whereas the Jesuits, before their expulsion from Latin America, organized on that continent the first communist experiment in modern history and possibly the only one that ever worked. It is not impossible that these paradoxes can be explained as an extension—or a revenge?—of the culture of the Renaissance.

### (iii) The Controversy about Asinity

Before publishing his treatise *On Occult Philosophy,* written in 1509–10,[2] Cornelius Agrippa in 1530 published a work which refuted the burgeoning "sciences," *De incertitudine et vanitate scientiarum atque artium.*[3] It is a bird's-eye view of worldly vanity sparing neither society with its defects, nor the professions, nor the sciences of the period, nor even theology and religion.

In expressing agreement with the spirit of the Reformation, Agrippa announces his opposition to the Catholic cult of images and relics. He stigmatizes the clergy's greed and evinces an intransigent hostility toward the Inquisition and all the monastic orders, "insolent gang of hooded monsters."[4] "It is the very language," Auguste Proste remarks, "of the most violent sectarians of the Reformation in the sixteenth century and the general tone of the adversaries of the Church of Rome of the period."[5]

But Agrippa is far from confining himself to that; in the best reformed tradition he goes on to say that "there are no men less prepared to receive Christ's doctrine than those whose mind is cultivated and enriched by knowledge."[6] And he embarks on lengthy praise of mental simplicity:[7]

> Let no one quarrel with me for having called the apostles donkeys. I wish to explain the mysterious worth and excellence of the donkey. In the eyes of Hebrew scholars the donkey is the symbol of strength and courage. He has all the qualities essential to a disciple of truth; he is satisfied with little and endures hunger and blows. Simple-minded, he does not know the difference between a head of lettuce and thistle; he loves peace, he carries burdens. A donkey saved Marius when he was pursued by Sylla. The philosopher Apuleius would never have been vouchsafed the mysteries of Isis had he not been transformed into a donkey. The donkey was useful in the triumph of Christ; the donkey was able to perceive the angel as Balaam had not done. The donkey's jaw supplied Samson with a victorious weapon. No animal had ever the honor to rise from the dead except the donkey, the donkey alone, to whom St. Germanus gave back life; and that suffices to prove that after this life the donkey will have his share of immortality.

This passage reveals the Christian tradition that must have inspired Robert Bresson to film *Au hasard Balthazar*. But it also casts light on Bruno's polemic against asinity (*asinitas*, the essential quality of the donkey). In fact he openly jeers at Agrippa in his Italian dialogue *Cabala del cavallo pegaseo* and especially in *De gl'heroici furori*. As a defender of the culture of the Renaissance, he cannot accept Agrippa's point of view. According to Bruno, careful distinction must be made between passive grace and active contemplation: the saint is simple-minded like a donkey bearing the sacraments of grace; the hero, representing "the excellence of human nature," is a "sacred thing" in himself.[8]

In another connection, Agrippa himself gave the lie to his own ideal of simplicity of mind. In his youth he had formed a secret society with colleagues at the Sorbonne who practiced alchemy. He seems to have been successful as a pyrotechnist in Spain; he had studied the occult

sciences and—claiming titles he did not have—practiced law and medicine; he was enamored of culture and thus was antipodal to the "donkey." Yet sometimes he evinces a reformist zeal which, though inspired
by the group surrounding Trithemius, is nonetheless strange in an individual like Agrippa.

In 1519 he was hired as town councillor of Metz, where, as usual, he
made himself unpopular, this time with the inquisitor for having forcefully intervened in defense of a so-called witch from the village of Woip-
py.[9] He had no misgivings, moreover, about abandoning this substantial sinecure because of a quarrel with the prior of the Dominicans on the
question—defended by Lefèvre d'Estaples—of the monogamy of St.
Anne. On this matter he shows a Puritan zeal probably explicable by
virtue of his contacts with Trithemius ten years earlier (Trithemius belonged to an association called Joachim, founded by Arnoldus Bostius of
Ghent, which upheld the idea of St. Anne's immaculate conception of
the Virgin).

But how can we explain Agrippa's ambivalence, which is the more
striking when we reflect that he had to leave Pavia in a hurry because he
had expounded a treatise by the cabbalist Reuchlin? Reuchlin undoubtedly belongs to the magic culture of the Renaissance, whereas the question of St. Anne's monogamy stems from the prudishness of a reformed
culture. The reason is that Agrippa—like Trithemius, incidentally—
straddled two eras whose contradictions he failed to grasp: he thought
he could be a magician and a man of religion, a hero and a donkey, at
one and the same time. Unluckily for him, he always showed the wrong
side in situations where he should have shown the other; had he been
pious in Pavia and cabbalistic in Metz, he might have aroused no one's
hatred.

But did he believe in the sciences of the Renaissance? There, too, his
own statements are ambivalent. In Lyon, Agrippa had once more found
steady employment as court physician. Urged by the queen mother,
Louise of Savoy, to draw up the horoscope of François I, he committed
the inexcusable gaffe of writing to the seneschal of France that he actually did not believe in astrology; moreover, according to that horoscope
the king's enemy, the duke of Bourbon, would be victorious within the
year (1526). It is not surprising that the poor doctor was once more deprived of his sinecure, or that it took him a long time to be sure that he
had been—since the king's party did not wish the duke of Bourbon to
attract to himself an individual whose reputation as a specialist in weapons of war went as far back as his early youth and his adventures in
Spain. At the beginning of 1527 the duke of Bourbon offered Agrippa a

prefecture in his army. Agrippa refused it but not without drawing up a horoscope favorable to him and probably after performing magic spells to benefit the king's enemy.[10] Unfortunately the horoscope proved to be incomplete on one point: the walls of Rome tumbled down according to Agrippa's prediction, but the duke himself, on May 6, 1527, was killed because they fell on *him!*[11]

How can we interpret Agrippa's letters to the seneschal of France? Did he truly scorn astrology, or was he such a conscientious astrologer that he did not feel he should interpret the information communicated to him by the stars in a manner favorable to the king?

As we have seen, ambiguities pile up within him. Agrippa is no longer a man of the Renaissance and not yet a man of the Reformation.

### (iv) The Wiles of Giordano Bruno

Giordano Bruno was undoubtedly one of the most complex individuals of the sixteenth century. In contrast to Agrippa, he is easy to classify: Bruno was a representative of the phantasmic era at the time of the Reformation. But the Reformation's influence upon him is not to be overlooked. At Nola, in the Dominican convent, he had bursts of iconoclasm which brought upon him persecution and rebuffs by the religious authorities. In England he played the role of defender of the Art of Memory against Ramism. Now, in the Puritan view, the mnemotechnics of the Renaissance were out-of-date and diabolical, unworthy of their general moral reforms, especially as they seemed to be linked in some way with the activities of the Catholic Church. Bruno, a foreigner in Italy, was no less foreign in Germany and in England.

Agrippa and Bruno were both impulsive men with an amazing incapacity to understand the people and situations surrounding them. But, whereas Agrippa seems to renounce (for the sake of form?) his past as an occultist and to enter the ranks of the reformers, Bruno aspires to defend his ideas even into martyrdom, convinced that people great in spirit do not flinch from physical pain. Agrippa is too naive to compromise but sufficiently realistic to retract his ideas; on the other hand, Bruno is too proud to retract, but, having yielded to impulse which let him down paths of no return, he still hopes to find a solution through compromise. Here again, he sins not through naïveté but its opposite, excessive guile, which has the same result.

We have cited some of Bruno's attempts to convert his followers to the use of the Art of Memory. We recall that his *Spaccio de la bestia trionfante* was a rejection of the signs of the zodiac, replacing them with a veritable cohort of virtues and vices. By such means Bruno meant to give to the system of astrological memory a more abstract and Christian character.

Bruno was not the first to have the concept of a "Christian sky." "The Middle Ages wished to replace all the signs of the zodiac by others, borrowed from the Bible—which Hippolytus rejected, warning against astro-theosophists. A Carolingian poet (the priest Opicinus de Canistris, of Santa Maria Capella) proposed replacing the Ram by the Lamb (Christ), and, in 1627, Julius Schiller suggested, in his *Coelum stellatum christianum*, substituting the apostles for the signs of the zodiac. *L'Astroscopium* by Wilhelm Schickhardt, in 1665, sees the Ram as the animal of Isaac's sacrifice, the Twins as Jacob and Esau, and connects the Fishes with the parable of the loaves and fishes. This was only one step removed from an entirely arbitrary interpretation. Opicinus de Canistris breached the gap by assimilation to Capricorn because his own sin was pride and sensuality."[12]

It is not surprising that these attempts proliferated in the seventeenth century, when the spirit of the Renaissance had not completely left western Europe and there was still hope for reconciliation between the austerity and rigidity of reformed Christianity and the "sciences" of the phantasmic era. I am looking at a map of the Christian heaven charted by Andreas Cellarius for his *Atlas Coelestis seu Harmonia Macrocosmica* (1661). On the *coeli stellati christiani haemispherium prius*, I see that St. James has been substituted for the constellation of Gemini, St. John for the constellation of Cancer, St. Thomas for Leo, St. James the Less for Virgo, St. Philip for Libra, and St. Bartholomew for Scorpio. In addition, the Lesser Bear was replaced by St. Michael, the Great Bear by St. Peter's boat, the Boreal signs by St. Peter himself, Serpentarius by St. Benedict, Centaurus by Abraham and Isaac, and so forth.

This effort by Andreas Cellarius presupposes an exercise of the imagination very close to the Art of Memory—an effort only conceivable, perhaps, by the Catholic side of the Reformation. It is appropriate to recall here that the Inquisition itself made ample use of the weapon of imagination, only it aimed it *against* the culture of the phantasmic age. The Christianization of the signs of the zodiac stems from a process of the same kind. However, no attempt of that sort had any chance of success with the English Puritans, who had yielded to the abstract mnemotechnics of Pierre de la Ramée. To the Puritans, who had cast icons out of their churches, an apostle or a beast of the zodiac merely represented idols conceived by the imagination. This is why Bruno speaks to the Puritans in language much better adapted to influencing them than the phantasies of Andreas Cellarius: he replaces the beasts of the zodiac with abstract entities. But, on that account, the concessions he makes to Ramism are so great that the principal characteristics of his own system of artificial memory eventually become blurred.

## (v) A Single Reformation

If the Catholic Church did not abandon its cult of images and the celibacy of its priests, there are other fields in which the Reformation, both Protestant and Catholic, arrived at the same results. We have only to think of the persecution of witches or the fight against astrology and magic.

In its eighteenth session, the Council of Trent exhorted bishops to censor all the books on astrology in their dioceses. This decision was followed by the bull *Coeli et Terrae Creator Deus* of Sixtus V (1586), to which we shall refer in the next pages.

In this context, the *Traitté curieux de l'astrologie judiciaire* published in 1641 by Claude Pithoys, less famous than the *Disputationes* of Pico della Mirandola or Agrippa's *De vanitate scientiarum*, has the merit of showing us how much Catholics and Protestants were in agreement about certain fundamental questions of the Reformation. Claude Pithoys (1587–1676), born at Vitry-le-Francois in Champagne, joined the Minorite Friars. His religious career does not concern us here.[13] In 1632, "he abjugated his vows and his faith and became a Protestant, placing himself under the protection of the duke of Bouillon, who guaranteed him a position in the Protestant academy of Sedan."[14] The Protestant community of Sedan had been there since the middle of the sixteenth century, instituting a totalitarian atmosphere that is well expressed by the wording of this ordinance of July 20, 1573: "All atheists, libertines, Anabaptists, and other outcast sects are accused of divine lèse-majesté and punished by death."[15] The academy, which deserved its reputation for strictness and dogmatism, was founded in 1578 by Henri de la Tour, duke of Bouillon. It was frequented by English, Dutch, and Silesian Calvinist students who studied under Pithoys, their professor of philosophy. Pithoys continued quietly to fill this post until 1675 (when he was eighty-eight) although Sedan had been ceded to France in 1651 and, under the rule of Marshal Fabert, had gradually returned to Catholic ways.[16]

The *Traitté curieux* was published, nevertheless, in 1641—the year Pithoys's protector, Frédéric-Maurice de la Tour, duke of Bouillon, had inflicted a crushing victory on the royalist troops at La Marfée. Pithoys's arguments against astrology are not at all original. He is only one of the many adversaries of the Genethliacs and "the hare-brained, exaggerated, and wretchedly perverted notions with which the demons colored them to cover up their diabolical imagery."[17] He accuses them of making a pact with the devil (pp. 192–93) and asserts that it is the devil who inspires the diviners with all their predictions.

> That can be accomplished by addressing them disguised as human beings. By mouthing a word in the air or in the ear of the diviner. By impressing on the diviner's imagination phantasms of the things they conjecture must occur. By confronting the diviner with letters, characters, shapes, signs, and symbols which will fit into the diviner's reckoning. (P. 197)

These are classic arguments, which we have already come across in the *Malleus maleficarum* and in the work of Johannes Wier or of the Jesuit Martin Del Rio. But the interesting thing about this refutation of astrology published *by a Calvinist* in 1641 is that it seems to have been drawn up at the time Pithoys was still a Minorite monk at Bracancour in the province of Champagne.[18] That seems all the more likely since Pithoys does not even bother to change his references, citing the bull of Sixtus V, *Coeli et Terrae Creator Deus* of 1586, which he uses for his *Traitté* in a French translation.[19] It is certain that he believes it applies to both sides of the Reformation:

> Here we find a Papal Censure that confirms all we have said about Astromancy and Genethlialogy. It calls them *perverse, presumptuous, bold, deceivers, and despicable* and their art *an invention of the devil*, their predictions *inspirations of devils*. It censures and condemns both them and their books as well as all those who read or own them. What can the Genethliacs say to that? Perhaps they will allege that the Priests, the Councils, and the Popes cannot excommunicate or anathematize them, or censure them severely on this account. To which I reply, as concerns their censure, that it can never be more legitimate, since all of Christianity considers their art magical. (P. 209)

Protestants and Catholics do not agree on outward religious observances or on the question of the celibacy of the clergy. But in the seventeenth century they seem to be at one concerning the impious nature of the culture of the phantasmic era and the imaginary in general. Catholics and Lutherans, to be sure, are slightly more tolerant than Calvinists; but they believe just as firmly that the practice of any kind of divination is inspired by demons. Now the site of communication between demon and man is the mechanism of phantasy. That is why the number one enemy which *all of Christianity* must combat is human phantasy.

## (vi)  The Change in Ways of Envisaging the World

The censure of the imaginary and the wholesale rejection by strict Christian circles of the culture of the phantasmic age result in a radical change in the human imagination.

Here again, the works of some historians of ideas betray an ineradicable prejudice: the belief that this change was caused by the advent of heliocentrism and the concept that the universe is infinite. There are writers to this day who assert *seriously* that Copernicus (or Bruno, which would be much more accurate) was at the bottom of a "revolution" that was not only scientific but psychological as well. According to them, the finite Thomist cosmos was able to quiet human anxieties, which exploded as soon as the belief in an infinite universe became generally accepted.

That would not be serious if it were only schoolboys that were taught fairy tales of this kind, though they too deserve something better. Unfortunately they circulate even in the most learned tracts and it would be in vain to hope for their immediate cessation. At issue are made-up ideas so convenient and superficial that no one bothers to refute them any more. They continue to circulate, from generation to generation, forming one of the most tenacious traditions of modern culture.

Responsible for this is a certain linear concept of the progress of history, which everywhere seeks signs of "change" and "evolution." Because he advanced a heliocentric image of our solar system, which is closer to scientific truth, Copernicus is identified with a key moment of change, of evolution, in short, of progress. It is noteworthy that those who still maintain that heliocentrism and the infinity of the universe have had a disastrous effect on the psychic equilibrium of the individual and the masses also share those ideas, since they do not doubt that the "guilty" are men like Copernicus and Bruno.

When we subject to more careful analysis the historic framework in which these important changes in perspective on the cosmos took place, we see that the cardinal of Cusa, Copernicus, and Bruno all have a hand in it.

First, let us ask ourselves whether the Ptolemaic-Thomist system could have had an equilibratory psychological influence on the individual. Not at all, since it taught that we were located, as it were, in the garbage can of the universe, at its lowest point. In Aristotelian cosmology, the essential idea is not simply that the earth is located at the center of the universe but that it occupies the lowest point of the universe: that it is, so to speak, the negative pole of the whole cosmos and that in this attribute it is characterized not by a superfluity of being but almost by a *want of being;* it amounts to less than what there is above it. It is against this concept that Nicholas of Cusa raises his voice in an effort to endow the earth with a dignity equal to that of every other star. In the Ptolemaic cosmos the individual is, in a way—not essentially, of course, but accidentally—refuse in the garbage can of the universe. The individual in the infinite cosmos of Nicholas of Cusa is a precious stone contributing to the beauty of the "piece of jewlry" (*kosmos*), to the harmony of the whole. It is impossible to say why the latter hypothesis should have been more "disequilibratory" than the former.

The same thing applies to heliocentrism, which the most inspired seventeenth-century theologians accepted willingly. Cardinal de Bérulle, in his *Discours de l'Estat et des Grandeurs de Jesus* (1622), wrote:

> This new idea, little heeded in the science of the Stars, is useful and should be adapted to the science of salvation. For Jesus is the Sun, immovable and steadfast in its greatness, and moving all things. Jesus is like his Father and, seated at his right, is immobile like him. Jesus is the Sun of our Souls, from which they receive all grace, light, and influence. And the Earth of our Hearts should be in unceasing motion towards him, in order to receive in all its parts and powers the favorable aspects and benign influences of this great Star.[20]

Two years later, in 1624, Father Mersenne, Robert Fludd's customary opponent, propounded more or less the same arguments, although he was not convinced of the astronomic validity of the system of heliocentrism.[21] This indicates, as Clémence Ramnoux has well demonstrated, that a whole theological imagination might easily have abandoned Thomism and invaded the terrain so magnificently prepared by Cardinal de Bérulle. That did not happen. A great pity.

When we go back to the heart of the dispute over the two systems of the universe, we come across the same arguments that were still being repeated a quarter of a century ago, so that we are amazed that our contemporaries have so little imagination.

The first argument that Smitho, a supporter of geocentrism, sets forth against Teofilo, a supporter of heliocentrism, in *La Cena de le ceneri* of Giordano Bruno is the following: "Holy Scripture . . . almost everywhere assumes the opposite" (*Op. it.*, I, p. 91). Teofilo replies that the Bible is not a philosophic tract (that is to say, scientific) and that, in addressing the masses, it is only concerned with appearances. Smitho grants that he is right but also remarks that to address the masses with speech which contradicts appearances would be sheer folly (p. 92). And he borrows from al-Ghazali an argument often to be found in public print right after World War II:

> The purpose of the laws is not primarily to seek the truth of things and of speculations but the good influence of customs; for the sake of understanding between peoples, ease of human intercourse, the maintenance of peace, and the progress of the republics. Often, and in many respects, it is stupider and more ignorant to speak the truth than to be guided by the event and by opportunity.

Instead of saying, "The sun rises, the sun sets, it moves toward the south, turns toward the north," might Ecclesiastes (1:5–6) have expressed himself thus: "The earth turns toward the east and goes past the sun, which disappears from sight"? His hearers would rightly have taken him for a lunatic.

True, Smitho carries this no farther, without maintaining that human psychology drew a sense of security from the idea of a universe arranged around the earth, its center, an idea that Giordano Bruno's system dispelled for all time. But he almost reached that conclusion because he was already on the way to it. The Puritan, Smitho, an adherent of the authority of Scripture, was on the same track as his colleague, a follower of Thomas Aquinas. But in neither case was it concern for truth that prompted this attitude; both men found it practical not to disturb peace of mind by hypotheses which were too daring. Such reasoning is much more in keeping with the Puritan than with the Thomist view, for the Ptolemaic system, in accounting for the apparent movements of the planets, is extremely complex: by comparison, the heliostatic system of Copernicus is child's play. From the time that simplification—aside from the contradiction between the apparent and the real movements of the stars—could only please the masses, from the time—witness Cardinal de Bérulle—that it could only reinforce theology, one continues to be amazed at the false argument offered us to justify a serious miscalculation in the interpretation of history.

Unfortunately de Bérulle's open mind was almost the only exception in the spiritual panorama of the seventeenth century. The entirely Puritan fear of estrangement from God as exemplified by a hardening of traditional attitudes, prevailed over the cardinal's balanced and optimistic judgment. Puritanism, with its excesses, spread and invaded the opposing camp. Its dazzling victory was also its defeat, because, by dint of wishing to save the soul from the contamination and abuses of science, it only led to expelling God from the world.

Blaise Pascal, born a year after the publication of the Cardinal de Bérulle's *Discours*, is the principal reference for this silence of God exiled from nature. Is there a polemical intent in the anguish of the convert forsaken among "the awful spaces of the Universe which surround [him]," in the feeling of being surrounded "everywhere by infinities" (*Pensées*, I)? Neither the one nor the other. Pascal, who even adds the little infinity to the great infinity, both equally mysterious and disturbing, seems to adopt the Puritan attitude and to fear it. Is this due to a yearning for the Thomist universe? That cannot be attributed to him. Is it due to the misleading effect the new system of the world will have on the masses? That is just as unlikely.

It has been said that, to some extent, Pascal is the herald of a new era, of a new way of experiencing the world. This existentialist interpretation of Pascal errs by neglecting the known quantity which distinguishes that thinker in favor of a quantity which was wholly unknown to him: the future. Before taking a "positive" attitude toward a nonexistent future, Pascal takes a negative attitude toward the past, which must have been familiar to him. He is the prophet of a new era only insofar as he himself contributes to its construction.

His choice seems to us to be unequivocal: he participates in the Puritan revolution, which, in its desire to return to its source, exerts an extraordinarily far-reaching activity on the whole intervening period, the period not only of the Church but also of the *covenant between Christianity and pagan philosophy*. Pascal's infinity, terrifying only because God is not there, is metaphysically and existentially antipodal to the infinity of Nicholas of Cusa and Giordano Bruno, to whom the presence of God is made manifest in every stone, in every grain of sand in the universe. Proclamation of the infinite transcendence of God, the rejection of pantheism, makes up the Puritan content of Pascal's message. Insofar as this nihilistic activity is exerted on the Platonic cosmos of the Renaissance, the only modern philosopher to whom Pascal can be compared is Nietzsche, whom he seems to foreshadow.

Let us not forget that Nietzsche made no distinction between Platonism and Christianity. To him, these two traditions formed one compact block, and his negation of Christianity is really a negation of Platonism.[22] Pascal lays the groundwork for Nietzsche insofar as he adopts the arid message of Puritanism, and thus repudiates Platonism, the Platonism which conceived of the whole, even in its infinity, as a living organism. What "terrifies" Pascal is precisely the *absence of life* in the universe.

We might say that Pascal's anguish was caused by clinging to a concept of the world which is too abstract and inhuman. It is not infinity that frightens Pascal and those he addresses; *it is the fact of being a Puritan.*

The idea of the infinitude of the universe is not the only one which, extolled in the Renaissance, strikes terror in succeeding eras. What a difference there is between the justification of human free will in Pico della Mirandola's *Oration on Human Dignity* and the agonizing sense of responsibility experienced by the Protestant Kierkegaard! The idea of liberty, which allowed man to belong to the higher beings, ends by becoming a crushing burden, for there are no longer any points of reference. As soon as God withdraws into his complete transcendence, every human attempt to examine his design runs into a ghastly silence. This "silence of God" is, in reality, silence of the world, silence of Nature.

To read in the "book of Nature" had been the fundamental experience in the Renaissance. The Reformation was tireless in seeking ways to close that book. Why? Because the Reformation thought of Nature not as a factor for rapprochement but as the *main thing responsible for the alienation of God from mankind.*

By dint of searching, the Reformation at last found the great culprit guilty of all the evils of individual and social existence: sinning Nature.

# 10| Doctor Faust, from Antioch to Seville

## (i) The Permissiveness of the Renaissance

The identification of woman with nature and man with cultural values was very common in a number of ancient societies. It was accepted in the ideology of the Christian Middle Ages, and the *Malleus maleficarum*, in stating that woman is an "evil of nature," only reiterates a rather traditional thought.

The climate of opinion from which Christianity arose is characterized by a dualistic tension between the divinity, which is transcendent, and existence in the natural world. Now, since man's true homeland, the haven of salvation, is heaven, nature is envisaged as a place of exile, and the body—according to the Platonic postulate—as a tomb. This situation implies, on the one hand, the constant seduction of man by nature, a seduction resulting in an increasingly pronounced effort—whose main instruments are religion and religious morality—to escape from the traps set by nature.

Nature is a mindless organism, endowed with beauty and a great capacity to fascinate, which engenders beings, nourishes and destroys them. On the other hand, religion represents an ensemble of laws with the purpose of saving man from natural destruction, ensuring him indestructibility on the spiritual plane. On the level of sexual differentiation, it is woman who assumes the role of nature and man the role of religion and its laws. It follows that the more beautiful a woman is, the more she evidences her natural functions (breeding, fertility, nutrition), and the more suspect she is from the religious point of view. Indeed, beauty means an increased capacity for seduction in view of the act of insemination and therefore a powerful danger to man, who must save himself from the defilement of sexual desire. The somatic signs of fertility and the nutritive function (the hips, the breasts) are what engender cupidity and sin. This is why the culture of the Middle Ages propounds its own ideal of beauty, which is contrary to natural beauty: the beauty of virtue acquired through contempt for and mortification of the body.

The history of women's fashion furnishes us with valuable information on this subject. Beyond its variations, dress has the primary function of concealing the female body entirely—including the hair of a married woman. The bust must be leveled and flat, since the ideal of virtuous beauty demands almost nonexistent breasts. The object of admiration until the end of the Middle Ages is woman's delicate figure, her fragile and virginal appearance: "You know how delicate is the waist of an ant," says Wolfram of Eschenbach, "but that of a young girl is even more so."[1] The custom of husband and wife sleeping together naked in the conjugal bed does not appear until the fourteenth century.[2] Before then, there is explicit evidence that forces us to believe it was not unusual for a man never to see his wife entirely nude. The Umbrian mystic poet, Jacopone da Todi, only found out upon the death of his wife that she used to wear a rough hair-shirt under her clothes which had badly wounded her body.

In the fourteenth century a marked change in custom occurred, evidenced by just as revolutionary a change in fashion. The *Chronique du Limbourg* informs us that the neckline was cut so low "that it was possible to see half of the breasts." Isabelle of Bavaria introduced "deep-necked dresses" cut down to the navel. Sometimes the breasts are completely bare, the nipples decorated with rouge or rings of precious stones and even pierced to permit insertion of little gold chains.[3] This fashion reached the villages, of course in a modified form. Peasants, too, chose low-necked dresses in bright colors. Geiler of Keisersberg, an early sixteenth-century moralist, is shocked by once having thus glimpsed the breasts of a young woman. But he is particularly overwhelmed by the village dances in which the young girl, having been tossed up into the air, "showed everything, behind and in front, as far up as the pubic bone"[4]— since those social circles at that period lacked underwear.

In the fifteenth century, though the "topless" style is rarely worn, a new standard of beauty arises which accentuates nature's charms to the detriment of the charms of virtue. Jan Hus, the Bohemian reformer, burned alive in Constance in 1415, denounces these women who "wore dresses with necklines cut so deep and wide that almost half their bosom was visible and everyone could see their dazzling skin everywhere, in the temples of God, in front of priests and clergy, as well as in the marketplace, but still more at home. *The part of the breasts which is covered is made so prominent that it looks like two horns.*" And elsewhere: "Then, they make two . . . horns on their bosom, very high up and artificially projected toward the front, even when nature has not endowed them with such important advantages; finally, thanks to the shape of their bodice and an excess of clothing, the horns of their bosom rise up."[5]

The preference for round and matronly shapes is accentuated in the course of the Renaissance.

> The slender young men and the fragile young girls of the fourteenth and fifteenth centuries have become strong and determined men with broad shoulders and mature, vigorous women with the ample dimensions of the sixteenth century that are familiar to us through the masterpieces of Leonardo da Vinci, Raphael, Michelangelo, Sansovino, Giorgione, Titian, Correggio, and others. The figure was sometimes revealed, sometimes accentuated by the costume. Catherine de' Medici introduced to the French court a fashion reminiscent of the Cretan. The low-cut neckline emphasized the bosom, which was hidden by a light and transparent material or else left completely bare.[6]

Italian fashion in the fifteenth century was high-waisted, which enabled the breasts to be exposed. This is even evident on the tombstone of a matron of Lucca, designed by Jacopo della Quercia (d. 1438) who sculpted the ample shapes of motherhood.[7] Sixteenth-century Italian fashion presages the low waist, the bosom covered by a "short bodice with a square neckline."[8] A fresco by Francesco del Cossa, *The Weavers* (1468–69), in the Schifanoia palace at Ferrara is a real fashion show of the high waist. On the other hand, Raphael's portraits of women reveal the dropped waist and the evolution of the neckline: his madonnas and his angels sometimes wear low-waisted dresses.

A certain balance is apparent in these variations in women's costumes: the high waist reveals the bosom, which is, however, covered; the low waist flattens it, but the neckline is sometimes so wide as to extend over the shoulder, exposing the "dazzling skin" that had so scandalized the reformer Jan Hus.

In conclusion, the fashion and costumes at the end of the Middle Ages and during the Renaissance show all the indications of permissiveness and even, in some cases—if we think of the mixed public baths or village dances[9]—of a promiscuity hitherto unknown. Literature does not contradict this general impression because, with the exception of fables,[10] erotic subjects had never been treated with the frankness of a Boccaccio, a Chaucer, a Machiavelli, a Rabelais, or a Bruno. Art also gives evidence of this change in customs. Not to delve into broad generalities, we have only to recall the great difference in portrayal of the human body between late Gothic art and fifteenth-century Renaissance art—the painting of Masaccio, for instance.[11] Subjects inspired by ancient mythology become—in the works of Pollaiuolo, Piero di Cosimo, Lorenzo di Credi,

Luca Signorelli, Botticelli, Leonardo, Michelangelo, etc.—a pretext for incredibly bold studies of female nudes.

A wind of independence was blowing everywhere, disquieting the religious authority. Luigi Cortusio, a jurist of Pavia who died July 17, 1418, left a rather strange will, which shows us how private mentality had been liberated from medieval tradition. Cortusio's main beneficiary was to be the member of his family who, in the funeral procession, wore the most *naturally* cheerful expression; on the other hand, those who wept were to be disinherited. Cortusio repudiated mourning and the tolling of bells; the house and the church where his body lay were to be decorated with garlands of flowers and green leaves. Fifty musicians playing Hallelujah were to accompany the procession to the cemetery. No monk dressed in black was to be allowed in the procession; by contrast, the catafalque was to be carried by twelve young girls dressed in green, singing merry refrains.[12]

We cannot say whether or not the permissiveness of the authorities went so far as to allow the provisions of Cortusio's will to be carried out. But the reaction to sexual emancipation, exhibitionist dress, and nonconformism was not late in coming. The moralistic sermons of a Jan Hus in Bohemia and of a Savonarola in Florence,[13] whose effectiveness and power of persuasion were tremendous, enable us to glimpse what was to become, in the sixteenth century, the mentality of Reformation.

**(ii)  It Will Be Hotter in Hell!**

Wherever the Reformation became established, customs changed. In women's fashion, this change was marked by the complete disappearance of low-cut dresses; instead, women wore dresses with a high collar and a double skirt, a purpose of which seems to have been to avoid attracting attention when dancing.[14] Mixed public baths, which had proliferated in the fourteenth century, hardly exist in the sixteenth.[15]

The German Reformation produce no unitary fashion. After 1540, the dominant influence came from Spain and quickly spread throughout Europe, including the Protestant countries.

The ideology responsible for Spanish fashion is clear and simple: woman is the blind instrument for seduction of nature, the symbol of temptation, sin, and evil. Besides her face, the principal baits of her allure are the signs of her fertility, hips and breasts, but also each millimeter of skin exhibited. The face, alas, must stay exposed, but it is possible for it to wear a rigid and manly expression. The neck can be enveloped in a high lace collar. As to the bosom, the treatment dealt it closely resembles the traditional deformation of the feet of Japanese women, being no less painful and unhealthy. The custom, which lasts unchanged until the beginning of the eighteenth century, is described thus by the countess of Aulnoy:[16] "Among [Spanish women] it is a sign of beauty to have no bosom, and they take early precautions to prevent it from appearing. When the Breasts begin to appear, they place little plates of lead on it and bind themselves up like the Children we swaddle. They have a bosom in one piece, almost like a piece of paper."

Since the lower parts of the body were taboo, a system was developed for making the skirt longer than the legs, especially by means of shoes with high soles of wood or cork. "This kind of footwear found unexpected allies in Church circles in Italy, who considered these uncomfortable shoes to be an effective weapon against the pleasures of this world and particularly against dancing. Women who wore them had a right to indulgences."[17] The color of the clothes was, of course, black.

Fashion certainly determines the threshold of sexual excitement: a permissive style which gives a woman an opportunity to exhibit all her natural charms results in a certain indifference between the sexes; on the other hand, a repressive style induces a proportionate lowering of the threshold of excitement. An example of this is that when Spanish fashion prevailed, "the supreme favor" a woman granted her suitor, the acme of happiness, was to show him her foot. In the nineteenth century the situation had not entirely changed, for Victor Hugo tells us in *Les Misérables* that Marius fell into a long erotic reverie, having glimpsed, by chance, Cosette's *ankle*.

The only country where Spanish fashion gained no foothold was Italy. The fact that Rome has always been the site of the Vatican, and that among the Roman Curia there have always been men endowed with remarkable intelligence and skepticism, saved Italy from the excesses of intolerance: it was, moreover, the only province of the Church that hardly experienced the mad fury of the persecution of witches. Baroque art is impregnated with sensuality, and the female costume of the seventeenth century is far from evincing the same rigid uniformity as in the rest of Europe.

The ideal of femininity propounded by the Reformation finds its most perfect expression in Spanish fashion: a woman defeminized, masculinized, whose role is no longer the nefarious seduction of man but to assist him on the difficult paths of moral perfection. The culture tends to destroy natural attractions by means of cruel or unhealthy practices: the bosom is flattened with lead plaques, the expressivity of the face is eliminated, the waistline is raised, and the woman is covered from neck to toes; in short, an attempt is made to give her an appearance as masculine as possible.

Natural femininity, overflowing, voluptuous, and sinful is categorized as unlawful. Henceforth only witches will dare to have wide hips, prominent breasts, conspicuous buttocks, long hair. We have only to look at Hans Baldung Grien's engravings or the illustrations for *Die Emeis* (Strasbourg, 1517) by Johannes Geiler of Keisersberg to realize the extraordinary vitality of the *maleficae*. In contrast to this picture of the natural, anticonformist, and destructive temptress is the rigid, uniform figure and emaciated face of the virtuous Spanish woman.

The literature and imagery relating to witchcraft border on the pornographic: the inhibitions of an entire era of repression are poured into it. All possible and impossible perversions are ascribed to witches and their fiendish partners. Hans Baldung Grien does not hesitate to represent naturalistically cunnilingus between a very voluptuous young heretic, long hair floating in the wind, and the dragon Leviathan, from whose mouth emerges a sort of penis in the form of a tendril (1515). The pictures of the witches' sabbath include scenes every bit as indelicate whose manifest intent is to edify the reader concerning the antisocial practices of witches. But the latent content of all this iconography is easy to grasp: taking as a pretext the erotic phantasies of the marginals who had surfaced during the transference process set in motion by the Inquisition, the persecutors themselves projected all their personal inhibitions onto them.

In the sixteenth and seventeenth centuries, if certain women were casual in their behavior this was sufficient reason "to make ready for them in this world the tortures of hell."[18] In engravings of the period we see them looking in the mirror and seeing not their own face but the backside of a demon. Untidy hair and clothes are enough to arouse suspicion of witchcraft. In Germany in the seventeenth century a woman is handed over to the authorities by her own husband, who came upon her unexpectedly *during the night*, not naked, but disheveled and unbuttoned![19] And if a coquette, unlacing her corset, should say, "It is too hot—do you mind?" her interlocutor would reply: "It will be still hotter in Hell!"[20]

### (iii) An Exhaustive Moralism: The Legend of Faust

The most perfect expression of the Reformation is the legend of Faust, which contains all the ideological characteristics already mentioned: censorship of the imaginary; the intrinsic guilt of nature and of its principal instrument, woman; and woman's masculinization.

There is also a historical tradition—documented by Trithemius, Wier, and others—which does not interest us in this context: that of the charlatan Jorg Faust, who assumed the Latinized name of Georgius Sabellicus. He must have lived between 1480 and 1540, and the villagers of Kittlingen still consider him their most famous son.

There are two ancient versions of the legend: the one by the "anonymous man of Wolfenbüttel,"[21] and the *Volksbuch* printed by Johann Spies in Frankfurt in 1587,[22] probably compiled by one Andreas Frei, head of the college of classics in Speyer.

In 1592, the *Volksbuch* was translated into English by P. F. Gent under the title *The History of the Damnable Life and Deserved Death of Doctor John Fausts.*[23] It thus became accessible to Christopher Marlowe.[24] The *Faustspiel*, adapted for the stage, for actors and for marionettes, was immediately exported to Holland.[25] Its great popularity with the Protestant Reformation brought it to the attention of Catholic circles, and in 1637 Calderón de la Barca did a free adaptation of it for Spanish audiences.

Whether the author of the *Volksbuch* was Andreas Frei or someone else, it was in any case the product of a well-read man whose pious inventiveness was drawn from ancient sources and combined with the German historical tradition. Strange as it may seem, the name of Faust does not seem to be borrowed from the German source but from the famous Simon Magus ("Simon the Magician"), contemporary of the apostles and surnamed *Faustus*. He was the antihero of various stories attributed to St. Clement of Rome and other sources of Late Antiquity diligently collected by Baronius, a sixteenth-century writer, in his *Annales* (*Ann.* 68, no. 21). Moreover, Simon Magus was also believed to be the earliest gnostic. In this capacity he claimed to be divine and had married a prostitute called Helen, to him the incarnation of Helen of Troy as well as of the Wisdom (*ennoia*) of God.[26] In the *Volksbuch*, Faust, through his magic acts, obtains the simulacrum of Helen of Troy, an episode explicable on the one hand, as deriving from the legend of Simon-Faustus and, on the other, from another ancient tradition: that of St. Cyprian of Antioch.

The legend of Cyprian is of Encratite origin: the Encratites represented a trend within eastern Christianity characterized by total repression of sexuality—including marriage—and by a strict ascetic regimen. The earliest version of the tale is in the apocryphal Acts of the apostle Andrew, written in Greek around the year 200, of which a fragmentary Coptic translation was recovered by Gilles Quispel among the manuscripts of the late Carl Schmidt.[27] In its canonical form the story—a very famous one—dates from the fourth century, when it occurs in no less than three drafts: the *Confessio seu poenitentia Cypriani,* pronounced heretical by Pope Gelasius I, who confuses Cyprian of Antioch with another Cyprian, bishop of Cathage; the *Conversio Sanctae Justinae virginis et Sancti Cypriani episcopi,* which perpetuates the same mistake; and, finally, the draft dealing with the martyrdom of the two saints. In 379, Gregory of Nazianzus mentions the legend in one of his sermons, while the ecclesiastical historian Photius, in one of his writings, sums up the contents of a heroic poem in three cantos on St. Cyprian, composed by Eudoxia, daughter of the philosopher Leontius, who became empress in 421. The work by Vincent de Beauvais and the *Legenda aurea* of Jacobus de Voragine ensure a wide readership to the tale of Cyprian and Justina. A second version of the legend was written in the tenth century by Symeon Metaphrastes, translated into Latin in 1558 by Aloysius Lipomanus, and republished by Laurentius Surius in 1580 and 1618 in an edifying work that was highly influential in its day.[28]

Calderón seems to have noted Surius's tale, but his two main sources remain the *Legenda aurea* and a collection of lives of the saints entitled *Flos Sanctorum.*[29]

Going beyond its numerous variations, the legend relates that Cyprian, a magician from Antioch—or a friend of his, Aglaidas—yearns for the beautiful Justina, unaware that she is a Christian and has taken a vow of chastity before God. Of course, he is haughtily rejected. All that is left for him to do is to make a pact with the devil, who promises to give him Justina in exchange for his soul. Lacking power over Christians, however, the devil cannot fulfill Cyprian's desire; he tries to deceive him, furnishing him with a simulacrum which, at a distance, resembles Justina but is actually only a diabolic apparition. Deeply impressed by the strength of Justina and her God, Cyprian himself is converted and follows her to martyrdom.

Apart from its conclusion, the structure of Faust's *Volksbuch* is quite similar; and in the form of drama, shorn of its many moralistic digressions of the prose version, it must resemble still more closely the legend of Cyprian and Justina: it deals with a magician who has recourse to a pact with the devil to obtain, among other favors, those of a young girl and the simulacrum of the beautiful Helen of Troy.

Let us imagine that someone had the opportunity to see a theatrical production of Faust, in English or in Dutch, without understanding a word of it. He would have taken it to be a pessimistic version of the legend of Cyprian in which the magician, instead of following Justina to martyrdom, was damned. It seems that this was the case with Calderón himself, who, according to his friend and editor J. de Vera Tassis y Villarroel, had spent ten years in His Majesty's service, first in Milan and then in the southern Netherlands. Later, his biographers reduced this period of time to include only the years 1623–25. In 1623, as it happens, English theatrical companies put on several plays in the Netherlands. Undoubtedly Calderón—who understood neither English nor Dutch— saw them.[30] The action enabled him to identify the legend of Cyprian. He saw the same scenes he must already have witnessed in Spanish drama: the pact with the devil which took place in various plays, including *El esclavo del demonio* and *El amparo de los hombres* by Mira de Amescua,[31] and the apparition of the simulacrum of Justina, which also resembled a scene in *El esclavo del demonio* (1612).[32] But he could also note the differences, which he put to use in his own drama. For example, in the English production, the pact took place on the stage; in Mira de Amescua's version, in the wings.[33] The English production began with Faust's monologue, the same monologue Goethe adapted in the famous "monologue of the *grübelnden Gelehrten.*" Calderón thought he had guessed the meaning from the stage presentation and made use of it not only in the *Magico prodigioso*, but also in his plays: *Los dos amantes del cielo, El José de las mujeres*, and *El gran principe de Fez.*[34] As for the name of Faust, Calderón used it in a surprising way in the first version of the *Magico prodigioso*, unpublished until 1877.[35] In the legend of Cyprian, the young girl, Justa, changes her name to Justina when she is baptized. In the first part of Calderón's play, she is not called Justa but *Faustina.*

The story of Cyprian and Justina had originated among the Encratites in the second century. Encratism forbade sexuality even when its goal was not pleasure but procreation. That is why the apocryphal acts of the apostles Andrew and Thomas relate various conversions effectuated by our heroes among married women whom they urged to practice continence. The brutal reactions of the husbands and the persecutions of the apostles should not surprise us: their message was a little extreme for this world.

The moral of the fourth-century story was apologetical: it showed the power of Christianity. The devil is helpless against a Christian girl who says her prayers. In the belief he had served weak and ineffectual masters, Cyprian gives up his profession of magician to embrace faith in a victorious god: the God of Justina.

Insofar as Cyprian's love for Justina seeks gratification, it can only find in it death since—due to the forcefulness of the Christian message—its object proves impregnable. Cyprian is obliged to sacrifice it because his erotic magic has not borne fruit. And his reasoning, to the very end, remains the reasoning of a sorcerer: its failure reveals Justina's *magic* power, which he can only gain by becoming a Christian himself. But Justina also exhorts him to bear witness (that is the etymological meaning of the word "martyr") to the supremacy of the Christian God, and the ex-magician can only hasten to respond to this gracious offer.

We can understand, to be sure, this pious *exemplum* of the era when the martyrdom of Christians was mandatory. But what could have been its message in the town of Yepes, in 1637—when the *Magico prodigioso* was performed for the first time? This time, Cyprian—like Johann or Jorg Faust—represents a symbol not of pagan antiquity vanquished by Christianity but of the Renaissance vanquished by the Reformation. Its message is therefore the repudiation of Renaissance values in favor of the values of the Reformation as portrayed by a young girl with flattened bosom called Faustina-Justina.

From the outset of Calderón's play, the sorcerer Cipriano is shown to be a disciple of the Renaissance, viewing the world as a fascinating work of art (lines 146–47, Morel-Fatio). In turn, the devil himself only repeats the same ideas, making it clear that he has been the pupil of Marsilio Ficino and Cornelius Agrippa. It is as though they were now identified with the devil in the new popular interpretation by the Reformation. Calderón's devil is no longer a transnatural apparition; he is merely an ideological fabrication who expresses himself like Ficino and Pico della Mirandola, the embodiment of the essence of a doctrine that the Reformed population had learned to despise and detest. Listen to him: *"Vien / En la fabrica gallarda / Del mundo se be, pues fue / Solo un concepto al obrarla. / Sola una voluntad luço / Esa arquitectura rara / Del cielo, una sola al sol, / Luna y estrellas viçarras, / Y una sola al hombre, que es / Pequeño mundo con alma."* Ficino's *Platonic theology* is the wellspring of the devil's misleading views: there, too, the world is envisaged as a work of art (*artificiosissimum mundi optificium*) and man, the microcosm (*parvus mundus*), as the artifice of brazen nature (*naturae audentissimum artificium*). The science the devil possesses is "Art," that is to say, magic (line 219); in particular, he can made the stars come down to earth (lines 1790 sq.) and convinces Cipriano of his talents by moving a mountain (lines 2579 sq.).

As to Cipriano himself, he learns necromancy, pyromancy, and palmistry and, in order to perform magic, he forms graphic symbols, ensuring the cooperation of the stars, the winds, and the spirits of the dead (lines 2720 sq.), in the tradition of Marsilio Ficino, Cornelius Agrippa, and Giordano Bruno.

Truth to tell, magic rites are described quite superficially in the *Magico prodigioso*. The important thing was to establish a direct relationship between magic and the devil, between the devil and the Renaissance, enemy number one of the Reformation. Calderón accomplishes this without any difficulty. He then concentrates on what we might call the equation Eros = magic, which also stems from the Renaissance. It is at this point that *Faustina* appears, whose name acquires a rather exact symbolism due to its connection with Faust.

Now, before being *essentially* a Christian (which Cipriano does not know), Faustina is a *woman*, a product of nature: a product perfect in beauty since she counts many admirers who do not hesitate to eliminate one another to obtain her favors. Without her knowledge or volition, Faustina was designed by nature to be an erotic object, a cause of covetous desire and dissension. The contradiction and tension between the *natural* destiny of Faustina and the *cultural* acosmic aspirations of Justina are focal to Calderón's scenario.

Like Goethe's *Faust*, the *Magico prodigioso* begins with a "prologue in heaven" in which the devil, who is under the domination of the Lord, intends to test the science of Cipriano and the virtue of Justina. There follows the "monologue of the *grübelnden Gelehrten*" in which the young Cipriano does not prove to be preoccupied, like Faust, by the problem of old age and the vanity of earthly things, but simply by a theological question he fails to resolve: that is, he would like to understand who this god is, described by Pliny as "absolute beauty, essence and cause, all-seeing and effective" (*todo vista y todo manos*, lines 261–63). While trying to separate two enraged suitors of the beautiful Justina, daughter of Lisandro, Cipriano himself is taken with this marvelous creature. Now he does not know that in reality Justina is the baptismal name of Faustina, who is not the daughter of Lisandro, and, moreover, that Lisandro is not the person he appears to be either. Lisandro and Justina are both crypto-Christians, Christians who hide within a hostile society; Lisandro adopted Faustina on the death of her mother, who had been a Christian martyr. And Cipriano also does not know that Justina has pledged her soul and her body to the same God to whom her mother had sacrificed her life.

At bottom, Cipriano sees in Justina only what she no longer is: the beautiful Faustina, a perfect product of nature, who exerts a powerful erotic fascination over him. Although innocent, the young girl cannot help casting natural magic spells all around her: it is she who *faustisizes* Cipriano, who changes him into Faust, who almost forces him to practice erotic magic.

In comparing the *Magico prodigioso* with the Christian legend, we see that for Calderón a more subtle erotic play enters the tale, a kind of play that corresponds perfectly to the concepts of the Reformation: nature herself is the sinner who engenders Eros; Faustina, at his behest, *faustisizes* all the males surrounding her. How to emerge from this dilemma? The young girl does not yet know how to use the methods refined by the culture to become unattractive, to flatten her chest, to assume masculine ways. To defend herself from the assaults of Cipriano and the others, all she has is the weapon of meditation and prayer. But Eros has his own methods: the more Cipriano is repulsed, the greater his passion grows. In order to obtain the object of his covetous desire, all he can do is to sign, in his own blood, a pact with the devil, promising him his soul in exchange for Justina. In turn, the devil sets loose powerful processes of erotic magic, designed to deliver Justina to him despite herself. Far from asking help from his grisly colleagues in the abysses of Hell the devil evokes, instead, through magic incantations, a *gentle erotic phantasm* with the purpose of exciting Justina, of awakening her dormant natural being, of reviving and encouraging her femininity. The principle behind this rests on the rules of erotic magic expressed by Ficino and developed by Bruno: one must act upon the subject's phantasies while taking account of his peculiarities. Now, besides having counted too much on the fact that Justina is also Faustina—that is, a product of nature as well as culture, a woman as well as a Christian—the devil had committed the irreparable mistake of not reading the *Institutio Sacerdotum* of Cardinal Francisco of Toledo (d. 1596), which had just come out in Rome,[36] before Calderón's departure for the Netherlands. Had he read it, the devil would have learned that it was impossible to influence anyone's free will; all he can do is produce phantasms to act on the imagination, but free will remains. The devil can be accused of some ignorance in the realm of theology but not of having failed to act in conformity with the rules of phantasmic magic. He had revealed to Justina the world of nature permeated by the winds of Eros, in order to arouse carnal appetites in her: "*Ea, infernal abismo, / Desesperado imperio de ti mismo, / De tu prison ingrata / Tus lascivios espiritus desata, / Amenaçando ruyna / Al virgen edificio de Justina. / Su casto pensamiento / De mil torpes fantasmas en el viento / Oy se informa, su honesta fantasia / Se llene, y con dulcissima armonia / Todo proboque amores, / Los pajaros, las plantas y las flores. / Nada miren su ojos / Que no sean de amor dulces despojos. / Nada oygan sus oydos / Que no sean de amor tiernos gemidos* (lines 2823 sq.).*"

Meditation and prayer safeguard the free will of Justina, removing her from the natural world and giving her a firm footing in the world of religious values. The "lascivious" devils of the lower regions do not succeed in drawing her into the world of nature, which, through its magic "chains," tempts all beings to appease their desire. The devil does not succeed in transforming Justina into Faustina, the subject of culture into a subject of nature. But his failure signifies not only the victory of the Reformation spirit over the Renaissance spirit but also the triumph of the reality principle over the pleasure principle. In fact, erotic magic, which presupposes the transmission of phantasms from the sender to the receiver, yields no results: the devil can only offer Cipriano a hideous shade of Justina, a demonic specter. This means that erotic magic is only capable of producing phantasms and that the fulfillment of desire it addresses is not real but is itself *phantasmic*. In other words, the performing of magic takes place in a closed circle: *erotic magic is a form of autism.*

This conclusion, to be sure, far outstrips Calderón's moralistic intent but is nonetheless implicit in the development of the plot. Later on, when the religious fervor of the Reformation is extinguished, this is all that remains: the strong contrast between the imagination (pleasure principle) and free will (reality principle) and the idea that magic autism has no *real* power.

By virtue of her victory over Faustina—her "natural" counterpart, her own femininity, her own right to desire and to enjoy—Justina ends by triumphing over Cipriano. The end of the play perfectly corresponds to the purposes of the Reformation and can easily be interpreted according to the historical facts of the period: Cipriano and Justina will be united in death, which means a complete victory of culture over nature, free will over imagination, the reality principle over the pleasure principle, Thanatos over Eros. The dual martyrdom has now become an anachronistic symbol: according to the standards of the Reformation, if Cipriano had been a young scholar salvaged by the Church and Justina a virtuous young girl with flattened breasts, they could have married and had children, provided that the flames of passion burning between them were forever extinguished.

The revolution in spirit and customs brought about by the Reformation led to the total destruction of Renaissance ideals. The Renaissance conceived of the natural and social world as a spiritual organism in which perpetual exchanges of phantasmic messages occurred. That was the principle of magic and of Eros, Eros itself being a form of magic.

The Reformation destroys this structure of phantasms in motion; it forbids the use of imagination and proclaims the necessity for total suppression of sinful nature. It even attempts artificially to make the sexes one and the same so that natural temptations might disappear.

At the time when the *religious* values of the Reformation are losing all their effectiveness, its theoretical and practical opposition to the spirit of the Renaissance receives an interpretation of a cultural and scientific kind. But it is a lesson that henceforth mankind takes for granted: the imaginary and the real are two separate and distinct realms, magic is a form of absorption in phantasy as an escape from reality, the reality principle is set over against the pleasure principle, and so forth.

### (iv) A Final Result?

Modern Western civilization is altogether a product of the Reformation—a Reformation which, void of its religious content, nevertheless kept its conventions and its rituals.

On the theoretical level, the pervasive censorship of the imaginary results in the advent of modern exact science and technology.

On the practical level, it results in the advent of modern institutions.

On the psychosocial level, it results in all our chronic neuroses, which are due to the entirely unilateral orientation of Reformation culture and its rejection of the *imaginary* on grounds of principle. We still live, so to speak, in a secularized appendix to the Reformation, and, on close examination, many phenomena of our era, for which we have never sought an historical explanation, go back to the great spiritual and political conflicts of the sixteenth and seventeenth centuries. We are accustomed to regarding the progress of military technology and the arms race as perfectly normal. We are therefore all the more surprised to find out that they, too, are attributable to the seventeenth century, primarily to a celebrity in his time, unknown to most people nowadays: the chemist Johann Rudolf Glauber.

Glauber, deeply affected by the events of the Thirty Years' War (1618–48) between the Catholic and the Protestant states, reached the conclusion—religious as well as practical—that only one power could ensure order and peace in Europe: Germany. To reach this goal it was imperative that Germany be proclaimed the *universal monarchy:* in order to accomplish this, the prerequisite had to be Germany's military and economic supremacy over the rest of the world, which it could only gain by developing more advanced military technology. Let us leave aside Glauber's economic solution, which was to hoard products against years of famine. His strategic solution is definitely more interesting and gives us the key to understanding the origin of the arms race. Glauber recommends the use of chemical weapons not only to ensure the military supremacy of Germany but also to stop the Turks from advancing in Europe. He himself invents a weapon more effective than gunpowder, namely, pressure tubes for pulverizing acids to spray on the enemy and also acid grenades and bombs that would make it possible to conquer the enemy's fortifications. Glauber believes the chemical weapon has a dual advantage: to guarantee victory to the army that possesses it, and to blind enemy soldiers without killing them. In that way, prisoners can be transformed into a cheap labor force, thus ensuring the economic supremacy of Germany as well.

Glauber is aware that the secret of the new weapons will eventually become known by the enemy—whether the Turks or other adversaries. He therefore envisages the existence of a group of scholars—"men endowed with a quick and penetrating mind"—whose only task must be to develop and perfect more and more sophisticated armaments. This will change the nature of war totally: war will no longer be won by brute force but by the intelligence of scholars and engineers: "Force will yield to skill, for skill often succeeds in overcoming force."[37]

Glauber's foresight was to prove correct: not only has Germany tried several times, unsuccessfully, to be the "universal monarchy," but the nature of modern warfare has actually changed to such an extent that it no longer takes place on the ground but only in the laboratories of the great powers.

All of the foregoing is not a mere curiosity of history but illuminating proof that our civilization continues to die in the trenches dug by the Reformation and by the political events that followed it. The modern West—as Nietzsche foresaw—is assuming the character of a *fatal* result of the Reformation. But is it also the *final* result, its lines of development fixed, once for all, in the sixteenth and seventeenth centuries?

On this question my book closes, without daring to express too clearly a hope that may be utopian: that a new Renaissance, a rebirth of the world, may overcome all our neuroses, all conflicts, and all divisions existing between us.

For such a Renaissance to appear a new Reformation must arise, effecting once again a profound modification of the human imagination in order to impress on it other paths and other goals. The only question is whether it will seem friendly and benign to those who experience its upheavals.

After all, the important thing is to provide an ecological climate in which a new "wingless fly" may crawl without being destroyed—so long as this genetic mutation is the one we might hope for!

*Bucharest, 1969—Chicago, 1986*

# Notes

**Introduction**
1. See Robert K. Merton, *Science, Technology and Society in Seventeenth Century England* (New York, 1970; 1st ed., 1938).
2. This is Max Weber's thesis in *The Protestant Ethic and the Spirit of Capitalism*.
3. Stephen Toulmin, *The Return to Cosmology: Postmodern Science and the Theology of Nature* (Berkeley and Los Angeles, 1982).

**Chapter 1**
1. The influence of the scholar W. Jaeger brought about the long-held belief that it was Aristotle who inspired the theories of the physician Diocles of Carystus; showing that Diocles was a contemporary if not a precursor of Aristotle, F. Kudlien reversed the data of the problem: cf. F. Kudlien, "Probleme um Diokles von Karystos" (1963), in H. Flashar (ed.), *Antike Medizin* (Darmstadt, 1971), pp. 192–201. Kurt Pollak, in *Die Heilkunde der Antike: Wissen und Weisheit der alten Ärzte*, vol. 2 (Düsseldorf and Vienna, 1969), pp. 140 ff., readily concedes that Diocles was probably the youngest contemporary of Plato and, like him, was profoundly influenced by the doctrines of Philistion, a Sicilian doctor who settled in Athens. Through the intermediary of Diocles, Aristotle is also indebted to the teachings of Empedoclean medicine.
2. The intellect is also *phantasma tis*; see *De anima*, 432a; cf. 428b.
3. Thomas Aquinas, *Summa theol.*, I, q. 89aI. It is strange that, in her book *The Art of Memory* (Chicago, 1966), p. 71, F. A. Yates forgets to quote the passage from Thomas Aquinas.
4. A true or a false hope? The historian of ideas must abstain from value judgment. However, most historians of science—even the most knowledgeable—exaggerate in the opposite direction, denying Renaissance science any "useful value." Toward the end of this book we shall discuss the scant relevance of the concept of "usefulness." Suffice it to specify here that the defection from premodern science is not due to its internal weaknesses; it is a matter of a closed system which, even minus its *absolute* usefulness, functions nonetheless, despite the error of its presuppositions; from the epistemological point of view, we must attribute to it a *relative* use value which is the equivalent, in its results, of any other scientific system including that of our era.
5. On Empedocles and his treatment of catalepsy, see my article "Iatroi kai manteis. Sulle strutture dell'estatismo greco," *Studi Storico-Religiosi* (Rome), n.s. 4 (1980), no. 2: 287–303, esp. 293–94. To this, further observations should be added, contained in my study *Psychanodia I: A Survey of the Evidence concerning the Ascension of the Soul and Its Relevance*, EPRO, 99 (Leiden, 1983).
6. See my article "Magia spirituale e magia demonica nel Rinascimento," *Rivista di Storia e Letteratura Religiosa* (Turin) 17 (1981): 360–408, esp. 373–74.
7. An exhaustive exposition of these theories is set forth in Gérard Verbeke's excellent work *L'Évolution de la doctrine du pneuma du stoïcisme à saint Augustin*

(Paris and Louvain, 1945), pp. 13–215; more recently in M. Putscher, *Pneuma Spiritus, Geist* (Wiesbaden, 1973).

8. See Verbeke, p. 14; Pollak, p. 140.

9. On the influence of the *Corpus hippocraticum* on the theories formulated by Plato in his *Timaeus* see the excellent work of Anders Olerud, *L'idée de macrocosmos et de microcosmos dans le Timée de Platon* (Uppsala, 1951).

10. Cf. Aetius, *Placita*, IV, 19, 1.

11. See note 1 above. The data of the problem are competently discussed in Kudlien's article (1963).

12. See Verbeke, p. 76.

13. The comparison is in Calcidius, *Commentary on the Timaeus*, chap. 220 (see J. H. Waszink's edition). The phrase *typosis en psychē* is from Zeno of Citium; cf. Verbeke, p. 32.

14. Verbeke, pp. 74 sq.; cf. Aetius, *Placita*, IV, 15, 3.

15. See Verbeke, pp. 75 sq.; see also the study by Giorgio Agamben, *Stanze: La parola e il fantasma nella cultura occidentale* (Turin, 1977), p. 108. On this book in general, see my review in *Aevum* (Milan) 54 (1980), 2:386b–87b.

16. Epictetus, *Diss.*, II, 23, 3. Cf. also Plutarch of Chaeronea, Platonist and contemporary of Epictetus the Stoic, in his *Quaest. conviv.*, V, 7.

17. See Verbeke, pp. 214–15. The classic work on the "Pneumatics" is Max Wellmann's *Die pneumatische Schule bis auf Archigenes in ihrer Entwicklung dargestellt* (Berlin, 1895).

18. On the works of Galen and the Latin translators of the Arab *materia medica*, see D. Campbell, *Arabian Medicine and Its Influence on the Middle Ages*, 2 vols. (London, 1926; repr., New York, 1973), esp. vol. 2. To be consulted with caution.

19. See my review of Barthomaeus Anglicus, *On the Properties of Soul and Body: De proprietatibus rerum libri III and IV* (Bibl. nationale, Latin ms. 16098), ed. R. James Long (Toronto, 1979), in *Aevum* 54 (1980): 391b–92a.

20. Long's edition contains only Bartolomaeus's books 3 and 4 according to manuscript copies of the work belonging to two Sorbonne doctors, Pierre de Limoges and the *doctor venerandus* Godefroy des Fontaines.

21. Translated into Latin by Mark of Toledo in the first half of the twelfth century; see Campbell, vol. 1, pp. 61–63.

22. Bartholomaeus's classifications vary according to the chapters; the one we have used is the most coherent.

23. Romantic generalizations have made the Renaissance a clearly defined era of universal history with its own "essence," which differs, for instance, from the "essence" of the Middle Ages or the Reformation. In opposition to this concept, Etienne Gilson stated that the cultural category "Renaissance," as described by Sismondi, Michelet, and Burckhardt, might apply just as well to the culture of the eleventh century. "There is no *essence* of the Middle Ages or of the Renaissance," he concluded; "that is why it cannot be defined." *Héloïse et Abélard: Études sur le Moyen Age et l'humanisme* (Paris, 1938), p. 164. Ernst Cassirer replied to him indirectly, writing some years later: "The historian of ideas does not ask, in the first place, what the *substance* of certain ideas is. He asks what their dynamics are. That which he seeks or ought to seek is less the content of ideas than their *dynamics*"; "Some Remarks on the Question of the Originality of the Renaissance," *Journal of the History of Ideas*, 4 (1943):49–56.

24. In French, English, and German the word "Renaissance" also applies to that period; it is followed by the specification "of the twelfth century." Italian historians have two words to differentiate between the two periods: *la Rinascita* (*romanica*) and the *Rinascimento.* Here we are dealing with *the Rinascita* (*romanica*)

and its importance in the crystallization of the ideational content of the *Rinascimento*.

25. On Ficino's relationship to the young Giovanni Cavalcanti, see the admirable study by Raymond Marcel, *Marsile Ficin (1433–1499)* (Paris, 1958); also André Chastel's succinct and precise *Arte e Umanesimo a Firenze al tempo di Lorenzo il Magnifico*, (Italian translation revised and amplified from the homonymous French work; Turin, 1964).

26. We shall have to take up this question later (see chap. 3, sec. 1).

27. See my review of Roger Boase, *The Origin and Meaning of Courtly Love: A Critical Study of European Scholarship*, (Manchester, 1977), *Aevum* 55 (1981): 360a–63a, esp. 360b–61a.

28. The school of Sicilian poetry started at the court of Frederick II, which gave refuge to many troubadours from France who were persecuted by the Church for (crypto) Catharism. Thus there exists an indirect historical connection between Provençal poetry and the Italian *dolce stil novo*.

29. My account, too short to avoid being schematic, is limited here to a very short inroad into the realm of erotic theories of the twelfth and thirteenth centuries. An almost desperate step—given the extent of that material as well as its importance at the time—which alone justifies the fact that the subject could not but be broached in this book.

30. See J.-P. Roux, *L'Islam en Occident: Europe-Afrique* (Paris, 1959), pp. 33 sq.

31. On Bogomilism, see D. Obolensky, *The Bogomils: A Study in Balkan Neo-Manichaeism* (Twickenham, 1972); on elements common to Catharism and Manichaeism, see H. Söderberg, *La Religion des cathares* (Uppsala, 1949); on the Bogomilist doctrine, see H.-Ch. Puech and A. Vaillant, *Le Traité contre les bogomiles de Cosmas le prêtre* (Paris, 1945). On Bogomilism in the global frame of medieval "heresies," see M. Lambert, *Mediæval Heresy* (London, 1977), pp. 12–13. Very important for the history of the Bogomils in Byzantium is J. Gouillard, "Le Synodikon de l'orthodoxie: Édition et commentaire," in *Travaux et Mémoires du Centre de recherche d'histoire et civilisation byzantines*, no. 2 (Paris, 1967), esp. pp. 228 sq. On Western dualistic trends, see my book *Les gnoses dualistes d'Occident* (Paris, 1987).

32. This theory seems, henceforth, to be proved: see Lambert, pp. 32 sq.

33. Ibid., pp. 26–27.

34. Ibid., p. 28.

35. Ibid., pp. 49–54.

36. Ibid., p. 55.

37. Ibid., p. 109. Studies on Catharism are so extensive in France that here we dare to cite only René Nelli's little masterpiece, *Dictionnaire des hérésies méridionales* (Toulouse, 1968), remarkably useful for new readers. It contains succinct but accurate information on all meridional "heresies," their history and dogma. For more information, see my book cited above, note 31.

38. Bernardus Guidonis, *Practica inquisitionis heretice pravitatis* (Paris, 1886), p. 130.

39. The civil authorities were no less concerned, for the Cathar "perfects," on the day of their *consolamentum*, promised not to take an oath (*quod non jurarent*) and also never to kill anyone (*nullo casu occidendum*), which was tantamount to refusal to do military service. This caused the Cathars to be told that the preachers of the Cross were all murderers, *quod predicatores Crucis sunt omnes homicidae*.

40. Boase, p. 79, referring to J.-Cl. Vadet, *L'Esprit courtois en Orient dans les cinq premiers siècles de l'Hégire* (Paris, 1968).

41. Boase, pp. 78–79.

42. See Henry Corbin, *Histoire de la philosophie islamique* (Paris, 1964), p. 282.

43. Translated in H. Massé, *Anthologie persane* (Paris, 1950).

44. See M. Asín Palacios, *El Islam cristianizado: Estudio del "sufismo" a través de las obras de Abenarabi de Murcia* (Madrid, 1931), pp. 83–84.

45. Cf. Henry Corbin, *L'Imagination créatrice dans le soufisme d'Ibn 'Arabî* (Paris, Flammarion, 1975), pp. 110–11.

46. Ibid., p. 112.

47. Ibid., pp. 113–14.

48. Asín Palacios, pp. 52–54.

49. For a suggestive evocation of courtly love, the reader can always refer to Denis de Rougemont's *L'Amour et l'Occident* (Paris, 1972).

50. *Andreae Capellani Regis Francorum, De Amore libri tres,* ed. E. Trojel (1892; Munich, 1964). The treatise was written around 1170 (see p. v).

51. See Agamben, pp. 21 and 133, n. 1. On *amor hereos* in general, see note 52 below.

52. Boase, Appendix I, 2, pp. 132–33, with bibliography. Bear in mind especially the study by John Livingstone Lowes, "The Loveres Maladye of Hereos," *Modern Philology* 11 (1913–14): 491–546. See also H. Crohns, "Zur Geschichte der Liebe als 'Krankheit,'" *Archiv für Kultur-Geschichte* (Berlin) 3 (1905): 66–86. The tradition of the passionate syndrome dates back to the Greek physician Oribasius (ca. A.D. 360), whose work had two Latin translations, in the sixth and tenth centuries.

53. This is the hypothesis preferred by Boase; see also Ficino, *Sopra lo amore o ver' Convito di Platone: Comento di Marsilio Ficino Fiorentino sopra il Convito di Platone,* ed. G. Ottaviano (Milan, 1973), VI, 5, p. 90.

54. This is the hypothesis used by Agamben, p. 20.

55. This tradition becomes a platitude of Neoplatonic demonology, in which heroes are always mentioned alongside gods and demons. See below, chap. 8, sec. 1.

56. *Causae et curae,* quoted by Agamben, p. 20.

57. *Sopra lo Amore,* VI, 9, p. 100: *Le quali cose osservando gli antichi medici dissono lo Amore essere una spezie di umore malinconico, e di pazzia: e Rafis medico comandò che e' si curasse per il coito, digiuno, ebrietà e esercizio.*

58. Melanchthon, *De amore,* quoted by Agamben, p. 22, n. 2.

59. On the life and work of Bernardus Gordonius, see L. E. Demaître, *Doctor Bernard de Gordon, Professor and Practitioner* (Leiden, 1980).

60. Quoted from Lowes, pp. 499–501.

61. From Lowes, pp. 52–53.

62. Asín Palacios, p. 51.

63. See my *Iter in silvis: Saggi scelti sulla gnosi e altri studi,* vol. 1 (Messina, 1981), p. 126.

64. *Poeti del Duecento,* ed. G. F. Contini (Milan and Naples, 1960), vol. 1, p. 49.

65. Agamben, p. 94, n. 1.

66. Ibid., pp. 94–95.

67. On spirit in Dante, see Robert Klein, "Spirito peregrino," in *La Forme et l'intelligible* (Paris, 1970), pp. 32–64.

68. On the erotic meaning of *significatio passiva,* see my study "Les fantasmes de l'éros chez M. Eminescu," *Neophilologus,* 1981, pp. 229–38.

69. "Heliostatic is a better word since Copernicus did not place the sun exactly at the center [of his universe]." A. G. Debus, *Man and Nature in the Renaissance* (Cambridge, 1978), p. 81.

70. See S. K. Henninger, Jr., "Pythagorean Cosmology and the Triumph of Heliocentrism," in *Le Soleil à la Renaissance: Science et mythes* (Brussels and Paris, 1965), pp. 35–53.

71. See the excellent article by J. Flamant, "Un témoin intéressant de la théorie héliocentrique d'Héraclide du Pont: Le ms. Vossianus lat. 79 q-to de Leyde," in M. B. de Boer and T. A. Edridge (eds.), *Hommages à M. J. Vermaseren* (Leiden, 1978), pp. 381–91. See also my article "Ordine e disordine delle sfere," *Aevum* 55 (1981): 96–110, esp. pp. 103–4.

72. See my article "Démonisation du cosmos et dualisme gnostique," *Revue de l'histoire des Religions* 196 (1979): 3–40 (now in *Iter in silvis*, vol. 1, pp. 15–52).

73. See M. de Gandillac's observations in *Le Soleil à la Renaissance*, p. 58.

74. *De docta ignorantia*, II, 12; cf. E. Cassirer, *Individuo e cosmo nella filosofia del Rinascimento*, Italian transl., (Florence, 1951), p. 50.

75. The name Nicholas of Cusa appears only once in the works of Marsilio Ficino; it was changed in "Nicolaus Caisius Cardinal" (see Cassirer, p. 76). It is a sign that Ficino had apparently not read him.

76. See Cassirer, pp. 74–80.

77. See A. G. Debus, pp. 92–95.

78. Ibid., p. 133.

79. See Gundel-Gundel, *Astrologumena*.

80. See my *Expériences de l'extase* (Paris 1984), pp. 119–44.

**Chapter 2**

1. For Ficino's work I have used the following editions: *Opera omnia* (Basel edition, 1576, 2 vols.), in the *Monumenta politica et philosophica rariora*, series I, 7–8, 2 vols., (Turin, 1962; anastatic reproduction of *Marsilii Ficini Florentini . . . Opera, et quae hactenus extitere . . . in duos Tomos digesta, Basileae, Ex Officina Henricpetrina, s.a.*). As for the *Theologia platonica*, I had a choice between Michele Schiavone's edition in two volumes (Bologna, 1965), in which some chapters especially important for our research were omitted, and the still unfinished but infinitely better edition by Raymond Marcel (Paris, 1964). I have therefore generally used the *Opera Omnia* edition. With respect to the *Commentary on the Symposium* or treatise *On love*, I had a choice between Raymond Marcel's edition (Paris, 1956) and Giorgio Ottaviano's more recent edition, in Italian, *Sopra lo amore o ver' Convito di Platone* (see above, chap. 1, note 53). Most citations are to the latter. Concerning the treatise *De vita coelitus comparanda*, which will be analyzed in detail in part 2 of this book, I have consulted various editions: *Opera*, Basel edition, 1561, vol. 1, pp. 531 sq.; *Opera*, Basel edition, 1576, vol. 1, pp. 529 sq.; the Venice edition, 1498, reproduced recently by Martin Plessner and F. Klein-Franke, *Marsilius Ficinus "De Vita libri tres," Kritischer Apparat, erklärende Anmerkungen, Namenregister und Nachwort von Martin Plessner. Nach dem Manuskript ediert von F. Klein-Franke* (Hildesheim and New York, 1978). See also my review in *Aevum* 54 (1980): 394a–b. Finally, an edition I used is inserted among the treatises on iatromathematics serving as appendix to the work of Johannes of Hasfurt (Johannes Virdung correspondent of the abbot Trithemius), *Ioannis Hasfurti Medici ac Astrologi Praestantissimi De Cognoscendis et medendis morbis ex corporum coelestium positione lib. III. Cum argumentis, et expositionibus Ioannis Paulli Gallucij Saloensis . . . ,Venetiis, Ex Officina Damiani Zenarij* (1584), f. 118 r sq. Since Plessner's edition seemed to me the most convenient (although in several places incorrect or unintelligible), I have used it in the majority of cases. I have therefore not given page references (pages are not numbered in that edition) but have cited directly in the text those chapters from which I have translated excerpts. The existing English translations of *On love* are infinitely better than my own. If, however, I have favored my own translations, it is because they conform to the conceptual system used throughout this book. The same observations apply to the translation of the treatise *De gl'heroici furori* by Giordano Bruno, available to

readers of French in P.-H. Michel's edition; I have not followed it only because a literal translation has the advantage of displaying certain technical terms that the stylistic efforts of the French translator have distorted. At any rate, it must be agreed that my translations from the Latin or the Italian, though accurate, lack elegance. I can recommend no better ones than those which already exist in English or French. With respect to technical details, readers should refer to works like the present book in order to understand their meaning in the cultural context of the period.

The treatise *De vita sana* (II, *Opera*, p. 496), from which this extract is drawn, is dedicated (undated) to Giorgio Antonio Vespucci and Giovan Battista Boninsegna. It was first published in Florence in 1489, with the two other *De vita* treatises.

2. *Vita coel.*, III, *Opera*, p. 535. The treatise is dedicated to the *Serenissimo pannoniae Regi semper invicto* dated July 10, 1489. The *Prooemium* contains the inevitable eulogy as well as astrological predictions concerning the fate of the sovereign. It is followed by an "Admonishment to the reader" ending with a *Protestatio catholici auctoris* including these words: *In omnibus quae hic aut alibi a me tractantur, tantum assertum esse volo, quantum ab ecclesia comprobatur* (cf. also my "Magia spirituale," p. 368). This protestation of faith did not spare Ficino some cause for anxiety; let us agree it was very convenient.

3. Epictetus, *Diss.*, II, 23, 3.

4. Cf. Agamben, p. 119, n. 1.

5. Agrippa of Nettesheim, *De occulta philosophia*, I, 65; cf. Viviana Pâques, *Les Sciences occultes d'après les documents littéraires italiens* (Paris, 1971), p. 155. On the "evil eye" in the Renaissance, see also S. Seligman, *Die Zauberkraft des Auges und das Berufen* (1921; repr. The Hague, n.d.), pp. 458–65. The author does not seem to grasp the precise meaning of the concept of mind and spirit in the Renaissance writers.

6. Pâques, p. 155.

7. Leonardo da Vinci, *Scritti letterari* (Milan, 1952), quoted in Pâques, p. 156.

8. My account of the Art of Memory has no original observations with the exception of Bruno's Italian writings and their interpretation. For the rest, though I have long since broached the subject of the study of *Ars combinatoria* by Ramon Llull and his commentaries (see *Raymundi Lullii Opera ea quae ad adinventam ab ipso artem universalem . . . , Argentorati-Sumptibus Haeredem Lazari Zetzneri*, 1651, 1110 + Index + 150 p., in-12), the incomplete nature of my research has necessitated giving priority to the commentaries of Paolo Rossi, F. A. Yates, and E. Gombrich. This part of my book might have been put in an appendix, had it not been indispensable for understanding all that is to follow.

9. Yates, p. 71; cf. Aristotle, *De anima*, 432a9, and *De memoria et reminiscentia*, 449b31; Yates, p. 32.

10. Yates, pp. 86–103; see also Paolo Rossi, *Clavis universalis* (Milan and Naples, 1962).

11. Yates, p. 112; Rossi, passim.

12. Published in Venice, 1533; see Yates, p. 115.

13. *Congestorium*, p. 119, according to Yates, fig. 6b, chap. V.

14. Rossellius, *Thesaurus artificiosae memoriae* (Venice, 1579), p. 119 v, according to Yates, p. 119.

15. Yates, pp. 130 sq.

16. Published at Udine in 1594; cf. D. P. Walker, *Spiritual and Demonic Magic from Ficino to Campanella* (London, 1958), p. 141.

17. That is Yates's opinion, p. 136.

18. Francisci Georgii Veneti Minoritae Familiae, *De Harmonia Mundi Totius Cantica Tria* (Venice, 1525).

19. Yates, p. 155.

20. Ibid., p. 136.

21. Cf. J. Flamant, *Macrobe* (Leiden, 1977), pp. 544 sq.

22. Giulio Camillo, "L'Idea del Teatro," in *Tutte le opere* (Florence, 1550), p. 67; cf. Yates, p. 140.

23. Ficino, *Vita coel.*, chap. 19.

24. *Opera*, II, p. 1768.

25. Cf. E. Gombrich, "Icones Symbolicae," in *Symbolic Images: Studies in the Art of the Renaissance II* (Oxford, 1978), p. 222, no. 82, and pp. 158–59.

26. Cf. E. Iversen, *The Myth of Egypt and its Hieroglyphs in European Tradition* (Copenhagen, 1961).

27. E. Garin, *Storia della filosofia italiana*, vol. 1 (Turin, 1966), p. 383.

28. *Comp. in Timeaum*, p. 27, in A. Chastel, *Marsile Ficin et l'Art* (Geneva, 1954), p. 105, no. 5.

29. *Theol. Plat.*, XV, 13; see also Garin, pp. 401–2. The tradition of this "inner eye" comes from Plotinus, *Enneads*, I, 6, 9. For Ficino, this is a phantasmic organ directed toward the summit (the intelligible world).

30. P. O. Kristeller, *Il pensiero filosofico di Marsilio Ficino*, Italian translation revised and augmented (Florence, 1953), pp. 218 sq.

31. See Verbeke, pp. 498–507.

32. For the history of the *oculus spiritalis*, see H. Lewy, *Chaldaean Oracles and Theurgy: Mysticism, Magic and Platonism in the Later Roman Empire* (Cairo, 1956; repr. Paris, 1978, through the good offices of M. Tardieu), pp. 370 sq.

33. Chastel, *Marcile Ficin et l'Art*, p. 147.

34. *Prooem. in Platonis Parmenidem* (*Opera*, II, p. 1137). This is simply the Latin translation of an expression Xenophon had used to designate the Socratic method (*paizein spoudē*). On the custom of the "serious games" of Ficino and his contemporaries, see Edgar Wind, *Pagan Mysteries in the Renaissance* 3d ed. (Oxford, 1980), pp. 236–38.

35. Wind attributes them to Nicholas of Cusa's disciple John Andreas of Bussi.

36. On the Orphic myth, see W. K. C. Guthrie, *Orphaeus and Greek Religion*, 2d ed. (London, 1952); H. Jeanmaire, *Dionysos: Histoire du culte de Bacchus* (Paris, Payot, 1950).

37. Heraclitus, fr. 52. On the "Orphic" interpretation of this fragment, see V. Macchioro, *Eraclito, nuovi studi sull' Orfismo* (Bari, 1922). On the interpretation pertaining to "initiation" in the game of Dionysus, see Andrew Lang, *Custom and Myth* (1885; reprint Ooserhout, 1970), pp. 29–44, esp. pp. 39–41; and R. Pettazzoni, *I misteri: Saggio di una teoria storico-religiosa* (Bologna, 1924). On the *ludus mundi*, by Karl Jaspers in particular, see D. L. Miller, *Gods and Games* (New York, 1973), pp. 163–64. On interpretation of fragment 52 by Heraclitus from Nietzsche to Heidegger, see G. Penzo, *Il nichilismo da Nietzsche a Sartre* (Rome, 1976).

38. *La Forme et l'Intelligible*, pp. 31–64.

39. On the biography of Brother F. Colonna, see M. T. Casella and G. Pozzi, *Francesco Colonna: Biografia e Opere*, (Padua, 1959).

40. See the edition by G. Pozzi and L. A. Ciapponi, *Hypnerotomachia Polifili* (Padua, 1964).

41. In 1463, Ficino, at thirty, translated the *Pimander* attributed to Hermes Trismegistus. Despite his precocity, his reputation did not reach Treviso from Florence before 1467.

42. Yates, pp. 123–24.

43. See *Hypnérotomachie*, ed. Guégan-Kerver, p. 309.

44. See my discussion of J. Flamant's thesis, *Macrobe et le néo-platonisme latin, à la fin du IV^e siècle* (Leiden, 1977) in *"Ordine e disordine delle sfere"* (cf. also my review of Flamant's book in *Aevum*, 1979). Two other passages from Ficino's work relate to the doctrine of the descent of the soul among the planetary spheres and the acquisition of vehicles. In his *Theologia platonica* (XVIII, 4–5), Ficino mentions three vehicles of the soul (celestial, aerial, and material), which seems to refer to Synesius of Cyrene's distinction between a *vehiculum divinioris animae*, which is ethereal, and a material vehicle, common to animals and to man (cf. my *Magia spirituale*, note 103). Proclus also makes this distinction (see my *"Ordine e disordine delle sfere"*). Ficino does not hold this position invariably, since in his commentary on Plotinus's *Enneads* (II, 6) we find this passage, akin to Proclus, Macrobius and Servius: *Ex eorum iterum animabus in nostris animis a Saturno contemplatio cautioque et conservatio diligens augetur, ab Jove civilis et prudens potissimum gubernatio, a Marte magnanimitas malorum iniuriarumque expultrix, a Mercurio inquisitio quaelibet et expressio, a Venere charitas et humanitas, a Sole honestatis cura pudorque et gloriae studium verioris, a Luna denique rerum vitae necessariam cura et providentia diligens* (*Opera*, II, p. 1619). The neo-Plotinian term "vehicle" does not appear here, nor do the planetary demons who appear in the text of the *Commentary to the Symposium*. It is very characteristic that, in the eighteenth book of his *Theologia platonica*, Ficino says he does not believe in the doctrine of the soul's passage through the spheres, which he calls "a phantasy of the Platonists." Since he sets it forth in his commentaries on *Enneads* and *Symposium*, however, it is very likely he does subscribe to this theory. Stranger yet, he does not even mention it where it deserves a place of honor, that is, in the book *De vita coelitus comparanda*. Actually, no theoretical justification for astrological magic is as simple as the idea that, in the course of its descent, the soul is enveloped in astral tunics that respond to the momentary influences of the planets. Walker (p. 39) believes that Ficino avoided this explanation because of its heretical nature: indeed, it seemed to presuppose the *preexistence* of souls that become incarnate, which represented a trace of Origenism or of the doctrine of reincarnation. Without being able to exclude Walker's interpretation, the absence of the doctrine of the soul's vehicle in the book *De vita coelitus comparanda*—containing sharp statements that border on heresy—is surprising.

45. Florence, Biblioteca Nazionale, Conventi soppressi I, 1, 28. The commentary to the quotation from Macrobius, *in Somn. Scip.*, I, 12, 13–14, is to be found in ff. 57v–58r of the ms.; cf. P. Dronke, *Fabula: Explorations into the Uses of Myth in Medieval Platonism* (Leiden and Cologne, 1974), p. 112: *A Saturno enim tristiciam, a Iove moderationem, a Marte animositatem, a Venere cupiditatem, a Mercurio interpretandi possibilitatem, a Sole calorem qui [est] etica, id est sentiendi vis, dicitur, a Luna phyticam accipit, quod appellatur incrementum.*

46. *Philosophia mundi*, IV, 10, in *Patrologiae latinae*, v. CLXXII, col. 88, ed. Dronke, p. 173. The same idea recurs in the commentary on Macrobius, f. 50r, cited by Dronke, ibid.

47. Letter to Filippo Valori of November 7, 1492, in *Opera*, p. 888, quoted by Chastel, *Ficin et l'Art*, p. 170.

48. See my review of Agamben, p. 387.

49. E. Panofsky and F. Saxl, *Dürers Melencholia I*, Leipzig and Berlin, 1923; cf. also E. Panofsky, *The Life and Art of Albrecht Dürer* (1943; Princeton, 1965), chap. 5; R. Klibansky, E. Panofsky, and F. Saxl, *Saturn and Melancholy* (London, 1964).

50. See Ficino, *Amore*, (ed. Ottaviano) VI, 9, pp. 100–101.

51. Johannes of Hasfurt, f. 4.

52. Ibid., f. 22v.

53. Ibid., f. 22r.

54. Ibid., f. 4r.
55. *Problemata*, XXX, 1: "Why are geniuses melancholic?" An exhaustive discussion of the question was undertaken by W. Müri, "Melancholie und schwarze Galle" (1953), in Flashar, *Antike Medizin*, pp. 165–91.
56. See Müri, p. 167.
57. *De memoria et reminiscentia*, quoted in Klibansky, Panofsky, and Saxl, pp. 69 sq.
58. *Theol. plat.*, XIII, 2.
59. *Vita coel.*, II: *Saturnus non facile communen significat humani generis qualitatem tamquam sortem* [see von Hasfurt, f. 162r; the text is apparently erroneous: *atque fortem*] *sed hominem ab aliis segregatum, divinum, aut brutum, beatum, aut extrema miseria pressum.*
60. Agamben, pp. 6–19.
61. Chastel, p. 165.
62. Kristeller, p. 230.
63. Letter to Matteo Corsino, in *Tomo Primo delle divine lettere del gran Marsilio Ficino, tradotte in linqua toscana per M. Felice Figliucii senese . . . , In Vinegia, Appresso Gabriel Giolitto de'Ferrari* (1546), 14r–v.
64. Campanella, in *Opere di Giordano Bruno e Tommaso Campanella, a cura di A. Guzzo e R. Amerio* (Milan and Naples, 1956), p. 1053.
65. Ibid., p. 1054.
66. Freud, *Metapsychology.*
67. Agamben, p. 13.
68. Agamben, p. 19, quoting William of Auvergne, *De universo*, I, 3, 7.
69. Sören Kierkegaard, *Enten-Eller: Un frammento di vita*, translated into Italian by A. Cortese, vol. I, Milan, 1976, p. 74.
70. Chastel, p. 168.
71. *Am.*, VI, 9, pp. 100–101.
72. *Theol. plat.*, XVI, 7.

## Chapter 3

1. Here is his portrait by the biographer Giovanni Corsi, in his *Vita* written in 1506 and published in Pisa in 1771: *Statura fuit admodum brevi, gracili corpore et aliquantum in utrisque humeris gibboso: lingua parumper haesitante, atque in prolatu dumtaxat litterae S balbutiente: et utraque sine gratia: cruribus, ac brachiis sed praecipue manibus oblongis: facies illi obducta: et quae mitem ac gratum adspectum praebent color sanguineus, capilli flavi, ac crispantes; ut qui super frontem in altum prominebant.* Besides Corsi's biography, there is another, probably by Pietro Caponsachi, in both a long and short version (cf. R. Marcel, *Marsile Ficin*, pp. 679 sq.). The following details are drawn from it: Ficino studied in two-hour stretches; during the intermissions he played the lyre to rest his spirit (ethereal body). He took great care of his health, which was delicate. To strengthen his spirit, he sipped wine; wherever he was invited to go, he took with him a bottle of his "good Valdarno wine," for changes of beverage were supposed to be bad for the complexion. This all goes to show that he himself followed the recommendations in his treatises *De vita.*
2. For the work of Pico della Mirandola, I have used the following reprint: Giovanni Pico della Mirandola-Gianfrancesco Pico, *Opera omnia (1557–1573). Con una introduzione di Cesare Vasoli* (Hildesheim, 1969), vol. 1 (a reproduction of the Basel edition: *Opera omnia Ioannis Pici Mirandulae Concordiaeque comitis . . .*). For the *Commento*, I have also used the complete E. Garin edition (Florence, 1942), the only one from which the passages concerning Marsilio Ficino have not been

expurgated. The more or less classic work on Pico is Eugenio Anagnine's *G. Pico della Mirandola: Sincretismo religioso-filosofico, 1463–1494* (Bari, 1937). There is a bibliography on Pico della Mirandola in the book by Henri de Lubac, *Pic de la Mirandole: Études et discussions* (Paris, 1974), In particular, there is discussion of the circumstances surrounding the writing of the *Commento*, pp. 84 sq. (for the text of the *Commento*, see *Opera*, I, pp. 898–923). Cf. also the study by Wind, "Amor as a God of Death," in *Pagan Mysteries*, pp. 152–70, esp. pp. 154–57.

3. Lubac, p. 85.
4. Ibid., p. 85, no. 2.
5. Op., I, p. 897a–b.
6. Ibid., p. 922a–b.
7. Garin, ed., pp. 466, 488, 499, 559.
8. The theme of *concordia discors* between Plotinus and the Gnostics (whom he fights—by proxy, so to speak—in his *Enneads*, II, 9; see my "Vol magique dans l'Antiquité tardive," *Revue de l'histoire des religions*, 1981, pp. 57–66, where the problem is only presented in its bare essentials) is one of the favorite subjects of Hans Jonas, who discusses it in the second part of his *Gnosis und spätantiker Geist* (Göttingen, 1954; it is actually the first part of the second volume of the work, which was never continued) and in other studies published subsequently. In 1975, however, he confided to me that he no longer feels up to realizing the dream of his youth—to write the long-planned book in which he would show that Plotinus is the metaphysical continuator of the Gnostics. In Jonas's excellent book *Gnostic Religion* (2d ed., 1963), the part concerning Plotinus has been deleted (see my review of the Italian translation of *Gnostic Religion* in *Aevum*, 1976). With respect to the analogies between gnostic mythology and Plotinus's thought, see the subtle study by H.-Ch. Puech, "Position spirituelle et signification de Plotin," in *En quête de la gnose I: La gnose et le temps* (Paris, 1978), pp. 55–82. I can no longer endorse C. Elsas's thesis, commented on and accepted in my article cited above, to wit, that the adversaries of Plotinus in *Enneads* II, 9, and the *uiri noui* of the Christian polemist Arnobius, were actually the same group surrounding Amelius, Plotinus's disciple. In substance, Plotinus's adversaries profess a doctrine with traces of Valentinian Gnosticism: they believe that the world and its creator are evil and that the very soul of the world has undergone a decline; as for Plotinus himself, the creator of the cosmos can only be good, the cosmos necessary to the perfection of the whole and the soul of the world being above mutability. It is only individual souls that fall. Nevertheless, Plotinus's schema of the emanation of Being (the so-called "Alexandrian schema") which is at the same time a gradual descent of Intellect towards matter, stems from a process of *devolution* (Hans Jonas's term) typical of the "syro-Egyptian" gnostic systems.

9. *Amore*, VII, 13.
10. See Kristeller, *Il pensiero filosofico*, p. 210. Pico makes use of this turn of phrase of Ficino's in his *Commento*, pp. 909b–10a.
11. *Theol. plat.*, III, 2; according to Kristeller, pp. 102 sq., this passage from Ficino derives from Plotinus, *Enneids*, IV, 2, 1.
12. *Theol. plat.*, XIV.
13. *Commento*, I, 11, p. 901a.
14. Ibid., p. 901b.
15. Ibid., III, 10, p. 919b.
16. Lubac, p. 308, no. 1, rules out this hypothesis: "A work as important as this one cannot be explained on such grounds."
17. *Commento*, p. 920a.
18. Ibid., p. 919b.

19. Lubac, pp. 325–26.
20. Ibid., p. 325.
21. Ibid.
22. *Commento*, p. 921a.
23. Ibid., III, 10, pp. 921a–b.
24. Ibid., III, 8, *in Stanza*, IV, pp. 915b–17b.
25. Ibid., p. 916b.
26. Ibid., p. 917a.
27. Ibid.
28. Ibid., p. 910a.
29. See Wind, p. 154.
30. Ibid., p. 155.
31. G. de Ruggiero, *Rinascimento Riforma e Controriforma* (Bari, 1966), p. 454.
32. Bruno's Italian writings have been edited by G. Gentile and V. Spampanato in three volumes, *Opere italiane* (I: *Dialoghi metafisici*, with notes by G. Gentile; II: *Dialoghi morali*, with notes by G. Gentile; III: *Candelaio. Commedia*, with introduction and notes by V. Spampanato), 2d ed. (Bari, 1923–25). This is the edition I have used. The Italian dialogues have been republished in one volume in conformity with the Gentile edition, by G. Aquilecchia (Florence, 1958). As to the Latin works, I have used the reprint of the national edition by Tocco, Vitelli, Imbriani, and Tallarigo: *Jordani Bruni Nolani Opera Latine conscripta: Faksimile-Neudruck der Ausgabe, 1879–1891*, 3 vols. in 8 parts (Stuttgart and Bad Cannstatt, 1961–62). For the Italian dialogues, I have also consulted the (incomplete) edition by A. Guzzo (Milan-Naples, 1956). For the dialogue *De gl'heroici furori*, I have also used F. Flora's edition (Turin, 1928), and one by P.-H. Michel with French translation (Paris, 1954). The bibliography on Bruno is enormous. This is evident in the *Bibliografia di Giordano Bruno* (1582–1950), edited by V. Salvestrini (Florence, 1958), (and its supplements). I have consulted many works; on consideration, it seems that the really important works on Bruno are not very numerous. Among them are: Luigi Firpo, *Il processo di Giordano Bruno* (Naples, 1949), an excellent—but incomplete—reconstruction of Bruno's trial; Antonio Corsano, *Il pensiero di Giordano Bruno nel suo svolgimento storico* (Florence, 1940), a work which, though very useful, systematically neglects Bruno's magic thought and mnemotechnics. This same defect is also evident in earlier studies: Erminio Troilo, *La filosofia Giordano Bruno*, 2 vols. (Turin and Rome, 1907–14), and *Giordano Bruno* (Rome, 1918); Giovanni Gentile, *Giordano Bruno e il pensiero del Rinascimento* (Florence, 1920); Leonardo Olschki, *Giordano Bruno* (Bari, 1927); Edgar Papu, *Giordano Bruno: Viata si opera* (Bucharest, 1947); Bertrando Spaventa, *Rinascimento, Riforma, Controriforma* (Venice, 1928); Augusto Guzzo, *I dialoghi di Giordano Bruno* (Turin, 1932), etc. Very valuable data on Bruno is to be found in P. O. Kristeller, *Eight Philosophers of the Italian Renaissance* (Stanford, 1964), and in E. Garin, *La cultura filosofica del Rinascimento italiano* (Florence, 1961), and *Storia della filosofia italiana*, vol. 2 (Turin, 1966). Nicola Badaloni's *La filosofia di Giordano Bruno* (Florence, 1955), is inspired by Marxism; and indirectly inspired by it is Hélène Védrine's book, *La Conception de la nature chez Giordano Bruno* (Paris, 1967). Frances A. Yates's book *Giordano Bruno and the Hermetic Tradition* (London and Chicago 1964) is still very important, especially as it is supplemented by observations on Bruno contained in *The Art of Memory* and, more recently, in *Astraea*. Yates's undeniable merit is to have integrated Bruno's *oeuvre* into its cultural context; for the first time in the history of modern philosophy, Bruno was not envisaged as the clumsy, grotesque, and "bacchanalian" precursor of modern thinking but as one of the most impressive representatives of Renaissance thought. It is, fundamentally, a question of applying different categories

and of measuring him by the standards of another era, and historians of ideas can never be sufficiently grateful to Yates for having patiently explained the difference. That does not prevent her from labeling as "Hermeticism" all sorts of doctrines of Late Antiquity of which Hermeticism did indeed make use but which did not have a "Hermetic" origin. The quotations in the text and in the footnotes conform to the editions of Bruno's works mentioned at the beginning of this footnote. The passage concerning the interrogation of May 30, 1592, is reproduced by Gentile, II, p. 211, no. 1.

33. These biographical data are indisputable. They are to be found in nearly all the works cited in n. 32 above.

34. J.-R. Charbonnel, *L'Ethique de Giordano Bruno et le deuxième dialogue du Spaccio . . . Contribution à l'étude des conceptions morales de la Renaissance* (Paris, 1919), p. 35.

35. Ibid., p. 276.

36. Henninger, p. 44.

37. See Keller's observation in *Le Soleil à la Renaissance*, pp. 63–64. On Digges's infinite empyrean heaven—an idea that was, at bottom, merely traditional—see also Debus, pp. 87–88.

38. Cf. Keith Thomas, *Religion and the Decline of Magic*, (Harmondsworth [1971], 1978), p. 412. On John Dee in general, see Peter J. French, *John Dee: The World of an Elizabethan Magus* (London, 1972).

39. *Op. it.*, I, p. 21.

40. Ibid.; cf. *De docta ignorantia*, II, pp. 11–12.

41. *Op. cit.*, I, p. 92.

42. P. Ramus, *De religione christiana*, Frankfurt ed., (1577), pp. 114–15, cited by Yates, *The Art of Memory*, p. 237.

43. Yates, ibid., pp. 234–35.

44. Ibid., p. 237.

45. Ibid., p. 261.

46. See n. 38 above.

47. Yates, *The Art of Memory*, pp. 266 sq.

48. Quoted by Yates, ibid., p. 278.

49. G. Perkins Cantabrigensis, *Antidicsonus* (London, 1584), p. 45, quoted by Yates, pp. 274–75. Fundamentally, Perkins was more correct than Yates thinks; it is true that with respect to Peter of Ravenna an absolutely inoffensive practice is at issue (he believes the image of an old love is particularly suited to being recorded by the memory, due to its emotional charge). However, in Bruno's case the technique assumes a systematic character, as evidenced by this very interesting passage from the *Sigillus sigillorum* (*Op. lat.*, II, 2, p. 166): *Excitent ergo, quae comitante discursu, cogitatione fortique phantasia movent affectum, quibusque zelantes, contemnentes, amantes, odientes, maerentes, gaudentes, admirantes, et ad sensuum trutinam referentes, cum zeli, contemptus, amoris, odii, maeroris, gaudii, admirationis et scrutinii speciebus, cum memorandae rei forma efficimur. Porro fortiores atque vehementiores fortius consequentia quadam atque vehementius imprimunt* (21). *Has autem si vel tua vel rei concipiendae natura non adferat, industria citet affectus. In istis enim exercitatio nedum ad optimos pessimosque mores viam aperit, sed et ad intelligentiam et (quantum per hominem fieri potest) omnium pro viribus eiusdem activitatem. Confirmatur hoc, quod populi et gentes, quibus promptior est libido et ira, sunt activiores; et ex iisdem intense odientes et amantes apprime impios, aut si se se vertant quo divinus eos agat amor atque zelus, apprime religiosos habes, ubi idem materiale principium summam ad virtutem pariter proximum esse atque ad vitium potes agnoscere* (22). *Hunc amorem omnium affectuum, studiorum et affectuum parentem (qui proxime allata causa geminus est) daemonem magnum appellavit antiquitas, quem si tibi affabre consiliaveris, omni*

*procul dubio nil tibi supererit difficile. Itaque, prout expedit, explicavimus, unde quasi per artem non solum rerum memoriam, sed et veritatem atque sapientiam per universum humanam possis assequi* (23). Bruno does not deny that emotions open the way toward the noblest as well as the most perverse customs; nevertheless, he is of the opinion that *all* emotions—including those which might be considered negative or immoral—are favorable to mnemotechnics.

50. P.-H. Michel, quoting Sellers, is certain that John Charlewood was the printer. See the foreword to Giordano Bruno, *Des fureurs héroïques* (Paris, 1954), p. 8.

51. Yates, *The Art of Memory*, p. 284.

52. *Ascl.*, IX; cf. Ficino, *Op.*, II, p. 1865; Bruno, *Op. it.*, II, p. 180.

53. *Op. lat.*, II, 2, p. 133; in its entirety, the passage reads: *Primus praecipuusque pictor est phantasica virtus, praecipuus primusque poëta est in cognitativae virtutis adpulsu, vel conatus vel inditus noviter quidam enthusiasmus, quo vel divino vel huic simili quodam afflatu ad convenienter aliquid praesentandum excogitatum concitantur. Idem ad utrumque proximum est principium; ideoque* philosophi sunt quodammodo pictores atque poëtae, poëtae pictores et philosophi, pictores philosophi et poëtae, *mutuoque veri poëtae, veri pictores et veri philosophi se diligunt et admirantur; non est enim philosophus, nisi qui fingit et pingit, unde non temere illud: "intelligere est phantasmata speculari, et intellectus est vel phantasia vel non sine ipsa"; non est pictor nisi quodammodo fingat et meditetur; et sine quandam meditatione atque pictura poëta non est. Phantasiam ergo pictorem, cogitativam poëtam, rationem philosophum primum intelligito, qui quidem ita ordinantur et copulantur, ut actus consequentis ab actu praecedentis non absolvatur.*

54. Yates, p. 253, translates this expression thus: "to understand is to speculate with images." But the verb *speculari*, in the expression *intelligere est phantasmata speculari*, can have no other meaning than to "contemplate, observe, look." In fact, the intellect comprehends by looking at the phantasms projected onto the screen of inner consciousness.

55. Quoted in Gombrich, p. 123.

56. I.e., Giorgio Agamben. Regarding the context of the dialogue, see John Charles Nelson, *Renaissance Theory of Love: The Context of Giordano Bruno's "Eroici furori"* (New York, 1958). We must agree that the title *Heroic Furors* is reminiscent of the name of the syndrome *amor hereos* or *heroycus*. But Giordano Bruno's meaning of the word "hero"—at least in the context of the dialogue—is not the current Neoplatonist meaning (a being from the worlds between, a higher disembodied soul, a kind of demon). On the contrary, here, Bruno's "hero" is a *human* figure who can manipulate phantasms at will and, by means of this procedure, which stems both from mnemotechnics and magic, is able to raise himself to knowledge of the intelligential world. The "heroic passion" is not, therefore, an atrabilious syndrome but a special faculty consisting in the correct channeling of emotions. Those who have it at their disposal are "the violent" (see n. 49 above), capable of intense love and hate which stimulate their imagination and their memory. It is they who can become "heroes," that is, who can master that access to the noetic world that is granted the saints through divine grace. The hero stands in contrast to the saint, and Bruno finds it preferable to be a hero rather than a saint. That is why the title *Heroic Furors* has nothing to do with *amor hereos*.

57. See my aforementioned article "Le vol magique. . . ."

58. R. Mondolfo, *Figure e idee della filosofia del Rinascimento*, Italian trans. (Florence, 1970), p. 73.

59. E. Garin, *La cultura filosofica*, p. 703.

60. G. Gentile, *Giordano Bruno e il pensiero del Rinascimento*, p. 91.

61. Cf. V. Spampanato, *L'antipetrarchismo di Giordano Bruno* (Milan, 1900).
62. Cf. H.-P. Duerr, *Traumzeit: Uber die Grenze zwischen Wildnis und Zivilisation* (Frankfurt, 1978), p. 73.
63. A. Sarno, "La genesi degli 'Eroici furori' di Giordano Bruno," *Giornale critico della filosofia italiana* (Rome), 1920, pp. 158–72; see also F. Flora's preface to his edition of *De gl'heroici furori*, p. xx, which agrees with Sarno's interpretation.
64. *Candelaio: Comedia del Bruno Nolano, Academico di nulla Academia, detto il Fastidito. In Parigi, Appresso Guglielmo Giuliano, Al Segno de l'Amicizia*, 1582 (*Op. it.*, III, 1923). The hero of the comedy, an untutored painter called Gioan Bernardo, was identified by Spampanato (p. xxxii) as being the Neapolitan painter Giovan Bernardo, pupil of Andrea Sabatini, who worked until 1600 and was famous in his day. However, we must not overlook the fact that Gioan Bernardo is the anagram of Giordano Bruno and that the latter likes to call himself a "painter," a philosophic painter and poet, whose canvas is the pneuma and whose colors are phantasms. It should also be made explicit that Bruno accepts, without comment in his works on magic, that same scholasticism of Ficino's that he mocks in the *Candelaio*. Suffice it to quote here this definition of spirit (*Theses de Magia*, XII, *Op. lat.*, III, p. 462): *Anima per se et immediate non est obligata corpori, sed mediante spiritu, hoc est subtilissima quandam substantia corporea, quae quodammodo media inter substantiam animalem est et elementarem; ratio vero istius nexus est, qui ipsa non est omnino substantia immaterialis.* And then this definition of the universal spirit (*De Magia*, ibid., pp. 408–9): *Et ex harum rerum experientia, aliis praetermissis rationibus, manifestum est omnem animam et spiritum habere quandam continuationem cum spiritu universi, ut non solum ibi intelligatur esse et includi, ubi sentit, ubi vivificat, sed etiam et immensum per suam essentiam et substantiam sit diffusus, ut multi Platonicorum et Pythagoricorum senserunt. . . . Porro animus ipse cum sua virtute praesens est quodammodo universo, utpote talis substantia, quae non est inclusa corpori per ipsam viventi, quamvis eidem obligata, adstricta. Itaque certis remotis impedimentis, statim subitoque praesentes habet species remotissimas, quae non per motum illi coniunguntur, ut nemo inficiabitur, ergo et per praesentiam quandam.* (But he believes, for instance, that a nose can be transplanted and the transplant is effective through the soul's virtue.)
65. Jacques du Fouilloux, *La Vénerie et l'adolescence*, ed. Gunnar Tilander (Karlshamn, 1967). In addition to the numerous French editions succeeding each other uninterruptedly until 1650, the work was translated into German, English, and Italian. Often imitated, it fell into disuse after the publication, in 1655, of the *Vénerie royale* by Robert de Salnove.
66. *Complainte du cerf à monsieur du Fouilloux*, by Guillaume Bouchet, pp. 180–83, Tilander.
67. This sonnet has been interpreted in many ways. I cite only a few: Olschki, pp. 96–97; Spaventa, pp. 224–25; Guzzo, pp. 153–55; Garin, in *Medioevo e Rinascimento* (Bari, 1954), pp. 198 and 210–11; Papu, pp. 98–100; Badaloni, pp. 54–63, etc.
68. *Sciolto dalli nodi de' perturbati sensi;* this expression, which resembles that of the Christian polemist Arnobius (fourth century), *liberati e nodis membrorum*, seems to belong to the *Chaldean Oracles* by Julian the Theurgist (see my article, "Le vol magique . . .").
69. This is Yates's interpretation, *The Art of Memory*, pp. 258–59. It refers to the *Sigillus sigillorum, Op. lat.*, II, 2, pp. 190–91. In this passage, Bruno actually speaks of St. Thomas, Zoroaster, and St. Paul, but does not state that he resembles them; he cites them as examples of individuals who have reached the highest state of ecstasy, in which the *imaginatum coelum* (the intelligential world as it is imagined by the performer while practicing the manipulation of phantasms)

corresponds to transcendental reality. Two pages later, however (p. 193), Bruno seems to refer to himself when he writes: *Ego eum, qui timet a corporeis, numquam divinis fuisse coniunctum facile crediderim; vere enim sapiens et virtuosus, cum dolorem non sentiat, est perfecte (ut praesentis vitae conditio ferre potest) beatus, si rem rationis oculto velis aspicere.* That probably explains his indifference when confronted by the death sentence.

70. Cf. S. Lunais, *Recherches sur la Lune*, I (Leiden, 1978), pp. 122 sq.

71. Cf. F. A. Yates, *Astraea: The Imperial Theme in the Sixteenth Century* (London and Boston, 1975), p. 85.

72. See my article *"Inter lunam terrasque . . . Incubazione, catalessi ed estasi in Plutarco,"* in G. Piccaluga (ed.), *Perennitas: Studi in onore di A. Brelich* (Rome, 1980), now in the volume *Iter in silvis*, I, pp. 53–76; *Expériences de l'extase*, pp. 103–17.

73. See J. Festugière, *La Philosophie de l'amour de Marsile Ficin et son influence sur la littérature française au XVIᵉ siècle* (Paris, 1941).

74. See Magendie, *La Politesse mondaine et les théories de l'honnêteté en France au XVIIᵉ siècle* (Paris, 1925), s.a., vol. 1, p. 271; Emile Picot, *Les Français italianisants au XVᵉ siècle* (Paris, 1906–7); E. Bourciez, *Les Moeurs polies et la littérature de cour sous Henri II* (Paris, 1886).

75. Cf. G. Weise, *L'ideale eroico del Rinascimento e le sue premesse umanistiche* (Naples, 1961), II, p. 104.

76. Ibid., pp. 52–103.

77. Ibid., p. 105.

78. Ibid., p. 49.

79. Ibid., pp. 76–77.

80. Cf. H. Champion, *Histoire poétique du XVIᵉ siècle* (Paris, 1923), I, p. 167, quoted by G. Weise, II, p. 45. J. Festugière attributes this phenomenon to the translations of courtly medieval romances: "They were so popular that, once again, the *Cours d'amour* were established among the entourage of François I and Henri II, with the code of fine manners and the whole amorous jurisprudence so dear to the ladies of the Middle Ages" (p. 3). As to G. Weise, he fails to establish the genetic connection, though an obvious one, between Ficino's Platonism and French love poetry in the sixteenth century.

81. Yates, *Astraea*, p. 52.

82. Ibid., p. 77. About a similar symbolism at the French court, see now Sheila Ffolliott, "Catherine de' Medici as Artemisia," in Margaret W. Ferguson and others (eds.), *Rewriting the Renaissance* (Chicago, 1986), pp. 227–41.

83. Yates, *Astraea*, p. 73.

84. Ibid.

85. Ibid., pp. 78 sq.

86. Ibid., p. 76.

87. Ibid., pp. 76–77.

88. Ibid.

89. Ibid., pp. 94–96.

90. The lunar Church (and the solar Christ) represents a cabbalistic tradition (see F. Secret, in *Le Soleil à la Renaissance*, p. 225).

91. Bruno, *Op. it.*, II, p. 479, n. 1 and p. 481, n. 1. On the symbolism of Circe, see my article "Giordano Bruno tra la Montagna di Circe e il Fiume delle Dame Leggiadre," in A. Audisio and R. Rinaldi (eds.), *Montagna e letteratura* (Turin, 1983), pp. 71–75.

92. Circe is very important in Bruno's mnemotechnics. She appears at least four times. First, in the *Sigillus sigillorum*, 30, *Op. lat.*, II, 2, p. 171: *A Circaeis demum veluti poculis abstinentes, caveamus ne animus a sensibilibus speciebus illectus,*

*ita sui in ipsi fixionem faciat, ut intelligibilis vitae privetur dilitiis, vinoque affectuum corporeorum et vulgaris authoritatis . . . ebrius, perpetuo in praesumtuosos, ignorantiae domicilium titubando pernoctet, ibidemque turbatae phantasiae velut insomniis exagitatus, amissis connatis alis intelligentiae, promet, et Protei contemplatus vultum, nunquam concinne formatam, in qua conquiescat, speciem inveniat.* This explains, moreover, the image of Circe in *De gl'heroici furori.* Of course she can have another function, a technical one, in the whole of Bruno's Art of Memory. In the *Triginta Sigillorum Explicatio* (ibid., pp. 148–49), she gives her name to one of the "seals"—which are spatial arrangements of phantasms and, probably, forms of meditation at the same time: *Circaeorum camporum, hortorum et antoroum, vicesimisexti videlicet sigilii, explicatio.* The four fields represent the four qualities (hot, cold, dry, humid). *Sigillum istum hoc in aenigmate quandoque implicavimus,* adds Bruno. A third time, Circe appears in the *Aenigma et Paradigma,* which open the *Ars Brevis alia,* which follows the *Ars Memoriae* and the *Ars Brevis,* integrated into *De Umbris idearum* dedicated to Henri III (*Op. lat.,* II, pp. 170–72). The significance of Circe here is the same as in the twenty-sixth "seal" of the thirtieth *sigil.* *Explicatio:*

> *Coge potens Circe succos tibi in atria septem*
> *Quaeque sit et species in genus acta suum.*

*Hinc medica Circe brevissimo levique studio memoriae inscriptas affixas habet simplicium omnium qualitates, et qualitatum gradus* (p. 171). In short, Circe is the main personage in the dialogue of the *Cantus Circaeus* (*ad eam memoriae praxim ordinatus quam ipse ludiciariam appellot*). *Ad altissimum Principem Henricum d'Angoulesme magnum Galliarum Priorem, in Provincia Regis locumtenentem . . . Parisiis, Apud Aegidium Gillium, via S. Ioannis Lateranensis, sub trium coronarum signo,* 1582; (*Op. lat.,* II, 179–210). This passage of the dialogue between Circe and Moeris is very interesting since it is an excellent characterization of the goddess Diana: *Te appello; Quam Hecaten, Latonam, Dianam, Phaeben, Lucinam, Triviam, Tergeminam, Deamque triformem dicimus. Si agilis, omnivaga, pulcherrima, clara, candida, casta, innupta, verecunda, pia, misericors, et intemerata. Iaculatrix, honesta, animosa venatrix, regina caeli, manium gubernatrix, dea noctis, rectrix elementorum, terra nutrix, animantium lactatrix, maris domina, roris mater, aëris nutrix, custos nemorum, sylvarum dominatrix, tartari domitrix, larvarum potentissima insectatrix, consors Apollinis* (p. 188). It will be observed that there is a veritable Diana litany, in the style of litanies to the Virgin. Since Bruno had already invented the Diana cult in 1582, he could not help being delighted to come across, in England, a whole school which venerated the same goddess. This is why the dialogue *De gl'heroici furori* cannot be interpreted as an Elizabethan allegory only; other more subtle meanings also come into play. (See also my article cited in n. 91.)

**Chapter 4**

1. See my article, "Magia spirituale e magia demonica," n. 118.

2. *Amatus,* "loved," and *amans,* "lover," are generic terms designating the two sexes. See above, chap. 3, n. 73.

3. Heroes are pneumatic beings superior to demons; see below, chap. 7, sec. 1.

4. .Concerning the Rosicrucians, readers can consult, with prudence, Paul Arnold's book (good when dealing with history but very generalized otherwise), *La Rose-Croix et ses rapports avec la Franc-Maçonnerie: Essai de synthèse historique* (Paris, 1970), and, most particularly F. A. Yates, *The Rosicrucian Enlightenment* (London, 1972), also rather generalized. As to the provenance of the Rosicrucian manifestos, there is no doubt that they were drawn up by the circle of friends surrounding Johann Valentin Andreae, who was the brains of the group.

5. *Theses de Magia*, vol. LVI, *Op. lat.*, III, p. 491. The expression *daemon magnus* stems from Ficino's *Commentary on the Symposium* and was conscientiously handed down by Ficino's followers, beginning with Pico della Mirandola.

6. See Edgar Morin, *Le Paradigme perdu: La nature humaine* (Paris, 1973), pp. 126–40, and I. P. Culianu, "Religione e accrescimento, del potere," in G. Romanato, R. G. Lombardo, and I. P. Culianu, *Religione e potere* (Turin, 1981), pp. 173–252, esp. pp. 182–85.

7. Here Bruno reacts against the renascent theories of beauty consisting in a certain *proportio* of the parts of the body (Firenzuola, etc.). In contradistinction, he proposes the idea that beauty is a subjective category which depends on certain transcendental givens. In this, he is merely following Ficino and the other renascent Platonists without, however, emphasizing the astrological correspondences which determine the attraction between individuals.

8. On Taoist practices, cf. Henri Maspéro, "Les procédés de 'nourrir le principe vital' dans la religion taoïste ancienne," in *Le Taoïsme et les religions chinoises* (Paris, 1971), pp. 467–589, and Robert van Gulik, *Sexual Life in Ancient China* (Leiden, 1961).

9. See Mircea Eliade, *Yoga: Immortality and Freedom*, 2d ed. (Princeton, 1970).

10. Cf. A. Coudert, "Some Theories of a Natural Language from the Renaissance to the Seventeenth Century," in *Magia Naturalis und die Entstehung der modernen Naturwissenschaften*, Studia Leibniziana, no. 7 (Wiesbaden, 1978), p. 63.

11. Ibid., p. 64.

12. Ibid., pp. 63 sq.

13. Ibid., p. 63.

14. At one time I thought this an expression of the *coincidentia oppositorum* (see "Motivul "coincidentia oppositorum" la Giordano Bruno," unpublished paper given in November 1970 at the University of Bucharest), especially as it was amply documented by Bruno's philosophical works. However, this interpretation was too greatly influenced by reading Mircea Eliade's *Patterns in Comparative Religion*. The oxymoron in Bruno's poetry can rather be explained as indicative of a technique and practice of a magical kind. We are dealing not with stylistic form but with *concrete* descriptions of controlled psychic functions.

### Chapter 5

1. Walker, *Spiritual and Demonic Magic*, pp. 82–83.

2. See Lubac, *Pic de la Mirandole*, pp. 130 sq.

3. Olerud, *L'idée de macrocosmos* . . . (see chap. 1, n. 9, above).

4. See my "Magia spirituale," n. 85.

5. See Verbeke, p. 53.

6. Ibid., p. 55.

7. Cicero informs us of this, *De divinatione*, I, 3, 6.

8. Ibid., I, 30, 63.

9. Ibid., I, 51, 115.

10. Ibid., I, 19, 37.

11. Cf. Verbeke, pp. 267 sq., with a list of writers who note this phenomenon.

12. Ibid., p. 327; cf. also my "Magia spirituale," p. 391.

13. The treatise *De (in) somniis* by Synesius is translated in volume II of Ficino's work. Its modern edition was done by Nicola Terzaghi *Synesii Cyreniensis Opuscula. Nicolaus Terzaghi recensuit* (Rome, 1944), pp. 143–87; Greek text, without translation. It is superior to that of the *Patrologia Graeca*, LXVI (with Latin translation).

14. See Verbeke, p. 32.

15. Ibid., p. 76.

16. Ibid., p. 161.

17. Epictetus, *Diss.*, III, 2, 20.

18. *De vita coelitus comparanda* was finished only a few months after the translation of Synesius's treatise *On Dreams* (*De somniis*). This (*Op.*, II, pp. 1968 sq.) was dedicated to Piero de' Medici on April 15, 1489, whereas the date of dedication of *De vita coelitus comparanda* is July 10, 1489.

19. Synesius, *Peri enhypniōn*, IV (134a sq.), p. 149, 16 sq. (Terzaghi).

20. Ibid.

21. This also applies to the Neoplatonist Iamblichus, *On the Mysteries of the Egyptians*, III, 14.

22. Synesius, *De somniis*, 135d–36a, pp. 152, 17–53, 5 (Terzaghi).

23. Cf. my article "Inter lunam terrasque."

24. *De defectu oraculorum*, 41, 432f sq.

25. *De somniis*, 137.

26. Ibid., 134–35.

27. Michel Foucault, "La prose du monde," in *Les Mots et les choses* (Paris, 1966), pp. 32–59.

28. Synesius, *De somniis*, 132b–c, p. 147, 1–7 (Terzaghi).

29. Ibid., 134.

30. Nicholas of Cusa, *Idiota triumphans*, III; *De mente*, 5.

31. *Vita coel. comp.*, XV.

32. Karl Preisendanz, *Papyri Graecae Magicae: Die griechischen Zauberpapyri*, 2 vols., edited by A. Henrichs, Stuttgart, 1973–1974.

33. Hans Dieter Betz, ed., *The Greek Magical Papyri in Translation, Including the Demotic Spells*, vol. 1 (Chicago, 1986).

34. The Arabic edition by H. Ritter, *Stud. Bibl. Warburg, XII, 1933*, German translation by H. Ritter and M. Plessner, *Studies of the Warburg Institute*, no. 27, 1962; the first two of the four books of the *Picatrix*, according to a French translation from the Latin, the most ancient of which goes back to 1739, are included in Sylvain Matton's collection *La Magie arabe traditionnelle* (Paris, 1976), pp. 245 sq. The mysterious name "Picatrix" is, perhaps, a distortion of Buqratis, mentioned in the text as translator of a treatise on talismans edited by Kriton; very likely it refers to the Greek physician Hippocrates, whose name carried sufficient weight to ensure the prestige of works of this kind.

35. See Plessner's edition of Ficino's treatises, *De vita*, and my review in *Aevum*, no. 54 (1980): 397a–b.

36. See Matton, *La Magie arabe traditionnelle*, p. 71; text, ibid., pp. 72 sq.

37. See Synesius, *De somniis*, in Ficino, *Opera*, II, p. 1969.

38. See A. Coudert, p. 59. This refers to the work of Franciscus Mercurius van Helmont, who believed the letters of the Hebrew alphabet represented phonetic diagrams indicating the position of the tongue when articulating sounds (ibid.).

39. See above, chap. 4, n. 6.

40. See my article "Iatroi kai manteis," where this theory is discussed from the point of view of its applicability to cases of Greek ecstatics; *Expériences de l'extase*, pp. 25–43.

41. *Tomo Primo delle Lettere*, p. 8r.

42. *Vita coel. comp.*, III; cf. *Picatrix*, p. 171, 7 (Ritter-Plessner).

43. See my "Magia spirituale."

44. See Arnold.

45. Walker, pp. 203 sq.

46. Ibid., pp. 54–145. For Agrippa, reference can always be made of the French translation by K.-F. Gaboriau, *La Philosophie occulte*, 5th ed., 4 vols. (Paris,

1979). A useful edition in modern German is H. Cornelius Agrippa von Nettesheim, *Die magischen Werken,* edited by K. Benesch (Wiesbaden, 1982).

**Chapter 6**

1. The adjective "celestial" or "heavenly" (*coelestis*) here means "ethereal" or "quintessential," since ether was the substance of sky. Let us remember that the human pneuma is of the same kind.

2. Psellus, "Commentaire des 'Oracles chaldaïques,'" p. 1132a, in *Oracles chaldaïques, avec un choix de commentaries anciens,* text compiled and translated by E. des Places (Paris, 1971), pp. 168–69.

3. Cf. H. Lewy, *Chaldean Oracles and Theurgy* (Cairo, 1956), p. 178.

4. Cf. G. Durand, "L'univers du symbole," *Revue de Sciences religieuses* 49 (1975): 3, 8–9.

5. S. M. Shirokogoroff, *Psychomental Complex of the Tungus* (London, 1935), p. 243a.

6. Ibid.

7. R. B. Onians, *The Origins of European Thought about the Body, the Mind, the Soul, the World, Time, and Fate: New Interpretation of Greek, Roman, and Kindred Evidence, Also of some Basic Jewish and Christian beliefs* (Cambridge, 1951). Onians's interpretations have been criticized by a number of scholars.

8. Olerud, *L'idée de macrocosmos.*

9. Onians, *Origins of European Thought.*

10. Onians, p. 119 sq.

11. Olerud, p. 23.

12. Ibid., p. 23.

13. Because of an objective anatomical datum (associated with elements of divination), the liver has a glossy and sleek surface enabling "visions" to be reflected in it.

14. "*Hermetis Trismegisti Iatromathematica (Hoc est, Medicinae cum Mathematica coniunctio) ad Ammonem Aegyptum conscripta, interprete Ioanne Stadio Leonnouthesio,*" in Johannes of Hasfurt, *De cognoscendis et medendis morbis,* f. 113r.

15. Ibid., f. 113v.

16. A rather far-reaching example of iatromathematical combinations with reference to phlebotomic man is found in Hasfurt, f. 5r–8v.

17. J. Seznec, *La Survivance des dieux antiques* (Paris, 1980), p. 50.

18. *Proinde necessarium est meminisse arietem praeesse capiti atque faciei, taurum collo, geminos brachiis atque humeris, cancrum pectori,* etc., up to: *pisces pedibus.*

19. See n. 16 above.

20. The erotic charms to which Ficino seems to refer were of folk origin. Abbot Trithemius speaks of them in his *Antipalus maleficiorum,* also mentioning rather peculiar remedies derived from medieval magic. The charms and remedies are corroborated by the Neapolitan G. B. Porta; cf. W.-E. Peuckert, *Pansophie: Ein Versuch zur Geschichte der weissen und schwarzen Magie* (Berlin, 1956), pp. 316 sq. Wolfgang Hildebrand adapted Porta's prescriptions, which then appeared in folk literature (in Germany in the form of what Peuckert calls *magische Hausväterliteratur*—an untranslatable idiom denoting lists and catalogues of information relating to astrology, meteorology, medicine, etc., indispensable to European peasants, patresfamilias, until the beginning of the twentieth century).

21. According to M. Plessner, this refers to the stone called *firuzağ* in Persian, which is the turquoise, not the sapphire. The example is taken from the *Picatrix,* p. 120, 14 sq. (Ritter-Plessner).

22. See *La Magie arabe traditionnelle,* p. 311.

23. *Picatrix*, bk. II, ibid.
24. *Picatrix*, translated in Seznec, *La Survivance*, p. 53.

**Chapter 7**
1. See Emile Grillot de Givry, *Illustrated Anthology of Sorcery, Magic and Alchemy* (New York, 1973); the iconology pertaining to demons in analyzed in Jurgis Baltrusaitis's masterpiece, *Le Moyen Age fantastique: Antiquités et exotismes dans l'art gothique* (Paris, Flammarion, 1981).
2. H. Lewy, p. 246.
3. *Or. chald.*, fr. 144, p. 102 (des Places).
4. On the *Iynges*, see Lewy, pp. 132–35.
5. Ibid., p. 4.
6. Ibid., pp. 190–92.
7. Ibid., pp. 252–54.
8. *Or. chald.*, fr. 90, p. 88 (des Places). I have changed the translation slightly. These same *chthonioi kynes* also reappear in another fragment (91, p. 89) next to aerial and aquatic dogs.
9. Lewy, pp. 289–92. The practice antedates the *Oracles*; it is mentioned by Plutarch (cf. Culianu, *Inter lunam terrasque* . . .). As to the statuettes, they were made in three colors of clay (red, white, black), symbolizing fiery ether, white air, and black earth. As binding material, vulture and crow fat were used. The statuettes represented an eagle and a snake. Wax in three colors was used for statues of Hecate; red, white, and black threads were part of the arsenal of magic.
10. I am following Marsilio Ficino's Latin translation, II, p. 1879. For a modern translation, see Iamblichus, *Les Mystères d'Egypte*, text compiled and translated by Edouard des Places (Paris, 1966).
11. Cf. Joseph Hansen, *Quellen und Untersuchungen zur Geschichte des Hexenwahns* (Bonn, 1901), p. 125; and also Henry Charles Lea, *Materials toward a History of Witchcraft* (New York and London, 1957), p. 272.
12. Lea, pp. 288–89.
13. Ibid., p. 553.
14. Ibid., p. 563.
15. Hansen, *Quellen*, pp. 197–98; Lea, p. 302.
16. Lea, pp. 922, 926.
17. Klein, *Examen* . . . , pref., nn. 3–4, cited by Lea, p. 929.
18. Lea, pp. 919–21.
19. Remy, *Daemonolatreia*, I, 6, nn. 7–13. Because of the term *focarius*, the translation is difficult. Though not foolproof, the "classical" translation followed here is better than the one given in the French edition of this book, p. 204.
20. Quoted by H. P. Duerr, *Traumzeit*, p. 65. To De Lancre, sodomy was a kind of erotic relationship preferred by the devil; for De Lancre's *Tableau de l'inconstance* . . . , see Bibliography.
21. Duerr, p. 262, n. 30. Once more it is Giordano Bruno who informs us of a folk practice of erotic magic which casts light on the very practices of witches. We quote the passage here without any changes (*Op. lat.*, II, p. 187: *Sigillus sigillorum*, 45; De undecima contractionis specie—"contractions" were spiritual phenomena whose effect could be positive or negative): "Let one add [to the list of contractions of spirit] a damnable kind of contraction which one finds in uncivilized people, dirty and hypocritical, whose black bile, thicker and more abundant than nature allows, is cause of the production of voluptuous pleasures and venereal liaisons, as well as so-called revelations which are fruitless and bestial, stemming from disturbances of their porcine phantasy. . . . Among this

kind of bestial personages there are some who eat raw and bitter grasses and distending vegetables and who, annointing themselves with baby fat, expose themselves nude to the fresh air, in the silence of night. It happens that the heat produced by those conditions moves to the interior of their body, and the fat penetrates through the pores of their skin. Thus it is that the receptacles of carnal desire fill up readily and produce an artificial semen [that is to say, not emitted during sexual intercourse]. Stimulated by venereal meditations caused by their initial procedures and all the rest, they reach a weak state of excitement in which they believe that their phantasmic cogitations are real acts. That lasts all night during which they eliminate this libidinal infatuation and juice, none of which remains when they awaken. But they are convinced of having spent the night in a voluptuous coupling with a man or a woman. It is likely and in conformity with nature that in the meantime they have experienced a very powerful phantasmic enjoyment. For the seminal emission is not developed during the whole of an ordinary sexual act but is produced later and more slowly, the body being in repose, solely by the movement of the imagination, transient infatuation and external humors having continuously penetrated through the libidinal channels." This passage seems to confirm the idea that many "sorcerers," through cutaneous absorption of hallucinogens, were only seeking sexual pleasures. Bruno's evidence was hitherto ignored.

22. Nider, *Formicarius*, V, 3, cited in Lea, p. 261.

23. Lea, p. 244.

24. Ibid., p. 187. This hypothesis is, however, highly questionable.

25. Ibid., pp. 179–80.

26. Ibid., p. 181, citing pseudo-Augustine, *Liber de Spiritu et Anima*, chap. XXVIII.

27. Ibid., p. 187, quoting Thomas Aquinas, *Quaestio unica*, 2, *ad* 14.

28. Ibid., pp. 260–61, quoting Nider, *Formicarius*, II, 4.

29. Hansen, *Quellen*, p. 196.

30. Ibid., p. 199.

31. Cf. Isidore Teirlink, *Flora Magica: De plant in de tooverwereld* (Antwerp, 1930), pp. 21–23 (six different prescriptions).

32. Ibid., pp. 86 and 90.

33. Ibid., p. 46.

34. I owe this information to Professor Van Os, who taught pharmacology at the University of Groningen. He has also been kind enough to provide me with the rudiments of a bibliography on this subject (especially R. E. Schultes and A. Hofmann, *The Botany and Chemistry of Hallucinogens*, Springfield, 1973). The alcaloids contained in the Solanaceae differ from the alcaloids contained in the hallucinogenic plants of Mexico and South America by virtue of their faculty of being absorbed through the skin. On the contrary, the latter are characterized by the presence, in their chemical structure, of a group called *indol*, which does not penetrate the skin. That explains the different customs of European sorcerers compared with the medicine men of Central and South America.

35. See M. Harner, "The Role of Hallucinogenic Plants in European Witchcraft," in M. Harner (ed.), *Hallucinogens and Shamanism* (Oxford University Press, 1973), pp. 125–50.

36. See Harner's and Duerr's point of view. As early as the beginning of the century, some scientists experimented with the action of "witches' unguents" made according to traditional prescriptions. Let us listen to the account one of them gives of the use of the active ingredients of the *Datura stramonium* and the *Hyoscyamus niger*: "Shortly after anointing myself I had the impression of flying through a tornado. When I had anointed armpits, shoulders, and the other parts

of the body I fell into a long sleep, and the following nights I had very vivid
dreams of fast trains and marvelous tropical landscapes. Several times I dreamed I
found myself on a high mountain and was speaking to people who lived in the
valley although, due to distance, the houses down there assumed tiny dimensions" (quoted by Teirlink, p. 23).

37. Related by Emile Grillot de Givry.

38. See H. Zimmer, "On the Significance of the Indian Tantric Yoga," in *Spiritual Disciplines*, Papers from Eranos Jahrbuch, no. 4 (New York, 1960), pp. 40–
53.

39. Paul Grillandi, *Tractatus de Sortilegiis* (Frankfurt-on-Main, 1592), p. 168, q.
XI, no. 1, cited in Lea, pp. 409–10.

40. Johannes Trithemius Abbas, *Liber Octo Quaestionum*, Oppenheim, 1515,
Q. 5, *"De Reprobis atque Maleficis,"* cited in Hansen, *Quellen*, pp. 292–93.

41. Printed at Ingolstadt in 1595; cf. Hansen, *Quellen*, pp. 295–96.

42. Peuckert, *Pansophie*, p. 76. One of those pseudo-epigraphs, under a kilo-
metric title, bears the date 1482. At that time, Trithemius, then hardly twenty,
had not yet written anything.

43. Peuckert, p. 71.

44. Ibid., pp. 72–73. Trithemius's bibliography is very extensive. We shall
deal only with matters relating to his *Steganography* of which we have used the
following edition by W. E. Heidel: *Johannis Trithemii Primo Spanheimensis deinde
Divi Jacobi Peapolitani Abbatis Steganographia. Quae Hucusq; a nemine intellecta, sed
passim ut supposititia, perniciosa, magica et necromantica, rejecta, elusa, damnata et
sententiam inquisitionis passa; Nunc tandem vindicata reserata et illustrata. Ubi post
vindicias Trithemii clarissime explicentur Coniurationes Spirituum ex Arabicis, Hebrai-
cis, Chaldaicis et Graecis Spirituum nominibus juxta quosdam conglobatae, aut secundum alios ex Barbaris et nihil significantibus verbis concinnatae. Deinde solvuntur et
exhibentur Artificia Nova Steganographica A Trithemio in Literis ad Arnoldum Bostium
et Polygraphia promissa, in hunc diem a nemine capta, sed pro paradoxis et impossibilibus
habita et summe desiderata. Authore Wolfgango Ernesto Heidel, Wormatiense. Moguntiae, Sumptibus Joannis Petri Zubrodt. Anno 1676* (1 vol. of 397 pp.). The classic
modern monograph on Trithemius is by Isidor Silbernagel, *Johannes Trithemius:
Eine Monographie* (1868; Regensburg, 1885). It is outstripped by P. Chacornac,
who, in his *Grandeur et adversité de Jean Trithème, bénédictin, abbé de Sponheim et de
Würzbourg, 1462–1516* (Paris, 1963), proves to be a good interpreter of the
*Steganography*, but confines himself to reproducing bibliographical data—often
erroneous—supplied by Heidel. The best monograph is also the most recent; it
is by Klaus Arnold, *Johannes Trithemius, 1462–1516* (Würzburg, 1971). Arnold
ably reconstructs Trithemius's personal history in the framework of the social
history of his era, but only deals superficially with Trithemius's magic. Regarding the latter, we can have recourse—exercising prudence—to the data given by
Peuckert in his *Pansophie* in the chapter entitled "Der Zauberer Trithemius," pp.
70–84. A scholar unequaled in the field of German occultism, Peuckert is the
most valuable source of a list of references on Trithemius; but he does not seem
to have closely studied interpretations of the *Steganography*. N. L. Brann's book,
*The Abbot Trithemius, 1462–1516* (Leiden, 1981), only deals with the monk's
career.

45. Peuckert, *Pansophie*, pp. 72–73.

46. Georg Willin, *Dissertatio historico-literaria de arte Trithemiana scribendi per
ignem* (Uppsala, 1728), p. 33, quoted by Klaus Arnold, *Johannes Trithemius*, p.
180.

47. Kurt Baschwitz, *Hexen und Hexenprozesse: Die Geschichte eines Massenwahns
und seiner Bekämpfung* (Munich, 1963), pp. 17 sq.

48. See Peuckert, pp. 72–73.

49. Ibid., p. 77.

50. *Fama confraternitatis*, in Yates, *The Rosicrucian Enlightenment*.

51. *Primo Poeta celeberrimus . . . Secundo . . . Orator facundissimus . . . Tertio . . . subtilissimus Philosophus . . . Quarto . . . Mathematicus . . . ingeniosissimus . . . Quinto . . . Historicus perfectus . . . Sexto . . . Theologus insignis* (Heidel, *Vita Johannes Trithemius Abb.*, pp. 34–35).

52. The city of Würzburg, where tradition concerning Trithemius lasted about two centuries, and the monastery of Sponheim are located near Heidelberg in the Palatinate, where the "farce" (*ludibrium*) of the Rosicrucians took place at the beginning of the seventeenth century. With respect to the "inextinguishable lamps" found in the tomb of Father Christian Rosenkreuz, it is probable that the authors of the *Fama confraternitatis* made use of an element of Trithemius's legend, according to information given by Bartholomeus Korndorff derived from Servatius Hochel.

53. Trithemius's complete bibliography is recorded by Klaus Arnold, pp. 228 sq.

54. Peuckert, p. 75.

55. Heidel, *Vita Johan. Trith. Abb.*, p. 1.

56. Arnold, p. 7.

57. Hans Ankwicz-Kleehoven, *Der wiener Humanist Johannes Cuspinian*, Graz-Köln, 1959, p. 16, quoted by Arnold, p. 56.

58. Arnold, p. 62.

59. Cited by Arnold, p. 61.

60. Ibid., p. 58.

61. *Antipalus*, I, 3; Peuckert furnishes a list which is almost complete, *Pansophie*, pp. 47–55.

62. The text of this letter is reproduced by Heidel, pp. 50–51; it is partially translated and summed up in its entirety by Peuckert, pp. 82–83.

63. On the whole case, see Thorndike, *History of Magic*, vol. 6, pp. 438–43. The letter is dated by Thorndike 1509.

64. The *Polygraphia* was finished March 21, 1508, and consigned to Emperor Maximilian June 8, 1508. It was translated into French by Gabriel de Collange in 1561.

65. *Joannis Wieri Opera Omnia . . . Editio nova . . . Amstelodami, Apud Petrum van den Berghe* (1660), p. 112 (*De Praestigiis Daemonum*, II, 6: "*De Johanne Trithemio, ejusque libro Steganographia inscripto*").

66. Adam Tanner, *Astrologia sacra: Hoc est, orationes et quaestiones quinque . . .* (Ingolstadt, 1615); see Arnold, p. 190.

67. Sigismund von Seeon, *Trithemius sui ipsius vindex, sive Steganographiae Joannis Trithemii apologetica defensio* (Ingolstadt, 1616); see Arnold, p. 190.

68. Gustav Selenus, *Cryptomenytices et cryptographiae libri IX. In quibus et planissima Steganographiae a Johanne Trithemio olim conscriptae enodatio traditur* (Lüneburg, 1624).

69. Johannes Caramuel y Lobkowitz, *Steganographiae nec non claviculae Salomonis Germani Joannis Trithemii Abbatis Spanheimensis Ordinis Sancti Benedicti (quae hucus a nemine intellecta, a multis fuerunt condemnatae, et necromantiae nota inustae) genuina, facilis, dilucidaque declaratio* (Cologne, n.d.; 1635 according to Arnold, p. 190).

70. Johannes d'Espières, *Specimen steganographiae Joannis Trithemii . . . quo auctoris ingenuitas demonstratur et opus a superstitione absolvitur, cum vindiciis Trithemianis* (Douai, 1641).

71. Athanasius Kircher, *Polygraphia nova et universalis* (Rome, 1663) (*Appendix apologetica ad polygraphiam novam, in qua Cryptologia Trithemiana discutitur*).

72. Heidel, *Vita Johan. Trith. Abb.*

73. Gaspar Schott, *Schola Steganographica* (Nuremberg, 1680); see Arnold, p. 190.

74. *Trithemius gehört das Verdienst, die erste umfassende Arbeit auf dem Gebiet der modernen Kryptographie veröffentlich und damit Vorbild und Anregung für die weitere Entwicklung gegeben zu haben* (K. Arnold, p. 192). Temurah is the cabbalistic system of permutation of the letters of the alphabet.

75. Heidel, p. 111.

76. Arnold, p. 188.

77. *De septem secundeis, id est intelligentiis sive spiritibus orbes post Deum moventibus;* see Arnold, pp. 162–63. Under the title *Traité des causes secondes* (preceded by a life of the author, a bibliography, and a preface and accompanied by notes), this writing appeared in Paris in 1898, becoming the first number of the Bibliothèque rosicrucienne. The translator is anonymous.

78. *Steganographia*, Heidel's edition, pp. 297 sq.

79. Ibid., pp. 310–11.

80. *Tractatus de Sortilegiis*, p. 168, q. XI, n. 1.

81. See Arnold, p. 184.

82. Agrippa, Epistle IV, 62, cited in Auguste Prost, *Les Sciences et les Arts occultes au XVIᵉ siècle: Corneille Agrippa. Sa vie et ses oeuvres*, 2 vols. (reprint of the Paris edition, 1881–82; Nieuwkoop, 1965), vol. 1, p. 156.

83. Epistle IV, 19, cited in Prost, pp. 204–5.

**Chapter 8**

1. See my *Religione e accrescimento del potere*.

2. See Debus, *Man and Nature in the Renaissance*, pp. 140–41. On Newton's alchemy, see B. J. T. Dobbs, *The Foundations of Newton's Alchemy, or "The Hunting of the Greene Lyon"* (Cambridge, 1975); Mircea Eliade, "Le Mythe de l'alchimie," *L'Herne* (Paris) 33 (1978): 157–67.

3. See Viviana Pâques, *Les Sciences occultes*.

4. Will-Erich Peuckert, *L'Astrologie: Son histoire, ses doctrines*, French trans. (Paris, 1980), p. 156.

5. Ibid., p. 165. On the treatment of conjunctions in medieval literature, see E. Garin, *La cultura filosofica del Rinascimento*, p. 157. Pietro of Abano wrote in his *Conciliator differentiarum* of 1277 (f. 15, quoted by Cantù, *Les Hérétiques d'Italie*, vol. 1, p. 386): *Ex coniunctione Saturni et Jovis in principio Arietis, quod quidem circa finem 960 contigit annorum, totus mundus inferior commutatur, ita quod non solum regna, sed et leges et prophetae consurgunt in mundo . . . sicut apparuit in adventu Nabuchodonosor, Moysis, Alexandri Magni, Nazarei, Mahometi* (his chronology must be taken with a grain of salt). As to Pierre d'Ailly, who seems to have predicted, in his *Concordia astronomiae cum historica veritate*, great changes for the still remote year 1789 (Pierre d'Ailly lived ca. 1350–1420), here is what he says about the coming of Christ (*Vigintiloquim*, Venice, 1490, quoted by Garin, *La cultura . . .*): *Sine temeraria assertione, sed cum humili reverentia dico quod benedicta Christi incarnatio et nativitas, licet in multis fuerit miraculosa et supernaturalis, tamen etiam quoad multa huic operi deifico conceptionis et nativitatis natura tamquam famula Domino suo et Creatori subserviens divinae omnipotentiae cooperari potest.* Roger Bacon assumes the role of interpreter of al-Kindī and Albumasar in his theory of the interrelations of the planets (or conjunctions) and the world's great religions: *Iudaisma*, he says for instance, *quod congruit planetae Saturni, quod omnes planetae iunguntur ei, et ipse nemini illorum iungitur . . .* (quoted by Garin, *La cultura . . .*). See also T. Gregory, "Temps astrologique et temps chrétien," in *Le Temps chrétien de la fin de l'Antiquité au Moyen Age* (Paris, 1984), pp. 557–73.

6. Kepler, *De vero anno* (1613), quoted by Peuckert, *L'Astrologie*, p. 148.

7. Peuckert, quoting Kepler, ibid.
8. Peuckert, p. 192.
9. See Yates, *The Rosicrucion Enlightenment.*
10. Peuckert, *L'Astrologie,* pp. 151–52.
11. Ibid., p. 190.
12. Quoted by Peuckert, p. 188.
13. See the *Disputationes adversus Astrologiam divinatricem* by Pico della Miran-dola, V, 1.
14. Peuckert, *L'Astrologie,* p. 120.
15. Lichtenberger, *Practica,* 1527 ed., pp. 31–33, quoted by Peuckert, *L'Astro-logie,* pp. 122–23.
16. Cf. H. Brabant and S. Zylberszac, "Le Soleil dans la médecine à la Renais-sance," in *Le Soleil à la Renaissance,* pp. 281–82. That only partly explains the term "French sickness," as Peuckert, pp. 217–18, may well have seen.
17. Brabant and Zylberszac, p. 282.
18. Quoted by Peuckert, *L'Astrologie,* p. 217.
19. Brabant and Zylberszac, p. 282.
20. Ibid., pp. 282–83.

**Chapter 9**
1. See Mircea Eliade, *Histoire des croyances et des idées religieuses,* vol. 1 (Paris, 1976), pp. 175 sq.; see also my *Mircea Eliade* (Assisi, 1978), pp. 139–40.
2. Agrippa had it printed in 1531. His fourth book is a fake, though written by someone very familiar with the first three books. It appears in the edition of the *Opera,* 2 vols. (Lyon, n.d., but 1565 or later) along with the others (vol. I, pp. 1–404).
3. *Opera,* II, pp. 1–247. The work was written about 1526.
4. Chaps. LXII and XCVI; see Auguste Prost, I, pp. 110–111.
5. Ibid., p. 111.
6. Chap. CI, quoted in Prost, p. 112.
7. Chap. CII, ibid., pp. 112–13.
8. I, pp. 332–33.
9. Prost, I, pp. 319 sq. With remarkable juridical energy and subtlety, Agrippa got the better of the inquisitor Nicole Savini, who got his revenge later (Prost, p. 327). In a letter to his friend Chansonnetti (*Cantiuncula; Ep.* II, 40), then in Basel, Agrippa denounces the irregularity of the procedures of the Inquisition (see Prost, p. 323).
10. On the "Lyon affair," see Prost, II, pp. 119 sq. Satisfied with the treat-ment that he and his family received at Lyon, Agrippa several times refused to leave the royal side to join the duke of Bourbon, who commanded the army of the Emperor Charles V in Italy. After the horoscope incident, Agrippa was left behind in Lyon by the royal family and deprived of his sinecure. Left without means of support, Agrippa sent desperate messages to his friends. He was later informed by a stranger of his irremediable disgrace vis-à-vis the queen mother.
11. Prost, II, p. 171.
12. Peuckert, *L'Astrologie,* p. 31.
13. Cf. P. J. S. Whitmore, *A Seventeenth-Century Exposure of Superstition: Se-lected Texts of Claude Pithoys, 1587–1676* (The Hague, 1972). Pithoys's career, though unremarkable, has some unusual aspects. It involves a story of demonic possession during which his attitude was similar to that of Agrippa in the Woip-py episode. Pithoys describes the whole business in a tract of 1621, entitled *Descouuerture des faux possedez.* A young widow of Nancy, Elisabeth Ranfaing, fell into the hands of a doctor who, after violating her, gave her medications

which caused convulsions. The widow was exorcised at Toul, November 9–11, 1620. Pithoys, who was present, arrived at the conclusion that the exorcism was futile, since the agent that had caused her torment was not diabolical but physical. He expressed his views in a letter to Jean de Porcelets, bishop of Toul (letter of January 6, 1621). The bishop summoned him in order to inform him that he found the exorcism valid nevertheless, upon which Pithoys could only "piously withdraw after a respectful bow." But he did not give up. Revealing considerable knowledge, he wrote the *Descouuerture*, in which, without denying the fundamentals of the practice of exorcism in general, he attacked the incongruous nature of the evidence against Elisabeth Ranfaing. The doctor replied, but, convicted of *mala fide*, he was burned at the stake with his assistant in 1622. Elisabeth recovered and, after taking her vows, founded, under the name of Marie-Elisabeth of the Cross, the order of Our Lady of Refuge (see Whitmore, pp. xv–xvi). This is the entire substance of the scant information that Whitmore furnishes about one of the most famous cases of demonic possession in the seventeenth century. On reading the study by E. Delcambre and J. Lhermitte (*Un cas de possession diabolique: Elisabeth de Ranfaing,* Nancy, 1956), we have such a different picture that we ask ourselves whether Pithoys's role was not more equivocal than it seemed to be. In fact, Elisabeth, who had received a Puritan upbringing (to the degree that she could not bear to have the servants see any part of her body uncovered other than face and hands, and had inflicted on herself a cruel treatment to make herself ugly, to reduce the sinful charms of nature) had been forced to marry a drunken ruffian who, on his early death, left her an inheritance of three children. Elisabeth's oneiric mortifications and phantasies reveal something as quite other than peace of soul: she was a person whose erotic frustration had, since adolescence, taken the form of a dangerous syndrome of abstinence. Having fallen ill, it is very likely that she fell in love with Dr. Poirot, who took care of her. When he held out a piece of meat to her during a picnic, she went into convulsions. The psychic illness, or the "seven years of demonic possession of Elisabeth de Ranfaing" (1618–25), represented the recourse, the refuge, of a person whose desire must momentarily have been stronger than religious inhibition. It is unlikely that Poirot administered a drug in the piece of meat; it was never proved, and, furthermore, Poirot was convicted on the evidence of one Anne-Marie Bouley, who revealed that the doctor had accompanied her to the witches' sabbath! As to Pithoy's theories concerning the nonsuit that the ecclesiastical authorities should have declared, they are very dubious when we learn that, in her delirium, Elisabeth went into a trance manifesting an astonishing muscular strength and emitted strange foreign utterances, and that the acts of telepathy, clairvoyance, and even total levitation ascribed to her were a sensation at the time. Hoax or not, the case of Elisabeth de Ranfaing was certainly one that the Church could feel it had the right to treat with exorcism. Pithoys's rationalism therefore seems to have innuendoes less praiseworthy than Whitmore thinks: it was not Elisabeth he wanted to save but the doctor he wanted to convict. Even granting that the doctor administered a drug in order to violate her, it is very unlikely that the effect of the drug could last seven years.

    14. Whitmore, p. xviii.

    15. Ibid.

    16. Ibid., pp. xx–xxv.

    17. *Traité curieux,* p. 163 (Whitmore).

    18. Whitmore, p. xvii, believes that this is the book mentioned by the General Corrector of the Order, Simon Bachelier, in a memorandum found in the Archives of the department of Moselle, at Metz.

19. *Traité curieux*, pp. 207–8 (Whitmore).
20. P. de Bérulle, *Discours de l'Estat et des Grandeurs de Jesus*, II, 2, p. 162, quoted by Clémence Ramnoux, "Héliocentrisme et Christocentrisme," in *Le Soleil à la Renaissance*, p. 450.
21. *L'Impiété des déistes* (Paris, 1624), p. 371, quoted by F. Secret in *Le Soleil à la Renaissance*, p. 213.
22. This is the interpretation that Heidegger gives to Nietzsche's maxim "God is dead"; see Martin Heidegger, *Holzwege*. The crux of Heidegger's interpretation is found in the following passage "That which previously conditioned and determined, concerning the mode and the measure of things, the essence of man, has lost its absolute and direct power of efficiency, the power infallibly efficient everywhere. The suprasensible world of ends and means no longer awakens and supports life. This world has itself become lifeless: dead. There is, to be sure, Christian faith here and there. But love, unfurled in such a world, is not the efficient and operative principle of what happens today. The suprasensible substance of the suprasensible world, taken as an efficient matter of fact of all reality, has itself become unreal. That is the metaphysical meaning of the saying considered metaphysically: 'God is dead.'" On a historico-cultural interpretation of the "death of God" assertion with respect to the Romantics and Nietzsche, see my article "Les fantasmes du nihilisme chez Mihai Eminescu," in *Cahiers d'Histoire des Littératures Romanes* 4 (1980) 422–33, and my essay *Religione e accrescimento del potere*, esp. pp. 222 sq.

### Chapter 10
1. L. Kybalová, O. Herbenová, and M. Lamarová, *Encyclopédie illustrée du costume et de la mode*, French trans. (Paris, 1980), p. 114.
2. See H. P. Duerr, *Traumzeit*, p. 67.
3. Ibid., p. 72.
4. Ibid.
5. *Encyclopédie du costume*, p. 139.
6. Ibid., p. 139.
7. See G. C. Argan, *Storia dell'arte italiana*, II, (Florence, 1968), fig. 133, p. 134.
8. *Encyclopédie du costume*, p. 139. This change of waistline in clothes begins to be manifest about 1495, as may be seen in art of the period, but the square neckline precedes it.
9. See Duerr, *Traumzeit*, p. 72.
10. See W. Noomen, "Structures narratives et force comique: les fabliaux," *Neophilologus*, 1979, pp. 361–73; by the same author, " 'Le chevalier qui fist . . .' : à propos du classement des genres narratifs brefs médiévaux," *Rapports* 50, 3 (1980): 110–23.
11. See Argan's excellent comparison between three *Adorations of the Magi*, painted respectively by Lorenzo Monaco, Gentile da Fabriano, and Masaccio, *Storia dell'arte italiana*, II, pp. 98 sq.
12. Cf. Cesare Cantù, *Les Hérétiques d'Italie*, French trans., I (Paris, 1869), p. 334.
13. On the reform of customs brought about by Savonarola in Florence, there exists a most interesting text, the *Riforma sancta et pretiosa* of the Florentine Domenico Cecchi, published in 1497. See U. Mazzone, *"El buon governo"*: *Un progetto di riforma generale nella Firenze savonaroliana* (Florence, 1978).
14. *Encyclopédie du costume*, p. 154.
15. Duerr, *Traumzeit*, p. 73.
16. Comtesse d'Aulnoy, *Relation du voyage d'Epagne*, II (The Hague, 1715), quoted by Duerr, p. 73. In this sense, it is typical that Giambattista della Porta—

the author of a *Magia Naturalis* which has not been discussed in this book since it does not belong to the tradition of "spiritual magic" started by Ficino—devotes a special paragraph to prescriptions to shrink the size of the breasts (II, 15: *Mamillarum incrementum phohibere, si volumus*). Peuckert has noted that this contains one of Porta's prescriptions, which, through the intermediary of Wolfgang Hildebrand, has entered the "literature of patresfamilias" in Germany, that is to say, one of the universal reference books considered indispensable for peasants. *Den Jungfrawen zuverhüten dass sie nicht grosse Brüste bekommen*, "Preventing maidens from having large breasts," was of no less importance, beginning in the second half of the sixteenth century, than making a love charm, ascertaining that a young girl would be fertile if still a virgin, or inducing sleep with the help of the sounds of the lyre. It is apparent that fashion decreed that young women have absolutely flat breasts (cf. Peuckert, *Pansophie*, p. 316).

17. *Encyclopédie du costume*, p. 164.
18. The anthropologist H. P. Duerr's expression, *Traumzeit*, p. 75.
19. Ibid., p. 77.
20. Ibid., p. 75.
21. This is obviously not the work of Reimarus commentated by Lessing. Our anonymous work is called "the *Faustbuch*" (to differentiate it from the *Volksbuch*) and was rediscovered in 1892 by the librarian G. Milschack. It was published the same year by J. Zwissler of Wolfenbüttel, under the title *Historia D. Johannis Faust des Zauberers*.
22. *Historia von D. Johann Fausten, dem weitbeschreyten Zauberer und Swartskünstler, Wie er sich gegen dem Teuffel auff eine benandte zeit verschrieben . . . , Gedruckt zu Frankfurt am Mayn, durch Johann Spies* (1587).
23. The two German texts and the English text have recently appeared in one edition commentated by M. E. d'Agostini and G. Silvani, *Faustbuch: Analisi comparata delle fonti inglesi e tedesche del Faust dal Volksbuch a Marlowe* (Naples, 1978).
24. The *Tragical History of Doctor Faust* by Marlowe has been republished in two separate versions: *Marlowe's Doctor Faust 1604–1616: Parallel Texts*, edited by W. W. Greg (Oxford, 1950).
25. Floris Groen produced the first version in Dutch around 1650, adapted by Jacob van Rijndorp before 1689: *De Hellevaart van Dokter Joan Faustus: Toneelspel* (Amsterdam, 1731).
26. Cf. Gilles Quispel, "Faust: Symbol of Western Man," in *Gnostic Studies*, II (Istanbul, 1975), pp. 288–307, esp. pp. 300–301.
27. Cf. G. Quispel, "An unknown Fragment of the Acts of Andrew," ibid., pp. 271–87. On page 10 of the codex (lines 6–37, trans. pp. 273–74) it tells of a virgin whom a magician wishes to seduce with the help of devils. She saves herself by prayer.
28. A. Lipomanus, *Sanctorum priscorum vitae* (Venice, 1558); cf. *De probatis sanctorum historiis ab Al. Lipomano olim conscriptis nunc primum a Laur: Surio emendatis et auctis* (Cologne, 1576–1581), V (1580), pp. 394–402, and 1610 reprint, III, pp. 296 sq.
29. Alfonso de Villegas, *Flos Sanctorum y Historia general de la vida y hechos de Jesucristo, Dios y Señor nuestro, y de todos los Santos de que raza y hace fiesta la Iglesia Católica* (Madrid, 1594), pp. 321–22.
30. This is the thesis of P. Ballestreros-Barahona, *Calderons erste Fassung von "El Mágico Prodigioso" und das Doktor-Faustus-Spiel der englischen Komödianten* (Berlin, 1972), p. 63.
31. Ibid., pp. 77 sq.
32. Ibid., pp. 94 sq.
33. Ibid., pp. 77 sq.

34. Ibid., pp. 67 sq.

35. *El Mágico prodigioso, Comedia famosa de Don Pedro Calderón de la Barca*, published according to the original manuscript from the library of the duke of Osuna, with two facsimiles, an introduction, variants, and notes by Alfred Morel-Fatio (Paris and Madrid, 1877). The version published in 1633 (*"La gran comedia del maxico prodigioso,"* in *Parte veinte de comedias varias nunca impressas, compuestas por los mejores ingenios de España*, Madrid) and reprinted in *Sexta parte de comedias del celebre poeta español Don P. Calderón de la Barca* by J. de Vera Tassis y Villarroel (Madrid, 1683), differs from the first in many ways, which are carefully analyzed in Ballestreros-Barahona.

36. Francisco de Toledo, *Institutio Sacerdotum. Cum additionibus Andreae Victorelli Bassaniensis* (Rome, 1618).

37. Glauber, cited in A. G. Debus, *Man and Nature*, pp. 138–40.

# Bibliography

Agamben, Giorgio. *Stanze: La parola e il fantasma nella cultura occidentale*. Turin: Einaudi, 1977.

*Albertus Magnus and the Sciences*. Commemorative Essays 1980, edited by James A. Weisheipl, OP. Toronto: Pontifical Institute of Mediaeval Studies, 1980.

Anagnine, Eugenio. G. *Pico della Mirandola: Sincretismo religioso-filosofico, 1463–1494*. Bari: Laterza, 1937.

Anglo, Sydney, ed. *The Damned Art: Essays in the Literature of Witchcraft*. London: Routledge & Kegan Paul, 1977.

Arnold, Klaus. *Johannes Trithemius (1642–1516)*. Würzburg: Kommissionsverlag F. Schöningh, 1971.

Arnold, Paul. *La Rose-Croix et ses rapports avec la Franc-Maçonnerie: Essai de synthèse historique*. Paris: Maisonneuve-Larose, 1970.

Barasch, Moshe. *Light and Color in the Italian Renaissance Theory of Art*. New York: New York University Press, 1981.

Bartholomaeus Anglicus. *On the Properties of Soul and Body: De proprietatibus rerum libri III et IV*. Edited by R. James Long. Toronto: Pontifical Institute of Mediaeval Studies, 1979.

Betz, Hans Dieter, ed. *The Greek Magical Papyri in Translation*. Vol. 1. Chicago: University of Chicago Press, 1986.

Boase, Roger. *The Origin and Meaning of Courtly Love*. Manchester: Rowman & Littlefield, 1977.

Boll, F., C. Bezold, and W. Gundel. *Storia dell'astrologia*. Preface by Eugenio Garin. Bari: Laterza, 1977.

Borst, Arno. *Les cathares*. Paris: Payot, 1974.

Bouché-Leclercq, A. *L'astrologie grecque*. Paris: E. Leroux, 1899.

Brann, Noël L. *The Abbot Trithemius (1462–1516): The Renaissance of Monastic Humanism*. Leiden: Brill, 1981.

Bruno, Giordano. *Jordani Bruni Nolani Opera latine conscripta*. Facsimile reprint of 1879–91 edition. 3 vols. in 8 parts. Stuttgart and Bad Canstatt: Friedrich Fromann Vg. Günther Holzboog, 1961–62.

———. *Opere italiane*. 2d ed. 3 vols. Bari: Laterza, 1923–25.

———. *Des fureurs héroïques*. Edited and translated by Paul-Henri Michel. Paris: Les Belles Lettres, 1954.

Chastel, André. *Marsile Ficin et l'Art*. Geneva: Droz, 1954.

———. *Arte e Umanesimo a Firenze al tempo di Lorenzo il Magnifico: Studi sul Rinascimento e sull'Umanesimo platonico*. Turin: Einaudi, 1964.

Christinger, Raymond. *Le Voyage dans l'imaginaire*. Paris: Stock, 1981.

Cornelius Agrippa, Henricus. *La Philosophie occulte, ou La Magie. . . .* 5th ed. 4 vols. Paris: Editions Traditionnelles, 1979–.

Cornford, Francis Macdonald. *Plato's Cosmology*. 2d ed. London: Routledge & Kegan Paul, 1948.

Couliano, Ioan P. *Expériences de l'extase*. Paris: Payot, 1984.

———. "Magia spirituale e magia demonica nel Rinascimento." *Rivista di Storia e Letteratura Religiosa* (Turin) 17 (1981): 360–408.

————. "Giordano Bruno tra la Montagna di Circe e il Fiume delle Dame leggiadre." In *Montagna e Letteratura*, edited by A. Audisio and R. Rinaldi, pp.
71–75. Turin: Museo della Montagna, 1983.

Crohns, Hjalmar. "Zur Geschichte der Liebe als 'Krankheit.'" *Archiv für Kultur-
Geschichte* (Berlin) 3 (1905): 66–86. Reprint, Vaduz: Kraus, 1965.

Culianu, Ioan P. *See* Couliano.

Debus, Allen G. *Man and Nature in the Renaissance*. Cambridge: Cambridge University Press, 1978.

————, ed. *Science, Medicine and Society in the Renaissance: Essays to Honor Walter
Pagel*. 2 vols. London: Heineman, 1972.

De Lancre, Pierre. *Tableau de l'inconstance des mauvais anges et demons où il est
amplement traité des sorciers et de la sorcellerie*. Introduction and notes by Nicole
Jacques-Chaquin. Paris: Aubier, 1982.

De Lubac, Henri. *Pic de la Mirandole: Etudes et discussions*. Paris: Aubier-Mon-
taigne, 1974.

Demaître, Luke E. *Doctor Bernard de Gordon: Professor and Practitioner*. Toronto:
Pontifical Institute of Mediaeval Studies, 1980.

Dreyer, J. L. E. *A History of Astronomy from Thales to Kepler*. 2d ed. New York:
Dover, 1953.

Dronke, Peter. *Fabula: Explorations into the Uses of Myth in Medieval Platonism*.
Leiden and Cologne: Brill, 1974.

Duerr, Hans Peter. *Traumzeit: Über die Grenze zwischen Wildnis und Zivilisation*.
Frankfurt: Syndikat, 1978.

Dupouy, Edmond. *Le Moyen Age médical*. Paris: Librairie Meurillon, 1888.

Evans, R. J. W. *Rudolph II and His World: A Study in Intellectual History, 1576–1612*.
Oxford: Clarendon Press, 1973.

*Faust*. Cahiers de l'Hermétisme. Paris: Albin Michel, 1977.

Festugière, Jean. *La Philosophie de l'amour de Marsile Ficin et son influence sur la
littérature française au XVIᵉ siècle*. Paris: Vrin, 1941.

Festugière, Le R. P., OP. *La Révélation d'Hermès Trismégiste I: L'Astrologie et les
Sciences occultes*. Reprint. Paris: Les Belles Lettres, 1983.

Ficinus, Marsilius. *Marsilii Ficini Florentini Opera, et quae hactenus extitere* (Basileae
1576). Reprint (*Opera omnia*). Turin: Bottega d'Erasmo, 1962.

————. *De Vita libri tres*. Edited and annotated by Martin Plessner. After the
manuscript edited by Felix Klein-Franke. Hildesheim and New York: Georg
Ohlms, 1978.

————. *Thèologie platonicienne de l'immortalité des Ames*. Edited and translated by
Raymond Marcel. 3 vols. Paris: Les Belles Lettres, 1964–.

————. *Teologia platonica*. Edited by Michele Schiavone. 2 vols. Bologna: Zani-
chelli, 1965.

————. *Commentaire sur le Banquet de Platon*. Edited and translated by Raymond
Marcel. Paris: Les Belles Lettres, 1955.

————. *Sopra lo amore o ver' Convito di Platone: Comento di Marsilio Ficini Florentino
sopra il Convito di Platone*. Edited by G. Ottaviano. Milan: CELUC, 1973.

French, Peter. *John Dee: The World of an Elizabethan Magus*. London: Routledge &
Kegan Paul, 1972.

Garin, Eugenio. *La cultura filosofica del Rinascimento italiano*. Florence: Sansoni,
1961.

————. *Storia della filosofia italiana*, vols. 1–2. Turin: Einaudi, 1966.

————. *Astrology in the Renaissance: The Zodiac of Life*. London: Routledge &
Kegan Paul, 1983.

Gundel, Wilhelm. *Sternglaube, Sternreligion und Sternorakel: Aus der Geschichte der
Astrologie*. 2d ed. Heidelberg: Quelle und Meyer, 1959.

Gundel, Wilhelm, and Hans Georg Gundel. *Astrologumena: Die astrologische Literatur in der Antike und ihre Geschichte.* Wiesbaden: Franz Steiner, 1966.

Hansen, Joseph. *Zauberwahn Inquisition und Hexenprozess im Mittelalter und die Entstehung der grossen Hexenverfolgung.* Munich and Leipzig: R. Oldenbourg, 1900.

*Hypnerotomachie, ou Discours du songe de Poliphile. . . .* Edited by Bertrand Guégan, after the Kerver edition. Paris: Payot, 1979.

*Kabbalistes chrétiens.* Cahiers de l'hermétisme. Paris: Albin Michel, 1979.

Koenigsberger, Dorothy. *Renaissance Man and Creative Thinking: A History of Concepts of Harmony, 1400–1700.* Atlantic Highlands, N.J.: Humanities Press, 1979.

Kristeller, P. O. *Il Pensiero filosofico di Marsilio Ficino.* Italian trans., revised and enlarged. Florence: Sansoni, 1953.

Lambert, Malcolm. *Medieval Heresy: Popular Movements from Bogomil to Hus.* London: Edward Arnold, 1977.

Lea, Henry Charles. *Materials toward a History of Witchcraft.* Edited by Arthur C. Howland. Introduction by George Lincoln Burr. 3 vols. 1939. Reprint New York and London: Thomas Yoseloff, 1957.

Leibbrand, Annemarie, and Werner Leibbrand. *Formen des Eros: Kultur- und Geistesgeschichte der Liebe.* 2 vols. Freiburg and Munich: Karl Aber, 1972.

Lewin, Louis. *Phantastica.* Paris: Payot, 1970.

Lewy, Hans. *Chaldean Oracles and Theurgy: Mysticism, Magic and Platonism in the Later Roman Empire.* Reprint of the 1956 Cairo edition. Paris: Etudes augustiniennes, 1978.

Lowes, John Livingstone. "The Loveres Maladye of Hereos." *Modern Philology* 11 (1913–14): 491–546.

*Magia Naturalis und die Entstehung der modernen Naturwissenschaften.* Studia Leibnitiana 7. Wiesbaden: Franz Steiner, 1978.

*La Magie arabe traditionelle. . . .* Introduction and notes by Sylvain Matton. Paris: Retz, 1977.

*Magie und Religion: Beiträge zu einer Theorie der Magie.* Edited by Leander Petzoldt. Darmstadt: Wissenschaftliche Buchgesellschaft, 1978.

Mandrou, Robert. *Magistrats et sorciers en France au XVIIᵉ siècle: Une analyse de psychologie historique.* Paris: Plon, 1968.

Marcel, Raymond. *Marsile Ficin (1433–1499).* Paris: Les Belles Lettres, 1958.

Masters, R. E. L. *Eros and Evil: The Sexual Psychopathology of Witchcraft.* New York: The Julian Press, 1962.

Nelson, John Charles. *Renaissance Theory of Love: The context of Giordano Bruno's "Eroici furori."* New York: Columbia University Press, 1958.

*Oracles chaldaïques, avec un choix de commentaires anciens.* Edited and translated by Edouard des Places, SJ. Paris: Les Belles Lettres, 1971.

Peuckert, Will-Erich. *Pansophie: Ein Versuch zur Geschichte der weissen un schwarzen Magie.* 2d ed. Berlin: Erich Schmidt, 1956.

——. *Gabalia: Ein Versuch zur Geschichte der magia naturalis im 16. bis 18. Jahrhundert (Pansophie, part 2).* Berlin: Erich Schmidt, 1967.

——. *L'Astrologie: Son histoire, ses doctrines.* Paris: Payot, 1980.

Pico della Mirandola, Giovanni. *Opera omnia Ioannis Pici, Mirandulae Concordiaeque comitis. . . .* Reprint of the 1557–73 Basel edition. 2 vols. Introduction by Cesare Vasoli. Hildesheim: Georg Olms, 1969.

Porta, Giambattista della. *Joh. Baptistae Portae Neapolitani, Magiae Naturalis Libri Viginti.* Amsterdam: Apud Elizeum Weyerstraten, 1664.

Prost, Auguste, *Les Sciences et les Arts occultes au XVIᵉ siècle: Corneille Agrippa, sa vie et ses œuvres.* Reprint of the 1881–82 Paris edition. 2 vols. Nieuwkoop: B. De Graaf, 1965.

Putscher, Marielene. *Pneuma, Spiritus, Geist: Vorstellungen vom Lebensantrieb in ihren geschichtlichen Wandlungen.* Wiesbaden: Franz Steiner, 1973.

Quispel, Gilles. *Gnostic Studies.* 2 vols. Istanbul: Nederlands Historisch-Archaeologisch Instituut, 1974–1975.

Rossi, Paolo. *Clavis universalis.* Milan and Naples: R. Ricciardi, 1962.

———. *Philosophy, Technology, and the Arts in the Early Modern Era.* New York: Harper and Row, 1970.

Russell, Jeffrey Burton. *Witchcraft in the Middle Ages.* Ithaca: Cornell University Press, 1972.

Shumaker, Wayne. *The Occult Sciences in the Renaissance: A Study in Intellectual Patterns.* Berkeley and Los Angeles: University of California Press, 1972.

Soleil. *Le Soleil à la Renaissance: Sciences et mythes.* Brussels and Paris: Presses Universitaires, 1965.

Spence, Jonathan D. *The Memory Palace of Matteo Ricci.* New York: Sifton/Penguin, 1983.

Tedeschi, John. "The Roman Inquisition and Witchcraft." *Revue de l'Histoire des Religions* 200 (1983): 163–88.

Teirlinck, Isidore. *Flora Magica: De plant in de Tooverwereld.* Anvers: De Sikkel, 1930.

*Le Temps chrétien de la fin de L'Antiquité au Moyen Age, IIIᵉ–XIIIᵉ siècles.* Paris: Editions du CNRS, 1984.

Thorndike, Lynn. *A History of Magic and Experimental Science.* Vols. 3–4, *Fourteenth and Fifteenth Centuries;* vols. 5–6, *The Sixteenth Century.* New York: Columbia University Press, 1934–41.

Toulmin, Stephen. *The Return to Cosmology: Postmodern Science and the Theology of Nature.* Berkeley and Los Angeles: University of California Press, 1982.

Trithemius, Johannes. *Johannis Trithemii . . . Steganographia. . . .* Edited by W. E. Heidel. Moguntiae, Sumptibus Joannis Petri Zubrodt, 1676.

Verbeke, Gérard. *L'Evolution de la doctrine du pneuma du stoïcisme à S. Augustin: Etude philosophique.* Paris and Louvain: D. De Brouwer, Editions Inst. Sup., 1945.

Walker, Daniel Pickering. *Spiritual and Demonic Magic from Ficino to Campanella.* London: The Warburg Institute, 1958.

———. *Unclean Spirits: Possession and Exorcism in France and England in the Late Sixteenth and Early Seventeenth Centuries.* London: Scolar Press, 1981.

Webster, Charles, ed. *Health, Medicine and Mortality in the Sixteenth Century.* Cambridge: Cambridge University Press.

Weise, Georg. *L'ideale eroïco del Rinascimento e le sue premesse umanistiche.* Naples: Edizioni Scientifiche Italiane, 1961.

Weisheipl, James A., ed. See *Albertus Magnus and the Sciences.*

Wier, Johannes. *Joannis Wieri . . . Opera omnia. . . .* Amsterdam: Apud Petrum van den Berge, 1660.

Wightman, W. D. P. *Science in a Renaissance Society.* London: Hutchinson University Library, 1972.

Wind, Edgar. *Pagan Mysteries in the Renaissance.* 3d ed. Oxford: Oxford University Press, 1980.

Yates, Frances Amelia. *The Art of Memory.* Chicago: University of Chicago Press, 1966.

———. *Astraea: The Imperial Theme in the Sixteenth Century.* London: Routledge & Kegan Paul, 1975.

———. *The Occult Philosophy in the Elizabethan Age.* London: Routledge & Kegan Paul, 1979.

———. *The Rosicrucian Enlightenment.* London, 1972.

# Index of Names